ALAIN CHARTIER

Routledge Medieval Texts

Routledge Medieval Texts makes the literary masterworks of the Middle Ages available in volumes translated by leading scholars. Suiting the needs of both general and advanced readers, each book contains an edition of the original with facing English translation. Based on the best available manuscripts, originals are presented in accurate, conservative versions, with minimal editorial or linguistic apparatus. Faithful, line-by-line translations in modern, colloquial English serve all audiences, from readers with no knowledge of the original language to those who need help with difficult constructions or unfamiliar vocabulary. Each volume features an introduction with a full discussion of important literary and critical questions, including the life of the author and the place of the work within either the authorial oeuvre or genre; the work's literary value and importance; the source materials drawn upon; the influence exerted on other writers; the manuscript tradition and printed history; and a select bibliography listing previous editions and major critical and historical studies. While the series includes texts from all medieval languages and literary traditions, important works from French, German, Italian, Occitan, Latin, and Hispanic literatures are its principal focus. Routledge Medieval Texts is overseen by an editorial board of eminent medievalists.

General Editors

Teresa Kennedy, Mary Washington College
R. Barton Palmer, Clemson University

Editorial Board

William W. Kibler, University of Texas
Norris J. Lacy, Pennsylvania State University
Giuseppe Mazzotta, Yale University
John M. Hill, United States Naval Academy
Stephen K. Wright, Catholic University of America

Series Titles

Eustache Deschamps
Selected Poems
Edited by Ian S. Laurie and Deborah M. Sinnreich-Levi
Translated by David Curzon and Jeffrey Fiskin

Walther von der Vogelweide
The Single-Stanza Lyrics
Edited and translated by Frederick Goldin

Alain Chartier
The Quarrel of the Belle dame sans mercy
Edited and translated by Joan E. McRae

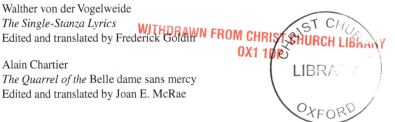

ALAIN CHARTIER

The Quarrel of the Belle dame sans mercy

Edited and translated by
JOAN E. McRAE

Routledge
Taylor & Francis Group

LONDON AND NEW YORK

Published 2014 by Routledge
2 Park Square, Milton Park, Abingdon, Oxfordshire OX14 4RN
711 Third Avenue, New York, NY, 10017, USA

First issued in paperback 2016

Routledge is an imprint of the Taylor & Francis Group, an informa business

Library of Congress Cataloging-in-Publication Data for this book is available from the Library of Congress

ISBN 13: 978-1-138-98843-9 (pbk)
ISBN 13: 978-0-415-96611-5 (hbk)

For Louise Justice Maloy

Contents

Acknowledgments

This book could not have been completed without the support of numerous people and the institutions they work with. I would like to thank especially Barton Palmer, who sought me out for this project; Virginie Greene at Harvard University, who prompted the project with her query about the availability of an English translation of the *Belle dame*; my students at Hampden-Sydney College, who helped with the translation of the *Belle dame*; professors of religion Gerald Carney and John David Ramsey at Hampden-Sydney College, for sharing their expertise on the medieval Catholic mass; Robert F. Cook, who in retirement still encourages and guides with unlimited wealth of knowledge on Old French and editing; David F. Hult, for his enthusiasm for the Quarrel poems; and Frances Perry McRae, who tirelessly read over the entire manuscript. William Nelles, Matthew Anderson, James Deviese, and Jim Pontuso also contributed their expertise. The support of the National Endowment for the Humanities, the Mednick Fellowship Committee of the Virginia Foundation for Independent Colleges, and the Committee for Professional Development and the Elliott Professorship Program at Hampden-Sydney College made this book possible, and I offer my sincere thanks. The research collections and manuscript libraries of the Bibliothèque Nationale de France, the Bibliothèque de l'Arsenal, the Jacquemart-André, and the Institut de Recherche et d'Histoire des Textes (IRHT), in Paris; the Musée Condé; the municipal library at Arnhem; the royal libraries of the Hague and

Copenhagen; and the staff and collection at the libraries of Hampden-Sydney College and the University of Virginia were limitless sources of information and help. To my husband, Ray Kleinlein, who offered his support and critical eye, I owe a great debt of gratitude. My companion, Yseut, too, deserves recognition for her tireless work beside me.

Introduction

La belle Dame sans mercy hath thee in thrall!

—John Keats

A sleeping man, aged and ugly, is approached by a beautiful and elegant young woman. She bends over him and sweetly kisses his lips. When reproached for this action by one of her followers, the young woman responds to the jealous courtier: "I did not kiss the man, but only his precious mouth, from which have issued so many witty words and virtuous remarks."[1] Quoted first by Jean Bouchet in the sixteenth century, this famous anecdote of Marguerite of Scotland kissing the sleeping Alain Chartier is a figurative expression of the extent of Chartier's reputation for oratory and literary excellence during his lifetime and long after his death. The Pre-Raphaelite painting by Edmund Blair Leighton depicting the kiss has brought this legend of Alain Chartier into the modern imagination. Pre-Raphaelite painters Waterhouse and Cowper made a subject of Alain Chartier's most notable character, the Belle dame sans mercy, who earlier in the nineteenth century had captured the attention of the Romantic poet John Keats.[2] The strong and beautiful femme fatale of the Middle Ages was reincarnated in the poem titled after her, "La Belle Dame Sans Merci," in which the story of her encounter with a forlorn lover is translated from the medieval court into a fairy forest. The melancholy influence of Romanticism underlies the fear that echoes in the narrator's words, evoking in their despair the fate of Chartier's lover, who was killed by the hardheartedness of this Belle dame. The poem's wistful portrait of her, fortified by the exquisite rendering of her beauty in the Pre-Raphaelite paintings, has ensured the image of the Belle dame in our consciousness as the woman whose beauty means death for an enthralled lover.

1

The medieval audience of Chartier's *Belle dame sans mercy* was equally enthralled by her. The scandal that surrounded the Belle dame's controversial character incited a literary debate, what we now refer to as the Quarrel of the Belle Dame Sans Mercy. The Quarrel testifies to the volatile reaction of some eighteen poetic voices of the middle of the fifteenth century. Begun with letters written to Chartier by ladies and courtiers of Charles VII's court shortly after the poem's appearance in 1424, the Quarrel centered on the courtly dilemma of whether the Belle dame was justified or not in refusing her lover. These erotico-juridical poems either continued or evaluated Chartier's poem. In four of the poems the Belle dame is put on trial for the murder of her lover; other poems of the Quarrel, including the two most popular ones edited here, rewrite the plot: either the Belle dame capitulates in the end, or the lover of the poem, instead of dying, is sent off for a cure.

Alain Chartier's renown grew as the poem was translated into Catalan, Italian, and English,[3] even as other of his works were imitated and adapted. The progression of the century and entry into the Renaissance saw his name repeatedly cited as a master of poetic style and as an authority to be invoked. He is one of the few authors of the Middle Ages, along with Jean de Meung, to be appreciated even through the sixteenth century. Some two hundred manuscripts and numerous early editions bear witness to the immense popularity of his works.[4]

The Life of Alain Chartier

Alain Chartier[5] was born in a brief oasis of peace amid the tumultuous events of the Hundred Years' War (1337–1453). The 1378 schism of the Church had split the papal authority between Rome and Avignon; dramatic extremes of weather conditions, years of ruined crops and famine, and many devastating bouts of plague traumatized the countryside. But there was peace between France and England to cradle Chartier at his birth. Although it was short-lived, lasting only from 1380 to 1396, the hope of renewed peace was forever to beckon him. The progressing madness of Charles VI and the political machinations of his wife, Isabeau de Bavière, exacerbated by the continued eruptions of internecine rivalries in a civil war between the Armagnacs (Orléanists) and Burgundians, left the French throne weak and vulnerable to the English, however, and war was soon to return.

The murder of peace-inclined Richard II, king of England and friend to Charles VI, paved the way for the succession of Henry V, who renewed the English demand for the French throne. Incensed by a dismissal of his demands by the French court, Henry V responded with an invasion of Normandy, and at the Battle of Agincourt in 1415 he profoundly wounded the French, body and soul, in one of the most devastating defeats in French history. Many of the bravest and highest of the French aristocracy were either killed or taken prisoner, among these Charles d'Orléans, who was held hostage for twenty-five years in England. The country was foundering in crisis. Alain Chartier, from this despair, was to find inspiration.

Dark circumstances molded the mind and work of the "simple clerc," Alain Chartier. He was born in Bayeux toward the end of the fourteenth century (1386?),[6] the oldest of three brothers whose father was Jean Chartier, a wealthy bourgeois of some stature in his town. All three of the Chartier brothers fared well in life: his brother Guillaume was to become the bishop of Paris, and his youngest brother, Thomas, followed his footsteps in the service of the king as secretary and notary. Alain went to the university in Paris for his degree as *maître ès arts*.[7] The self-portrait he inscribed in a letter to his brother on scholarly life disclosed a contemplative, humble, and dedicated student who preferred the company of his elders to that of his peers.[8] Though his health may have been feeble,[9] his determination to follow the wisdom of his teachers and the ancients drove him to succeed. Around 1409 he joined the entourage of Yolande of Anjou, the mother of Marie d'Anjou, to whom Charles of France, son of Charles VI, was engaged and with whom, in keeping with tradition, the prince lived for five years before his marriage.[10] When Charles became the Dauphin in 1417 and set up his own household, Chartier joined him, even following him into exile in Bourges when the Burgundians took control of Paris in 1418. He would never again be allowed to return to Paris.

As secretary and notary to the Dauphin, later king, Chartier performed many and varied services, including writing letters and royal acts, supporting the royal authority and the public good, and accompanying ambassadors on political missions. The job offered abundant opportunities to a young writer: access to books and writing materials, a salary to support himself, association with other authors and poets, the excitement and glamour of the royal court, and the occasion to travel. Yet the work was arduous and strictly controlled by the rule of the Confraternity. From the details of his life at court revealed in his *Curial* and *Livre de l'espérance*, Alain was not only exhausted and enfeebled by his work and the peregrinations required of him, but also embittered and melancholic—sentiments that crept into many of his writings, subtly underlying his courtliness and patriotism.

The politics of the itinerant Dauphin were in a desperate state in the early years of the fifteenth century, as he continued to claim the legitimacy denied him by his father, Charles VI, in the Treaty of Troyes (1420). This treaty, drafted by the English-allied Burgundians, disinherited the Dauphin in favor of Henry V upon the death of Charles VI. But the death of Henry in 1422, followed three months later by the death of Charles VI, put the question of succession again in doubt. Charles VII was eager to reestablish his claim as the legitimate inheritor of the French throne, and used all his resources to this end. Chartier, especially after 1424, was sent on dangerous and influential diplomatic missions, charged as ambassador and orator: to Hungary, to negotiate an alliance with Sigismund; to Venice, as mediator between Sigismund and the Republic of Venice; to Bruges (by way of Tournai) to discuss peace with the duke of Burgundy; to Scotland, to enlist aid from the Scottish against the English and arrange a marriage between the young daughter of James I, Marguerite, and the future Louis XI, an encounter that is most probably the source of the legend of the kiss.

In addition to his work for Charles VII, Chartier was appointed to several ecclesiastical positions: as canon of Tours, as canon and archdeacon[11] of Paris (titles that were purely honorary, since he was exiled from Paris), as rector of the parish of Saint-Lambert-des-Levées in Angers, and as chancellor and canon of Bayeux, his hometown. It is probable that Chartier was admitted to full orders sometime after 1425.

In July of 1429 Chartier witnessed the triumph of Joan of Arc in Rheims cathedral at the coronation ceremony of Charles VII and wrote with hope of her glorious career in a letter most likely destined for the duke of Milan. This was his last written letter, and possibly his last official duty. He died shortly thereafter, sometime in 1430, in Avignon.[12] The reason for his visit to the former papal city remains a mystery, as do the circumstances of his death.

Due to his career as secretary to the Dauphin, Chartier's authorial activity was more limited than that of many writers of his age, but also perhaps more varied. He wrote in both Latin and French, poetry and prose, ballads, letters, and treatises, compiling a total of fifty-five texts: fourteen in Latin, forty-one in French; sixteen in prose, thirty-nine in verse. His works include lyric and didactic subjects, and he did not shy from mixing the two as he scrutinized the world around him, anxious to make sense of the turbulent times and eager to reestablish the dignity and peace of France. His works, both prose and poetry, reveal him as an engaged servant of his king, a determined diplomat, a courtly gentleman, and, most of all, an inspired author and great poet. This study will focus primarily on his poetry, since it is in this arena that Chartier found his greatest fame and success with the publication of his *Belle dame sans mercy*.

There is little evidence to help us date Chartier's works, and so much of the chronology of the poems as reconstructed by scholars is based on a healthy amount of reasonable supposition. However, throughout Chartier's works we can detect glimpses of biographical information revealed by a reoccurring melancholic narrator, by which we might surmise a hypothetical time line. The *Lai de plaisance* [*Lay of Pleasure*] (196 verses, seventeen manuscripts), for example, presents a narrator who claims that he has never been blessed with love and is currently without a lover—"sans dame suy" (ed. Laidlaw v. 10)—but who encourages his friend to seek the virtues of love and pleasure rather than melancholy. Laidlaw claims that "both the tone and the construction of the *Lai de plaisance* confirm that it is an early work" (29). By the same standard, the *Débat des deux fortunes d'amours* [*Debate of the Fortunate and Unfortunate in Love*] also known as the *Débat du gras et du maigre*; 1,246 verses, twenty-seven manuscripts) may also be considered an early work, as its narrator claims to be inexperienced in love when he agrees hesitatingly to record the debate between the fat knight, who hails the benefits of love over its sorrows, and the thin knight, who claims the contrary. Continuing to follow this "poetic I" through the course of amatory development, we find a narrator who is now secretly in love in the *Livre des quatre dames* [*The Book of the Four Ladies*] (3,531 verses), having recovered from the rejection of a lady two years earlier. This popular work, conserved in thirty-two manuscripts, was surely written shortly after the Battle of Agincourt (October 1415). The narrator introduces us to four ladies who debate which one of them has been dealt the most unhappy fate: the first laments the death of her lover in the battle, the second her lover's capture;[13] the third is tormented by uncertainty, for she does not know whether her lover is dead, alive, or captured; the fourth decries the shame of her lover's flight. The narrator offers the poem to his lady to decide who among them is the most miserable. The satirical *Débat du herault, du vassault et du villain* [*Debate of the Herald, the Vassal and the Peasant*] (or the *Débat patriotique*; 440 verses, one manuscript) again addresses this discussion of the plight of France, echoing the criticisms of the ladies of his previous work and denouncing the egoism of knights who neglect their duty to fight for the king and the nation. More sophisticated, the prose *Quadrilogue invectif* [*The Four-Voiced Invective*] (forty manuscripts) presents an allegorical France as she listens to the voices of the three estates, filled with recriminations and complaints about the others as well as the state of the nation. The final discourse of the Clergy encourages the people and knights to join with him in favor of the king and against the enemy. An expression of the desire to encourage knights to better themselves is the subject of the *Breviaire des nobles* [*The Breviary of Noblemen*] (454 verses, fifty-three manuscripts), in which Chartier encourages knights to embrace these twelve virtues of knighthood: Faith, Loyalty, Honor, Uprightness, Prowess, Love, Courtesy, Diligence, Honesty, Generosity, Sobriety, and Perseverance.

Love, the other side of courtliness, inspires *Réveille matin* [*Awake at Dawn*] (368 verses, thirty-seven manuscripts), which Laidlaw next orders in Chartier's poetic oeuvre. A debate between two friends, one distressed by love, the other sleepy yet forced to listen and comment on his friend's anguished thoughts, presages many of the themes and rhetorical strategies we will see in the *Belle dame sans mercy*. Chartier adopts the stanzaic form of his precursor, Oton de Grandson: the octosyllabic eight-line stanza of three interlaced rhymes *ababbcbc*, made

famous with the *Belle dame sans mercy* and the ensuing Quarrel, all the poems of
which are written in this same form. Bypassing the *Belle dame sans mercy* and the
Excusation [*The Excuse of Master Alain*] for the moment, the *Complainte* [the *Complaint*] (184 verses, thirty-seven manuscripts) reveals a narrator in the throes of
grief over the death of his lady. Probably written around the same time as the *Belle
dame*, this poem is closely associated with it and is copied in close proximity to it
in almost all of the manuscripts. Both Charles d'Orleans and Villon imitated its
versification some years later. The *Lay de paix* [*Lay of Peace*] (284 verses, forty-
eight manuscripts) foregrounds the subject so dear to Chartier's heart: peace. But it
is a general, if passionate, presentation, and its short verses hasten the reader
unduly to its end. The circumstances and date of its composition are still unsure,
although four manuscripts testify that it was written for or sent to Philip, duke of
Burgundy, around the time of Chartier's diplomatic mission to Bruges in 1426 in
an attempt to restore national unity. The poem's dedication, "A vous, Princes nez
du lis precïeux," is too vague to confirm the association.[14] Others have deduced
that the poem was composed when the princes gathered at Angers in October of
1424.[15] Chartier's shorter compositions, his ballads and rondeaux, should also be
mentioned here. Laidlaw posits that these twenty-seven poems were written over
the course of his career, since some echo the aspirations of his earlier works, while
others reveal the maturity of his later concerns. Chartier's final work in French
prose and verse, the *Livre de l'espérance* [*The Book of Hope*] (some thirty manuscripts), was never completed. A work of maturity and one of the first examples of
prosimètre, which the Rhétoriqueurs would eagerly embrace, it reveals Chartier as a
great poet and one of the finest prose writers of the French tradition.

The following tentative chronology of Chartier's works in French is based on
information compiled by Laidlaw and Walravens:

1412–14 *Lai de plaisance* [The Lay of Pleasure]

1412–14 *Débat des deux fortunés en amour (Le Gras et le maigre)* [Debate of the
Fortunate and Unfortunate in Love, or the Fat and the Thin]

1416 *Livre des quatres dames* [The Book of the Four Ladies]

1422 *Quadrilogue invective* [The Four-voiced Invective]

1421–25 *Débat du herault, du vassault et du villain (Débat patriotique)* [Debate
of the Herald, the Vassal and the Peasant]

1422–26 *Breviaire des nobles* [The Breviary of Noblemen]

1424–26 *Lay de paix* [The Lay of Peace]

1422–24? *Réveille matin* [Awake at Dawn]

1424 *Complainte* [The Complaint]

1424 *La belle dame sans mercy* [The Beautiful Lady Without Mercy]

1425 *L'excusation de Maistre Alain* [The Excuse of Master Alain]

1428–29 *Livre de l'espérance* [The Book of Hope]

1410–25 *Rondeaux et ballades* [Rondeau and Ballads]

The *Belle dame sans mercy* and the Quarrel

Chartier's most widely read poem, The *Belle dame sans mercy*, presents a debate between a lover and his inflexible lady. The narrator, a character we have met in the previous poems, has now lost his lady and laments her death. Stumbling upon a party, he witnesses a lover dressed in black who cannot keep his eyes from one particular lady. Sympathizing with him but tiring of the party, the narrator goes off alone into the garden, only to happen upon the couple shortly thereafter. The narrator listens discreetly as the lover attempts to persuade his lady to grant him her favors, using all the courtly rhetorical strategies stylized since Andreas Capellanus's twelfth-century *Art of Courtly Love*. The lady, however, refuses to believe the sincerity of his words and responds to his appeals brusquely, frankly, and skeptically, calling the lover to return to reason. Upon her final rebuff, the lover sadly retreats. The surprise ending is then revealed by the narrator: he has heard that the lover, after pulling out all of his hair, died of grief. In the envoi, the narrator appeals to lovers to eschew the company of fickle lovers and slanderers, and to the ladies not to be without pity, as was this woman. He ends the poem thus as a warning, reminding his readers of the laws of a courtesy menaced by the degradation of morals and manners.

Such dialogue between lady and lover is grounded in the tradition of the poetry of courtly love dating back to the troubadours, and Chartier does not hesitate to imitate and respond to his predecessors and contemporaries. The poem entitled *The Belle Dame Who Has Mercy*, attributed to Oton de Grandson by Piaget (thus predating the *Belle dame sans mercy*, yet included among the Quarrel poems), provides not only the verse form that Chartier adopts (eight-line stanzas of octosyllables, rhyming *ababbcbc*), but also much of the verbal interplay. The sappy sweet capitulation of the lady provides impetus enough to rewrite the ending.[16] Christine de Pizan's *Cent ballades d'amant et de dame* [*One Hundred Ballads of Lover and Lady*], too, was a direct source of inspiration for Chartier. The lady's voice describes not only the frustration of love but also betrayal. Her fears were well warranted with regard to her lover, for his promises of faithfulness proved false. Chartier's lady will not be so gullible. The influence of another *Cent ballades* [*One Hundred Ballads*] the collaborative work of Jean le Seneschal, Philippe d'Artois, Boucicaut le Jeune, and Jean de Crésecque, is evident even in the initial line, which Chartier modifies from the earlier "Une fois pieça chevauchoie" to his *Belle dame*'s "Naguieres, chevauchant, pensoie." The discussions therein over the importance of loyalty in love will prove especially relevant in the Quarrel poems.

The situation of the eavesdropping narrator who frames the story, familiar to Chartier from the *dits* of Machaut, is appropriated within the context of a debate. Already Machaut's *Jugement du roy de Bohème* [*Judgment of the King of Bohemia*] and *Jugement du roy de Navarre* [*Judgment of the King of Navarre*] had transformed the *tensos* and *jeux partis* of an earlier aesthetic into a narrative debate. Chartier modified Machaut's form only by alternating voices by stanza: the lover speaks, then the lady responds. Even though the *Belle dame* does not, properly speaking, fit into the allegorical tradition, as its characters are not allegorical figures, the incalculable authority of *The Romance of the Rose* underlies the language and expectations of the poem: the Belle dame speaks in the voice of Reason, even as she has learned the lessons of the Old Woman. The allegorical context of the *Rose* does not hesitate long to appear; it molds the form and characters of the entire Quarrel sequence.

The *Belle dame sans mercy* offers no internal evidence by which it might be dated; however, the first documents of the Quarrel, coupled with the evidence of Chartier's diplomatic missions, allow us to reconstruct a date of 1424. Shortly after this date Chartier received two letters from Issoudun: the first written by three ladies of the court, Katherine, Jeanne, and Marie, and dated the last day of January, whose purpose was to inform him of the second letter, a complaint to them from some courtiers regarding Chartier's new poem, the *Belle dame sans mercy*. These letters initiate the Quarrel by their criticisms of Chartier and his Belle dame character, and also suggest evidence for dating the affair. Specifically mentioned is that Chartier is away and engaged in some mission on which he might be killed or captured; as we know from a document dated December 31, 1424, Chartier was supposed to have left the court sometime during the first week of January 1425 on a diplomatic mission with Arthaud de Granval to the emperor of Germany, Sigismund. The ladies' letter further insists that Chartier come before them on the first of April to justify his poem and its pitiless lady; however, he may not have received it until some months after the letter had been sent and after the date set for his appearance before the ladies, on New Year's Day, April 8, 1425. This is the date on which he composes his response to them, writing in his Excuse: "Listen to the harsh news I heard on New Year's Day. . . . " Indeed, Chartier was engaged for the better part of the year on his mission and so was unable to appear before the ladies. He seems to have taken the request of the ladies seriously enough, however, to respond to their concerns in the form of a dreamed debate between himself and the God of Love, *The Excuse of Master Alain*, which we can reasonably date to spring or summer 1425, shortly after his receipt of the ladies' letter.

In this poem the God of Love, brandishing his bow and arrow, threatens to abandon him forever for the "unfortunate book" he has written. The God of

Love's diatribe against Chartier and his literary creation echoes the complaints made in the courtiers' letter: Chartier is bitter and spiteful toward Love and lovers, his poem threatens to take from women the virtuous quality of pity, and the poem should be destroyed. Chartier has obviously read the Issoudun courtiers' request sent to the ladies, forwarded to him by the ladies, and responds directly to them, whose complaints he flatteringly reiterates from the God of Love's mouth. Chartier begs the God of Love to read the whole book before judging it, and his defense of his poem is twofold. First, the God of Love should agree with him that women do not, nor should they, always bestow their grace on anyone who requests it. Second, should he be condemned when he is just the writer of words he has overheard? He has earlier professed his devotion to the God of Love and women. Now he has shown that he has been accused unjustly. The God of Love is content with the responses of the dreaming Chartier. After the God of Love remands the case back to the ladies and disappears, Chartier begs the ladies to forgive him, promises to come before them, and ends his *Excuse* with a quatrain playing on his first name.[17]

But was he forgiven? How seriously should we take this controversy, which proved to be the genesis of the Quarrel? Evidence of what happened next is found in the form of a response from the ladies to Chartier's *Excuse*. This third letter in verse form, *The Response of the Ladies*, is extant in only four manuscripts, compared to some twenty-five manuscripts of the first letters and Chartier's *Excuse*. More severe in tone than the ladies' original letter, Chartier is threatened with being hung or burned alive if he does not "amend his folly." The ladies are offended by his portrait of a lady as cruel, which they claim defames them all. If he does not repent of his sins or agree to pay reparations, they intend to bring the case before the court of Love and condemn him with the help of their lawyers, "Dessarteaulx" and "Chastel."[18] We do not know if Chartier ever presented himself before the ladies, but we do find in the *Lai de guerre* [*Lay of War*] of Pierre de Nesson (dated before 1429), written in response to Chartier's *Lai de paix* [*Lay of Peace*], a curious passage referring to Alain:

Ainsi que dit son ribault Charretier,
Qui d'elle [Peace] fit une rime avant'ier,
En blasmant ceulx que je norris et paix,
Et l'appelle, le truant, Lay de Paix
Et dit qu'elle est fille du roy des cieulx
Et qu'elle fait tant de bien et de mieulx,
L'ort infame de loyaulté mescreu
Qui ne devroit estre tesmoin ne creu,
Lui qui jadis fut anmy d'Issouldun,

Present son roy et trestout le commun,
Publicquement banni a son de trompe.

—*Lai de guerre*, ed. Piaget/Droz, vv. 49–59

(Just as was said by the depraved Chartier, who made a poem about her not long ago, blaming those that I govern and feed, and that scoundrel calls it the *Lay of Peace* and says that she [Peace] is the daughter of the king of Heaven and that she provides many good things and many advantages, [and is] the disgraceful source of faithless loyalty whose testimony should never be believed, [and Chartier is] the one who formerly was the enemy of Issoudun, and before the king and the entire community he was publicly banished at the sound of the trumpet.)

The allegorical figure War adds that it was Nesson himself who "defamed [Chartier] publicly" (v. 64) at Issoudun, a town neighboring Berry, seat of the exiled Dauphin's court at this time, and the same locale noted in the first letter of the ladies to Chartier. The obvious irony of the context questions the serious nature of the anecdote. The evidence of friendship and professional rivalry between Nesson and Chartier suggests that this "banishment" was a joke. In addition, the scribe of one manuscript in which the *Lay of War* is extant[19] glossed the passage in this way: "Nesson, estant le roy a Issodun, trova une crie de la ville faisant ung cry de par le roy et estoit ladicte crie yvre; si fist Nesson banner maistre Alain par mocquerie par tous les carrefours et de ce parle Gerre en ce lieu" (Nesson, being the king at Issoudun, found a town crier who was working a cry for the king, and this crier was drunk, thus Nesson had Master Alain Chartier banished in mockery in all the town squares, and this is what War is speaking of here).[20]

Never a question of banishment from the court of Charles VII (since Chartier continued to engage in diplomatic missions until his death in 1430), this "banishment" could only have been social if it happened at all. The Court referenced may well be that Cour amoureuse of which Pierre de Hauteville was prince and which entertained the retinue of Charles VI and Charles VII. This social and literary society, founded in 1400 at Tournai, purportedly to promote love and the glory of women, hosted a monthly *puy d'amours* to encourage poetry writing. It also provided a judicial procedure by which actions considered crimes of love might be prosecuted. This must be the court before which the ladies called Chartier; indeed, one of the lawyers they intend to employ, Christine de Pizan's son Chastel, is listed as a member.[21] Whether any sort of banishment took place or not may never be determined; however, what is evident is that the Quarrel captured the imagination of the court, that of Charles VII as well perhaps, since many members of the Cour amoureuse and the poetically inclined were inspired to lift their quills to pen their response.

Borrowing the verse form, and often the characters, of Chartier's *Belle dame*, some eighteen poems catalogued by Piaget participate in the Quarrel.[22] Four of these poems act as sequels to the *Belle dame*; in the continuing narrative, the Belle dame is held responsible for her lover's death of a broken heart and indicted for murder before the allegorical court of love. Some fourteen other poems classified by Piaget rewrite Chartier's poem, correcting either character or consequence of the amorous debate between lover and lady. Found extant in varying number and distribution in thirty-one of the fifty or so *Belle dame* and Quarrel manuscripts, these poems make allusion to the Belle dame or to the Quarrel as they record differing reactions to the *Belle dame*; from their titles one can see how they treat the myriad of interpretations provoked by Chartier's poem.

1. *Les accusations contre la Belle dame sans mercy* or *Le parlement d'amours* [*The Accusations against the Belle dame sans mercy*]
2. *La dame loyalle en amour* [*The Lady Loyal in Love*]
3. *La cruelle femme en amour* [*The Cruel Lady in Love*]
4. *Les erreurs du jugement de la Belle dame sans mercy* [*The Errors of Judgment of the Belle dame sans mercy*]
5. *Dialogue d'un amoureux et de sa dame* [*Dialogue of a Lover and His Lady*]
6. *Le jugement de l'amant banny*[23] [*The Judgment of the Banished Lover*]
7. *Les erreurs de jugement de l'amant banny* [*The Errors of Judgment of the Banished Lover*]
8. *L'amant rendu cordelier à l'observance d'amours* [*The Lover Who Became a Monk in the Rule of Love*]
9. *L'hopital d'amours* [*The Hospital of Love*]
10. *Le traité du reveille qui dort* [*The Treatise of the One Awake While Sleeping*]
11. *Le débat sans conclusion* [*The Debate with No End*]
12. *Le desconseillé d'amours* [*The Bewildered One in Love*]
13. *Le loyal amant refusé* [*The Loyal Lover Refused*]
14. *La desserte du desloyal* [*The Desert of the Disloyal*]
15. *La sepulture d'amours* [*The Tomb of Love*]
16. *Le martyr d'Amour* [*The Martyr of Love*]
17. *Le débat de la dame et de l'ecuyer* [*The Debate of the Lady and the Squire*]
18. *La belle dame ou a mercy* [*The Beautiful Woman Who Has Mercy*].[24]

The Accusations against the Belle Dame Sans Mercy, **Baudet Herenc**

For centuries the *Accusations* was attributed to Chartier. Du Chesne, in his 1617 edition, believed that he might have rediscovered a work of Chartier in his manuscript base, B.N. fr. 1727 (Pe), and so includes it among Chartier's other poems. But in 1894 Piaget revealed in manuscript 3521 (Pn) of the Arsenal library an incipit that attributed the poem to Baudet: "Traittié fait par Baudart Hereng correspondent a la Belle dame sans mercy." (Note that Besançon 554, f. 76r has a similar incipit: "Accusation contre la belle dame sans mercy faicte par maistre Baudet.") He then pieced together details that Gaston Paris had published earlier: Baudet was the author of a *Doctrinal de la seconde rhétorique* contained in Vatican Re.g., 1468. Though the attribution of the *Doctrinal* was originally deciphered to read "Baoldt Hercut," Paris and E. Langlois realized and corrected the mistake with reference to the name of a poet who had received payment on April 7, 1449,[25] from Charles d'Orléans and his wife, Marie de Clèves.[26] According to the accounts of Blois, this poet had presented certain compositions for them in Chalon and had been paid 4 livres, 2 sous, and 6 derniers, not a negligible sum in those days, for his effort.[27] Although Piaget believes that these ballades must now be lost, there is no reason not to believe that among the "balades" presented to the couple was, in fact, the earlier composed *Accusations,* particularly since one of Marie de Clèves's manuscripts (Pj) includes a copy of this text (see description of manuscripts).

Biographical details of Baudet's life are scarce. Unwilling to place his origins in Chalon-sur-Saône despite the Blois entry, Piaget posits that he is from Lille, by association with Pierre de Hauteville, the prince of the Cour amoureuse of Charles VI, who lived in Tournai until 1424 and then moved to Lille. Piaget asserts that in the fifteenth century there lived in Lille a family named Herenc, and that they were connected to the Prince of Love. The evidence he cites is an epitaph put up in a church by a Jehan Herenc, notary, in 1480, which refers to Pierre de Hauteville, "dit le Prinche d'Amours," lord of Ars in Beauvoisis and steward and cup-bearer of the king Charles VI, and at his death (in 1447) counselor and *maitre d'ostel* of the duke of Burgundy.[28]

Ernest Langlois included an edition of Baudet's *Doctrinal de la seconde rhétorique* in his compilation of such treatises, the *Recueil d'arts de seconde rhétorique.* In the introduction to his edition, he comes to more refined conclusions than Piaget about Baudet's origins. Having found and closely studied the only other work we know to have been written by Baudet, Langlois bases his hypothesis on philological evidence of this treatise, dated 1432. The Blois account, he says, confirms what we find in the text: that Baudet knew the Chalonnais region well. Many of the spelling and rhyming words listed in his tables are towns or landmarks of Burgundy: "Bama, qui est une abbaye en Bourgongne," "Iamble, le bon vignoble," la "riviere d'Oce," le "chastel de Rie," "lé, part en Bourgongne," "bois d'anne, qu'on appelle verne en Bourgongne." Moreover, there is complementary evidence that our author was quite familiar with Artois and Flanders: "Louvain, la maistresse ville de Brabant," "Zeriser, une ville de Hollande," "Terremond en Flandres," "Mons en Bareul, qui est ung vilaige prèz de Lile en Flandres," "kuquelins, qui sont petites rondes guaffres en Picardie," "kuque, qui est gastel en Flandres," "une faille, que les femmes portent en Flandres." Langlois concludes that Baudet was living in Flanders when he wrote the *Doctrinal* since there is even greater abundance of references reflecting these locales. In addition, the author's dialectical traits are characteristic of Picardy, and the poetic forms he presents as representative models of poetic form come from that region: *serventois* that are written "A Lisle en Flandres, le premier dimanche devant l'Assumption Nostre Dame," *sottes amoureuses* that are written "a Amiens, le jour de l'an noeuf," and *pastourelles* written "a Bethune en Artoys, chascun an, le dimanche apr la feste Dieu." Such a conclusion, however, need not conflict with the Blois account, for, as he states: "L'oeuvre est d'un pays, l'auteur est d'un autre" (xxxix). Indeed, the author was probably from Burgundy, lived in Flanders for a period (during which he wrote his *Doctrinal*), perhaps even in Lille, and then returned to his hometown of Chalon-sur-Saône.

The *Accusations* of Baudet is the first sequel of the *Belle dame sans mercy*. It is known by several titles in the manuscript tradition: *Les accusations contre la belle dame sans mercy* in Pb,[29] *Le proceix contre la belle damme sans mercy* in Pg, *Le traitie du jugement de la belle dame sans mercy* in Pj, and in Qj as *La cruelle femme en amours*, a title that was probably written in error. In the *Jardin de plaisance* (1501) it is first called the *Parlement d'Amour*, a title repeated by Du Chesne in his edition (1617) and reprinted by Piaget. Since the most common and most descriptive title is the *Accusations contre la belle dame sans mercy* [*Accusations against the Belle Dame Sans Mercy*], that is the title chosen for this edition.

The narrator, while struggling over a ballad to offer to his sweetheart, falls asleep. At this point, the action of the poem takes place in a dream populated with allegorical figures, in imitation of the *Romance of the Rose*. The narrator strolls through the most beautiful garden he has ever seen and comes upon the spot where the court of Love is to be held. Free Will is the president of the twelve judges, Hope is the prosecutor for Love, Desire is the lead attorney, and Memory is the clerk of the court. Sweet Thought, the bailiff, calls the Belle dame, alone and red with shame, before the court, where Desire accuses her of murder, claiming that refusal to grant her pity to the lover caused his death. He also accuses her of treason against Love for her portrait of him as "foolish" and "unwise." Desire seeks to indict the Belle dame by the evidence of her own words, repeated in approximation from Chartier's poem. After he has presented his case, Free Will invites her to launch a defense, but when she asks for a lawyer to volunteer to defend her, none dares because of the words she has spoken against Love. She requests and is granted a stay for lack of representation. The narrator awakens, takes up his pen, and records all that he has seen in a ballad, which he will offer to his lady in the hope that she will not treat him as the Belle dame treated her lover.

There is no internal evidence by which the poem might be dated; Piaget, however, imagines that it must have been written soon after Chartier's *Excuse*, and certainly before Baudet wrote his *Doctrinal*, by the logic that Baudet would never claim not to be proficient at writing verse (lines 14–15) after having composed a treatise on poetry. While we might object that "one does not have to be a good poet to elaborate a good theory of poetry,"[30] his assumptions are certainly reasonable. None of the manuscripts in which the poem is extant, however, can be dated before the middle of the fifteenth century. We do know, as mentioned above, that Baudet performed before Marie de Clèves and Charles d'Orléans in 1449. Marie's copy of the *Accusations* found in Pj[31] is abbreviated: it ends at line 560, just before Free Will calls for the Belle dame's defense and she is forced to ask for a stay. As the poem reads, the trial appears complete: the accused is found guilty and sentenced to be locked up in the prison of pain. Could it be that this is the earliest version of the poem and that the tantalizingly unresolved ending was written later, in a deliberate attempt to prolong the debate?[32] While the poem was probably written before 1440 (see below), Marie may still have managed to preserve one of the earliest manifestations of the Quarrel by having Baudet's early version of the poem recopied in her codex.

The Lady Loyal in Love, **Anonymous**

Although the poet's identity remains unknown, Piaget suspects he must have been a part of the literary circle surrounding Pierre de Hauteville, the Prince of Love of the Cour amoureuse. The *Lady Loyal in Love* begins where the *Accusations* ended. Its author indicates in numerous passages an intimate knowledge of the preceding poem. At the close of the *Accusations*, the Belle dame was in tears because no lawyer would agree to take her case. She asked for and was granted a delay in the proceedings. In the *Loyal*, a new narrator, remembering a traumatic moment when his lady refused him, consoles himself by going hunting. In a valley strewn with the caskets and tombs of unfaithful lovers, he finds the Belle dame crying inconsolably. He cajoles her into telling him what has upset her: she has been accused unjustly of a crime. Suddenly the messengers of the God of Love appear. The case of the Belle dame must continue; the narrator must accompany her to serve as witness to the proceedings. They are whisked away up into the sky, passing first through a red sky reserved for those too proud in love, then through a green sky where fickle lovers reside, then through a sky of white and blue, where they see the loyal lovers of old before ultimately passing into a sky that encompasses the others and in which is held the court of Love. Set down before the judges' thrones, the Belle dame is asked to choose a lawyer to represent her. She requests the services of Loyalty and Truth. After Desire's reiteration of his conclusion in the previous poem, the defense lawyers argue before the court that the Belle dame is not responsible for the death of the lover. In a surprising narrative twist, it is revealed that the reason the lady refused the lover's advances was because she already had a secret lover to whom she wished to remain loyal. The doctrines of love, whereby a lady is given the freedom to choose her lover but then required to rest faithful to him, are entered as justifications for the lady's actions. Her name should be the Lady Loyal in Love, not the Lady without Mercy. In a typical defensive strategy, the Belle dame's lawyers point the blame first at the lover, who was deluding himself, then at the author of the poem, Alain Chartier, who must have had it in for her, and finally at Desire and Hope, who inflamed the lover beyond hope. After Love convenes his counsel, Gracious Speech announces the verdict: the lady will be called the Lady Loyal in Love. Moreover, Desire and Hope will be called to trial for their crimes. Suddenly the narrator finds himself alone in the valley. He realizes that it is prudent to beware of too ardent a desire.

The date of the poem is uncertain, except that it must have been written after the *Accusations,* for the author of the poem refutes point by point the criticisms of the lady that were raised in the *Accusations.* But the introduction of new information, that of a secret lover, was apparently unpalatable to the supporters of the defunct lover, and the next poem in the series sought a conclusive end to the Belle dame.

The Cruel Woman in Love, Achilles Caulier

What little we know of Achilles Caulier's life is also based on Piaget. He posits that our author may be from Tournai and may well have participated in an association known as the "Chapel vert," a presumption drawn from a reference within the *Cruel Woman* to pilgrims putting a "vert chapel" around the neck of Venus in order to win the goddess's favor (line 198). According to Piaget, the members of the "Chapel vert" were required to wear "un chapelte vert sur la teste ou au col" at dinner and other ceremonies (317). Three poems are attributed to Achilles Caulier. The first is *The Cruel Woman in Love,* of which the last stanza gives an acrostic of his first name, A-C-I-L-E-S. *The Hospital of Love,* considered one of the imitation poems and closely linked in the manuscript tradition with the *Belle dame sans mercy* and the Quarrel, was for a long time attributed to Alain Chartier and published with his works in the earliest printed editions. The first verses of the first six stanzas of this poem form the same acrostic, A-C-I-L-E-S. The third work attributed to him is *The Lay in Honor of Our Lady,* a short (244 lines) religious poem extant in only four manuscripts, attributed to him in Pn. The dates of *The Cruel Woman* and the *Hospital of Love* are uncertain. We know that the *Cruel Woman* was written after the *Accusations* and the *Loyal,* both of which are referred to in this poem. The *Hospital* makes specific reference to the *Cruel Woman* when he recalls the sentence handed down to her:

Entre ces faulx amants couchoit
La ditte dame que l'en dit
"Sans mercy," laquelle y estoit
Gettee comme par despit.
Elle avoit esté sans respit
Nouvellement noiee en plours,
Et la nommoit l'en par escript
La cruelle femme en amours

(Among these unfaithful lovers was the aforementioned lady named "with no mercy"; she had been tossed away as if in contempt. Condemned without appeal and recently drowned in tears, she was renamed in writing the Cruel Woman in Love.)

The *Hospital* in turn is alluded to in Martin Le Franc's *Champion des Dames* [*Champion of Ladies*]: "Elle n'est pas a l'ospital / Comme ne sçay qui l'a songié" (She is not at the hospital, as was dreamed by who knows who) (1905–6). The *Champion* has been dated before the end of 1441 or the beginning of 1442, when it is presumed that Martin Le Franc presented this 24,384-line defense of women to Phillippe of Burgundy. In addition, the poet mentions Chartier's death in the *Cruel Woman* (lines 481–88) and locates his tombstone in the cemetery of the *Hospital* (lines 426–27). Assuming accuracy in the dating of the *Champion des Dames*, both the *Cruel Woman* and the *Hospital of Love* must be dated after 1430 and before 1441.

The *Cruel Woman* seeks to repudiate the judgment of the *Loyal* and again, point by point, refers to it. In this third poem of the series, the narrator, in a state of extreme sadness and confusion, rides out into a valley devoid of all joy and pleasure. Brooding on his sadness, he enters into a trancelike state and has a vision. He finds himself in a palace of the most amazing construction, with walls depicting literary scenes as well as images of the past and the future. Whisked away in a cloud, he then is introduced to a marvelous city wherein is located the Hall of Justice (called the Hall of Hope), where those who are in amorous quest live. He visits the temple of Venus to pay homage, then passes through a cemetery where loyal lovers are buried. Returning to the court of Love, he spies a young squire dressed in black, a friend of the defunct lover, who requests an appeal of the verdict of the previous trial, claiming that it had been won by trickery, for Truth and Loyalty, the Belle dame's lawyers, were none other than Fiction and Falsity, disguised to pass as the more noble figures. Truth is called in to verify the claim and proves the deception of the previous case by pointing out that the Belle dame herself denied having any lover. Since her innocence was based on this evidence, the verdict is overturned and the trial begins again. The accusations against the Belle dame are once more introduced, the probity of her creator, Alain Chartier, reestablished, and the heartless lady forced to confess. Condemned to drown in the well of tears, the Belle dame is punished in the most severe terms. The narrator awakens in the valley and returns to his house, where he writes down what he has seen. In a final stanza, he appeals to ladies, especially to the one he loves, not to resemble this Belle dame sans mercy.

The nut of the Quarrel has taken a curious transformation. The original criticisms of the courtiers and the ladies against Alain Chartier, poet, have been transferred to his character, the Belle dame. His name and reputation as author are placed above reproach, rehabilitated from the earlier poem, the *Lady Loyal in Love*, which criticized him but praised his Belle dame for playing the game of love faithfully, having learned the lesson of the *Châtelaine de Vergy* and kept her love a secret. The other character who plays a role in this courtroom drama, the defunct lover, undergoes a series of transformations as well. He, created by Chartier as the perfect courtly lover who strives to attain the inaccessible woman of stone, is recast in the *Loyal* as the very scoundrel Chartier warned against, before finally being resuscitated as a martyr of love. The play of the literary quarrel, too, changes tone, as the litigious proceedings and the specter of death take center stage. Chartier's favored topoi of patriotism and courtliness are eclipsed, his original message lost in the reception of his work. The language of the legal system replaces the poetry, and in the final phase of the trial presented in the *Errors of Judgment of the Belle dame sans mercy*, the process becomes almost absurd.

The Errors of Judgment of the Belle Dame Sans Mercy, **Anonymous**

This poem is extant in only three manuscripts; it was not a widely read text of the Quarrel and appears to be one or several poets' attempt to keep going a cycle that had already moved beyond the trial series. At great length are repeated all the arguments of the previous poems, written in much the same way that legal cases were recorded: in third person with little discourse. Its syntax is generally simple: each line is a phrase and each stanza a sentence. The language is even more saturated with legalese, and while the allegorical characters are still present, the plaintiffs and defendants, heirs of the Belle dame and the dead lover, are the primary characters. The poem displays an evolution of the poetic legal game that concentrates more on legal contortions and humor than on poetics. Allusions and responses are made to unidentified sources, which suggests that this work is several steps removed from the first three trial poems, although no intermediary poems have been found. Moreover, it is never listed as one of the "books of the Belle dame," as are the other poems, and may have been written sometime afterward: the three manuscripts in which it is extant date to the end of the fifteenth century.

The poem is recounted by a narrator who is all but invisible until the final lines of the poem. The heirs of the defunct Belle dame, now known as the Cruel Woman, return to the court to request that the judgment rendered in the *Cruel Woman in Love* be modified. They explain that the lover had evil intentions; their relative was justified in her refusal of such a rogue. In addition, they feel that the sentence was far too harsh. Not only has the punishment for her crime cost the Belle dame her life and destroyed her reputation, but it also damaged the reputation of her noble family. In the hope that the court will take mercy on them, they present the following twelve legal errors as grounds for the judgment to be rescinded.

1. Because the belle dame was of noble birth, she should not have been put to death in such a cruel way in public (121–28).
2. The Belle dame tried to dissuade the lover from his hopeless endeavor, but he refused to heed her words (129–36).
3. The Belle dame did the lover no physical harm, despite his intention to dishonor her. In addition, she had every right to refuse his advances if she so wished, as is the right of all ladies (17–60).
4. The court based its decision on hearsay: that of a malicious writer who wished to defame the Belle dame (161–68).
5. According to the decrees of Love, no lover can complain if he has not been three times refused. This lover had addressed the Belle dame no more than twice and had been refused only once (169–84).
6. The Belle dame had no legal defense at her final trial (185–92).
7. Her confession was given under extreme duress and therefore should not be admitted as evidence (193–208).
8. In a capital murder case, all the judges must be present. In this case several of the lords were wandering around the halls when deliberations were held (209–16).
9. The cause of the lover's death has not been established and may not have been attributable to the Belle dame's refusal, for the lover traveled around and lived a full month after his encounter with her (217–32).
10. In the lover's last will and testament, he blamed no one for his death, but granted forgiveness to everyone (233–40).
11. The court should have taken into account the Belle dame's youth and beauty (241–48).
12. The goddesses Mercy, Peace, and Concord were not allowed by the court to testify in her behalf (249–56).

The defendants, the lover's heirs, respond to and attempt to refute all twelve of these alleged errors with explanations and justifications as creative and long-winded as the plaintiffs'. The plaintiffs rebut the defense and emphasize the shame endured by the family of the convicted Belle dame. Even though the unjustly executed lady cannot be raised from the dead, the court could have mercy on the family and relieve them of this miserable reputation. After deliberation, the court pronounces that the original verdict will be upheld. However, in view of the hardship and grief suffered by the Belle dame's descendants, they will be allowed to collect the bones of their relative from the well of tears and bury them in a cemetery, though no tombstone will be allowed. Before the court can finish its pronouncement, two courtiers enter the chambers with birds. They have, however, forgotten their gloves, and the birds escape, disrupting the proceedings. The president of the court, in a fury, dismisses the court and reschedules the session to a later date, which our narrator intends to attend, no matter what the cost of staying in town, since he wishes to accurately report all he has seen.

The Hospital of Love, **Achilles Caulier**

The *Hospital of Love* was attributed for many years to Alain Chartier. Despite Clément Marot's claim that the poem was unworthy of Chartier,[33] Du Chesne included the poem in his 1617 edition of Chartier's works. Now knowing the name of the author, we can decipher the acrostic A-C-I-L-E-S in the initial of the first six stanzas of the poem. *The Hospital* is the imitation poem most frequently copied with the *Belle dame* and is considered an integral part of the Quarrel even though it does not introduce the same characters or continue the trial. Instead Achilles introduces himself as a narrator in much the same position as the lover of the Belle dame, but instead of dying of his grief, he will make his way to the Hospital of Love for treatment. The Belle dame's lover's fate is thus recast: the lover, who achieves limited success with regard to a formerly pitiless lady, is given the promise of recovery.

Restless with desire, the narrator arrives at a party, where he spies his lady. After he reveals his love for her, she rebuffs him, and he wanders off alone, overcome with heartache. He finds himself on the road named Too Harsh Response, which leads him through a macabre valley strewn with the corpses of famous lovers and past the fountain of Narcissus. Patience and Hope come to him, help him escape from this place, and leave him in front of the Hospital of Love. Fair Welcoming is the porter, Pity the prioress, Courtesy the nurse, and Hope the physician. After being triaged by Courtesy and put in a sumptuous bed, Hope brings him a potion of Sweet Thought. This medicine heals him enough to ask Pity permission for a kiss from his lady. After obtaining the kiss, he feels better and strolls through the cemetery, where he sees the tombs of loyal lovers, including Alain Chartier and the lover who died from the Belle dame's refusal. On the other side he sees the graves of unfaithful lovers, including that of the one called the Cruel Woman in Love. Suddenly he is beset by Desire and falls ill again. Understanding and Hope visit him in his hospital bed, and then he falls asleep. In his dream the God of Love comes to him to remind him of his teachings, which the narrator has forgotten. Love recounts the story of the emblematic lover, not omitting any of the tribulations or tortures that must be endured before his lady finally listens to the lover's request and grants her grace. The narrator awakens and immediately returns to his lady for another kiss, but he must then leave because of the threats of Envy and Foul Mouth. He returns to the Hospital of Love, where he graciously thanks those who helped him. The sleeping narrator is disturbed by the sound of voices and gets up to write down this dream, which he plans to present to his lady.

The Belle Dame Who Has Mercy

Extant in eighteen manuscripts, *The Belle Dame Who Has Mercy* was given a new title in almost every manuscript copy: *La belle dame ou a mercy, La dame qui eut mercy de son amant, La belle dame a mercy, Complainte d'amours et response faicte par maistre Alain Charretier . . . , Complainte d'amant a amye, Ung traittie en maniere de prieres en amours, etc.* It was published by Pierre Le Caron in the earliest edition of Chartier's works and in all subsequent incunabula; the poem also circulated in several single-work editions.

Attributed to Chartier in several manuscripts and in all of the early editions, the author of the poem remains uncertain. In 1890 Piaget suggested that the poem was by Oton de Grandson, yet in his edition of Oton de Grandson's collected works (dated 1941) *The Belle Dame Who Has Mercy* is not included or even mentioned. It appears that Piaget changed his mind, not surprisingly. The ending of the poem is uncharacteristic of the reputation of Oton de Grandson's poetry, renowned for his depiction of a heartless woman in the *Livre messire ode*, and a fickle one in *Complainte de Saint Valentin*. As Kelly puts it: "The Image of the *unfaithful and unattainable lady* was to give Oton de Grandson a popularity and influence far beyond what his talents as a poet would lead one to expect" (italics added).[34] Grenier-Winther still suggests that Achilles Caulier may be the author,[35] but has not yet provided sufficient evidence for positive attribution.

This antipode to Chartier's *Belle dame sans mercy* seeks to correct the response of the lady by having her capitulate to the lover's prayers. With no narratorial introduction, the lover woos his Belle dame with flattery and pleas for mercy. She is as resistant and skeptical as Chartier's Belle dame, though more polite about listening to the lover's speeches. She mentions a husband (living or dead?), who provides the reason for her initial refusal. After thirty-three stanzas, however, she is quite suddenly overwhelmed with passion for the lover; extracting a promise from him to be discreet and faithful, she commits to being his sweetheart. The sexual allusions (beyond a kiss), usually revealed in double entendres, are rampant; by their frequency they distinguish this poem from other Quarrel poems.

The Manuscripts

The poems presented in this edition are closely linked intertextually by their direct references to each other, as well as externally by their manuscript environment and their titles. Some thirty-five manuscripts that contain the Piaget "imitation" poems have been identified. The manuscripts range in quality from luxuriously decorated copies made for members of the nobility or the royal family to those one might refer to as "working manuscripts" of paper, with frequent corrections and other marginal indications, little or no decoration, and often arranged so that each item is contained in its own quire. The *"Belle dame"* is extant in forty-four manuscripts, of which thirty-one contain the letters and the *Excuse*. The sequel poems are contained in twenty-four manuscripts collectively; in nineteen of these twenty-four the *"Belle dame"* is also copied. The frequency of occurrence of the poems together in these manuscripts confirms the idea that there was a contemporary notion of a cycle of the *Belle dame*. None of the manuscripts that collect the sequel poems can be dated before 1445, which is curious since Piaget postulates that the imitation poems were probably written soon after the *Belle dame* — around 1430, just after Chartier's death.

Manuscript sigla used are those chosen by Laidlaw for the *Poetical Works* (43–60). They are based on a system that designates manuscripts containing the *Belle dame* and imitation poems that are found in Paris as P, manuscripts containing the *Belle dame* and imitation poems found outside of Paris as Q. Five manuscripts that do not contain Chartier's works require sigla: Pq, Px, Qs, Qt, Qx. They have been labeled following the principals of Laidlaw's system.

Pa	Paris BNF, fr. 833
Pb	Paris BNF, fr. 924
Pc	Paris BNF, fr. 1131
Pd	Paris, BNF, fr. 1642
Pe	Paris, BNF, fr. 1727
Pf	Paris, BNF, fr. 2230
Pg	Paris, BNF, fr. 2264
Ph	Paris, BNF, fr. 19131
Pj	Paris, BNF, fr. 20026

Pk   Paris, BNF, fr. 24440
Pl   Paris, BNF, Fonds Rothschild 440 (I.4.31)
Pm   Paris, BNF, fr. 1661
Pn   Paris, Arsenal, 3521
Po   Paris, Arsenal, 3523
Pp   Paris, Musée Jacquemar-André, 11
Pq   Paris, BNF, fr. 1661
Px   Paris, BNF, n.ac. 4237 (labeled Pr by Hult; Px by Hurlbut)
Qa   Besançon, Bibl. Mun., 554
Qb   Carpentras, Bibl. Mun., 390
Qc   Chantilly, Musée Condé, 686
Qd   Toulouse, Bibl. Mun., 826
Qf   Bibl. Arnhem, prov. de Gueldre, 79
Qh   Copenhagen, Bib. Roy. Ny Kgl., S. 1768.2
Qi   Fribourg-Diesbach [private collection, currently lost]
Qk   La Haye, Bib. Roy., 71.E.49
Ql   St. Petersburg, Bib. Saltikov-Schedrin, fr. f. V.XIV.7
Qm   London, British Museum, Royal 19.A.iii
Qn   London, Sotheby Clumber sale (06/12/37), no. 941 [currently
     lost]
Qp   Turin, Bib. Naz. Univ., L.II.12
Qq   Rome, Vat. Lat., 4794
Qr   Vienna, Bib. Nat., 2619
Qs   Turin, Bib. Naz. Univ., L.IV.3
Qt   Rom, Vat. Re.g., 1363
Qx   London, Westminster Abbey, Ms. 21

The poems are extant in varying number and distribution. The manuscripts for
each poem are listed below, along with their incipit and explicit wherever possible.

I.   The *Belle dame sans mercy*, 44 manuscripts; see Laidlaw, p. 328
II.   *The Request Sent to the Ladies*, 25 manuscripts
III.   *The Letter of the Ladies Sent to Chartier*, 25 manuscripts
IV.   *The Excuse of Master Alain*, 31 manuscripts
V.   *The Response of the Ladies*, 4 manuscripts
       1. Pn   Arsenal 3521 f. 74–75v
       2. Qa   Besançon, Bib. Mun. f. 77–79

3. Qj   Fribourg Diesbach f. 30–30v

4. Qf   Arnhem f. 45r

VI. *The Accusations against the Belle Dame Sans Mercy,* Baudet Herenc, 18 manuscripts

1. Pb   f. 27–39v. Incipit: "Accusacions contre la belle dame sans mercy." Explicit: "A quoi serons contre la belle dame sans mercy" in the hand of Jacques Thiboust.

2. Pc   f. 108v–116v. No incipit. "Explicit."

3. Pd   f. 253–261v. Incipit: "S'ensuivent les accusacions faictes et donnees par Desir et Espoir contre la dame sans mercy." Explicit: "Cy finissent les accusacions faictes contre la dame sans mercy ou elle demanda et eut estat par absence de conseil."

4. Pe   f. 136–144v. No incipit. "Explicit."

5. Pf   f. 148v–160. Incipit: "Apres s'ensuit comment la belle dame sans mercy fut traittee en jugement en la court du dieu d'Amours pour respondre aux articles contre lui imposees . . ." Explicit: "Le traittie du jugement de la belle dame sans mercy en la court du dieu d'Amours."

6. Pg   f. 19v–32. Incipit: "Cy commance le proceix contre la belle damme sans mercy." Explicit: "Le proceix contre la belle damme sans mercy."

7. Pj   f. 28–37. Explicit: "Le traitie du jugement de la belle dame sans mercy en la court du dieu d'Amours."

8. Pk   f. 121v–129. Incipit: "Le Parlement d'Amours" in a more modern hand. No explicit.

9. Pn   f. 76–85. Incipit: "Traittie faict par Budet Hereng correspondant a la belle dame sans mercy." No explicit.

10. Po   f. 165–186. Incipit: "La Responce de la belle dame sans mercy." No explicit.

11. Qa   f. 32–44v. Incipit: "Accusation contre la Belle dame sans mercy faicte par maistre Baudet." No explicit.

12. Qf   f. 17–26. Incipit: "La confession de la belle dame sans mercy devant Amour." "Explicit."

13. Qh   f. 24–33v. "Accusacions contre la belle dams sans mercy." "Explicit."

14. Qj   f. 44v–56v. Incipit: "La Cruelle femme en amours et comment elle fu jugie et accusee devant Amours." Explicit: "Comment la belle dame sans mercy fut jugie et accusee devant Amours et appellee la cruelle femme en amours."

15. Qk f. 29–38v. Incipit: "Accusacions contre la belle dame sans mercy." Explicit: "La Response et accusacion de la belle dame dans mercy."

16. Ql f. 132v–144v. Incipit: "Le Procés contre la belle dame sans mercy dont elle demanda deslay." Explicit: "Le Jugement de la belle dame sans mercy."

17. Qm f. 17–28v. Beginning is incomplete. Explicit: "Les Accusations contre la belle dame sans mercy."

18. Qs f. 99–108. Incipit: "Balade faicte par maistre Alain." No explicit.[36]

VII. *The Lady Loyal in Love,* anonymous, 13 manuscripts

1. Pb f. 71–89v. Incipit: "La Loyalle dame en amours." "Explicit la loyalle dame en amours."

2. Pc f. 117–130v. No title. "Explicit."

3. Pq f. 107–126v. Incipit: "La dame lealle en amours." "Explicit la dame leale en amours."

4. Pd f. 240–252. Incipit: "S'ensuit le jugement comme la dame qu'on disoit estre sans mercy fut trouvee loyalle en amours." "Explicit le jugement et arrest donné par la cour et parlement du dieu d'amours au prouffit de la belle dame sans mercy, laquelle a esté trouvee loyalle en amours."

5. Pg f. 32–40. Incomplete. Incipit: "Si commance l'excusation de la belle damme sans mercy." Last line: "Mais il y a une autre loy."

6. Pk f. 129–142v. No title.

7. Pn f. 86–99. Incipit: "La dame leale en amours."

8. Qa f. 45r. Incipit: "Parlement contre la belle dame."

9. Qf f. 27–40v. Incipit: "La dame leale en amours." "Explicit.'

10. Qh f. 34–47v. Incipit: "La loyalle dame en amours." "Explicit."

11. Qi f. 57–79v. Incipit: "Cy commence ly second livre sur la belle damme, et est appellee la leale dame en amours." "Explicit le second livre fait pour la belle damme et devise comment ly dicte belle dame fut appelle par jugement devant amour la leale damme en amours contre ce que ly livre precedant cestuy l'appelle la cruelle femme en amours."

12. Qk f. 50–64. No incipit. "Explicit la loyalle dame en amours nommee par sentence."

13. Ql f. 115–132v. Incipit: "Le jugement comment la dame fut trouve loyale en amours." Explicit: "Le jugement de la dame trouve loyalle en amours."

VIII. *The Cruel Woman in Love,* Achilles Caulier, 16 manuscripts

1. Pb f. 51–70v. Incipit: "La condempnacion et jugement de la belle dame sans mercy." Explicit: "La cruelle dame en amours qui est la condemnation et jugement de la belle dame sans mercy."

2. Pc   f. 131–146. Incipit: "La cruelle femme en amours, que on dit le procés de la belle dame sans mercy." Explicit: "Cy fine la cruelle femme en amours que on dist le procés de la belle dame sans mercy."

3. Pq   f. 127–143. Incipit: "Le jugement contraire a la leale dame en amours." "Explicit le jugement."

4. Pd   f. 262–272v. Incomplete. Incipit: "Cy commence le jugement de la belle dame sans mercy par lequel est nommee la cruelle dame en amours et desgradee de non avoir jamais nom de dame." Last line: "Et soit l'amant a tort finé."

5. Pk   f. 142v–157. No title.

6. Pn   f. 100–114. "S'ensuit la cruelle femme en amours."

7. Po   pp. 187–218. "S'ensuit les erreurs contraires a la belle dame en amours."

8. Qc   f. 71r. No title.

9. Qf   f. 53–57v. Incipit: "La cruelle femme en amours." Explicit: "Cy finit les erreurs de la belle dame sans mercy."

10. Qh   f. 56v–70v. "Cy commence la condemnation et jugement de la belle dame sans mercy."

11. Qj   f. 75–94. Incipit: "Cy commence ly tier livre fait sur la belle damme, devisant comment ly belle damme derichief fut appellee par jugement devant Amours ly cruelle femme en amours et comment ly jugement cy devant de la leale damme fu reprouvé." Explicit: "Cy finist comment derechief ly belle damme sans mercy fut jugie d'estre nommee la cruelle femme en amour et comment ly jugement ouquel elle fu appellee ly leale damme fu reprouvé."

12. Qk   f. 65–79v. No title. "Explicit les erreurs et jugements de la belle dame sans mercy."

13. Ql   f. 98–114v. Incipit: "Cy commence la cruelle dame en amours." Explicit: "Cy fine la cruelle femme en amours qu'on dist le procés de la belle dame sans mercy."

14. Qn   f. 122. Incipit: "Le Procès et Condemnation de la Belle Dame sans Mercy."

15. Qq   f. 31–45v. Incipit: "Condamnation de la dame sans mercy." No explicit. (Formerly thought to be *Accusations*, see note.)

16. Qr   f. 80–85. Incipit: "Cy commence le jugement et condanpnacion de la belle dame sans mercy."

IX. *The Errors of Judgment of the Belle dame sans mercy,* anonymous, 3 manuscripts

    1.   Pb   f. 90–111v. "Les erreurs de la belle dame sans mercy."

    2.   Qh   f. 71r–87r. "Cy comancent les erreurs de la belle dame sans mercy."

    3.   Qt   f. 217r–249r. "Cy commencent les erreurs du jugement de la belle dame sans mercy."

X. *The Hospital of Love,* Achilles Caulier, 22 manuscripts

    1.   Pa   f. 162v–172. No incipit.

    2.   Pb   f. 112–138. "L'ospital d'Amours."

    3.   Pc   f.146–166v. "L'Hospital d'Amours."

    4.   Pd   f. 205r–224r. "Cy commence l'ospital d'amours."

    5.   Pf   f. 184–211v. "Cy commence l'ospital d'amours."

    6.   Ph   f. 358–403.

    7.   Px   f. 77v. Incomplete.

    8.   Pl   f. 115–139v.

    9.   Pm   f. 217–235v.

    10.   Pn   f. 115–134v. "L'Ospital d'amours."

    11.   Po   pp. 281–320. "L'ospital d'amours."

    12.   Pp   pp. 1–41. "L'ospital d'amours" (called Lib. Morgand by Piaget), *Romania* 34, 560, and Hult (Hult and McRae p. 327, note 1, and thus mistakenly counted twice; Morgand was the name of the sales catalogue of 1893 in which the manuscript was listed before being purchased by Mme. Jacquemart-André).

    13.   Qa   f. 107v. "Ospital d'amour."

    14.   Qb   f. 21r–37v.

    15.   Qe   f. 14–38v.

    16.   Qh   f. 159r. "Cy commence l'opital d'amour."

    17.   Qk   f. 151–170. No incipit.

    18.   Qn   f. 113v. "Le livre de l'Hopital d'amour."

    19.   Qo   f. 37.

    20.   Qp   f. 131v–141. Burned, not listed by Hurlbut.

    21.   Qq   f. 46–65. Hurlbut writes 4798.

    22.   Qr   fol. 135v–142v. "Cy apres commance l'ospital d'amours fait par achilles caulier."

XI. *The Belle Dame Who Has Mercy,* attributed to Oton de Grandson, 19 manuscripts

    1.   Pa   f. 128.

    2.   Pb   f. 19r. "La belle dame ou a mercy."

    3.   Pc   f. 184r. "La dame qui eut mercy de son amant."

4.   Pd   f. 285–290. "La belle dame a mercy."

5.   Pe   f. 124r. "Complaincte d'amours et responce faicte par maistre Alain Charretier, secretaire du roy."

6.   Pf   f. 160r. "Apres s'enssuit le traitte de la belle dame a mercy."

7.   Pj   f. 39v. "Appres s'enssuit la dame a mercy."

8.   Pk   f. 160. "Complainte d'amant a amye."

9.   Pl   f. 107. No incipit.

10. Po   f. 339. "Dialogue entre l'amant et la dame."

11. P   pp. 75. "Ung traittie en maniere de prieres en amours."

12. Qa   f. 79v. "Cy s'ensuit une complainte d'amours que l'on dit autrement la belle dame a mercy faicte par maistre Alain Charretier."

13. Qb   fol. 61r–69v.

14. Qh   f. 16r. "Cy commence la belle dame a mercy."

15. Qn   f. 102r. "La Belle dame ou mercy."

16. Qp   f. 103r.

17. Qq   f. 25r–30v. "La belle dame ou a mercy." Missing first line.

18. Qr   f. 143d–146a.

19. Qx   f. 78.

Choice of Base Manuscripts

The choice of a base manuscript is rarely an easy one. Since the manuscript tradition of the Quarrel documents seems to be founded to some extent on the circulation of individual poems, the quality of the texts in a given manuscript can vary widely, with the exception of manuscripts that appear to have been copied directly from another—Pk from Pc, for example, Pf from Pj, or Qh from Pb. The Quarrel is represented in the manuscript tradition in its many stages of development, or according to the interests of the buyer of a manuscript who chooses which texts to include in the codex. Thus we see manuscripts that contain several of the texts but not all, as well as manuscripts that collect almost the entire series of poems.[37] Since the Quarrel grew and expanded, it seemed logical to choose base manuscripts that witness the development of the Quarrel.[38] Pj was selected as base for the first stage of the saga: the *Belle dame sans mercy*, the *Letter of the Ladies to Alain*, the *Request Sent to the Ladies*, the *Excuse of Master Alain*, the *Accusations*, and the *Belle Dame Who Has Mercy*, along with the closely related Pf, from which the *Hospital of Love* has been edited. None of the manuscripts has all the poems and letters of the Belle dame's trial. However, in eleven of the manuscripts are collected the five essential Quarrel poems with two letters. Pn has been chosen to represent this progression of the Quarrel through the condemnation of the lady: the *Lady Loyal in Love* and the *Cruel Woman in Love*, as well as the third letter, the *Response of the Ladies,* have been edited from this manuscript. The final poem of the trial series, the less popular *Errors of Judgement of the Belle Dame Sans Mercy,* a postmortem trial on behalf of the heirs of the Belle dame, has been abridged and edited from Pb, a manuscript that contains all of the Quarrel documents except the *Response of the Ladies* but often presents heavily edited copies of the texts.

Descriptions of the Manuscripts[39]

Bibliothèque National, Fonds Français, 20026 (Pj)

This manuscript is made of parchment, contains 179 folios plus three flyleaves, and measures 220 by 150 mm (135 by 70 written area), with thirty lines per page. The collation as recorded by Laidlaw is as follows: A[4] (first folio canceled): 1–22 quires of 8: B[4]. The parchment is not of the highest quality: it is yellow, well worn in margins, many places are stitched, the edges are often short. The pricking is still visible on some leaves, as are the catchwords. Initials of new items are gilded and decorated, as are the borders.[40] The manuscript was commissioned for Marie de Clèves, the third wife of Charles d'Orléans. In the financial records of the duke of Orléans, we see that Marie was fond of having books recopied or rebound; this manuscript appears to have been recopied, at least partially, from poems belonging to her husband. Charles's paper copy of the *Quatre dames*, attested to in his 1442 record of the books he kept with him in captivity ("ung viel livre des Quatre Dames, en papier, couvert de viel parchemin"; Champion, *Librairie* 30) likely served as exemplar for the final text of this new codex. Charles may have had copies of other texts that also served as exemplars; indeed, he may also have owned an early copy of the *Belle dame sans mercy.* Records indicate some confusion over whether a certain paper booklet was the *Cent ballades* or the *Belle dame,* identified by its first line once as the *Cent ballades* ("Une fois chavchant [*sic*] pensoye") and another time as the *Belle dame* ("Nagueres chevauchant pensoie").[41] As mentioned earlier, Baudet Herenc performed before Marie and Charles in April 1449 at Chalon-sur-Saône. The copy of the *Accusations* may well have been given to the couple by Baudet himself. The exemplar of Machaut's *Jugement du roi de Bohème* could be the "Machault" owned by the Bastard of Orléans[42] (Charles was notorious for lending manuscripts; we can presume that he also borrowed them) or perhaps is one of the many unnamed manuscripts in Charles's collection.

The date accorded to the codex is the mid-fifteenth century, certainly after 1440, the date of Charles's release from English captivity and his marriage to Marie. Her coat of arms appears three times on the front folio: the arms of Orléans and Clèves impaled. In addition, her device, "Rien ne m'est plus," adopted from Charles's mother, Valentine de Milan, is written on scrolls in the decoration of the margin. The manuscript appears to have originally been covered in blue velvet (a trace of this fabric still remains in the back flyleaf), a common color for royal books, since the remains of clothing fabric were often used for book covers. In the eighteenth century it was recovered in pounced parchment and then in 1967 recovered again in blue velvet.[43]

Most fascinating about the manuscript is the plethora of signatures adorning its flyleaves, which indicates to us that this codex was used as a conversation point for one or more courtly gatherings; indeed, the margins of the first items, the *Belle dame sans mercy* and Quarrel documents, are well thumbed. Among the fifty-eight signatures and devices are: Marie de Clèves, "Rien ne m'est plus"; René d'Anjou, "FVT," as well as his son, Jean (who signed his name "Lorrainne"), with the device "Ce mieulx ne puis" and daughter Yolande d'Anjou; Charles d'Orléans, who signs "De bon cuer le vouz donnray"; and the future Louis XII, who signs "Loys d'Orleans" with the device "Riens n'y demeure." The other identifiable signatures are of friends and members of the household services of Charles d'Orléans and his good friend King René.[44] Some of these same signatures also appear in the flyleaves of Pf. A poem that appears to be by René d'Anjou is found on the front flyleaf and introduces the codex:

Ung oeil en		Sur tout occasion
ung regard		Sans faillir le larron
Doulz semblant	FvT	Cellui qui l'emporta
Espoir si		Qui plus me conforta
	Quant le perdy mon cuer par mesprison	
Ung desir		plus ardant que charbon
Ung plaisir	FvT	sans rime ne raison
	Qui de ce faire en tel point en horta	
Ung gemir		lors ouy abas son
Ung soupir		rempli de passion
Ung penser	FvT	qu'aultre soing debouta
Ung vouloir		qui le povoir m'osta
	Et le donna a aultruy habandon	
	Ung oeil en fut sur tout occasion	

Contents, with common title, authorial attribution, and incipit:

1r. *The Belle dame sans mercy*, Chartier. No incipit.

17v. *The Request Sent to the Ladies Against Alain.* "Cy est la requeste baillee aux [*sic*] contre maistre alain."

18v. *The Letter of the Ladies Sent to Alain.* "Cy sont les letres envoiees par les dames audit maistre alain."

19r. *The Excuse of Master Alain*, Chartier. "Cy après est l'excusacion de maistre Alain contre ceulx qui dient quil a parle contre les dames sans mercy/Comment maistre alain respond." 24v. "Explicit le livre de la belle dame sans mercy."

24v. *The Complaint of Master Alain*, Chartier. "Apres s'ensuit la complainte maistre Alain contre la mort, en disant ainsi."

27v. *The Accusations Against the Belle Dame Sans Mercy*, Baudet Herenc. "Apres s'ensuit comment la belle dame sans mercy fut traitié en jugement en la court du dieu d'amours pour respondre aux articles contre lui imposes." 39v. "Explicit le traitie du jugement de la belle dame sans mercy en la court du dieu d'amours."

39v. *The Belle Dame Who Has Mercy*, attributed by Piaget to Oton de Grandson. "Apres s'enssuit la dame a mercy."

47v. *Awake at Dawn [Réveille matin]*, Chartier. "Apres s'ensuit le debat reveille matin de deux amoureux."

54v. *Lay of peace [Lai de paix]*, Chartier. "Apres s'enssuit le lay de paix d'amour et d'amitié."

60v. *The Debate of the Fortunate and Unfortunate in Love [Le débat des deux fortunés d'amours (or Le gras et le maigre)]*, Chartier. "Apres s'enssuit le debat du bien et du mal d'amours."

81v. *The Judgment of King of Bohemia [Le jugement du roi de Bohème]*, Machaut.

115r. "Complainte d'un amoureux par maniere de requeste d'une sentence donnée par sa dame contre lui a tort et sans cause," unidentified.

121v. *The Book of the Four Ladies [Le livre des quatre dames]*, Chartier. No incipit. (Note: fol. 175–176 are blank.)

Bibliothèque Nationale, Fonds Français, 2230 (Pf)

The binding is of red morocco from the seventeenth century with the stamp of the royal library of Louis XIV on the front cover; it was restored in 1978. The manuscript can be dated to after 1450.[45] Written on parchment, the 248 folios with two accompanying flyleaves measure 210 by 155 mm (140 by 75 written area), with thirty lines per page; prickings are still visible in the outer margin. The collation is as follows: A(1): 1–15 quires of 8: 16–31 quires of 8: B(1). Catchwords and traces of quire signatures written in a later hand are visible. Initials are gilded, decorated, and colored, as are the borders of new items with acanthus, fruits, and flowers. One miniature at fol. 211v, the beginning of the *Débat des deux soeurs*, depicts two ladies before a fireplace inside a room being spied upon from outside the window by two men (there are four more spaces with rubrics left for minia-tures in this item, and another sketch of angels at the beginning of item 22). Fol. 1r presents an ornate border of acanthus, a knot, a swan wounded by an arrow, a frame of the roped initials *J* and *M*, and a coat of arms: the impaled arms of Angoulême and Rohan, identifying its possessor as Marguerite de Rohan, married to Jean d'Angoulême in 1445, the brother of Charles d'Orleans, also held captive until 1445. The couple were great bibliophiles and collected a consider-able library, including copies of Chartier's *Curial* and *Bréviaire des nobles*, Christine de Pizan's *Corps de policie* and *Cité des dames*, a *Roman de la rose*, and Chaucer's *Canterbury Tales*.[46] The manuscript was probably copied from Pj by the same scribe: the hand and idiosyncrasies are identical to Pj, and the decoration, too, is strikingly similar, as are the readings of the texts of the two manuscripts. The parchment of this codex, however, is of superior quality: whiter and more flexible, with less translucence. Like Marie's book, the flyleaves are filled with signatures and devices, including those of Marie. Some of the names are found in both manuscripts. The first contents of this manuscript are identical to those of Marie's manuscript; even the sequence of items is the same, and the layout of the first page of the *Belle dame* is identical. But a decision seems to have been made to rearrange the order of works just prior to the completion of illustration: Pf appears to have been split after the fifteenth quire, and the two halves are bound in opposite order, perhaps to more adequately accommodate the added *Hospital of Love* and *Bréviaire des nobles,* arranged thus in close proximity to the book of the *Belle dame.* It is worth noting that the final ten items by Jean Vaillant, also not in Pj, are clearly of personal importance for Marguerite: the only miniature is here, as well as spaces left for more miniatures. The date of composition of these texts, after 1450, is notably later than the Chartier and Machaut texts.

Contents of the manuscript, with common title, authorial attribution, and incipit:

1r. *The Lay of Peace* [*Le lai de paix*], Chartier. No incipit.

6v. *The Debate of the Fortunate and Unfortunate in Love* [*Le débat des deux for-tunés d'amours* (*Le gras et le maigre*)], Chartier. "Apres s'enssuit le debat du bien et du mal d'amours."

27r. *The Judgment of the King of Bohemia* [*Le jugement du roi de Bohème*], Machaut. No incipit.

61r. "Complainte d'un amoureux, par maniere de requeste d'une sentence donnée par sa dame contre lui à tort et sans cause." The same unidenti-fied poem as item 12 in Pj.

68r. *The Book of Four Ladies* [*Le livre des quatre dames*], Chartier. No incipit.

121r. *The Belle dame sans mercy*, Chartier. No incipit.

137v. *The Request Given to the Ladies against Alain.* "Cy est la requeste baillee aux dames contre maistre alain chartier."

138v. *The Letter of the Ladies Sent to Alain.* "Cy sont les lettres envoiees par les dames audit maistre Alain."

139r. *The Excuse of Master Alain*, Chartier. "Cy après est l'excusacion de maistre Alain contre ceulx qui dient quil a parle contre les dames sans mercy." 144v. "Explicit livre de la belle dame sans mercy."

144v. *The Complaint of Master Alain*, Chartier. "Apres s'enssuit la complainte maistre Alain contre la mort, en disant ainsy."

148r. *The Accusations against the Belle Dame Sans Mercy*, Baudet Herenc. "Apres s'ensuit comment la belle dame sans mercy fut traittee en jugement en la court du dieu d'amours pour respondre aux articles contre lui imposes etc." 160r. "Explicit le traittie du jugement de la belle dame sans mercy en la court du dieu d'amours."

160r. *The Belle Dame Who Has Mercy*, attributed by Piaget to Oton de Grandson. "Apres s'enssuit le traitté de la dame a mercy."

168r. *Awake at Dawn* [*Réveille matin*], Chartier. "Apres s'enssuit le debat reveille matin de deux amoureux."

175r. *The Breviary of Noblemen* [*Le bréviaire des nobles*], Chartier. "Cy après s'ensuit le breviaire des nobles que tous gentilz hommes doivent aprendre."

184v. *The Hospital of Love*, Achilles Caulier. "Cy commence l'ospital d'amours."

211r. *The Debate of Two Sisters* [*Le débat des deux soeurs*], Jean Vaillant.[47] "Cy après s'ensuit le debat des deux seurs."

233r. "Rondeau," Vaillant.

233v. "Lettres envoieez," Vaillant.

236r. "Rondeau layey," Vaillant.

236v. "Bergerete," Vaillant.

237r–v. Three rondeaux, Vaillant.

237v. "Cy s'enssuit la cornerie des anges de paradis que chascun doit noter," Vaillant.

239v–248r. Two bergeretes, ten rondeaux, one ballade, Vaillant.

245r. "Lettres en prose." 247v. "Vostre humble et leal serviteur / cellui qui par mon createur / povez nommer votre vaillant," Vaillant.

248r. "Ballade faitte sus le mot de Jaquet [heart] qui est a [heart] vaillant rien impossible," Vaillant. Written in the margin in another hand: "C'est jacques coeur."

Bibliothèque de l'Arsenal, 3521 (Pn)

The manuscript is bound in red morocco, with gilded page edges, and can be dated after 1461.[48] Written on paper, the 299 folios measure 280 by 195 mm (170 by 90 written area) with thirty to thirty-four lines per page. The collation is as follows: 1–3[12] (first quire includes A–D, table of contents): 4[10]: 5[12]: 6[10]: 7[12]: 8[12]: 9[14]: 10–16[12]: 17–19[12]: 20–21[12]: 22–23[12]: 24[14]: 25[12] (last canceled). Catchwords and signatures are still visible in the lower margins. The manuscript has been numbered three times: in Roman numerals, in Arabic numerals, and finally with a set of Arabic numerals in pencil that correct at fol. 24 the previous Arabic numerals. Like Laidlaw, I have followed the numbering in pencil. There is no decoration, but space was left for larger initials in item 1. The explicits are often "AMEN." A contemporary table of contents that occupies fol. Ar-Cr. Laidlaw (115) records the following watermarks:

a unicorn with its head lowered, 100 or 105 mm long, fixed to chain lines about 26 mm apart

a unicorn with its head erect, 95 or 100 mm long, across chain lines 35 mm apart

an ox head surmounted by a cross, between lightly sewn chain lines 38 mm apart; 60 or 65 mm long; most like Briquet 14239 (1478–83)

a coat of arms (quarterly, 1 and 4, a fleur-de-lys; 2 and 3, a dolphin), 40 mm long, between chain lines 35 mm apart

Contents, with common title, authorial attribution, and incipit:

1r. "Livre intitullé l'instruction d'un josne prince pour soy bien gouverner envers Dieu et le monde" (title given in table of contents), attributed to Georges Chastelain.

30r. *The Breviary of Noblemen* [*Le breviaire des nobles*], Chartier. "S'ensuit le breviaire des nobles que fist maistre allain charretier."

38r. *The Lay of Peace* [*Le lai de paix*], Chartier. "Lay de paix fait par maistre Allain chartier."

43r. "Lay."

46r. "Ethismologisation de paris."

47r. "Lay de Nostre Dame."

48r. *The Psalter of the Peasants* [*Le psaultier des villains*], Michault Taillevant.[49] "Le psaultier des villains."

56v. *The Complaint of Master Alain*, Chartier. "Complainte de Maistre Allain Charretier."

59v. *The Belle dame sans mercy*, Chartier. "S'ensuit la belle dame sans mercy."

72r. *The Letter of the Ladies to Alain*.

72r–v. *The Request Given to the Ladies Against Alain.*

   73r. *The Excuse of Master Alain,* Chartier: "L'excusacion de maistre allain."

   77r. *The Response of the Ladies.* "La Response des dames faite a maistre allain."

   79r. *The Accusations against the Belle Dame Sans Mercy,* Baudet Herenc. "Traittié fait par Baudart Hereng, correspondent a la belle dame sans mercy." 88v. Blank

   89r. *The Lady Loyal in Love,* anonymous. "S'ensuit la dame lealle en amours."

  103r. *The Cruel Woman in Love,* Achilles Caulier. "S'ensuit la cruelle femme en Amours."

  118r. *The Hospital of Love,* Achilles Caulier. "S'ensuit l'ospital d'amours."

  137r. *Awake at Dawn [Reveille matin],* Chartier. "S'ensuit le debat resveille matin."

  143r. *Lay of Pleasure [Lay de plaisance],* Chartier. "Lay de plaisance."

  147v. "S'ensuit l'ostelerie de joye."[50]

  149r. *The Debate of the Heart and the Eye [Le debat du cuer et de l'oeil],* Michault Taillevant (1444).

  162r. "La Confession d'amours."

  169v. "Passio cuiusdam monachi." In Latin.

  171r. *The Debate of the Fortunate and Unfortunate in Love [Le debat des deux fortunes d'Amours,* or *Le gras et le maigre],* Chartier. "Le debat de deux chevaliers sur les plaisirs et dolleurs qui peuvent estre en amours fait par maistre Allain Charetier." No stanza division.

  187r. "La lamentacion de Gresse, oppressee des Turcs, et la consolacion qui lui donne France et Angleterre du tresfort lyon d'occident son futur reparateur." 194v. blank page.

  195r. *The Trial of the Honor of Ladies [Le proces de l'honneur feminin],* Pierre Michault (after 1461). "Sensuit la Deduction du proces de honneur femenin . . ."

  218v. Ballade.

  219r. *The Rule of Fortune [Le regime de fortune],* Michault Taillevent (c. 1445). "S'ensuit le Regime de fortune fait par Michault Taillevent."

  223r. "Lay fait par Michault Taillevent." "Ha mort mort tresdure mort." 226v. Blank.

  227r. *Time Past [Le passe temps],* Michault Taillevent (c. 1440). "Sensuit le passetemps de Michault Taillevant."

238r. *Time Lost* [*Le temps perdu*], Pierre Chastellain (before 1450). "Sensuit le le temps perdu de Pierre Chastellain correspondant au passe temps de michault taillevent."

247r. *Goodbye to Love* [*Congé d'amours*], Michault Taillevent (after 1440). "Cy apres d'amours le congie en la forme de six ballades par michault fait et abregie."

250r. *A Fine Departure* [*Bien allee*], Michault Taillevent (after 1440). "S'ensuit en ce petit cayer la bien allee de Michault la quelle a amours vault payer pour ce que d'amer ne lui chault."

253v. "Icy commence l'Ediffice de l'ostel dollereux d'amours ou amans de leur droit office font souvent plaints et clamours, fait par ledit Michault Taill-evant."

256v. "Sensuit du dolloureux hostel la Ressourse et reliefvement, lisies le s'il vous plaist au tel qu'il est fait bien nouvellement."

259v. *Lay in Honor of Our Lady* [*Lai en l'honneur de Notre-Dame*], Achilles Caulier. "Lay fait par Achilles Caulier a l'onneur de la vierge Marie."

261v. "Exhortacion prouffitable a salut de creature humaine."

264v. "Comment l'estat de ce monde puet estre compare au jeu des eschecz."

267v. "Meditacion a l'ymage du crucefix."

268r. *The Path of Death* [*Le pas de la mort*]. "Cy traittie cy pour enseignier fist george l'aventurier afin que chacun ait remort de penser au pas de la mort . . . ," George Chastelain (?).

276r. *Vers a la louange des seigneurs illustre en France.* "France du Roy." 284v. Blank.

285r. "Ballade." Eight ballads.

289r. "Sensuit l'istoire du temple de Mars."

294r. "Piece de vers ajoutee" in later hand.

Bibliothèque Nationale, Fonds Français, 924 (Pb)

Rebound in white leather in 1975, the manuscript dates to the late fifteenth century. It is written on 282 folios of paper and parchment (sheet 1/18) measuring 275 by 190 mm (200 by 100 written area) with twenty-one to twenty-four lines per page, ruled by stylus and by folding. Two sets of page numbering in Roman and Arabic numerals fill the top right margin; neither was written by the scribe. The complicated collation, designed to accommodate one item per folio, is as follows: 1^{18}: 2^8: 3^{14} (last canceled): 4^{12} (last canceled): 5^{20}: 6^{20} (last canceled): 7^{22}: 8^{14}: 9^{14} (last canceled): 10^{16}: 11^{18} (first canceled): 12^{14}: 13^{12}: 14^{24} (first canceled): 15^8: 16^8: 17^6: 18^4: 19^{16}: 20^{10}: 21^{14} (first canceled, last three canceled, new leaf inserted at end). Catchwords are visible in items copied on more than one quire. Fol. 1r has a decorated border and initial, and space for a miniature, in which a possessor (Thiboust) has written, "Ce present livre appartient a Maistre Jaques Thiboust Notaire et secretaire du Roy et Seigneur esleu en Berry et seigneur de Quantilly Et contiens les xxii livres de feu M. Alain Chartier en son vivant notaire et secretaire du Roy de la coronne et maison de france et swervoit du temps de Roy Charles Vii de ce nom Qui morut ou chateau de mehun sur Evre en l'an M.IIIIcLXI. Et premierement le livre de la belle dame sans mercy." (See McRae, 383–386.) Throughout the remainder of the text, a large red initial followed by six to twelve large black letters of text introduce a new item. Titles to the poems are written in the upper margin; some of them, in a sixteenth-century hand, add titles that Piaget believes to have been taken from the early printed editions. Numerous corrections have been made in several hands, including the hand of the possessor Thiboust. The last folio of the final item is in a different hand (probably Thiboust's). Laidlaw records the following watermarks:

a barred *P* surmounted by a fleuron and cross; 70 mm long, between chain lines 33 mm apart; Briquet 8693 (1475)

a unicorn 90 mm long, across chain lines 33 mm apart; Briquet 9994 (1467–70)

a coat of arms (quarterly, 1 and 4, a fleur-de-lys; 2 and 3, a dolphin) crowned, 63 mm long, fixed to chain lines 37 mm apart; very like Briquet 1655 (1477–93)

a pot surmounted by a cross, 80 mm long, chain lines 33 mm apart; very like Briquet 12482 (1474–80)

an unidentified mark, perhaps a balance or a weathervane, 30 mm long and fixed to a chain line; lines 23 mm apart

Contents, with common title, authorial attribution, and incipit:

> 1r. The *Belle dame sans mercy*, Chartier. 18r–v. Blank.
>
> 19r. *The Belle Dame Who Has Mercy*, attributed to Oton de Grandson. "La belle dame ou a mercy."
>
> 27r. *Accusations against the Belle Dame Sans Mercy*, Chartier. "Accusacions contre la belle dame sans mercy."
>
> 40r. *The Complaint of Master Alain*, Chartier. "La complainte et regretz maistre alain chartier [continues in another hand] contre la Mort que luy a tollu sa maistresse."
>
> 43v. *The Letter of the Ladies Sent to Alain.* "Coppie des lectres envoiees par les dames a maistre alain chartier."
>
> 44r. *The Request Given to the Ladies against Alain.* "Coppie de la requeste baillee aux dames."

Establishment of the Text

The text has been established with as little editorial intervention as possible to the base manuscript reading. For the most part, the use of diacritical marks follows the conventions outlined by Alfred Foulet and Mary Blakely Speer. The three marks used, therefore, are the acute accent to distinguish tonic from atonic *e*, the dieresis to indicate hiatus in a group of two or more vowels, and the cedilla to specify *c* as a sibilant. Spelling of the base text has not been modified except for the substitution of *v* for consonant *u* and *j* for consonant *i*. Modern punctuation has been added to help guide the reader through the intricate syntax of late

Middle French. Direct discourse is set off by quotation marks, and quotes within quotes, frequently seen as the Belle dame and Lover are cited in the Quarrel poems, are marked with single quotation marks. The manuscripts all capitalize the first letter of a line; these capitals have been retained, and capitals have been added to proper names, especially in the case of allegorical figures, and to mark the start of a sentence within a line. Apostrophes are used to separate elided articles from the following word as well as to indicate the third person singular *il* or third person plural *ils*, which when elided with *si* or *qui* gives the reading *s'i* or *qu'i*.

Every fourth line has been numbered and each stanza marked with a roman numeral. The stanzas of the translation have also been marked with roman numerals for more convenient reference. Rejected readings and variant readings are gathered at the end in separate paragraphs and keyed by line number; the origin of the replacement variant is given by the siglum of the appropriate manuscript. The most common reason for replacing the reading of the base text is scansion. The need to count eight syllables is complicated by the Middle French flexibility regarding atonic final *e* before a word beginning with a vowel, as well as the instability of the mute *e* in the interior of words. Thus *elle*, whose two syllables would render the line hypermetric, can easily be modified with *el*—a correction frequently made in the later, more carefully prepared manuscripts such as Pc. Such emendations have been made when more convenient for the reader. Likewise, there are words whose mute *e* is sometimes included in the syllable count and sometimes not. For example, *veoir* can be monosyllabic (BD160) or *vĕoir* disyllabic (H53), depending on the scansion needs of the verse. The third person plural ending *-ent* is counted or not, again depending on the scansion needs of the verse (E392/E397).

In Pj, Pf, and Pn, it can be difficult to distinguish *c* from *t*, especially in such words as *dittier* or *dictier*. *Que* is used for *qui*, *en* for *on*, and *se* for *ce*; because these are common in Middle French, they have not been amended, though variant readings have been noted.

The Translation

The translation attempts to retain as faithfully as meaningful the reading of the original text. Because the syntax of Middle French can be so intricate, at times it has been necessary to rearrange a sentence or repeat the subject or referent implied in the original. Since it is not possible to create a readable translation line for line, I have marked the stanzas of the translation to correspond to the stanza of the original. I have tried to keep in mind the interest of the reader to follow closely the original reading guided by the translation; nevertheless, at times it has been necessary to modify the literal translation so that the English text reads coherently. Some lines do not translate well at all, such as the Middle French proverbs that have no equivalent in English. These have been translated literally with a note explaining the meaning or various possible translations.

Notes

1. Jehan Bouchet, *Les Annalles d'Acquitaine . . .* , Paris: Jehan Mace, 1537, fo. S.i.v. "Je n'ay pas baisé l'homme, mais la precieuse bouche de laquelle sont yssuz et sortis tant de bons motz et vertueuses parolles." Chartier was reputed to be very ugly.

2. Keats may have discovered the *Belle dame* in the Richard Ros translation once thought to have been reworked by Chaucer (see more in note 3).

3. See, for example, the *Belle dame sans mercy*, translated by Sir Richard Ros in 1460, the edition of Chartier's "delectable demaundes, and pleasaunt questions, with their severall aunswers, in matters of love, naturall causes, with morall and politique devises" edited by John Cawood in 1566, Francesc Oliver's 1460 Catalan translation of the Belle dame, and Carlo di Piero dal Nero's 1476 Italian translation, edited by Werner Söderjhelm.

4. See Hoffman, *Alain Chartier*, especially the chapter "Reputation," 209–72, for specific references made to Chartier pertaining to his reputation. See Laidlaw, "The Manuscripts," for more information on the manuscripts that contain Chartier's works.

5. As is so common with medieval authors, the details of Chartier's life have been difficult to piece together, and many facts are still controversial. Since Du Chesne's 1617 publication of a brief biography to precede his edition of Chartier's collected works, many scholars have attempted to reconstruct the erasures of time and the errors of the past. J. C. Laidlaw, *The Poetical Works of Alain Chartier*, Cambridge: Cambridge University Press, 1977; C. J. H. Walravens, *Alain Chartier: études biographiques, suivies de pièces justificatives, d'une description des éditions et d'une édition des ouvrages inédits*, Amsterdam: Meulenhoff-Didier, 1971; and E. J. Hoffman, *Alain Chartier: His Work and Reputation*, New York: Wittes Press, 1942, are today considered the authoritative voices on Chartier's life, and the summary is based on their extensive research.

6. For a complete discussion of the controversy over establishing the date of Alain's birth, see Walravens 10–14, and Hoffman 9–11.

7. One manuscript, B. N. ms. lat. 5748, attributes a doctoral degree to him, but this may well be a misinformed appropriation of brother Guillaume's title (Walravens 19).

8. Walravens 254–56, *"Alanus ad fratem suum iuvenem."*

9. In the *Quadrilogue invective*, France encourages Alain to act politically not with physical force or arms, with which God has not blessed him, but with his true talent, writing (Bouchet 124). We could well interpret this injunctive as a comment on Alain's poor physical health, as does Walravens (22).

10. Laidlaw suggests that Chartier may have served in the house of Charles VI because he signs his name as "Alain Charretier humble secretaire du roy et de mon tresre-doubte seigneur monseigneur le regent" (*Quadrilogue invective*)." However, the Dauphin also appropriated the title of Regent in his exile, so Chartier may have been referring, again, to his service for the Dauphin.

11. The authenticity of this title is disputed. See Walravens 38.

12. As much controversy has surrounded the particulars of Chartier's death as his birth. See Walravens 40–48, Laidlaw 15–18, and Hoffman 19–33.

13. Laidlaw identifies this lady as most likely the second wife of Charles d'Orleans, Bonne of Armagnac, who died before his release from English captivity in 1440 (35–36). Charles had in his possession then a copy of the *Quatre dames*: "Ung viel livre des Quatre Dames, en papier, couvert de viel parchemin" (P. Champion, *La Librairie de Charles d'Orléans,* Paris: Bibliothèque du XVe siècle, 1910: 30).

14. Laidlaw 11.

15. P. Champion, *Histoire poètique du XVe siècle,* I, Paris: Bibliothèque du XVe siècle, 184–85, with reference to Pierre de Nesson's *Lai de guerre.*

16. This ending is uncharacteristic of the reputation of Oton de Grandson's poetry, renowned for his depiction of a heartless woman in the *Livre messire ode,* and a fickle one in "Complainte de Saint Valentin." As Kelly puts it: "The Image of the unfaithful and unattainable lady was to give Oton de Grandson a popularity and influence far bejond what his talents as a poet would lead one to expect" (D. Kelly, *Medieval Imagination,* Madison: University of Wisconsin Press, 1978: 182). Perhaps this is why Piaget did not reaffirm his attribution of the *Belle Dame Who Has Mercy* to Oton de Grandson in his book on this author. See *Oton de Grandson: sa vie et ses poésies,* Mémoires et documents publiés par la Société d'histoire de la Suisse Romande, vol. 1, Geneva: Librairie Payot, TK, 1941, to discover that nowhere in the book is this poem mentioned, despite his attribution made some years earlier in "Oton de Granson et ses poésies," *Romania* 19 (1890): 403–48.

17. This quatrain is not included in all manuscripts.

18. Chastel, son of Christine de Pizan, was a poet as well as a member of the Cour amoureuse of Charles VI and Charles VII. The letter implies a link between the Quarrel documents and the Cour amourouse.

19. Vatican reg. lat. 1363 (Qt).

20. As mentioned above, the tone and form of the *Response of the Ladies* is quite different from that of the earlier letter of the ladies. The reader may notice that this last letter is written in decasyllabic verse, the same meter as Nesson's *Lay of War* (all other documents of the Quarrel are written in prose or octosyllabic verse). Given the history of rivalry between Nesson and Chartier, one might suspect that it was not the ladies who penned the *Response,* but the prankster Nesson.

21. On the Cour amoureuse, see Piaget, "La Cour amourseuse dite de Charles VI," *Romania,* 20 (1891): 417–54, and Bozzolo and Loyau, *La Cour amoureuse dite de Charles VI,* Paris: Le Léopard d'Or, 1982.

22. See A. Piaget, "*La belle dame sans mercy* et ses imitations." *Romania,* 30 (1901): 22–48, 317–51; 31 (1902): 315–39; 33 (1904): 179–208; 34 (1905): 375–428, 559–602.

23. The *Jugement du povre triste amant banny* is not really, as claim Martí de Riquer and Helen Solterer, a part of the *Belle dame* cycle, but is part of a cycle in imitation of this cycle.

24. *La belle dame ou a mercy* technically should not be included in this grouping because manuscript evidence indicates that the poem was written before Chartier's poem, not in imitation of it. For greater detail on this subject, see Piaget's article in *Romania* 33 (1904): 203.

25. Recorded as 1448, before the calendar was corrected.

26. See Paris, *Romania* 15 (1886): 135.

27. Comte de Laborde, *Les ducs de bourgogne: études sur les lettres, les arts, et l'industrie pendant le XVe siècle. Seconde partie: preuves*, III, Paris: Plon Frères,1852, 842.

28. See Piaget, *Romania* 23 (1894): 256–257.

29. Sigla for the manuscripts are listed on page TK.

30. U. Eco, *Experiences in Translation*, trans. A. McEwen, Toronto: University of Toronto Press, 2001, 5.

31. Also in Pf, a manuscript belonging to her sister-in-law.

32. See Adrian Armstrong's article for a discussion of the impulse to continue the debate.

33. *Oeuvres complètes de Marot*, vol. IV, p. 195.

34. D. Kelly, *Medieval Imagination*, Madison: University of Wisconsin Press, 1978, 182. See Note 16.

35. In the introduction to her Web page: http://www.innoved.org/belledame/.

36. Qq (Rome, Bib. Vaticane 4794) was mistakenly included in the list of manuscripts for the *Accusations*, but in fact this poem is the *Cruel Woman in Love*.

37. See J. E. McRae, "The Trials of Alain Chartier's *Belle Dame Sans Mercy:* The Poems in Their Cyclical and Manuscript Context," 46–89, 374–79.

38. In addition, the poems have already been edited based on Pb (McRae) and Pc (Hult and McRae), which witness to the tradition of a carefully constituted cycle, even beyond consideration of Piaget's editions.

39. See Laidlaw, *Poetical Works,* 101–16 for his meticulous codicological descriptions of the manuscripts.

40. The codicological measurements and collations are based on Laidlaw, *Poetical Works*, 101–16.

41. The first citation reads "ung autre [petit livre] en papier, de Balades commençant: Une fois chavchant [*sic;* chevauchant] pensoye" (The *Cent ballades* reads "Une fois pieca chevauchoie"), and the second "Ung autre livre de balades, en paper, commencant: Nagueres chevauchant pensoie, appelle les Cent Ballades." Despite this last citation's claim that the poem is called *Cent ballades*, the incipit is the distinctive beginning of Chartier's *Belle dame sans mercy.* Perhaps the incipit given is a scribal error, but perhaps it is not, since in this same collection where Marie had recopied the *Quatre dames* she also had copied the *Belle dame.* The first is cited by Champion in the *Librairie de Charles d'Orléans*, then verified by looking at BN français 22571, p. 176. an eighteenth-century copy of the first list; the second is quoted from De Labord, *Ducs de Bourgogne, Preuves*, p. 323 [6553], based on Archive nationales K. 534. This list was made November 5, 1440, in Saint Omer by Hugues Perrier and Etienne le Gout.

42. Champion, *Librairie* 125–26.

43. Mme. Lafitte, in charge of book binding restauration at the Bibliothèque nationale in Paris, generously provided this information. The restoration number, 2217, is marked on the flyleaf.

44. For more information on this "liber amicorum" of Marie de Clèves, as well as information on the people who signed her book, see Piaget, "Un liber amicorum du XVe siècle," *Revue des bibliothèques*, XX (1910): 320–36.

45. Item 16, the *Debat des deux soeurs* (*Embusche Vaillant*), can be dated to after 1450, as it mentions the Order of the Croissant, created by René d'Anjou in 1448. In addition, the poem about Jacques Coeur was likely written after his fall from grace, 1450. The manuscript must have been constructed after this date. See Note 47.

46. For a complete list of the books in Jean d'Angoûleme's library, see Champion, *Librairie*, 119–24.

47. The items after the *Hospital of Love* were written by "Vaillant," presumably a certain Jean Vaillant, squire of Gaston IV de Foix, who offered a "petit traicté d'amors" to René d'Anjou on March 14, 1457. This "petit traictié" is probably this poem, the *Débat des deux soeurs*, also called the *Embusche Vaillant* (1450–70?) a debate between two sisters that echoes the *Cent ballades*: the elder prefers to keep many lovers around her, and the younger loyally loves only one. The ending lines offer the debate to Gaston IV and René d'Anjou for arbitration. Two poems signed Vaillant, a ballad and a rondeau, are recorded in the literary tournament at Charles d'Orléans's chateau in Blois around 1455. *Dictionnaire des lettres françaises* I: 1470; Poirion, *Le Poète et le Prince*, 159.

48. The earliest date of composition for item 26, *Le procès de l'honneur feminine*, by Pierre Michault, is 1461.

49. The *Psaultier des villains* was written after 1440 in response to Chartier's *Breviaire des nobles*.

50. *L'hostelerie de joye*: twelve eight-line stanzas of octosyllabic rhymes *ababbcbc*; short allegorical tale about a hotel of joy.

51. *Miroir des dames*, attributed to Durand de Champagne (fourteenth century). *Dictionnaire des lettres*, 1017.

La belle dame sans mercy

Alain Chartier

Translated with the collaboration of
Demas Boudreaux, Henrik Rasmussen, and Dale Cornett

I   Naguieres, chevauchant, pensoie,   [1r]
    Com homme triste et douloureux,
    Au dueil ou il fault que je soie
    Le plus doulent des amoureux,   4
    Puis que par son dart rigoureux
    La Mort m'a tollu ma maistresse
    Et me laisse seul, langoureux,
    En la conduite de Tristresse.   8

II   Sy disoie: Il fault que je cesse
    De ditter et de rimoier,
    Et que je habandonne et delaisse
    Le rire pour le lermoier.   12
    La me fault mon temps amploier,
    Car plus n'ay sentement ne aise,
    Soit d'escripre, soit d'envoier
    Chose qu'a moy n'a aultrui plaise.   16

III   Qui vouldroit mon vouloir contraindre
    A joyeuses choses escripre,
    Ma plume n'y sauroit attaindre,
    Non feroit ma langue a les dire.   20
    Je n'ay bouche qui puisse rire
    Que les yeulx ne la demantissent,
    Car le cuer l'envoieroit desdire
    Par les lermes qui des yeulx yssent.   24

IV   Je laisse aux amoureux malades   [1v]
    Qui ont espoir d'alegement
    Faire chançons, dis, et balades,
    Chascun a son entendement,   28
    Car ma dame a son testament
    Print a la mort,—Dieu en ait l'ame—
    Et emporta mon sentement,
    Qui gist o elle soubz la lame.   32

I

Not so long ago, while out riding, I was thinking,
as a man sad and grieving does,
of the woeful state I was in,
being the saddest of lovers
for, by his cruel sword,
Death has taken my mistress from me
and left me alone and languishing,
guided only by Sadness.

II

So I said: I must stop
the writing and rhyming of happy verses;
Now I must trade
laughter for tears.
This is how I will spend my time,
for I no longer find delight
in writing or sharing with others
something that pleases neither me nor anyone else.

III

No matter who might wish to change my mind,
insisting that I write joyful things,
neither my pen nor my tongue
would be able to produce them.
My mouth might not laugh
but that my eyes would belie it,
for my heart would reveal the lie
by the tears that flow from my eyes.

IV

I leave to those languishing lovers
who have hope of some relief
to write and sing songs and ballades,
each to his own talent.
For my lady, in her will,
took with her in death, God rest her soul,
every emotion I had within me, and
these lie now with her in the tomb.

V
Desormais est temps de me taire,
Car de dire suis je lassé.
Je laisse aux aultres amans faire:
Leur temps est, le mien est passé.   36
Fortune a le forcier cassé
Ou je prenoie ma richesse
Et le bien que j'ay amassé
Ou meilleur temps de ma jeunesse.   40

VI
Amour a gouverné mon sens:
Se faulte y a, Dieu me pardonne;
Se j'ay bien fait, plus ne m'en sens.
Cela ne me tolt ne ne donne,   44
Car au trespas de la tresbonne
Tout mon bien fait se trespassa.
La Mort m'assist illec sa bonne,
Oncques mon cuer puis n'y passa.   48

VII
En ce penser et en ce soing   [2r]
Chevauchay toute matinee,
Tant que je ne fus gueres loing
Du lieu ou estoit la disnee;   52
Et quant j'euz ma voie affinee
Et que je cuide herbegier,
J'ouÿ par droitte destinee
Des menestriers en ung vergier.   56

VIII
Sy me retrehÿ voulentiers
En ung lieu tout coy et privé,
Mes deux bons amis et entiers
Sceurent que je fuz arrivé   60
Et vindrent. Tant ont estrivé,
Moitié force, moitié requeste,
Que je n'ay oncques eschevé
Qu'i ne me mainent a la feste.   64

V   It is time that I be silent,
for I am grown tired of speaking;
I leave it to others to take over:
it is their time now, mine has passed.
Fortune has crushed the coffer
in which I was saving my riches,
as well as the wealth that I amassed
in the better days of my youth.

VI   Until now Love has governed my spirit;
if that be a fault, God forgive me.
And if I have done well, I do not know it,
nor do I really care,
for at the death of the Very Best
all my good was destroyed.
This is the barrier that Death has placed before me,
one that my heart will never pass beyond.

VII   In such a reverie and such a state of mind,
I rode my horse the entire morning,
for so long that I came upon
the place where I was to dine.
And when I had arrived there,
thinking I would find a place to rest,
I happened to hear
music coming from the garden.

VIII   So I withdrew myself willingly
to a calm and isolated spot,
but two of my good friends
learned of my arrival.
They came there, and with their
prodding and pleadings,
which I could not refuse,
they succeeded in leading me to the feast.

IX   A l'entree fus bien recueilly
       Des dames et des demoyselles,
       Et de celles bien acueilly
       Qui toutes sont bonnes et belles.   68
       Et de la courtoisie d'elles
       Me tindrent illec toute jour,
       En plaisans parolles nouvelles
       Et en tresgracïeux seiour.   72

X   Disner fut prest et tables mises. [2v]
       Les dames a table s'assirent
       Et quant elles furent assisez,
       Des plus gracïeux les servirent. 76
       Telz y ot qui ad ce jour virent
       En la compaignie leans
       Leurs juges (dont semblant n'en firent)
       Qui les tiennent en leurs liens 80

XI   Ung entre les aultres y vy,
       Qui souvent aloit et venoit,
       En pensant com home ravi,
       Et guieres de bruit ne menoit. 84
       Son semblant fort contretenoit,
       Mais desir passoit sa raison,
       Qui souvent son regart menoit
       Tel foiz qu'i n'estoit pas saison. 88

XII   De faire chiere s'efforçoit
       Et menoit une joie fainte,
       Et a chanter son cuer forçoit,
       Non paz pour plaisir ne pour crainte: 92
       Car tous jours en relais de plainte
       Sus laissoit au son de sa voix;
       Puis revenoit a son attainte
       Comme l'oysel au chant du boys. 96

IX
At the entrance, I was greeted
by all the ladies and maidens
and welcomed by them,
so polite and pretty all.
Their company was so pleasurable
that I spent the whole day entertained
with pleasant and witty words
in such a delightful manner.

X
Dinner was ready and the tables set.
The ladies went to be seated,
and when they were settled,
the most gracious men came to wait upon them.
Some saw there that day
among the company assembled,
their judges, who held them in thrall,
though they concealed it well.

XI
There among the others, I saw one
who paced back and forth.
He was like a man possessed by some madness
though he made no sound.
He tried to control the expression of his face,
but his desire was stronger than his will,
and his glance continually returned to one spot
so often that his intent could not be concealed.

XII
He forced a cheerful expression,
keeping his countenance gay,
and compelled his heart to sing
not from pleasure, but from fear:
for though his speech
was disrupted with heavy sighs,
he repeatedly recommenced it,
as a bird will when chirping its song.

XIII   Des aultres y eust plaine sale,   [3r]
                    Mais cellui trop bien me sembloit
                    Ennuyé, mesgre, blesme et pale,
                    Et la parole lui trembloit.   100
                    Guieres aux aultres ne sambloit.
                    Le noir portoit en sa devise,
                    Et trop bien homme ressambloit
                    Qui n'a pas son cuer en franchise.   104

XIV   De toutes festoier faignoit:
                    Bien le fist et bien lui sëoit,
                    Mais a la foiz le contraingnoit
                    Amours, qui fort son cuer ardoit   108
                    Par sa maistresse qu'i vëoit,
                    Que je choisi lors clerement
                    A son regart qu'il assëoit
                    Sus elle si piteusement.   112

XV   Assez sa face destournoit
                    Pour regarder en aultres lieux,
                    Mais au travers, l'ueil retournoit
                    Au lieu qui lui plaisoit le mieulx.   116
                    J'apperceu le trait de ses yeulx,
                    Tout empané d'umbles requestes,
                    Si dis a par moy, "se m'aist Dieux,
                    Autel fus je comme vous estez."   120

XVI   A la fois a part se tiroit   [3v]
                    Pour rasseoir sa contenance,
                    Et trestendrement soupiroit
                    Par douloureuse souvenance.   124
                    Puis reprenoit son ordonnance
                    Et venoit pour servir les mes,
                    Mais a bien jugier sa samblance,
                    C'estoit ung piteux entreméz.   128

XIII   A crowd of people filled the hall,
but this one seemed to be
so thin, distressed, and pale
that his words trembled,
and he would not mingle with the others.
He was dressed all in black, with no crest to identify him,
and appeared to me to be a man
whose heart was no longer free.

XIV   He pretended to participate in the festivities,
feigning his enjoyment, and it suited him well,
but at the same time he was besieged
by Love, who was burning his heart
with the sight of his beloved,
whom I identified easily
by his persistent glances, which
settled on her so pitifully.

XV   He tried to force his eyes
to look away in other directions,
but from each distraction his eye returned
to the place that pleased him the most.
I saw the arrow that shot from his eyes,
carrying his humble appeal,
and I said to myself: "So help me God,
I was once as you are now."

XVI   From time to time he withdrew from the others
to compose himself,
and he sighed tenderly,
overwhelmed by his unshakable sorrow.
Then, recovering his composure,
he would return to serving the courses;
but, judging by his appearance,
these interludes did him no good.

XVII
Aprés disner on s'avança
De dancer chascun et chascune,
Lors le triste amoureux dança
Puis a l'autre, puis a l'une.   132
A toutes fist chiere commune,
A chascune a son tour aloit,
Mais tousjours retournoit a une,
Dont sur toutes mieulx lui chaloit.   136

XVIII
Bien avoit a mon gré visé
Entre celles que je vy lors,
S'il eust au gré du cuer visé
Autant qu'a la beaulté du corps: 140
Qui croist de legier les rappors
De ses yeulx, sans aultre esperance,
Pourroit mourir de mille mors
Avant qu'ataindre a sa plaisance.   144

XIX
En la dame ne failloit riens,   [4r]
Ne plus avant ne plus arriere.
C'estoit garnison de tous biens
Pour faire aux cuers d'amans frontiere: 148
Jeune, gente, fresche, et entiere;
Maintien rassis et sans changier;
Doulce parolle et grant maniere,
Dessoubz l'estandart de Dangier.   152

XX
De celle feste me lassay,
Car joye triste cuer traveille,
Et hors de presse je passay;
Et m'assis derriere une traille,   156
Drue de fueilles a merveille,
Entrelacee de saulz vers,
Si qu'es nul pour l'espesseur d'elle[1]
Ne me peüst veoir au travers.   160

XVII   After the dinner was finished,
the ladies and gentlemen all began to dance;
and the sad lover danced
first with one, then with another.
He presented the same courteous face to all
and accompanied each lady for a round,
but he always returned to the one
whom he preferred above all the rest.

XVIII   To my mind, he had chosen well
among those that I saw there.
If only he had considered graciousness of heart
as well as beauty of form!
He who believes too easily
what his eyes see, without any other reason for hope,
could die a thousand times
before attaining his joy.

XIX   In the lady there was nothing lacking,
neither too much nor too little of anything.
She was blessed with all good qualities,
capable of stopping the heart of many a lover.
Young, noble, fresh, and pure,
serene and calm of countenance,
she spoke sweet words with perfect courtesy,
safe behind the flag of Resistance.

XX   I grew tired of the party,
for rejoicing torments a sad heart,
so I slipped away from the crowd
and settled myself behind a trellis,
marvelously thick with leaves,
interlaced with weeping willow,
so that no one, thanks to the density of the foliage,
could spy me through it.

XXI   L'amoureus sa dame menoit
           Dancer quant venoit a son tour,
           Et puis sëoir s'en revenoit
           Sus ung vert prëau au retour.   164
           Nulz aultres n'avoit alentour
           Assiz, fors seullement les deulx;
           Et n'y avoit aultre destour
           Fors la traille entre moy et eulx.   168

XXII   J'ouÿ l'amant qui souspiroit,   [4v]
           Car qui plus prés est plus desire,
           Et la grant doulour qu'i tiroit
           Ne savoit taire et n'osoit dire.   172
           Il languissoit au prés du mire
           Qui nuisoit a sa gairison,
           Car qui art ne se puet plus nuyre
           Qu'aprouchier le feu du tison.   176

XXIII   Le cuer ens ou corps lui croissoit,
           D'angoisse et de päour estraint,
           Tant qu'a bien pou qu'i ne froissoit
           Quant l'un a l'autre le contraint.   180
           Desir boute, Crainte reffraint;
           L'un eslargist, l'autre resserre;
           Si n'a pas pou de mal empraint
           Qui porte a son cuer telle guerre.   184

XXIV   De parler souvent s'efforça
           Se Crainte ne l'eust destourné,
           Mais en la fin son cuer força
           Quant il eust assez sejourné.   188
           Puis s'est vers sa dame tourné
           Et dist bas, en pleurant adoncques:
           "Mal jour fut pour moy adjourné,
           Ma dame, quant je vous vis oncques.   192

XXI	The Lover led his lady to the dance when it was his turn, and then returned to sit in a small enclosed garden. No one else was in this corner, except the two of them, and there was no other barrier but the trellis to separate them from me.
XXII	I heard the lover sighing, for proximity enflames desire, and the great pain that he felt he could no longer hide, yet he dared not reveal. So he languished ill, so close to his physician, spoiling all hope of healing: for he who burns can do himself no more harm than to touch the flaming brand!
XXIII	His heart in his chest was straining, swollen with anguish and fear such that he almost fainted, as one, then the other, exerted its force. Desire arising, Fear restraining, one pushes him forward, the other holds him back He whose heart is in such a war can do little to conceal its effects.
XXIV	He made frequent attempts to speak, but Fear would not allow it, yet finally his heart won out after struggling within long enough. He turned to the lady and said softly, almost in tears: "A bad day dawned for me my lady, when I first laid eyes on you.

L'amant

XXV   Je seuffre mal ardant et chault,   [5r]
                  Dont je meurs pour vous bien vouloir,
                  Et si voy qu'i ne vous en chault
                  Et n'avez d'y penser vouloir;   196
                  Mais entremoins qu'a non chaloir
                  Le mettez quant je le vous compte,
                  Car vous n'en povez pis valoir
                  N'avoir moins honneur ne plus honte.   200

L'amant

XXVI   Helas! Que vous griefve, ma dame,
                  S'ung franc cuer d'omme vous veult bien,
                  Et se par honneur et sans blasme
                  Je suis vostre et vostre me tien?   204
                  De droit je n'y chalenge rien,
                  Car ma voulenté s'est soubzmise
                  A vostre gré, non pas au mien,
                  Pour plus asservir ma franchise.   208

L'amant

XXVII   Ja soit ce que pas ne desserve
                  Vostre grace par mon servir,
                  Souffrez au moins que je vous serve
                  Sans vostre mal gré desservir.   212
                  Je serviray sans desservir
                  En ma loyaulté observant,
                  Et pour ce me fist asservir
                  Amours d'estre vostre servant."   216

La dame

XXVIII   Quant la dame ouÿt ce langaige,   [5v]
                  Elle respondi bassement,
                  Sans müer couleur ne couraige,
                  Mais tout amesureement: 220
                  "Beau sire, ce fol pensement,
                  Ne vous laissera il jamais?
                  Ne penserez vous aultrement
                  De donner a vostre cuer paix?"   224

The Lover

XXV
         I suffer from a pain that burns and enflames me
         and is killing me, for want of you.
         And yet you do not seem to care,
         refusing even to notice it,
         and are indifferent
         when I speak to you about it,
         and yet your reputation will not suffer;
         neither will you lose honor or incur any shame.

The Lover

XXVI
         Alas! How can it cause you pain, my lady,
         if the heart of a sincere man so desires you,
         and if, with honor and beyond reproach,
         I declare and consider myself yours?
         As is right, I ask for nothing in return,
         for my will is submitted
         to your pleasure, not to my own,
         and my freedom enslaved to you.

The Lover

XXVII
         Although I do not deserve
         your grace for my service,
         at least permit me to serve you
         without incurring your displeasure.
         I will serve though I am not worthy,
         keeping true to my troth,
         for this is the service Love requires:
         that I be your humble servant."

The Lady

XXVIII
         When the lady heard these words,
         she responded in a low voice,
         without changing color or comportment,
         but in an evenly measured fashion:
         "My dear sir, will these foolish thoughts
         never leave you?
         Will you not find another way
         to bring peace to your heart?"

L'amant

XXIX   Nully n'y pourroit la paix mettre
                   Fors vous qui la guerre y meïstez
                   Quant vos yeulx escriprent la lettre
                   Par quoy deffier me feïstes,   228
                   Et que Doulz Regart me transmëistes
                   Herault de celle deffiance,
                   Par lequel vous me promeïstes,
                   En deffiant, bonne fiance.   232

La dame

XXX   Il a grant fain de vivre en dueil
                   Et fait de son cuer lache garde,
                   Qui, contre ung tout seul regart d'ueil,
                   Sa paix et sa joye ne garde.   236
                   Se moy ou aultre vous regarde,
                   Les yeulx sont faiz pour regarder.
                   Je n'y prens point autrement garde:
                   Qui y sent mal s'en doit garder.   240

L'amant

XXXI   S'aucun blesce aultruy d'avanture   [6r]
                   Sans coulpe de cellui qui blesse,
                   Quoy qu'il n'en peust maiz par droitture,
                   Si en a il dueil et tristresse.   244
                   Et puis que Fortune ou Rudesse
                   Ne m'ont fait mie ce meshaing,
                   Mais vostre tresbelle jennesse,
                   Pour quoy m'avez vous en desdaing?   248

La dame

XXXII   Contre vous nul desdaing n'ataine
                   N'euz oncques ne ne veulz avoir,
                   Ne trop grant amour ne grant hayne,
                   Ne vostre priveté sçavoir.   252
                   Se Cuider vous fait decevoir
                   Que pou de chose veult trop plaire,
                   Et vous vous voulez decevoir,
                   Ce ne vueil je pas pour tant faire.   256

The Lover

XXIX

No one can bring peace to my heart
but you, who wage the war within it.
Ever since your eyes wrote the letter
that gave the charge
that then Sweet Look transmitted
(as herald of this challenge)
by which you promised.
in challenging me, a good engagement.

The Lady

XXX

He must really wish to live in misery
who keeps such a loose hold on his heart
and, for the sake of one quick glance,
would lose his peace and joy.
If I, or another, should look your way,
eyes were made for looking.
I mean nothing else by it.
He who might suffer from it should protect himself.

The Lover

XXXI

If someone wounds another by chance
it is not his fault,
and even though by right he can do nothing about it,
he still feels pity and sadness.
And since neither Fortune nor Hardship,
but your most beautiful youth
has caused my misfortune,
why do you feel such disdain for me?

The Lady

XXXII

I have no disdain for you,
never did, nor ever will have;
neither too much love nor too much hate,
nor do I wish to know your personal intimacies.
If Presumption has made you believe
that a small thing should please so much,
and you wish to deceive yourself so,
well, this is something I do not wish to do.

L'amant

XXXIII   Qui que m'ait ce mal pourchassé,
       Cuider ne m'a point deceü;
       Mais Amour m'a si bien chassé
       Que je suis en voz laz cheü.   260
       Et puis qu'ainsi m'est escheü
       D'estre cheü entre voz mains,
       S'il m'est au chëoir mescheü,
       Qui plus tost meurt en languist moins. 264

La dame

XXXIV   Sy gracïeuse maladie   [6v]
       Ne met gueres de gens a mort,
       Mais il chiet bien que l'on le die
       Pour plus tost attraire confort.   268
       Tel se plaint et guermente fort
       Qui n'a pas les plus aspres dueuz;
       Et s'amour greve tant, au fort,
       Mieulx en vault ung dolent que deux. 272

L'amant

XXXV   Helas! ma dame, il vault trop mieulx,
       Pour courtoisie et bonté faire,
       D'un dolant faire deux joyeux
       Que le doulent du tout deffaire.   276
       Je n'ay desir në aultre affaire
       Fors que mon service vous plaise
       Pour eschangier, sans rien meffaire,
       Deulx plaisirs en lieu d'un mesaize. 280

La dame

XXXVI   D'amours ne quier courroux n'aisance,
       Ne grant espoir ne grant desir,
       Et si n'ay de voz maulx plaisance
       Ne regart a vostre plaisir.   284
       Choisisse qui vouldra choisir:
       Je suis franche et franche vueil estre,
       Sans moy de mon cuer dessaisir
       Pour en fairë ung aultre maistre. 288

The Lover

XXXIII   No matter who might have caused this ill,
                    I tell you: Presumption has not deceived me.
                    But Love has given such hard chase
                    that I am now entangled in your trap.
                    And since it has thus befallen
                    to have fallen into your hands,
                    if this proves a fatal fall,
                    then at least I shall die quickly, and languish less.

The Lady

XXXIV   Such a gracious malady
                    causes the death of no one,
                    but it serves well to say so,
                    to win consolation all the sooner.
                    They who complain and cry out loud
                    do not suffer the most serious pain,
                    but if Love doles out such affliction,
                    better for one to suffer than two!

The Lover

XXXV   Alas, my lady, it is better,
                    for courtesy and kindness's sake,
                    to make from one suffering, two joyful,
                    rather than destroy the sufferer in such a way.
                    I have no desire nor any intention
                    other than to please you with my service—
                    to exchange, without doing any disservice,
                    two pleasures for one torment.

The Lady

XXXVI   I seek neither the pain nor the pleasure of love,
                    neither grand hope nor great desire;
                    so, even as I get no joy from your sadness,
                    neither am I concerned about your pleasure.
                    I will choose whom I wish to choose:
                    I am free and wish to remain so,
                    and will not let my heart go
                    so that another can become its master.

L'amant

XXXVII   Amours, qui joye et dueil depart,   [7r]
                  Mist les dames hors de servage
                  Et leur ordonna pour leur part
                  Maistrise et franc segnourïage.   292
                  Les servans n'y ont d'avantage
                  Fors tant seulement le pourchaz;
                  Et qui fait une foiz hommage,
                  Bien chier en coustent les rachaz.   296

La dame

XXXVIII   Dames ne sont mie si lourdes,
                  Si mal entendans, ne si folles,
                  Que pour ung pou de plaisans bourdes
                  Confites en belles parolles,   300
                  Dont vous aultres tenez escolles
                  Pour leur faire croire merveillez,
                  Elles changent si tost leurs colles:
                  Aux beaulx parleurs, closes oreilles.   304

L'amant

XXXIX   Il n'est jangleur, tant y meïst
                  De sens, d'ententë ou de paine,
                  Qui si triste plainte feïst
                  Comme cellui qui le mal maine.   308
                  Car qui se plaint de teste saine
                  A paine sa faintise queuvre;
                  Mais pensee de douleur plaine
                  Preuve ses parolles par l'euvre.   312

La dame

XL   Amours est crüeux losengier,   [7v]
                  Aspre en fait et doulx en mentir,
                  Et se scet bien de ceux vengier
                  Qui cuident ses secretz sentir: 316
                  Il les fait a soy consentir
                  Par une entree de chierté;
                  Mais quant ce vient au repentir,
                  Lors se descueuvre sa fierté.   320

The Lover

XXXVII   Love, which distributes both joy and pain,
                        puts ladies above the bonds of servitude,
                        and gives them instead
                        sovereignty and autonomy.
                        Their servants can do no more
                        save continue in their efforts,
                        and he who has once rendered his homage
                        would buy it back at too high a price.

The Lady

XXXVIII   Ladies are not so naïve,
                        so stupid, or so foolish
                        that, for a few words of flattery
                        crafted of pretty words,
                        which you and yours have learned at school
                        to make them believe in miracles,
                        they will so easily change their minds:
                        to such sweet talkers, we close our ears.

The Lover

XXXIX   There is no bard, no matter how much
                        feeling, knowledge, or pain that he might bring to bear,
                        who can make as sad a complaint
                        as he whom tragedy has befallen.
                        For he who makes his complaint in a healthy state of mind
                        can scarce disguise his pretense;
                        but when a man is truly full of pain
                        his words are proven by his deeds.

The Lady

XL   Love is a cruel flatterer,
                        bitter in deed yet sweet in his lying,
                        knowing well how to take revenge
                        on those who claim to understand his secrets.
                        He makes them promise their loyalty
                        with a show of affection,
                        and it is not until one repents
                        that he reveals his ferocious side.

L'amant

XLI   De tant plus que Dieu et Nature
                      Ont fait plaisirs d'amours plus hault,
                      Tant plus aspre en est la pointure
                      Et plus desplaisant le deffault.   324
                      Qui n'a froit n'a cure de chault;
                      L'un contraire est pour l'autre quis,
                      Et ne scet nul que plaisir vault
                      S'i ne l'a par douleur conquis.   328

La dame

XLII   Plaisir n'est mie par tout ung;
                      Ce vous est doulx qui m'est amer,
                      Si ne povez vous ou aucun
                      A vostre gré me faire amer.   332
                      Nul ne se doibt amy clamer
                      Si non par cueur ains que par livre,
                      Car force ne puet entamer
                      La voulenté franche et delivre.   336

L'amant

XLIII   Ha, ma dame! Ja Dieu ne plaise   [8r]
                      Qu'autre droit y veulle querir
                      Fors de vous monstrer mon mesaise
                      Et vostre mercy requerir.   340
                      Se vostre honneur veul surquerir,
                      Dieu et Fortune me confonde
                      Et ne me doint ja acquerir
                      Une seule joye en ce monde.   344

La dame

XLIV   Vous et aultres qui ainsy jurent
                      Et se condempnent et mauldient,
                      Ne cuident que leurs sermens durent
                      Fors tant que les motz se dient,   348
                      Et que Dieu et les sains s'en rient,
                      Mais en telz sermens n'a riens fermes,
                      Et les chetives qui s'i fient
                      En pleurent aprés maintes lermes.   352

The Lover

XLI   As high as God and Nature
      have placed the pleasures of love,
      so painful is its pricking,
      and even more unpleasant the disappointment of not attaining it.
      He who is not cold has no need for warmth;
      the contrary serves to define its opposite.
      And who can appreciate pleasure
      if he has not achieved it by ardent suffering?

The Lady

XLII   Not everyone takes pleasure in the same things:
      what to you is sweet, to me may be bitter.
      And so neither you, nor anyone else, can make me love
      according to your desire.
      No one should call himself lover
      unless it comes from the heart, rather than from a book,
      for force cannot break
      a free and independent will.

The Lover

XLIII   Ha, my lady! May it never please God
      that I might seek any privilege other
      than simply to show you my distress,
      and humbly request your pity.
      If my goal is to compromise your honor
      may God and Fortune confound me
      and grant that I never receive
      one single joy in this world.

The Lady

XLIV   You, and others who swear like this,
      calling condemnation if you break your pledge,
      do not believe your oaths to last any longer
      than the brief second it takes to pronounce the words.
      God and the saints mock your sport,
      for no one takes such oaths seriously,
      but the poor women who do trust in them
      afterward shed many tears.

L'amant

XLV   Cellui n'a pas courage d'omme
                 Qui quiert son plaisir en reprouche,
                 Et n'est pas digne qu'on le nomme
                 Ne que air ou terre lui atouche.   356
                 Loyal cuer et voir disant bouche
                 Sont le chatey[2] d'omme parfait,
                 Et qui de legier sa foy touche,
                 Son honneur pour aultrui deffait.   360

La dame

XLVI   Villain cueur et bouche courtoise   [8v]
                 Ne sont mie bien d'une sorte,
                 Mais Faintise tous les acoise
                 Qui par malice les asorte.   364
                 Et mesgniee Faulx Semblant porte
                 Son honneur en sa langue fainte,
                 Mais honneur est en leur cuer morte
                 Sans estre pleuree ne plainte.   368

L'amant

XLVII   Qui pense mal, bien ne lui viengne!
                 Dieux doint a chascun sa desserte!
                 Mais, pour Dieu mercy, vous souviengne
                 De la douleur que j'ay soufferte,   372
                 Car de ma mort ne de ma perte
                 N'a pas vostre doulceur envie;
                 Et se vo grace m'est ouverte,
                 Vous estez garant de ma vie.   376

La dame

XLVIII   Legier cuer et plaisant folie,
                 Qui est meilleur tant plus est brieve,
                 Vous font ceste melencolie;
                 Mais c'est ung mal dont on relieve.   380
                 Faitez a vostre pensee treve,
                 Car de plus beaulx jeux on se lasse.
                 Je ne vous aide ne ne greve:
                 Qui ne m'en croira, je m'en passe.   384

The Lover

XLV   He has not the true heart of a man,
       who seeks pleasure in what should be reproached;
       he does not merit even being called a man,
       nor deserve the recognition of earth or heaven.
       A loyal heart and truthful tongue
       are the qualities of a good man,
       and he who gives out promises lightly,
       compromises his own honor in his pursuit of another's.

The Lady

XLVI   A base heart and a courteous tongue
       are not a compatible pair.
       Yet Deception easily smoothes their differences
       by forging an alliance in her perfidious way.
       The followers of False Seeming are able to maintain
       their honor by deceiving with hollow words,
       even though honor is dead in their hearts
       and is not even missed or mourned.

The Lover

XLVII   To him who thinks ill, no good will come.
       God gives to each what he deserves.
       But, for the love of God, please remember
       the pain that I have suffered,
       for I know you cannot wish
       my death or my ruin;
       and if your grace is offered to me,
       you will be the redeemer of my life.

The Lady

XLVIII   A light heart and pleasant foolishness,
       the merrier for their brevity,
       have convinced you of this melancholy;
       but it is an illness from which one recovers quickly.
       Call a truce for your thoughts,
       for one can tire of even the most enjoyable games.
       I cannot help you or do you harm.
       If you don't want to believe this, I wash my hands of it.

L'amant

XLIX   Qui a faulcon, oysel, ou chien   [9r]
        Qui le suit, aime, craint et doubte,
        Le tiengne chier et garde bien
        Et ne le chace ne reboute.   388
        Et je, qui ay m'entente toute
        A vous, sans faintise et sans change,
        Suis rebouté plus bas en soulte
        Et moins prisé q'ung tout estrange. 392

La dame

L   Se je faiz bonne chiere a tous
        Par honneur et par franc courage,
        Je ne la veuil pas faire a vous
        Pour eschever vostre dommage,   396
        Car Amours est si petit saige
        Et de crëance si legiere
        Qu'i prent tout a son avantage
        Chose qui ne lui sert de guiere.   400

L'amant

LI   Se par amour et fëaulté
        Je pers l'acueil qu'estranges ont,
        Donc me vauldra ma loyaulté
        Moins qu'a ceulx qui viennent et vont 404
        Et qui de riens vostres ne sont.
        Et sembleroit en vous perie
        Courtoisie, qui vous semont
        Qu'amour soit par amour merie.   408

La dame

LII   Courtoisie si est aliee   [9v]
        D'omme, qui l'aime et la tient chiere,
        Et ne veult estre a riens liee,
        Ne pour donner ne pour priere;   412
        Mais depart de sa bonne chiere
        Ou il lui plaist et bon lui semble.
        Guerredon, contraint a l'enchiere,
        Et elle ne vont point ensamble.   416

The Lover

XLIX   He who has a falcon or a dog,
and hunts with it, loves it, and worries over it,
he holds it dear and takes good care of it,
and does not neglect or reject it.
Yet I, who have focused all my intentions
on you, with no falseness or inconstancy,
am relegated lower on the scale
and receive less appreciation than a complete stranger!

The Lady

L   If I give to everyone a warm welcome
in a civilized manner and with an honest heart,
I do not wish to do the same for you
to ease your dolorous state;
for Love is so foolish,
so facile, and so credulous, that
he will take as a positive sign
something that really is just a trifle.

The Lover

LI   If for Love and Loyalty's sake,
I lose the welcome that strangers receive,
then my faith makes me worth less
than those who casually come and go,
who are not at all devoted to you!
It would seem that in you has perished
Courtesy, who should have taught you
that love receives just compensation from love.

The Lady

LII   Courtesy is so closely allied
to Man, who loves and holds her dear,
that she does not wish to be influenced
either by gifts or by pleading,
but prefers to bestow her smiling grace
where it pleases her the most.
Recompense, constraint, and promises of greater goods
do not go hand in hand with Courtesy.

L'amant

LIII   Je ne quier point de guerredon,
               Car le desservir m'est trop hault;
               Je demande grace et pardon,
               Puis que mort ou mercy me fault.   420
               Donner le bien ou il deffault
               Est courtoisie raisonnable,
               Mais aux siens encore plus vault
               Qu'estre aux estranges amiable.   424

La dame

LIV   Ne sçay que vous appelez "bien"
               (Mal emprunte sus aultrui nom!)
               Mais il est trop large du sien
               Qui par donner pert son renom.   428
               On ne doit faire aultrui, si non
               Quant la requeste est avenant,
               Car se honneur ne retenon,
               Trop petit est le remenant.   432

L'amant

LV   Oncques homme mortel nasqui,   [10r]
               Ou pourroit naistre, soubz les cieulx,
               Et n'est autre, fors vous, a qui
               Vostre honneur touche plus ou mieulx   436
               Qu'a moy, qui n'atens jeune ne vieux
               Le mien fors par vostre service.
               Et n'ay cuer, scens, bouche ou yeulx
               Qui soit donné a aultre office.   440

La dame

LVI   D'assez grant charge se chevit
               Qui son honneur garde et maintient;
               Mais a dangier traveille et vit
               Qui en aultrui main l'entretient.   444
               Cil a qui l'onneur appartient
               Ne s'en doit a aultrui attendre,
               Car tant moins du sien en retient
               Qui trop veult a l'aultrui entendre.   448

The Lover

LIII
I am seeking no recompense,
for I am far from deserving that.
I ask for your goodness, pure and simple,
for I must receive either pity or death by your hand.
It is a reasonable act of grace
To give where there is need,
and it is better to show friendship
to one's own people rather than to strangers.

The Lady

LIV
I do not know what you call "goodness"
(evil goes by many names);
but she shows herself too generous who,
by her giving, loses her good reputation.
One does not ever owe anyone anything, even if
the request is made properly,
for if we do not carefully guard our honor,
what else will be left to us?

The Lover

LV
There is not a man in the world
now living or yet to be born,
nor any other creature alive, save yourself
who is more concerned with your honor
than I. I, young and old at the same time,
look to acquire my honor only in your service.
My heart, mind, lips, and eyes
are dedicated solely to this purpose.

The Lady

LVI
It is quite a heavy charge
to maintain and protect one's own honor;
but to entrust it to another, surely,
is to live dangerously.
He who has honor
need not rely on another for its care,
for the man busy worrying about his neighbors' needs
takes little care of his own.

L'amant

LVII
Vos yeulx ont si empraint leur marche
En mon cuer que, quoy qu'il adviengne,
Se j'ay honneur ou je le serche,
Il convient que de vous y viengne.   452
Fortune a voulu que je tiengne
Ma vie en vostre mercy close,
Si est bien droit qu'i me souviengne
De vostre honneur sur toute chose.   456

La dame

LVIII
A vostre honneur seul entendez   [10v]
Pour vostre temps mieulx emploier:
Du mien a moy vous attendez
Sans prendre painne a foloier.   460
Bon fait vaincre et assoupploier
Ung cuer follement deceü,
Car rompre vault pis que ploier
Et esbranlé mieulx que cheü.   464

L'amant

LIX
Pensez, ma dame, que depuis
Qu'Amours mon cuer vous delivra,
Il ne pourroit (ne je ne puis)
Estre a aultre, tant qu'il vivra.   468
Tout quicte et franc le vous livra:
Ce don ne se peut abollir.
J'attens ce qui s'en ensuivra;
Je n'y puis mettre ne tollir.   472

La dame

LX
Je ne tiens mie pour donné
Ce qu'on offre qu'i ne le prent,
Car le don est habandonné
Se le donneur ne le reprent.   476
Trop a de cuers qui entreprent
D'en donner a qui les reffuse,
Mais il est saige qui aprent
A s'en retraire qu'i ne muse.   480

The Lover

LVII

Your eyes have so engraved their mark
in my heart that, no matter what happens,
whether I now have honor or still seek it,
it is from you that it must finally come.
Fortune has decided that I will live
my life waiting on your gracious pity,
so it is right and just that he should keep
your honor always on my mind, above all else.

The Lady

LVIII

Be attentive to your honor alone,
to make better use of your time.
As for my honor, entrust it back to me.
Stop causing yourself so much pain, or you will go mad.
It is wise to beware of encouraging
a heart so woefully deceived,
for breaking is worse than bending,
and fearful is better than fallen.

The Lover

LIX

Know for certain, my lady, that since
Love delivered my heart to you
it cannot be (nor can I be) any other way
as long as he is living.
He gave my heart to you truly, entirely, and with no obligation:
this gift cannot be returned!
So I patiently await the next step,
for it is out of my control to add or retract a single thing.

The Lady

LX

I do not consider given
what has simply been offered and not taken,
for the gift is just abandoned
if the giver will not take it back.
Too many hearts try to give
to those who then refuse,
but he is wise who takes his
gift back, so as not to waste his time.

L'amant

LXI   Il ne doit pas cuider muser   [11r]
                       Qui sert dame de si hault pris.
                       Se jë y doy mon temps user,
                       Au moins ne puis je estre repris   484
                       De cuer failli ne de mespris
                       Quant envers vous faiz cette queste,
                       Par qui Amours a entrepris
                       De tant de bons cuers la conqueste.   488

La dame

LXII   Se mon conseil voulez ouÿr,
                       Querez aillieurs plus noble et gente
                       Qui d'amours se veulle esjouÿr
                       Et mieulx sortisse a vostre entente.   492
                       Trop loing de confort se tourmente
                       Qui apart soy pour deux se trouble,
                       Et cellui pert le jeu d'attente
                       Qui ne scet faire son point double.   496

L'amant

LXIII   Ce conseil que vous me donnez
                       Se peust mieulx dire que exploitier.
                       Du non croire me pardonnez,
                       Car j'ay cuer tel et si entier   500
                       Qu'i ne se pourroit affaittier
                       A chose ou Loyaulté n'acorde;
                       N'autre conseil ne m'a mestier
                       Fors pitié et misericorde.   504

La dame

LXIV   Saige est qui folie encommance   [11v]
                       Quant departir s'en scet et veult;
                       Maiz il a faulte de scïence
                       Qui la veult conduire et ne peut.   508
                       Qui par conseil ne se desmeut,
                       Desespoir se met de sa suite;
                       Et tout le bien qu'il en requeut,
                       C'est de mourir en la poursuite.   512

The Lover

LXI

He should not consider it a waste of time
to serve a lady of such great worth.
For if I devote my days to this duty,
at least I will not be blamed
for having a faint or fickle heart
as I continue for you in this quest,
a test by which Love has often succeeded
in the conquest of many a fine heart.

The Lady

LXII

If you want to hear my advice,
seek elsewhere a girl more noble and more courtly,
who wishes to enjoy Love's delights,
and who will thus prove more to your liking.
He who takes upon himself the worry of two hearts
torments himself without hope of relief;
and he will lose the waiting game
if he does not know how to play.

The Lover

LXIII

The advice you give me
is easier said than done.
Forgive me for not following it,
but my heart is so wholly decided
that it could not possibly do
a thing that Loyalty would not assent to.
The only advice I need now
is that of Pity and Compassion!

The Lady

LXIV

He is wise who, having once acted foolishly,
finds a way out of the situation, recognizing his folly.
But he who cannot so restrain himself, even though he wishes to,
is sadly lacking in savoir faire.
He who does not follow good advice
is bound to find nothing but despair,
and the only good he receives for his effort
is to die in hapless pursuit.

L'amant

LXV   Je poursuivray tant que pourray
                    Et que vie me durera,
                    Et lors qu'en loyaulté mourray,
                    Ceste mort ne me grevera;   516
                    Mais quant vo durté me fera
                    Mourir loyaulx et douloureux,
                    Encores moins grief me fera
                    Que de vivre faulx amoureux.   520

La dame

LXVI   De rien a moy ne vous prenez.
                    Je ne vous suis aspre ne dure,
                    Et n'est droit que vous me tenez
                    Envers vous ne doulce ne sure.   524
                    Qui se quiert le mal, si l'endure,
                    Aultre confort donner n'y sçay
                    Ne de l'apprendre n'ay je cure:
                    Qui en veult en face l'essay.   528

L'amant

LXVII   Une fois le fault essayer   [12r]
                    A tous les bons a leur endroit,
                    Et le devoir d'Amours paier,
                    Qui sus frans cuers a prise et droit,   532
                    Car Franc Vouloir maintient et croit
                    Que c'est durté et mesprison
                    Tenir ung hault cuer si estroit
                    Qu'il n'ait qu'ung seul corps en prison.   536

La dame

LXVIII   J'en voy tant de cas merveilleux
                    Qu'il m'en doit assez souvenir,
                    Car l'entree en est perilleux
                    Et encor plus le revenir.   540
                    A tart en peut bien advenir:
                    Pour ce n'ay vouloir de cerchier
                    Ung mal plaisant au mieulx venir,
                    Pour l'essay en couster si chier.   544

The Lover

LXV   I will persevere in this way,
with hope, for as long as I live.
And when I die, still loyal to my troth,
my death will not displease me.
But when your hard-heartedness does kill me,
still true and in great pain,
know that dying grieves me less
than would living known as a fickle lover.

The Lady

LXVI   You have nothing to reproach me for.
I am not bitter or harsh with you,
and it is not fair that you should judge me
either sweet or sour toward you:
he who seeks evil can always find it.
I do not know how to give you comfort,
nor do I wish to learn how.
Let one who wishes to try give her best effort.

The Lover

LXVII   But you should make at least some effort;
everyone worthy must, at least once,
pay tribute to Love's power,
which rightly influences sincere hearts!
For Free Will believes and considers
that it is haughty, and even wrong,
to guard a noble heart so closely
that he be imprisoned alone, in a single body.

The Lady

LXVIII   I have heard such stories told and retold[3]
and so I remember all too easily
the perils of embarking on this path,
the return even more unsure.
In these affairs, the best is slow to come.
Therefore, I have no desire to chase after
what might be, at best, a pleasant evil,
but for which the price would be too dear.

L'amant

LXIX   Vous n'avez cause de doubter
                  Ne que souspeçon vous esmeuve
                  A m'esloingnier ne debouter,
                  Car vostre bonté voy et treuve   548
                  Car j'ay fait l'essay et l'espreuve
                  Par quoy ma loyaulté appert.
                  La longue attente et seure espreuve
                  Ne se peut celer: il appert.   552

La dame

LXX   Il se peut loyal appeller—   [12v]
                  Et se nom lui doit et affiert—
                  Qui scet deservir et celer
                  Et garder le bien, s'il acquiert.   556
                  Qui encor poursuit et requiert
                  N'a pas loyaulté esprouvee,
                  Mais tel pourchasse grace et quiert
                  Qui la pert puis qu'il l'a trouvee.   560

L'amant

LXXI   Se ma loyaulté s'avanture
                  D'amer ce qui ne m'aime mie,
                  Et tant cherist ce qui me tue,
                  Ce m'est amoureuse ennemye,   564
                  Quant Pitié, qui est endormye,
                  Mettroit en mes maulx fin et terme,
                  Ce gracïeux confort d'amye
                  Feroit ma loyaulté plus ferme.   568

La dame

LXXII   Ung douloureux pense tousdiz
                  Du plus joyeulx le droit revers,
                  Et le penser du maladis
                  Est entre les sains tout divers.   572
                  Assez est il de cuers travers
                  Qu'Amours fait tantost empirer
                  Et loyaulté mettre a l'envers,
                  Dont ilz souloient souspirer.   576

The Lover

LXIX   You have no cause to doubt me,
nor suspicion that might induce you
to send me away or spurn my love.
For the goodness in you must see and approve
that I have passed the test
and openly proven my loyalty.
This long-abiding and true service
cannot be ignored: the proof is plain to see.

The Lady

LXX   A man has the right to call himself "loyal,"
and this is fitting and right,
only when he has learned to deserve the reward,
and hide it and keep it safe: only then will it finally be granted.
He who is still seeking and begging
has not yet proven his loyalty,
for there are many who, requesting such grace,
throw it away as soon as they have attained it.

The Lover

LXXI   If my Loyalty risks
loving that which loves me not,
and so cherishes that which is killing me
and to me is an enemy of love,
then Pity, who now is sleeping,
will put an end to my suffering,
and such gracious comfort from a lover
will make my Loyalty even more devout.

The Lady

LXXII   A sad man is always thinking
the opposite of what the joyful man thinks,
and the thoughts of a sick man
are, in the midst of the healthy, out of place.
There are many corrupt hearts who,
as soon as they have something valuable,
just as soon degrade it,
and thus act contrary to Loyalty,
in whose name they used to sigh so wishfully.

L'amant

LXXIII   De tous soit cellui deguerpiz,   [13r]
                  D'onneur, de grace, et defait,
                  Qui descongnoist et tourne en pis
                  Le don de grace et de bienfait   580
                  De sa dame, qui l'a reffait
                  Et ramené de mort a vie.
                  Qui se soubzmet a tel meffait
                  A plus d'une mort desservie.   584

La dame

LXXIV   Sus telz meffaiz n'a court ne juge
                  A qui on puisse racourir.
                  L'ung les mauldit, l'autre les juge,
                  Maiz je n'en ay veu nulz mourir.   588
                  On leur laisse leurs cuers courir
                  En commançant pis de rechief,
                  Et tristes dames encourir
                  D'aultrui peine, coulpe, et meschief.   592

L'amant

LXXV   Combien qu'on ne naye ou pende
                  Cellui qui en tel crime chiet,
                  Je suis certain, quoy qu'il attende,
                  Qu'en la fin si lui en meschiet   596
                  Et que honneur et bien lui dechiet,
                  Car Faulceté est si mauldite
                  Que jamaiz hault honneur n'escheit
                  Dessus cellui ou elle habite.   600

La dame

LXXVI   De ce n'ont mie grant paour   [13v]
                  Ceulx qui dient et qui maintiennent
                  Que loyaulté n'est pas eür
                  A ceulx qui longuement la tiennent.   604
                  Leurs cueurs s'en vont et puis reviennent,
                  Car ilz les ont bien reclaméz
                  Et si bien aprins qu'i retiennent
                  A changier des qu'ilz sont améz.   608

The Lover

LXXIII   He should be abandoned by everyone,
by honor and grace, and then destroyed,
who does not recognize or appreciate
the gift of grace and the righteousness
of his lady, who has remade him
and brought him from death to life.
He who lowers himself to this crime
deserves to die a thousand deaths.

The Lady

LXXIV   For this crime there is no court nor judge
before whom one can seek any recourse.
One can condemn such miscreants, or even judge them,
but I have yet to see one put to death;
they are allowed to continue their course
and do even worse damage
to poor unsuspecting women,
exposing them to pain, blame, and grief.

The Lover

LXXV   Even though we do not drown or even hang
him who is guilty of such crimes,
I am certain that no matter what happens now,
eventually he will get his due
and lose all honor and worldly goods
because Falseness is so ruinous
that true Honor can never live
in him within whom Falseness resides.

The Lady

LXXVI   They have no fear,
the ones who maintain that
Loyalty does not bring happiness to
those who hold it so dear and for so long.
The hearts of these people come
and just as quickly go, for they have trained themselves well
to change their hearts again
just as soon as they are loved in return.

L'amant

LXXVII   Quant on a son cuer bien assis
                    En bonne et loyalle partie,
                    On doit estre entier et rassis
                    A tousjours mais sans departie.   612
                    Si tost qu'amours est my partie,
                    Et le hault plaisir en est hors;
                    Si ne sera par moy partie
                    Tant que l'ame me bate ou corps.   616

La dame

LXXVIII   De amer bien ce qu'amer devez
                    Ne pourriez vous pas mesprendre;
                    Mais s'ainsi vous vous decevez
                    Par legierement entreprendre,   620
                    Vous mesmes vous povez reprendre
                    Et avoir a Raison recours
                    Plus tost qu'en Fol Espoir attendre
                    Ung tres desesperé secours.   624

L'amant

LXXIX   Raison, Advis, Conseil, et Sens   [14r]
                    Sont soubz l'arrest d'Amours selez.
                    A tel arrest je m'y consens,
                    Car nul d'eulx ne s'est rebelléz.   628
                    Ilz sont par my Desir mesléz
                    Et si fort enlasséz es laz
                    Que ja ne seront desmesléz
                    Se Pitié ne brise les laz.   632

La dame

LXXX   Qui n'a en soy mesme amitié
                    De toute amour est deffiéz;
                    Et se de vous n'avez pitié,
                    D'aultrui pitié ne vous fiez.   636
                    Maiz soiez tout certiffiéz
                    Que je suis celle que je fus:
                    D'avoir mieulx ne vous affiez
                    Et prenez en gré le reffuz.   640

The Lover

LXXVII   When one has placed his heart in the care
of a good and loyal lover,
one should be devoted entirely to her
forevermore, with never a thought otherwise,
because as soon as love is divided,
its sublime nature is deformed.
Therefore this love will never be fractured by me
for as long as this heart beats in my chest.

The Lady

LXXVIII   Certainly you cannot go wrong by
loving that which it is your duty to love;
but, should you mistake your duty
by undertaking something too lightly,
your duty is then to get hold of yourself,
and be reasonable,
rather than waiting on help from
foolish Hope: such a rescue is surely hopeless![4]

The Lover

LXXIX   Reason, Wisdom, Advice, and Good Sense
are all to be found in Love's court,
and to such authority do I, too, subject myself,
for none of them has seen reason to rebel.
Yet they are all so tied up by Desire,
so entwined in his laces, alas!
that they will never be unbound,
unless Pity come to cut the ties.

The Lady

LXXX   He who has no love for himself
is forbidden from loving another.
Likewise, if you have no pity for yourself,
how can you expect pity from another?
Have no doubt that I am still exactly
as I have always been;
do not presume that things will change.
Resign yourself to rejection!

L'amant

LXXXI   J'ay mon esperance fermee
                Qu'en tel dame ne doit faillir
                Pitié, mais elle est enfermee
                Et laisse Dangier m'assaillir,   644
                Et c'elle voit ma vertu faillir
                Pour bien amer, elle s'en sauldra.
                Vers sa demeure et tart saillir
                Ce moult bien souffrir me fauldra.   648

La dame

LXXXII   Ostés vous hors de ce propos   [14v]
                Car tant plus vous y attendez,
                Moins avrez joyë et repos
                Et jamaiz au bout n'en vendrez.   652
                Quant a Espoir vous attendez,
                Vous vous en trouverez abestiz,
                Et en la fin vous aprendrez
                Qu'Esperance paist les chetifz.   656

L'amant

LXXXIII   Vous direz ce que vous vouldrez—
                Et du povoir avez assez—
                Mais ja Espoir ne me touldrez,
                Par qui j'ay tant de maulx passéz.   660
                Car quant Nature a enchasséz
                En vous des biens a telz effors,
                Elle ne les y amasséz
                Pour en mettre Pitié dehors.   664

La dame

LXXXIV   Pitié doit estre raisonnable
                Et a nul desavantageuse,
                Et aux besongneux prouffitable
                Et aux piteux non maulgracieuse.   668
                Se dame est a aultrui piteuse
                Pour estre a soy mesmes crüelle,
                Sa pitié devient despiteuse
                Et son amour hayne mortelle.   672

The Lover

LXXXI
I, in my hope, am firmly convinced
that Pity cannot be lacking in such a lady as you;
but it must be locked up,
and leaves Resistance to attack me,
from which I will surely die, a martyr
of true love, unless Pity escapes.
Then her tardy arrival and my long suffering
will serve to my advantage.

The Lady

LXXXII
Stop this foolish talk,
for the more you persist,
the less you will have of joy and peace;
you will never see the end of it!
If you continue to rely on Hope,
you will end up looking asinine,
for ultimately you will see
that Hope simply puts out to pasture the sheepish ones.

The Lover

LXXXIII
Say what you will—
you have the power to do so—
but you will never take away my Hope,
which has helped me through so much hardship;
when Nature bestowed upon you
so many good qualities,
she could never have collected such an assembly,
only to leave Pity out!

The Lady

LXXXIV
Pity must be reasonable, however,
and to none disadvantageous;
beneficial to those who are in need,
and gracious to the broken-hearted.
If a lady treats someone with pity
and in so doing is cruel to herself,
her pity becomes pitiless
and her sweet love changes to mortal hatred.

L'amant

LXXXV   Conforter les desconfortéz   [15r]
                   N'est pas crüaulté, maiz est loz;
                   Mais vous, qui si dur cuer portez
                   En si beau corps, se dire l'oz,   676
                   Gaigniez le blasme et le desloz
                   De crüaulté, qui mal y siet,
                   Quant Pitié qui depart les lotz
                   En vostre hault cuer ne s'assiet.   680

La dame

LXXXVI   Qui me dit que je suis amee:
                   Se bien croire je le vouloye,
                   Me doit il tenir pour blasmee
                   S'a son vouloir je ne folloye.   684
                   Se de telz confors me mesloye,
                   Ce seroit pitié sans maniere;
                   Et depuis ce, je m'en douloie
                   S'en est la souldee derreniere.   688

L'amant

LXXXVII   Ha! cuer plus dur que le noir marbre,
                   En qui Mercy ne puet entrer,
                   Plus fort a ploier qu'ung fort arbre,
                   Que vous vault tel rigueur monstrer?   692
                   Vous plaist il mieulx me veoir oultrer
                   Mort devant vous pour vostre esbat,
                   Que pour ung confort demonstrer
                   Respiter la Mort qui m'abat?   696

La dame

LXXXVIII   De vos maulx guerir vous pourrez,   [15v]
                   Car des miens ne vous requerray;
                   Ne pour mon plaisir ne mourrez,
                   Ne pour vous guerir ne guerray.   700
                   Mon cuer pour aultrui ne harray,
                   Crient, pleurent, rient ou chantent;
                   Mais se je puis, je pourverray
                   Que vous në aultres ne s'en vantent.   704

The Lover

LXXXV To comfort those who are discomforted
is not cruel but laudable.
As for you, who hide a heart so hard
in such a lovely body, if I dare to say,
you shall incur reproach and accusation of cruelty
for this, which would suit you badly,
unless Pity, who determines each man's worth,
is found in your haughty heart.

The Lady

LXXXVI I am told that I am dearly loved.
Even if I wished to believe this,
does he have the right to hold me up to reproach
because I do not do as he requests?
Were I to become involved in giving out comfort,
that would be too pitiful,
especially if later I were to suffer for it.
That would be a fine profit for my efforts!

The Lover

LXXXVII Oh! What a heart, harder than the blackest marble,
in which no Pity can even enter,
harder to bend than a thick tree;
how does it serve you to be so harsh?
Will it please you more to see me laid out
dead before you for your enjoyment,
rather than offer me some small comfort
to hold back Death, who so beats me down?

The Lady

LXXXVIII You are quite capable of healing yourself
and have no need of me.
You will not die for my pleasure,
nor will I put myself out to heal you.
I will not compromise my honor for others,
though they shout, cry, laugh, or sing;
and, as I am able, I will make sure
that neither you nor any others can say anything about it.

L'amant

LXXXIX   Je ne suis pas bon chanteurs—
      Aussi m'avient mieulx le pleurer—
      Mais je ne fuz oncques vanteurs:
      J'ayme plus tout coy demourer.   708
      Nul ne se doit enamourer
      S'il n'a cuer de celer l'emprise,
      Car vanteur n'est a honnourer
      Puisque sa langue le desprise.   712

La dame

XC   Male Bouche tient bien grant court:
      Chascun a mesdire estudie.
      Faulx amoureux au temps qui court
      Si servent tous de gouliardie.   716
      Le plus secret veult bien qu'on die
      Qu'il est d'aucune mescreüz,
      Et pour riens que homme a dame die
      Il ne peust estre jamaiz creüz.   720

L'amant

XCI   D'uns et d'aultres est et sera.   [16r]
      La terre n'est pas toute onnye:
      Des bons le bien se monstrera
      Et des mauvaiz la villanie.   724
      Est ce droit, s'aucuns ont honnie
      Leur langue en mesdit eshonté,
      Que Reffus en excommenie
      Les bons avec leur bonté?   728

La dame

XCII   Quant meschans meschant parler eussent,
      Ce meschief seroit pardonnéz;
      Mais ceulx qui mieulx faire deüssent
      Et que Noblesse a ordonnéz   732
      D'estre bien condicionnéz
      Sont les plus avant en la fangue,
      Et ont leurs cueurs habandonnéz
      A courte foy et longue langue.   736

The Lover

LXXXIX   I am not an able singer,
                  tears, in fact, are better suited to me,
                  and I have never talked out of line —
                  I prefer to stay silent about such things.
                  No one should engage in loving
                  if he cannot keep quiet,
                  for a braggart should not be honored
                  since his tongue is so despicable.

The Lady

XC   Foul Mouth reigns over a large court,
                  each well studied at slander.
                  False lovers nowadays
                  serve everyone a share of their debauchery.
                  The most discreet really wants to be spoken of,
                  to let it be known that certain women suspect him,
                  And so, no matter what a man says to a woman,
                  I say, he should not be believed.

The Lover

XCI   For some it has always been and will always be,
                  but everyone is not the same.
                  The good of the virtuous cannot be concealed
                  and the infamy of the vicious will be revealed.
                  Let us admit that certain men have dishonored their lips
                  with shameful slander; is it right that, in consequence,
                  Refusal should excommunicate at the same time
                  the good with all their goodness?

The Lady

XCII   When wretched men speak wretchedly
                  their sin should be pardoned.
                  But those who know better how to behave
                  and whom Noblesse has taught well
                  how to love
                  are the worst of the lot:
                  these have abandoned their noble hearts
                  to flattering tongues and brief engagements.

L'amant

XCIII   Or congnoiz je bien cy endroit
                       Que pour bien faire on est honnyz,
                       Puis que Pitié, Justice et Droit
                       Sont de cuer de dame banis.   740
                       Fault il faire dont tous unis
                       Les humbles servans et les faulx,
                       Et que les bons soient pugniz
                       Pour le pechié des desloyaulx?   744

La dame

XCIV   Je n'ay le povoir de grever   [16v]
                       Ne de pugnir aultre ne vous,
                       Mais pour les mauvaiz eschever
                       Il se fait bon garder de tous.   748
                       Faulx Semblant fait l'umble et le doulx
                       Pour prendre dames en aguet,
                       Et pour ce chascune de nous
                       Y doit bien l'escoute et le guet.   752

L'amant

XCV   Puis que de grace ung tout seul mot
                       De vostre rigoureux cuer n'yst,
                       J'appelle devant Dieu qui m'ot
                       De la durté qui me honnist;   756
                       Et me plains qu'i ne parfournist
                       Pitié, qu'en vous il oublïa,
                       Ou que ma vie ne fenist
                       Que si tost mis en oubli a.   760

La dame

XCVI   Mon cuer ne moy ne vous feïsmes
                       Onc riens dont plaindre vous doiez.
                       Riens ne vous nuyst fors vous meïsmes:
                       De vous mesmes juges soiez.   764
                       Une foiz pour toutes croiez
                       Que vous demourez escondit.
                       De tant redire m'ennuyez,
                       Car je vous en ay assez dit.   768

The Lover

XCIII
So then, I see now
that doing the right thing incurs shame,
because Pity, Justice, and Righteousness
are banished from the hearts of ladies.
Must you see everyone as the same,
the loyal servants as well as the wicked,
and hold that the good should be punished
for the sins of the unfaithful?

The Lady

XCIV
I do not have the power to hurt
or to punish anyone, not even you.
But in order to escape the bad ones,
it is best to protect oneself from them all.
False Seeming plays humble and sweet
to ensnare ladies in his trap,
and for this reason, each one of us
would do well to pay attention and be on guard.

The Lover

XCV
Since not a single word of grace
comes from your hardened heart,
I appeal to God, who will save me
from this harshness that devastates me,
and I complain that He has not brought forth
Pity, whom he seems to have neglected to put in you.
And I pray that I find death more quickly,
to end this life, which he has forgotten so soon.

The Lady

XCVI
Neither my heart nor I have done anything to you
that gives you reason to complain.
The only thing that harms you is yourself:
therefore be your own judge.
Once and for all, try to understand
that you have been refused without respite.
You annoy me with your repetitions,
for I have already said enough to you.

L'acteur

XCVII

Adonc le doulant se leva   [17r]
Et part de la feste pleurant.
A pou que son cuer ne creva
Comme a homme qui va mourant,   772
Et dist: Mort, vien a moy courant
Ains que mon scens se decongnoisse,
Et m'abrege le demourant
De ma vie plaine d'angoisse.   776

L'acteur

XCVIII

Depuis ne sceüs qu'il devint
Ne quel part il se transporta;
Mais a sa dame n'en souvint
Qui aux dances se deporta.   780
Et depuis on me rapporta
Qu'il avoit ses cheveux desroups,
Et que tant se desconforta
Qu'il en estoit mort de courroux.   784

L'acteur

XCIX

Sy vous pri, amoureux, fuiez
Ces vanteurs et ces mesdisans,
Et comme infames les huiez,
Car ilz sont a voz faiz nuysans.   788
Pour les faire non voir disans,
Reffuz a ses chastiaux bastiz,
Car ilz ont mis trop puis. x. ans
Le païs d'Amours a pastiz.   792

L'acteur

C

Et vous, dames et damoiselles,   [17v]
En qui honneur croist et s'assemble,
Ne soiez mie si crüelles,
Chascune ne toutes ensamble.   796
Que ja nulle de vous ressemble
Celle que m'oyez nommer cy,
Qu'on peut appeller, se me samble,
La belle dame sans mercy.[5]   800

The Narrator

XCVII   At these words, the grieving man arose,
and left the party with tears in his eyes.
His heart was practically bursting
like that of a dying man,
and to himself he cried: "Death, come quickly,
before I lose my mind
and shorten the rest of this life,
which is so filled with anguish."

The Narrator

XCVIII   I do not know what became of him afterward
nor to where he fled,
but he was quickly forgotten by his lady,
who went back to dance with the others.
Not long after, someone told me
that he had torn out all of his hair,
and that he was so miserable,
that finally he had died of his distress.

The Narrator

XCIX   Thus I beseech you, men in love, flee
these braggarts and scandalmongers,
and call them traitors,
because they will impede your progress.
Refusal has built a fortress against them
so that their words will not be taken as truth,
for they have had too much control
over the land of love in recent times.

The Narrator

C   As for you, ladies and young maidens,
in whom honor is born and collected,
be not so cruel as this one,
neither individually nor collectively.
Would that none of you resemble
this lady whom you will now hear me name,
and who should be called, it seems to me,
The Belle Dame Sans Mercy.[6,7]

Notes

1. This line, also in Pf, attests the rhyme *merveille/elle*.

2. Chatey: "goods, possession."

3. The "stories": likely the *Châtelaine de Vergy*, a text often cited in the Quarrel cycle to show the consequences of unfaithful love, as well as Christine de Pizan's *Cent ballades*.

4. The narrator has already given us a foreshadowing of the impossibility of reciprocal love in this affair, for the lover is responding to the desire inspired by her eyes meeting his, with no further evidence that the lady will respond positively to his advances. See lines 141–44.

5. In Pp after the explicit are written the first four lines of the *Loyal Lady in Love*, as if an envoi.

6. *Belle dame sans mercy*, rejected readings: 2. Comme triste Qd; 30. P. la mort (-1) PcPnPpQd; 36. temps le mien (-1) PcPnPpQd; 50. Chevauchie PcPnQd; 65. resveillé PcPfQd; 67. acueille PcPfQd; 77. avait +1 PcPnQd; 83. ung h. (+1) Pf; 153. lasse (-1) PcPfQd; 155. j. passe (-1) PcPfQd; 154. jeuz t. PcQd; 229. me tramitez PbPcPnQd; 179. a pou quil (-1) PcPnQd; 231. proumitez PbPcPfPnQd; 249. vous d. (-1) Pn; 267. l'on dit (-1) PcPf; 279. estanchier PcQd; 281. Amours n. PcQd; 305. mist (-1) Pc; 307. fist (-1) Pc; 319. v. au r. -1 Pb; 347. serment; 363. acorde PcQd; 375. Et se vostre g. n'y est o. (+2) Pc; 393. foiz Pf; 413. depart sa (-1) PbPcPnQd; 418. servir (-1) Pc; 478. le Pc; 502. ne s'acorde (+1) Pc; 507. de bonne science (+2) PbPcPnQd; 557. encores (+1) Qd; 559. requiert (+1) Pc; 586. racouurir; 589. couurir; 591. encouurir; 596. Quon PcPfQd; 604. detiennent (+1) Pc; 606. y les ont Pc; 607. qui r. Qd; 616. on Pc; 642. telle (+1) Qd; 726. et a honte PcQd; 734. S. plus (-1) Pc; 762. r. de quoy p. (+1) Pc; 763. mesmes rhyme, -1 Qd; 781. Et puis (-1) Pc; 782. desromps (rhyme) Pc; 788. il sont; 791. il ont.

7. *Belle dame sans mercy*, variant readings: 6. me tolly PcPn; 13. le t. PnPhQd; 15. D'escripre ne de ennoier Pn; 20. Non saurait m. Pn; 23. l'en vouldroit PcPn; 30. Prist Pc; 34. de dittier Pp; 35. veul laisser aux aultres PcPnPp; 38. esparnoye PcPnPp; 44. ne moste Pn; 47. la Pc; 48. C'oncques puis m. c. n'y pensa Pp; 52. ma d. Pn; 53. v. affinee Pn; 54. cuiday PcPp; 56. Menestreux dedens Pc, Menestrerelz en Pp; 59. Maiz d. mes bons a. Pc, Mais quant PnPp; 65. A l'entrer PcQd; 66. De d. et de d. Pc; 70. t. le j. PcPn; tout ce j. Qd; 83. Et pensoit c. h. Pc, Et sembloit bien h. r. Oj; 84. entretenoit Pc; 92. mais pour Pc; 94. S'enlachoit au ton Pc; 97. ot Pc; 102. et sans Pc; 108. A. qui son cuer maistrioit Pn; 120. A. fusmes Pc PnQd; 121. se trayoit Pc, s. tournoit Pn; 122. P. raffermir Pc, P. reformer Pn; 129. d. or Pc; 131. Et Pc; 132. Ades o l. PcPn; 135. revenoit Pc; 136. sus toutes plus Pc; 144. Ainchoiz q. Pc; 148. a cuer [damans Pc] d'amant PnQd; 154. C. jeuz t. Pf; 156. desoiubx Pn; 159 l'espesse fueille PcPnQd; 163. sen retournoit Pn; 170. plus est p. Pn; 171. avoit Pn, sentoit Pc; 174. Et Pc; 181. restraint Qd; 194. muir Pc; 197. en trop moins PnQd, M. a t. m. Pc; 198. conte Pc; 199. Et si n'en p. PcPnQd; 210. pour PcPf; 220. asseureement Pn; XXXVII–XLII precede XXXI–XXXVI in Pn; 248 mavez v. Pn; 251. n. trop h. Qd; 253. percevoir Pn; 257. le m. PcQd; 262. en mercy Pc; 265. amoureuse m. Pc; 279. eschangier PbPcPf; 281. De vous Pf; 284. n. regret Pc; 294. leur p. Pf; 304. beau par-

ler PbPcQd; 306. d'estudie et PbPc; 320. Alors d. NjPn; 326. par Pc; 28. acquiz Pc; 338 je Pc; 339. ma Pc; 341. Se je tens h. Np; 347. N. cuidez Nj; 358. chatel Pc; chastel Pf, chasteau Pb; 359 couche NpPbPc; 367. pitie Pf; 360. l'autruy Qd; 369. ne pense bien, ne luy v. Pc; 378. m. quant NjQd; 381. vos pensees Qd; 387. ayme b. Pc; 391. qu'en s. Pc; 395. le Pc; 401. pour PcQd; 402. estrangiers Pf; 410. d'onneur PbPcQd; 411. en rien Pc; 412. N. p. avoir Pc, N. p. devoir Qd; 415. et renchiere PcPfPn; 419. g. en pur don Qd; 426. M. em bien aultruy non PcPnQd; 429. octroy si non PcQd; 432. vault le demourant Pn, est le demourant Pf; 439. ne y. Pf; 449. merche Qd; 461. refraindre Pn; 471. ensuira Pc; 474. s'on n. Pc; 480. n'y m. Qd; 486. telle q. Pc; 490. belle PbPcPnQd; 511. requeust Qd; 519. sera Pc; 530. en son endroit Pc; 536. pour p. Pc; 537. Jen oy Pc, J. say PnQd; 538. men droit Pf; 539. Que Pc; 544. Dont l'essay cousteroit Pc, puet couster s. c. PnQd; 546. Ne souspechon qui Pc; 547. rebouter PcQd; 549. Que j. f. l. e. la preuve PcQd; 552. il y pert PcQd; 554. ce Pc; 556. si l. Pc, sil l. Qd; 561. s'esvertue PcQd; 574. Quamours font moult t. e. Pc, Qu'avoir bien fait tost Qd; 578. (D'onneur PcQd) Damours desgradé et deffait Pb; 581. soulle de PcQd; 587. Chascun les mauldit et conivre Pf; 590. Et commencher Pc; 591. encourir PfQd; 593. pende ou arde Pn arde ne pende PbPc; 595. bien c. q. q. tarde Pn; 599. ne chiet Pc; 611. Il d. Qd; 613. impartie Pn; 619. s'en debvoir vous Pc; 621. debves r. Pc; 626. celez Pn; 630. helas Pc; 631. n'en seray d. Pc; 637. tous c. Qd; 638. telle q. Pc; 645. Dont je mourray, certes, martir PcQl; 646. ou el sauldra Pc; 647. Lors s. d. a t. s. Pc; 648. vauldra PbPcQd; 650. v. vous y tendres Pc; 653. actendres PbPc; 661. entasses PbPc; 668. non domageuse Pc; 674. ains e. l. PcPfQd; 680. Se Pc; 681. On m. Pc; 684. souploye Pc; 691. gros PcPfQd; 700. n. querray Pn; 701. M'onnour Pc; 706. me duit m. Qd; 708. p. tost QdNj; 714. a mal dire Pc; 719. a femme Pc; 720. Jamais ne doit e. c Pp, n. doit plus e. Qd; 722. unie Pp; 729. Q. m. fol p. e. PnQd; 740. cueurs de dames PcPp; 741. onnys PcPfQd; 750. p. baillier Pc; 756. vo d. Pn; 794. naist Pc, asemble Qd; 799. Qu'on appellera PnQd.

Letters

Cy est la requeste baillee aux (dames) contre maistre Alain

[17v] Supplient humblement voz humbles serviteurs, les attendans vostre tres doulce grace et poursuivans la queste du don d'amoureuse mercy, et comme ilz ayent donné leur cuer a penser, leur corps a traveillier, leur vouloir a desirer, leur bouche a requerir, leur temps a pourchasser le riche don de Pitié que Dangier, Reffus et Crainte ont embusché et retrait en la gaste Forest de Longue Attente, et ne leur soit demouré compaignie ne conduit qui ne les ait laisséz en la poursuite, fors seul bon Espoir, qui encores demeure derriere laz et traveillié du long chemin et de la tresennuyeuse queste; et qu'a ung pas qui se [18r] nomme Dure Responce ilz ont esté plusieurs foiz destrousséz de joye et desers de lyesse par les brigans et souldoiers de Reffuz. Et neantmoins entretiennent tousjours leur queste pour y mettre la vie du corps qui leur est demouré, maiz que Espoir ne les laisse au besoing; et encores aroient attente a vostre secours mais que Doulx Acueil et Bel Attrait les remissent sus, se ne fust qu'il est venu a congnoissance que aucuns ont escript en vers riméz certaines nouvelles ou y n'ont gueres pensé. Et peut estre que Ennvye, Reboutement d'Amours, ou Faulte de Cuer, qui les ont fait demourer recreuz en chemin et laisser la queste qu'ilz avoient encommencee avec nous qui les a fait ainsi parler et escripre; et ont tant fait, comme ont dit, pour destourner aux aultres la joye a quoy ilz ont failli, que leurs escrips sont venuz en vos mains et, pour le trait d'aucunes parolles doulces qui sont dedens, qui l'ont amusé a lire que l'on appelle *La belle dame sans mercy*, ouquel, soubz ung langage affaitié, les conmencemens et ouvertures sont de mettre rimeur en la court amoureuse, et rompre la queste des humbles serviteurs, et vous tollir l'eureux non de [18v] Pitié, qui est le parement et la richesse de voz aultres vertuz. Et en vendra dommage et eslongnement aux humbles serviteurs, et amendrissement de vostre povoir. Qu'il vous plaise de vostre grace destourner vos yeulx de lire si desraisonnables escriptures et n'y donner foy ne audience, mais les faire rompre et casser par tout ou trouver se pourront et des faiseurs ordonner telle pugnicion que ce soit exemple aux aultres et que voz humbles serviteurs puissent leur queste parfaire a vostre honneur et a leur joye; et monstrer par euvres et bien brief que en vous a pitié et mercy. Et Amours prieront qu'i vous doint tousjours tant de joye et de liesse que aux aultres en puissiez departir.

The Request Sent to the Ladies against Master Alain

Coming before you on bended knee, your loyal servants, attendants of your sweet grace and participants in the quest of the gift of loving mercy, having given their hearts to reflect, their bodies to work, their passion to desire, their mouths to request, and their time to pursue the rich gift of Pity that Resistance, Refusal, and Fear have ambushed and hidden in the wild Forest of Long Awaiting, leaving them alone with no company nor guide left to accompany them except Hope, who stays behind still, completely exhausted from the long trail and the difficult quest; and they who seek her, on a path named Harsh Response, have many times been robbed of joy and stripped of happiness by the brigands and mercenaries of Refusal, nevertheless they keep up the quest, giving all the strength of their body to it, but Hope leaves them languishing and in need of your help, as well as that of Sweet Welcoming and Fair Courtesy,[1] and they would be waiting still if it had not come to their attention that some persons had written in rhymed verse a certain new piece that has never been heard of before, and it may be that Envy, Rejection of Love, or Weak Heart might have made them renounce the path and abandon that quest that they had begun with us and thus made them speak and write in such a way, and wishing to take away any joy from that pursuit in which they had failed, which writings have fallen in your hands, and in the interest of several sweet words which can be found therein, it might amuse you to read their little book, which is called "The Beautiful Lady with No Mercy,"[2] in which, under the guise of courtly language, are hidden the beginnings and means to start rumors in the court of love, and to destroy the quest of humble servants, and to steal from you the blessed name of Pity, which is the adornment and richness of your other virtues, besides which would bring harm to and estrangement from your humble servants, as well as the weakening of your power if you do not prevent it. May it please you by your grace to turn your eyes from reading such unreasonable words and to give them neither credence nor attention, and to tear them up and crush them wherever they might be found and also to order punishment for the writers of such words so that this might serve as example to others. And grant that your humble servants might achieve their quest to your honor and their joy, showing by example that in you is lodged mercy and pity, and they will pray to Love to give you always so much delight that you will share it willingly with others.

Cy sont les letres envoiees par les dames audit maistre Alain

Honnouré frere, nous nous recommandons a vous et vous faisons assavoir que naguieres par aucuns a esté envoié et baillé aux dames certaine requeste qui grandement touche vostre honneur et le desavanchement de vostre tresgracieux loz et bonne grace que vous avez tousjours acquis vers elles. Et pour [19r] ce que nous vous cuidons tel et que bien vous saurez excuser et deffendre de ceste charge quant vous en serez adverti, nous vous en envoions le double, esperans que vous mettrez paine a vous getter hors de ce blasme a vostre honneur et au rejouissement de ceulx qui plus voulentiers verroient vostre loz faire croistre que amendrir. Et comme escript vous a esté par aultres lettres de voz amis, journee est assignee au premier jour d'apvril a vous et a voz parties adverses, auquel jour vous pensons veoir se vous n'estez mort ou prins, dont Dieu vous gart, laquelle chose vous doubterez moins que de demourer en ceste charge. Honnouré frere, Nostre Seigneur vous doint autant de joye comme nous vouldrions et brief retourner, car se vous estiez par deça, tel parle de vous qui se tairoit. Escript a Yssoldun, le derrenier jour de janvier.

Estoit escript en la marge dessoubz les lettres: Katherine, Marie, Jehanne.

La Response des dames faicte a maistre Allain[3]

I	Puis qu'ainsy est, Allain, feu nostre ami,	[77r]
	Qu'en ton meffait chiet mercy et amende,	
	Et tu escrips que dame est sans mercy,	
	Par quoy Amours le jugement conmande	4
	Du tout a nous et le cas recommande,	
	Autant vauldroit qu'Amours meismes jugast,	
	S'aultre conseil ta follie n'amende,	
	Qu'on te pendeist ou que l'en te brullast.	8
II	Car quant tu as escript premierement	
	Que serviteur es et seras aux dames,	
	L'excuse aprez que metz premiere ment	
	Par tes escrips, esquelz tu nous diffames	12
	Tant grandement que se fuissons infames,	
	Sy que le sens pers, a ce qu'on t'oit dire.	
	Ne charge point ta frenesie aux femmes,	
	Mais prens conseil et recours a ton mire.	16

Copy of the Letter Sent by the Ladies to Master Alain

Honored brother, we send our warmest regards and wish to let you know that very recently a certain request has been brought to the ladies which gravely affects your honor to the detriment of the generous glory and grace that you have already acquired with regard to them. And since we believe that you might well explain and defend yourself of this accusation, when you are advised, we send you a copy of it, hoping that you will take the trouble to extricate yourself of this blemish to your honor and to indulge the pleasure of those who would willingly see your glory grow rather than fade. And as has been written to you in other words of friends, a date of the first of April has been assigned to you and your adversaries, on which we believe to see you if you are not dead or captured, God keep you safe, a fate that you would dread less than to remain accused on this charge. Honored brother, may our Lord grant you as much joy as we would wish for you. Return soon, for if you are here, this gossip against you will be silenced. Written at Issodun, the last day of January.

Written in the margin below the letters: Katherine, Marie, and Jeanne.

The Response of the Ladies to Master Alain

I   Since it is thus, Alain, our erstwhile friend,
                 that you let pity and compensation expire in your malfeasance'
                 when you write that a lady is without mercy,
                 For which Love remits the adjudication
                 of the affair to us, and hands over the case
                 in as much as it would be worthwhile that Love himself judge
                 (if no other counsel can correct your folly)
                 that you be hung or burned alive.

II   For when you first wrote
                 that you are a devoted servant of ladies and will always be;[4]
                 the apology that follows is shown to be a lie
                 by your verses, in which you defame us
                 so greatly that we seem to be ignoble,
                 until the point that you lose your senses, by what one hears you say.
                 Do not blame your frenzy on the ladies
                 but instead take advice and refuge through your physician.

III   Tu tesmoignes que telles et sy belles
           Sommes que Dieu y a tout bien comprins,
           Et puis escrips que nous sommes crüelles,
           Dont nous donnes villain blasme pour pris.   20
           Et quant a ce que tu as tant apris
           Que crüaulté metz sans divisïon
           Aveucq tous buens en sy pou de pourpris,
           Tu es ainsy comme l'escorpïon.   24

IV   Tu oingz, tu poins, tu flattes, tu offens,
           Tu honnoures, tu fais bien, tu le casses,
           Tu t'acuses et puis tu t'en deffens,
           Tu dis le bien, tu l'escrips, tu l'effaces.   28
           Mais se ton bien et notre honneur amasses,
           N'eusses escript en franchois ne en latin
           Chose par quoy tellement pourchassasses
           Qu'on te nommast fils au Prestre Martin.   32

V   Se jeune estois, tu ferois a reprendre,   [77v]
           Mais vieulx deviens et nous savons bien toutes
           Qu'on doit pugnir homme jeune et viel pendre.
           Ce sauras tu s'a nostre court te boutes,   36
           Car se t'atens a mercy et ne doubtes
           Toy submettrë a nostre jugement,
           Tu en morras, puis que Pitié nous ostes,
           Pour acomplir sans plus ton dampnement.   40

VI   Se tu cuidez en nous trouver secours
           Sans corrigier ton faulx mensongier livre,
           Tous tes cuidiers te seront a ce cours,
           Et les amis qui te pourront poursuivre,   44
           Ains que soyes de ton meffait delivre,
           Se n'affermes plainement devant tous
           Que menty as com hors du sens ou yvre,
           Querant pardon a chacune de nous.   48

III   You declare that we are so beautiful
and so on, that God neglected nothing in our composition,[5]
yet then you write that we are cruel,
which offers us only vile blame as reward!
And as for how you have learned
to include cruelty without distinction
among all the virtues of ladies in such a small space,
well, you are just like the scorpion.[6]

IV   You coat them with ointment, you sting, you flatter, you offend,
you honor, you do a good deed, you destroy it,
you blame yourself and then you justify your offense,
you say it well, you write it down, you erase it.
but if you really loved your acclaim and our goodness
you would not have written in French nor in Latin
something for which you are begging
to be called the son of Father Martin.[7]

V   If you were younger, you would merit a reprimand,
but you are getting old and we all know well
that one should punish the young and hang the old.
This fact you will know if you come to our court,
for if you are hoping for mercy and do not fear
to submit yourself to our judgment,
you will certainly die, for you have removed Pity from us
and thus assure without doubt your condemnation.

VI   If you believe that you will get help from us
without correcting your perfidious, lying book,
all of your assumptions will be put to the test,
as well as the friends who could support you,
until you be deliverd from your sin
and admit openly before everyone
that you lied, as if you were out of your mind or drunk,[8]
when begging for pardon from each one of us ladies.

VII   Et puis aprés ce fait et advenu
                   Qu'esvertüé l'on verra ton effort
                   Jusques ad ce que soyes devenu
                   Parfait lëal et requeras confort,   52
                   Tu trouveras, et le verras au fort,
                   Que Lëaulté, Doulceur, Bonté, Franchise,
                   Portent la clef du chastel ferme et fort
                   Ou Honneur a nostre pitié soubsmise.   56

VIII   Et ne croy point qu'on te tiengne a failly
                   De corrigier ton deslëal ouvrage,
                   Car il eschiet, depuis qu'on a failly,
                   Changier conseil et est fait d'homme sage.   60
                   Rappelle dont ton orgueil et oultraige,
                   Car tu vois bien, se tu scez qu'honneur monte,
                   Que le vray sens de ton double langaige
                   Nous donroit tost aultrement blasme et honte.   64

IX   Honnie soit d'entre nous qui vouldra   [78r]
                   De tel honte le grief meffait couvrir,
                   Ne que jamais du pechie t'assouldra
                   Pour quelque mal qu'en ayes a souffrir,   68
                   S'on ne te voit a ce fairë offrir
                   Que l'en t'a dit, sans y espargnier rien,
                   Car nul ne puet a hault honneur venir
                   S'il n'a chier son honneur sur toute rien.   72

X   Tu dis moult bien, quë on ne doit pas croire,
                   Pour cuidier toy et ton livre excuser,
                   Et que l'effort d'Amours t'a fait recroire
                   De bien parler et de bon sens user.   76
                   Mais encores te voit on abuser
                   Comme heritë en ce quë as escript
                   Que, s'on te veult de mespris accuser,
                   Tu en veulz bien respondre par escript.   80

VII   And then, after this has happened
               and been accomplished, one sees your effort
               until you have become
               perfectly loyal, and then you will ask again for consolation
               you will find and will see, for certain,
               that Loyalty, Sweetness, Goodness, Freedom
               carry the key to the castle, strong and fortified
               where Honor watches over our pity.

VIII   Do not believe for a moment that we do not consider you a coward
               to correct your disloyal work
               for it is opportune, when one has failed,
               to change counsel and thus is the act of a wise man.
               Take back your arrogance and insults
               for you see, if you recognize that honor is cumulative,
               that the true meaning of your double talk
               would give us in every way fault and shame.

IX   He should be ashamed who among us will wish
               that such shame may cover up this grievous offense.
               You will never be acquitted of this sin
               no matter how much trouble you suffer for it.
               If one can't see that you propose
               to do what they told you to,
               without sparing a single thing
               for no one can cultivate high honor
               if he does not hold his honor more dear than anything else.

X   You speak well, but no one should believe a word of it
               to make us believe you and to excuse your book,
               and even that the effort of Love has convinced you
               to speak correctly and to use good sense.
               But, again, we see you lying
               like a heretic in what you have written,
               which states that if one wishes to accuse you of malfeasance
               that you will repond in writing.[9]

XI   Or escrips ce quë escripre vouldras,
            Car en tout ce que tu savras escripre
            Le jugement a raison ne touldras
            De ton meffait que nostre loz empire.   84
            Pour ce choisy de ces deux le moins pire,
            Sans pourchasser qui deffende ou debate:
            Ou tu mouras, ou il t'en fault desdire,
            Car point n'affiert que femme t'en combatte.   88

XII   Et pour mettrë en ce conclusïon,
            Veu quë a nous du tout te recommandes,
            Toutes sommes de ceste oppinïon:
            Sy t'en desdiz et humblement demandes   92
            Grace et pardon, et ton faulx livre amendes.
            En ce faisant tu respites la mort;
            Ou aultrement gaigeras les amendes
            D'un herite qui en herese mort.   96

XIII   Riens plus n'avras de nous, c'est somme toute.
            Mais s'il t'appert qu'on te face injustice
            Par trop vëoir ou par n'y vëoir goutte,[10]
            Comme dit as glosant ton mallefice,   100
            Requiers Amours qu'il t'en face justice,
            Par devant lui appellant en cas tel,
            Et nous ferons pour moustrer ton mallice
            Nos advocatz Dessarteaulx et Chastel.   104

Explicit

XI   You can write whatever you wish to write
            for no matter what you might know how to compose
            you will not impede a right judgment
            on your misdeed that damages our reputation.
            And so choose the least of these two courses
            without seeking to defend or debate:
            either you die, or you must take back your words
            because it is not fitting that a woman combat you.

XII   And to bring this to an end,
            given that you in every way recommend yourself to us
            we are all of this opinion:
            Either you take back your words and humbly beg
            for grace and pardon, and then correct your false book
            and in so doing you will escape death,
            or else you will receive the penalty
            of a heretic who dies in his heresy.

XIII   Nothing more can you expect from us, this is it.
            But if you perceive that we have been unjust to you
            by either looking too hard or not looking at it all
            as you said in interpreting your insulting work,
            Ask Love to give you justice,
            and call your case before him
            and we will engage our lawyers Dessarteaulx and Chastel
            to demonstrate your malice.[11]

The End

Notes

1. Line 12: "Doulx Acueil et Bel Attrait": the other manuscripts (except Pf) read "Bel Acueil et Doux Attrait." Is this a scribal error or perhaps a deliberate attempt to modify the names of these allegorical figures established by the *Romance of the Rose*?

2. Line 17: Chartier is being accused more obliquely by his inclusion in a group of those who, like him, would try to spoil the lovers' chances. The subject is thus plural, instead of the singular that one would expect.

3. The text of the Reponse is found in four mss: Pn, Qa, Qf, Qj ; in No the heading "Reponse" follows the letters and *Excuse* but the poem has not been copied. This third letter was apparently not as widely read as the first two; no references are made to it in the Quarrel poems edited here. In fact, none of the editions of Chartier's work

includes it, even though they include the first two letters and the *Excuse*. Pierre de Nesson seems to be the only one to comment on it in his *Lay of War*.

4. *Resp.* lines 9–10: reference to the *Excuse*, vv. 145–46.

5. *Resp.* lines 17–18: *Excuse,* vv. 89–92 *(these are, however, Love's words); vv. 137–44.*

6. *Resp.* line 24: The analogy is presumably based on the fact that the scorpion packs a powerful and deadly poison in a tiny body.

7. *Resp.* line 32. Prestre Martin, a proverbial character who talks out of both sides of his mouth (usually both in French and Latin), "only knows how to sing by reading the book" or "who sings and responds to himself." See also *Hospital of Love, line* 910 (Hassell 161, Di Stephano 728).

8. Line 47: reference to *Excuse, line* 25.

9. Line 80: reference to *Excuse, line* 224

10. Cited from *Excuse,* v. 200.

11. *Resp.* line 104: Chastel is Jean Chastel, poet and member of Pierre de Hauteville's *Cour Amoureuse* who was also the son of Christine de Pizan; 'Dessarteaulx' remains unidentified.

The Excuse of Master Alain

Cy apres est l'excusacion de maistre Alain contre ceulx qui dient qu'i l'a parlé contre les dames sans mercy. Comment maistre Alain respond.

I

        Mes dames et mes damoiselles,
        Se Dieu vous doint joye prochaine,   [19v]
        Escoutez les dures nouvelles
        Que j'ouÿ le jour de l'estraine;   4
        Et entendez ce qui me maine,
        Car je n'ay fors a vous recours;
        Et me donnez par grace plaine
        Conseil, confort, aide et secours.   8

II

        Le jour m'avint en mon dormant,
        Attendant le souleil levant,
        Moitié dormant, moitié veillant,
        Environ l'aube et pou avant,   12
        Qu'Amours s'apparut au devant
        De mon lit a l'arc tout tendu,
        Et me dist: Desloyal servant,
        Ton loyer te sera rendu.   16

III

        Je t'ay long temps tenu des miens
        A l'eure que bien me servoies,
        Et te gardoie de grans biens
        Trop plus que tu ne desservoies;   20
        Et quant ta loyaulté devoiez
        Vers moy garder en tous endroiz,
        Tu faiz et escripz et envoies
        Nouveaulx livres contre mes droiz.   24

IV

        Es tu fol, hors du scens ou yvre,
        Qui veulx contre moy guerre prendre,
        Qui as fait le maleureux livre
        Dont chascun te devroit reprandre,   28
        Pour enseignier et pour aprendre
        Les dames a getter au loing
        Pitié, debonnairë et tendre,
        De qui tout le monde a besoing?   32

Here follows the excuse of Master Alain against those who say that he spoke against the ladies without mercy. How Master Alain responds:

I

My ladies and maidens,
may God grant you imminent joy!
Listen to the harsh news
I heard on New Year's day and
know what brings me forward,
for I have no one to turn to but you.
Grant me by your grace
advice, comfort, aid, and succor.

II

I was sleeping on this morn,
waiting for the sun to rise,
half asleep, half awake,
at dawn or just before,
when Love appeared
before my bed, his bow extended,
and said to me, "Disloyal servant,
your due will be returned to you.

III

For a long time I have considered you
one of my faithful servants. You were serving me well,
and I have been saving up many riches for you,
more even than you merited.
But at this time when you should remain loyal
to me in every way,
you imagine, write down, and publish
new books that go against my laws.

IV

Are you crazy, have you lost your mind, are you drunk?
Or do you wish to engage in war against me?
You have written this unfortunate book,
for which everyone should chastise you,
because it teaches
ladies to throw aside
Pity, the debonair and tender,
who is needed by every one!

V   Se tu as ta melencolie
               Prise de non amer jamais,
               Doivent acheter ta folie
               Les aultres qui n'en peuent maiz?   36
               Laisse faire aultrui et te tais!
               Que de deuil ait le cuer nercy
               Qui ja croira, comme tu faiz,
               C'onques dame fust sans mercy!   40

VI   Tu mouras de ce pechié quicte;
               Et se briëf ne t'en desdiz,
               Preschier te feray comme herite
               Et bruler ton livre et tes diz.   44
               En la loy d'Amours sont mauldiz,
               Et chascun m'en fait les clameurs.
               Le lire est a tous interdiz
               De par l'inquisiteur d'Amours.   48

VII   Veulx tu mon povoir abollir   [20v]
               Et que bonté et honneur s'efface,
               Quant tu quiers des dames tollir
               Pitié, mercy, doulceur et grace.   52
               Cuides tu doncques que Dieu face
               Entre les hommes sus la terre
               Si beau corps et si belle face
               Pour leur porter rigueur et guerre?   56

VIII   Nennyl non! Il n'y pensa oncques,
               Car ja faitez ne les eüst
               Plus plaisans que chose quelconques
               Que sus terre faire peüst,   60
               Se Il ne veïst bien et sceüst
               Qu'elles devroient l'eur porter
               Qui par droit les hommes deüst
               Resiouïr et reconforter.   64

V   If your melancholy comes from the fact
that you have never known love,
should others who know nothing of this
be forced to pay the price of your madness?
Let the others do as they please and you keep quiet!
What pain must grip a heart blackened with misery
that will believe, as you do,
that ever there was a woman without pity!

VI   You will die of this very sin.
And if you do not renounce it,
I will proclaim you a heretic
and burn your book and all your poems,
which are cursed by the law of Love
and about which everyone keeps complaining to me.
Reading these books is forbidden to everyone,
by command of the Inquisitor of Love.

VII   Do you wish to eradicate my power
and make honor and goodness disappear
by trying to take from ladies
pity, compassion, sweetness, and good will?
Do you really believe that God created
creatures of such a beautiful body and sweet face
for men on this earth,
in order to bring them harshness and even war?

VIII   Not at all! He never had the slightest intention of doing so,
for He would never have made them
more charming than any other being
he put on this earth,
if he had not seen and known
that they should be the bearers of the happiness
which by right should serve
to exult and comfort all men.

IX
Ne seroit ce pas grant dommaige
Que Dieu, qui soustient homme en vie,
Eust faicte si parfaicte ymaige
Par droitte excellence assouvie   68
Que la pensee fust ravie
Des hommes par force de plaire?
Se Dieu leur portoit telle envie
Qu'i leur donnast pour adversaire?   72

X
Cuides tu faire baziliques,   [21r]
Qui occïent les gens des yeulx,
Ces doulx visaiges angeliques
Qui samblent estre faiz es cieulx?   76
Dieu ne les a mie faiz tieulx
Pour desdaignier et non chaloir,
Mais pour croistre de bien en mieulx
Ceux qui ont desir de valoir.   80

XI
Doulceur, courtoisie, amitié
Sont les vertuz de noble femme,
Et le droit mirouer de Pitié
Est ens ou cuer de belle dame.   84
S'il falloit par ton livre infame
Pitié dont de dame banir,
Autant vauldroit qu'i ne fust ame
Et que le monde deust fenir.   88

XII
Puis que Nature s'entremist
De taillier si noble figure,
Qu'il est ottroié qu'elle y mist
De tous biens a comble mesure.   92
Dangier y est soubz couverture
De Nature la tresbenigne,
Et pour adoulcir la pointure,
Y mist Pitié son medicine.   96

IX
Would it not be a crying shame
if God, who gives life to man,
had created an image so perfect,
so irrevocably excellent
that it ravished a man's mind
because it pleased so greatly?
Can one imagine that God is so jealous
that this is what He gave to men as adversary?

X
Do you believe them to be basilisks,[1]
who kill people by looking them in the eye,
these sweet angelic faces
that seem to be made in heaven?
They were certainly not made
to be disdainful and indifferent,
but rather to encourage the development of good to better
within those who have the desire to be worthy.

XI
Goodness, courtesy, and friendship
are the virtues of a noble lady,
and the true home of Pity
is found in the heart of a beautiful woman.
If it were necessary, as your little book says,
to banish Pity from the hearts of ladies,
it would be better that no soul continue to live,
thus bringing the world to an end.

XII
Since Nature set about
sculpting such a noble figure,
it is a given that she included
a full measure of all her riches.
Resistance is also there under cover
of Nature, the benevolent,
and to soften the barb of Resistance,
she put in Pity, her physician.

XIII   Pour garder homme en charité,   [21v]
            Raison y mist Honte et Dangier,
            Et voult tout Desdaing et Fierté
            Du tout des dames estrangier;   100
            Mais Pitié y peut chalengier
            Tout son droit, car quant el fauldroit,
            El pourroit la bonté changier,
            Puis que nully mieulx n'en vauldroit.   104

XIV   Tu veulx, par ton oultrecuidance
            Et les faulx vers que tu as faiz,
            Tollir aux dames leur puissance,
            Toutes vertuz et leurs biens faiz,   108
            Quant ainsi leur pitié deffaiz,
            Par quoy maint loyal cuer s'amende;
            Si veul chastïer tes mesfaiz
            Ou que tu m'en gaiges l'amende.²   112

XV   Quant j'euz ces parolles oÿ
            Et je vy la fleche en la corde,
            Tout le sang au cuer me fouÿ.
            Oncq n'euz tel paour dont me recorde?   116
            Si dy: Pour Dieu misericorde,
            Escoutez moy excuser, sire.
            Il respondit: Je le t'acorde.
            Or dy ce que tu vouldras dire.   120

XVI   Ha! sire, ne me mescroiez,   [22r]
            Ne les dames samblablement,
            Se vous ne lisez et voiez
            Le livre tout premierement.   124
            Je suis aux dames ligement,
            Et ce pou qu'anques j'ay de bien,
            D'onneur et de bon sentement,
            Vint d'elles et d'elles le tien.   128

XIII
To keep man in the state of love,
Reason included Shame and Resistance,
but chose to exclude completely
Disdain and Arrogance from ladies.
Nevertheless, Pity can certainly claim
all her rights, for if she should fail,
she would alter the level of goodness,
and even the best would not be worthy enough.

XIV
You must want, by your presumption,
as well as through the lying verses that you have composed,
to take away from ladies all their power,
all of their virtues, and all of their good deeds,
when you tear to pieces their pity in this manner,
pity through which many loyal hearts find succor.
For this reason, I wish to chastise your misdeeds
if you do agree to pay the penalty."

XV
When I had heard these words
and noticed the arrow ready at the bow,
all the blood drained from my heart.
I do not remember ever having been so frightened,
so I said: "For the mercy of God,
listen as I explain, lord."
He responded: "I grant you your request.
Do tell me what you wish to say."

XVI
Oh, please do not doubt me, lord,
nor you ladies, either,
before having read and closely considered
the book in its entirety.
I am fully obliged to these ladies,
for the little I have ever had of pleasure,
honor, and good sense
comes from them and in their name do I retain it.

XVII   Quant est de faire telle faulte³
            Mon cuer choisiroit qu'il mouroit
            La folie seroit si haulte
            Que jamaiz ne la pardonroit.   132
            Bien est vil cellui qui vouldroit
            A l'onneur des dames meffaire
            Sans lesquelles nul ne pourroit
            Jamaiz bien dire ne bien faire.   136

XVIII   Par elles et pour elles sommes:
            C'est la source de nostre joye;
            C'est l'adresse des nobles hommes;
            C'est d'onneur la droite montjoye;   140
            C'est ce qui les bons cuers resioye;
            C'est le comble de noz desirs;
            C'est ce qui d'espoir nous pourvoie;
            C'est ce qu'est des mondains plaisirs.   144

XIX   Leur serviteur veuil demourer   [22v]
            Et en leur service mourray,
            Je ne les puis trop honnourer
            N'aultrement ja ne le vouldray;   148
            Et tant que je vif demourray,
            A garder honneur qui leur touche
            Amploieray ou je pourray
            Cuer, corps, sens, langue, plume et bouche.   152

XX   Pitié en cuer de dame siet
            Ainsi qu'en l'or le dÿamant
            N'en sa vertu pas ne s'assiet
            Tousjours au plaisir de l'amant;   156
            Mais fault reffrener ung servant
            Quant Crainte tient Pitié enclose
            Et en ce reffrain reffregnant,
            Souffrir sa douleur une pose.   160

XVII

My heart would rather die
than commit such an error,
for the folly would be so great
that it would never be pardoned.
He is truly vile who would wish
to debase the honor of ladies
without whom no one
could ever say or do anything of merit.

XVIII

Our very existence comes from them and for them we live.
They are the well of our joy;
they are the reparation of noble men;
they are the height of honor;
they are the comfort in which good hearts rejoice;
they are the sum of all our desires;
they are the providers of hope;
they are the essence of all pleasure in this world.

XIX

I wish to remain their servant
and in their service will I die;
I cannot honor them too highly
nor would I wish to do otherwise.
As long as I live,
I will employ where I might,
in order to protect their honor, my heart, my body,
my mind, my tongue, my pen, and my lips.

XX

Pity is fixed in the heart of a lady
just as a diamond is set in gold,
but her virtue does not always serve
the pleasure of the lover;
rather it is necessary to restrain an eager servant,
as when Fear keeps Pity under guard,
and in restraining this refrain,
he suffers in pain for a short while.

XXI   Pitié se tient close et couverte
               Et ne veult forces ne contraintes,
               Ne sa porte n'est ja ouverte
               Fors par soupirs et longues plaintes.   164
               Attendre y fault de guerres maintes,
               Maiz l'attente bien se requeuvre,
               Car toutes doulours sont estaintes
               Aussi tost que sa porte s'euvre.   168

XXII   S'el ne gardoit sa seignourie,   [23r]
               Chacun luy feroit l'ennuyeux;
               Et sa bonté seroit perie,
               Car elle auroit trop d'envïeux.   172
               Pour ce son tresor gracïeux
               N'euvre pas a toutes requestes,
               Neantmoins q'ung jouel precïeux
               Qu'on ne doit monstrer qu'aux grans festes.   176

XXIII   Se j'osoie dire ou songier
               Qu'onques dame fust despiteuse,
               Je seroie faulx mensongier
               Et ma parolle maulgracieuse.   180
               Jamaiz en dame gracïeuse
               Ne failly mercy ne respit,
               Ains est erreur presumptüeuse
               Qu'en dame ait orgueul ne despit.   184

XXIV   Comme la rose tourne en lermes
               Au fourneau sa force et valeur,
               Ainsy rent Pitié aux enfermes,
               Par feu d'amoureuse chaleur,   188
               Pleurs qui garissent la douleur
               Par leur vertu puissant et digne;
               Mais quant le dangier n'est pas leur
               Plus en prise la medecine.   192

XXI	Pity keeps herself cloistered and concealed
	and accepts neither force nor constraint;
	one cannot make her door open
	except by sighs and moans.
	It is necessary to wait the span of many wars,
	but the wait is well rewarded,
	for all suffering is extinguished
	as soon as the door swings open.

XXII	If she did not guard her authority carefully,
	one could make trouble for her
	and her goodness would be used up,
	for she would have too many who wanted her.
	This is why her most precious treasure
	is not opened at just any request,
	much like a costly jewel
	that one should not show at grand parties.

XXIII	If I dared to say or even dream
	that ever a woman was without pity,
	I would be a dastardly liar,
	and my words undeserved.
	For never has any gracious lady
	lacked sufficient mercy or pardon.
	Thus it is a presumptuous error
	to say that a lady be arrogant or scornful.

XXIV	Like the rose whose vitality and beauty
	turn into tears under a scorching heat,
	so sick lovers, melted
	by the heat of the fire of love, are given by Pity
	tears that heal the wound
	by their powerful and worthy virtue;
	but since control over it is not in lovers' hands,
	the medicine is all the more valuable.

XXV	Mon livre, qui pou vault et monte,	[23v]
	A nullë aultre fin ne tend	
	Si non a recorder le conte	
	D'un triste amoureux mal content	196
	Qui pleure et plaint que trop attend,	
	Et comme Reffuz le reboute.	
	Et qui aultre chosë y tend,	
	Il voit trop ou y n'y voit goute.	200
XXVI	Quant ung amant si est estraint,	
	De forcennerie mortelle,	
	Que force d'amer le contraint	
	D'appeler sa dame crüelle,	204
	Doit il penser qu'elle soit telle?	
	Nanil, car le grief mal d'amer	
	Y met fievre continüelle	
	Qui fait sembler le doulx amer.	208
XXVII	Puis que son mal luy a fait dire,	
	Et apres lui pour pour temps passer	
	J'ay voulu ses plaintes escripre	
	Sans ung seul mot en trespasser,	212
	S'en doit tout le monde amasser	
	Contre moy, a tort et en vain,	
	Pour le chetif livre casser	
	Dont je ne suis que l'escripvain?	216
XXVIII	S'aucuns me veullent accuser	[24r]
	D'avoir ou failli ou mesprins,	
	Devant vous m'en veuil excuser,	
	Que j'ay pieça pour juge prins;	220
	Et combien comme pou aprins,	
	S'ilz en ont rien dit ou escript	
	Par quoy j'en puisse estre reprins,	
	Je leur respondray par escript.	224

XXV   My book, of little importance or value,
is written to no other end
than to simply record the account
of a sad and unhappy lover
who cries and moans that he has been waiting too long
and that Refusal rebuffs him.
He who understands anything different,
either is looking too hard or is not looking at all.

XXVI   When a lover is so oppressed
by fatal madness
that the force of acrimony compels him
to call his lady cruel
must it be believed that this is true?
Not at all, for the grievous malady of love
feeds a continual fire
that makes a sweet thing seem bitter.

XXVII   Just because it was his illness that made him speak so,
and then after he spoke, I tried
to transcribe his complaint to pass the time,
without omitting a single word,
must everyone assemble
against me, wrongly and without cause,
in order to tear apart this miserable book
of which I am only the scribe?

XXVIII   If certain persons wish to accuse me
of having made a mistake or done some wrong
before you, I wish to offer my apologies before
you whom I earlier chose to be my judge;
and in spite of my feeble ken,
if they have said or written anything
for which I might be reproached,
I will respond to them in writing."

XXIX	Quant Amours eust oÿ mon cas	
	Et vit qu'a bonne foy tendy,	
	Il remist la flesche ou carquas	
	Et l'arc amoureux destendy:	228
	Et tel responce me rendy:	
	Puis qu'a ma court tu te reclames,	
	Je suis content et tant t'en dy	
	Que j'en remet la cause aux dames.	232
XXX	Lors m'esveillay soubit et court,	
	Et puis entour moy rien ne vy.	
	Pour ce me rens a vostre court,	
	Mes dames, et la foy plevy	236
	D'obeÿr a droit sans ennuy,	
	Ainsi qu'Amours l'a commandé;	
	Maiz se j'en n'ay mal desservy,	
	Ayez moy pour recommandé.⁴	240

Explicit le livre de la belle dame sans mercy   [24v]

XXIX   When Love had listened to my side of the affair
              and realized that my intentions were good,
              he put the arrow back in his quiver
              and released his bow of love,
              and gave me this response:
              "Because you have brought your case before my court,
              I am pleased, and furthermore, I say to you
              that I will remit the case back to the ladies."

XXX   Then suddenly I awoke,
              but saw nothing and no one around.
              For this reason, my ladies, I remand myself to your court
              and pledge my faith
              to obey rightly and without begrudging,
              just as Love commanded me;
              and if I deserve no punishment,
              please accept that I commend myself to you.[5,6]

The end of the Belle dame sans mercy.

Notes

1. *Excuse* line 73: the basilisk is a mythical serpent-like reptile with a crown on its head said to be hatched by a serpent from a cock's egg. Its breath or look inflicts death.

2. *Excuse* line 112 in Pk, a rubric reads: "Comme le dieu damours tient larc enteze et la fleche en la corde oyant lexcusacion de maistre alain."

3. *Excuse* Stanza XVII replaced in PcPnQl with the following:

   De leur bonte vient et habonde
   Sur joye et confort en dueil
   C'est lexemple des bien du monde
   Aise de cuer et deduit d'oeul
   C'est le rabas de tout orgueil
   Et le patron pour les bons faire
   Sans ce que nul franc cuer ait le vueil
   De riens leur mesdire ou meffaire

4. *Excuse*: PcPnQd includes the following quatrain at the end of the poem as signature:

   Vostre humble serviteur, Allain,
   Qui Beaulté print pieça a l'ain
   Du trait d'uns tresdoulx rians yeulx,

Dont il languist, attendant mieulx.

5. *The Excuse of Master Alain,* rejected readings: 6. secours PcQd; 60. f. deust PnQl; 62. le leur Pc; 93. Doncques PcPnQd; 102. elle f. +1 PcQd; 103. Elle +1 PcQd; 116. Oncques +1 Qd; 143. ce que desespoir +1 PcQd; 153. cuer dame -1 Pc; 154. Ainsi com l'or, perle, ou diament PcQd; 169. Selle +1 Pc; 184. respite Pc; 210. Dont priez lui PcPf; 212. Pour ung ung seul mot contrepenser Pf.

6. *The Excuse of Master Alain,* variant readings: Le j. [me vint Pc], m'avint en sommeillant QdPcPn; 19. de g. b. Qd; 40. fust Pc; 42. briefment Pc; 47. Les l. Qd; 55. doulce PcQd; 67. bel i. Pn; 77. Ilz ne furent pas fourmés PcPnQd; 83. logeis PcQd; 84. d'unne noble femme Pc; 86. d'entre PcQd; 90. digne PcPn; 91. a croyrre PcPfPnQd; 94. Mais nature PcPn; 97. g. honneur et chierté PcPnQd; 103. feroit PcQd, la chance c. Pn; P. quoy Pf; 109 Puis a. Pn; 122. d. pareillement Pn; 126. euz PcQd; 139. l'espargne PcPn; 141. le penser qui plus PcPn; 150. les Pc; 157. deffermer ung fermant PcPn; 159. fermeur desfermant PcPnQd; 165. heures PcPnQd; 168. sa p. Qd; 180. injurieuse PcPnQd; 182. N'ait il PcPnQd; 183. Qui dit de voix PcQd; 184. despit PcPnQd; 190. Tant est l. haulte v. d. PnQd; 191–92. Mais au cueur gist la pitié leur/ Plus parfont que l'or en la mine PcPnQd; 193. M. livret PcPn; 202. Comme en reverie PcPnQd; 203. de mal PcPnQd; 210. Et en apres Pn, empres l. Qd; 211. J'ay veu s. Pf; 226. fin PcPfQd; 237. envie PcQd.

Accusations against the Belle dame sans mercy

Baudet Herenc

Apres s'ensuit comment la belle dame sans mercy fut traitié en jugement en la court du dieu d'amours pour respondre aux articles contre lui imposees

I   Le jour que l'en se renouvelle,   [28r]
              Amours me fist commandement
              De faire balade nouvelle,
              Et me ordonna expressement   4
              Que j'en estrinasse humblement
              Celle a qui serf me suis rendu,
              De laquelle j'ay longuement
              La doulce mercy attendu.   8

II   Quant ainsi je me vy contraint
              D'Amours a la balade faire,
              De soucy me trouvay estraint,
              Pour ce que doubtoie forfaire   12
              Les biens d'Amours dont j'ay affaire;
              Car oncques n'aprins le mestier
              De rimer en aucun affaire
              Mais pour lors me fust bien mestier.   16

III   Et pour obeïr a Amours,
              Papier, plume et encre alay prendre,
              Et le nouveau dit sans demours
              Commençay, lors cuidant comprendre   20
              De la belle ou n'a que reprandre
              Les beaultéz, l'onneur, et le sens,
              Dont je fis folie d'emprandre
              Si haulte euvre, a ce que je sens.   24

IV   Car se toutes langues en une   [28v]
              Estoient pour ses biens raconter,
              Elles fauldroient, chose est commune,
              D'iceulx proprement raconter: 28
              Tant bien l'ont voulu appointer
              Dieu et Nature a leur vouloir
              Qu'on n'y sçaroit mettre n'oster
              Pour elle faire mieulx valoir.   32

Here follows how the Belle dame sans mercy was brought to trial in the court of the God of Love in order to respond to the accusations made against her.

I

On the day the year is renewed,[1]
Love commanded me
to compose a new ballad
and ordered explicitly
that I humbly present it as a New Year's gift
before her to whom I have rendered myself serf
and from whom I have so long
awaited the most tender grace.

II

Finding myself thus compelled
by Love to compose this ballad,
I was seized with anxiety
because I feared to forfeit
the benefits of Love, of which I was in great need,
for never in my training had I learned the skill
of making rhymes for this situation in which I found myself,
even though it would certainly have been useful for me now![2]

III

So to obey Love
I went to gather paper, pen, and ink
and without hesitation,
I began to write the new poem
believing to take account of
the beauty, honor, and character
of this beautiful lady beyond reproach.
In fact, it was foolish to undertake
such a difficult and sublime task, in my humble opinion,

IV

for even if all languages were combined
in order to speak of her perfections,
this language, too, would fail
to describe her accurately, it is well known.
For God and Nature have ordained,
in accordance with their will,
that no one might add or remove from her
a single thing that could render her more sublime.

V   Et pour ce faire ne sçavoie
        Ceste ballade a mon plaisir,
        Car le sentement point n'avoie,
        Dont au cuer avoie desplaisir.   36
        Par quoy il me couvient gesir
        Par desconfort sus une couche
        Ou, maulgré moy, prins le lesir
        De clorre mes yeulx et ma bouche.   40

VI   Car par sommeil fu asserviz
        De dormir une longue espace;
        Et en dormant m'estoit advis
        Que je vëoie l'oultrepasse   44
        De tous les vergés qu'on compasse
        En l'air, sus une vive roche
        De tres reluisant pierre en masse,
        Ou Amours tenoit l'arc en coche.   48

VII   Du vergier m'approchay si prés   [29r]
        Que je vy toutes ses beaultéz:
        Clos estoit d'arbres de cyprés
        Et de rosiers par my plantéz;   52
        La porte estoit de tous costéz
        Forte de lys et de muguet,
        Et sus icelle estoit montéz
        Dangier pour y faire le guet;   56

VIII   Par my estoit de romarins,
        Entre lesquelz tousdiz chantoient
        Chardonnerelles et tarins;
        Et es quatre cornes estoient   60
        Cleres fontainnes qui sourdoient
        Par celle superfluïté
        Que tout le vergier arousoient
        Pour le maintenir en beaulté.   64

V
    And this is why I could not write
    the ballad to suit myself,
    for I lacked the insight to do it
    a fact that pained my heart grievously.
    So I had to lie down
    out of pure despair on a little bed
    where, despite myself, I took the leisure
    to close my eyes and lips.

VI
    Drowsiness overcame me
    and lulled me to sleep a long while;
    and while sleeping it happened
    that I saw the most splendid
    of all gardens imaginable,
    up high in the air, atop a shining cliff
    made of huge sparkling rocks,
    where Love stood with a nocked arrow in his bow.

VII
    I drew close to the garden
    in order to see all of its marvels.
    It was enclosed by cypress trees
    with rosebushes planted among them.
    The door was entirely covered on all sides
    with lily of the valley and other lilies,
    and above the door was perched
    Resistance, to keep a lookout.

VIII
    Around the garden were planted rosemary bushes,
    in whose branches were forever singing
    goldfinches and siskins.
    In the four corners were
    fountains of clear water that gushed forth
    with such abundance
    that they watered the entire garden
    to maintain its beauty.

IX   Et ou milieu, une auditoire
            Vis toute d'erbe, marjolaine,
            Et d'aultres fleurs; puis vis l'istoire
            faite de Paris et de Helainne,[3]   68
            Du Vergier de la Chastellaine,
            Qui servirent Amours jadiz
            Sans avoir reprouche villaine
            En faiz, en pensers, ou en diz.   72

X   Le siëge ou Amours vis estre   [29v]
            Estoit de d'amoureuses fleurettez
            Tendu a dexstre, et a senexstre
            De gracïeuses violettez,   76
            Couvert d'un tapis de fleurettez
            De lys et de fleurs d'orengés,
            Ou maintz rossignolx et linotez
            C'estoient pour chanter logés.   80

XI   Et au dehors escript avoit
            De tresbeaulx diz sans mesprison
            Qu'Amours son parlement devoit
            Tenir en ce lieu, par raison   84
            Faire de ceux qui desraison
            Avoient fait en son service:
            Car lui qui n'a comparaison
            Ne peut souffrir en son serf vice.   88

XII   Il avoit douze presidans:
            Le premier estoit Franc Vouloir;
            Et Espoir, qui est tant prudens
            Qui riens ne met en nonchaloir   92
            Pour les amans faire valoir,
            Estoit le procureus des cas
            Desquelz on se vouloit douloir;
            Et Desir estoit l'avocas.   96

IX

In the middle I saw a plot for a tribunal
made from herbs, marjoram,
and other flowers; I also saw fashioned the story
of Paris and of Helen,
and of the Châtelaine de Vergy,[4]
who served Love in years gone by
with never a single reproach
in thought, word, or deed.

X

The throne where I saw Love sitting
was also made of lovely flowers:
to the right and to the left
were the most delicate violets.
It was covered by a tapestry of silk
woven with lilies and orange blossoms
and on it many nightingales and larks
perched to sing their songs.

XI

On the outside was written
in beautiful words and without error,
that Love would be holding court
in this place, in order to bring justice
to those who had committed injustice
while in his service:
for Love, who has no equal,
cannot tolerate any vice in his servants.

XII

There were twelve judges there;
the presiding judge was Free Will.
Hope, who is so prudent
that he never neglects anything
that might make lovers more worthy,
was the prosecutor for those cases
that were the subject of complaint;
and Desire was the lead attorney.[5]

XIII   A ce parlement vis venir   [30r]
                        Amans plusieurs et a grant nombre
                        Qui alerent vers Souvenir,
                        Le greffier d'Amours et soubz umbre   100
                        D'eulx presenter, car dur encombre
                        Pensoient avoir de deffault faire.
                        Et aprés se mistrent en l'ombre
                        Des rosiers par plaisant affaire.   104

XIV   Doulx Parler, l'uissier, commanda
                        Qu'en ce lieu fust faite silence,
                        Et puis le greffier lui manda
                        Qu'il appellast en audïence   108
                        Celle qui, oultre la deffence
                        D'Amours, avoit cuer endurci,
                        Qu'on appelloit en ma presence
                        La belle dame sans mercy.   112

XV   Aussi tost qu'appellee fust,
                        Seulete devant Amours vint,
                        Coulouree comme le feu
                        Pour la honte qui lui advint;   116
                        Et de fait perdre lui couvint
                        Toute maniere et contenance
                        En gettant pleurs et soupirs mains,
                        Tant avoit d'Amours grant doubtance.   120

XVI   Lors furent les prerogatives   [30v]
                        D'Amours par Desir proposees
                        Et ses haultes vertus actives
                        Par plaisans raisons exposees,   124
                        Qui tellement sont composees
                        Qu'amer font ung cuer sans contraire
                        Quant Amours les a disposees
                        A plaisant regart a lui traire.   128

XIII   I saw coming into the court
many lovers, in great crowds,
who approached Memory,
the clerk of the court, under the pretext
of introducing themselves, for some great adversity
they feared might ensue if they failed to appear there,
after which they retreated to the shade
of the rosebushes to enjoy themselves.

XIV   Sweet Thought, the bailiff, gave the command
that silence be observed in this place,
and then the clerk of the court commanded
that she be called before the court
who, against the laws
of Love, had a hardened heart,
who was named in my presence
"La belle dame sans mercy."

XV   As soon as she was called,
she presented herself all alone before Love,
her face colored like fire
for the shame that had come upon her.
Indeed, she completely lost
her poise and composure
and burst into great sobs,
because she dreaded and feared Love exceedingly.

XVI   Then were the prerogatives
of Love declared by Desire,
and his most high and powerful virtues
extolled in an eloquent speech:
those very virtues that are so constituted
to oblige a heart to love without limit
from the moment that Love disposes them
to draw a heart to himself by means of a pleasant look.

XVII   Car par sa puissance nobile
       Doulx Regard trait ou bon lui semble,
       Tant est son arc fort et habille,
       Lequel a aultre ne ressamble: 132
       Par son traire deux cueurs assemble
       En ung seul amoureux penser,
       Et les fait demourer ensamble
       Pour le temps en joye passer.   136

XVIII   Quant Desir, l'avocat parfait,
       Avec qui Espoir fu adjoint,
       Eust d'Amours conclu tout le fait,
       Il replica de point en point   140
       Les cas proposéz mal apoint
       Contre la dame sus nommee
       A la quelle il ne donna point
       En amours bonne renommee.   144

XIX   Et dist: Amoureux Dieu haultain,   [31r]
       A nous pleust une foiz commettre
       Ung vostre serviteur certain
       A lui humblement entremettre   148
       De sa pensee et son cuer mettre
       En ceste dame que voiez,
       Auquel voulez faire promettre
       D'estre loyal servant trouvéz.   152

XX   Il a sa promesse tenue,
       Comme bon serviteur doit faire,
       Et loyaulté entretenue,
       Doubtant vostre grace forfaire.   156
       Et ceste dame a la deffaire
       S'est efforcee tellement
       Que la mort par son dur affaire
       L'a desconfist mortellement.   160

XVII
For by Love's noble authority,
Sweet Look strikes wherever he pleases,
and his bow is strong and able.
There is no other like it:
by his shot two hearts are united
in one single amorous thought,
and he makes them stay together
so that they might pass the time in joy.

XVIII
When Desire, the perfect attorney,
with whom Hope is closely associated,
had concluded his introduction before Love,
he recalled point by point
the facts disadvantageously disposed
against the aforementioned lady,[6]
to whom he did not credit
a worthy reputation in love.

XIX
And said: "Most high God of Love,
at one time it pleased us to commit
one of your faithful servants
to undertake most humbly
a pledge of his heart and mind
to this woman that you see here,
toward whom you accepted the lover's promise
to conduct himself as a proven and loyal servant.

XX
He has kept his promise,
as a good servant should,
and has remained loyal,
fearing to forfeit your grace.
But this lady, in order to destroy him,
has put forth so much effort
that from her cruel treatment, death
has mortally vanquished him.

XXI   Et les causes je vous veuil dire:
                     Quant premierement fust requise
                     De l'amant ou n'avoit point d'ire,
                     Elle lui respondy que acquise   164
                     Avoit folle pensee et quise
                     La guerre pour son cuer grever;
                     Si pensast que par luy conquise
                     fust Paix pour joye recouvrer.   168

XXII   C'estoit dit contre vostre loy,   [31v]
                     Hault et puissant Dieu Amoureux,
                     Car vous estes de tel aloy
                     Et en voz faiz tant vertüeux   172
                     Qu'a celuy qui est curïeux
                     De choisir dame pour amer
                     Penser luy donnez Gracïeux
                     Pour mercy querir sans amer.   176

XXIII   Car si tost que vous avez trait
                     Regard en cuer du vray amant,
                     Doulx Penser aussi si retrait,
                     Comme le fer vers l'aÿment,   180
                     Qui ne le laisse pas dormant.
                     Car nuyt et jour en pensant veille
                     Comment faire peust le command
                     De celle pour qui se traveille,   184

XXIV   Qui doit estre, selon nature,
                     Doulce, courtoise, et amiable,
                     Et contre la griefve pointure
                     D'Envie la desraisonnable   188
                     Avoir Pitié, l'incomparable
                     Comme doulce phisicïenne,
                     Pour garir son servant fiable
                     De sa douleur cotidïenne.   192

XXI   And I wish to explain to you the causes of this affair.
When she was first courted
by the lover, in whom there was no discontent,
she said that he
was obsessed with foolish thoughts and was begging for
war to wound his own heart,
and that instead he should seek
Peace in order to recover his happiness.[7]

XXII   These words are contrary to your law,
almighty and most high God of Love,
for you are of such a mind
and in your deeds so upright,
that to him who is inclined
to choose a lady to love,
you grant Gracious Thought,
so that he might seek grace without bitterness.

XXIII   For as soon as you have pierced
the heart of a true lover with a look,
Sweet Thought is attracted there, too,
like iron to a magnet
and will not let the lover sleep.
Night and day he stays up thinking
of ways to follow the orders
of her for whom he slaves.

XXIV   She is and should be, according to her nature,
tender, courteous, and amiable,
and counter the painful wound
of Envy, the irrational one.
She must have Pity, the incomparable,
as her sweet physician,
in order to heal her faithful servant
of his daily suffering.

XXV   Pour souldre ce qu'elle disoit
             Que l'amant pensast d'enquerir
             Paix pour son cuer qui languissoit
             Quant vers lui cuidoit acquerir   196
             Confort pour mercy requerir:
             Elle estoit fiere et despiteuse,
             Par quoy ne povait conquerir
             Paix, la tresbonne et gracïeuse.   200

XXVI   Expressement vous commandez
             Que nulle dame ne soit fiere,
             Et au surplus vous lui mandez
             Qu'en elle desdaing ne se fiere,   204
             Car ce n'est chose qui affiere
             A une dame, d'estre telle
             Que son servant de reffus fiere
             Si qu'es au cuer ait plaie mortelle.   208

XXVII   Apres Desir lui replica,
             Sur ce qu'elle avoit dit qu'en dueil
             L'amant demourer s'aplica
             Pour ce que contre ung regart d'ueil   212
             Sa paix ne gardoit a son vueil,
             Et que les yeulx a celle estoient
             Acompaigniés de Bel Acueil
             Pour regarder ou qu'i vouloient: 216

XXVIII   On scet bien que les yeulx sont faiz   [32v]
             Pour a leur plaisir regarder,
             Maintz de faulx regars contreffaiz
             Que aucuns font se doit on garder,   220
             Qui semblant monstrent d'amender
             Les griefs douleurs que aux amans donnent,
             Et y font leurs biens retarder
             Pour la trahison qu'ilz en ordonnent.   224

XXV   To refute the words this lady spoke,
when she said that the lover should seek
peace for his languishing heart[8]
instead of thinking he could obtain
consolation by requesting her grace:
she was proud indeed and without pity!
That is why he could not find
Peace, the benevolent and most gracious one.

XXVI   Explicitly you command
that no lady be cruel;
moreover, you forbid
that she pride herself on showing disdain,
for it is not befitting
a lady to act thus–
refusing her lover so harshly
that he receive a mortal wound to the heart.

XXVII   Next, Desire responded
to her comment that the lover
was trying to live in grief
if, after a quick glance of the eye,
he did not choose to protect his peace of mind;
furthermore, that her eyes,
accompanied by Fair Welcoming,[9]
were made in order to look where they wished.

XXVIII   It is well known that eyes were made
to look wherever they wish.
However, the deceptive and fake looks
thrown around by some eyes must be guarded against,
for they seem to show promise of soothing
the grave pain that they inflict on lovers,
but in fact they prevent the reception of these benefits
because of the treachery they command.

XXIX   Se le cueur n'est aux yeulx d'acort,
              Regart du tout l'amant abuze,
              Car par leur desloyal discort
              En tristece nuit et jour muse,   228
              Pensant qu'en douleur son temps use.
              Et ceste femme en tel party
              Mist l'amant par la faulce ruze
              Du regart qui d'elle party.   232

XXX   Encores pour grever plus fort
              Le bon et loyal serviteur,
              Quant vers elle queroit confort
              Pour alegier sa grant douleur,   236
              Elle disoit que grant cuideur
              Estoit trop d'y plaisir avoir
              En chose de pou de valeur,
              Et qu'il s'en voulait decevoir.   240

XXXI   Se Cuider en cuer d'amant n'a,   [33r]
              Il ne puet nulz maulx endurer.
              Amours par ce point ordonna
              Cuider en l'amant pour durer,   244
              Car se fol Dangier en yvrer
              Devoit ung amoureux loyal
              Pour cuider mercy recouvrer,
              Il portera en gré son mal.   248

XXXII   Et n'est pas donc ung pou de chose
              De cuider mercy conquerir,
              Qui est en cuer de dame enclose,
              Qu'on va par long temps requerir.   252
              Par quoy a icelle acquerir
              Il ne doit penser decevance,
              Car a la longuement querir
              L'amant acquiert paix et plaisance.   256

XXIX	If the heart is not in harmony with the eyes,
	then the look only deceives the lover,
	and because of this perfidious disaccord,
	in sadness the lover night and day will dream,
	thinking that he is passing his time in anguish.
	And this woman has put him
	in such a state by the subterfuge
	of the glance coming from her eyes.

XXX	And to wound even more profoundly
	the good and loyal servant,
	when he came before her seeking consolation
	in order to alleviate his great pain
	she told him that he was truly bumptious
	to believe that he could take pleasure
	from something of such little value
	and that he was deliberately deceiving himself.[10]

XXXI	Now, if Belief were not in the heart of a lover,
	he could not endure any of the heartaches of Love.
	Love, for this reason, commanded
	Belief to live forever within a lover;
	for if foolish Resistance
	inebriates the loyal lover
	in order to make him believe that he has received grace,
	he takes only pleasure in the other's pain.

XXXII	It is not, then, a little thing
	to believe in achieving the grace
	that is enclosed in a lady's heart
	and for which one must entreat a long while.
	This is why to acquire such grace,
	he must not think to employ deception,
	for only by seeking a long while,
	will he acquire peace and pleasure.

XXXIII   Mais trouvé a tout le revers
            Cellui dont je faiz mencion,
            Par affaitiéz samblans divers
            Engendrez de decepcion;   260
            Car, pour quelque admiracion
            Qu'il sceust faire de ceste femme,
            N'a peu avoir pour garison
            De mercy une seule drame.   264

XXXIV   Et affin que plus fort grevez   [33v]
            Il fust, elle lui disoit 'celle
            Maladie que vous avez
            Ne pourroit pas etre mortelle.   268
            Au fort, s'elle estoit si crüelle
            Qu'i faulsist qu'aucuns en mourussent,
            Mieulx en vault de ceste cordelle
            Ung lïer que les deulx le fussent.'   272

XXXV   Ce fut moult terrible parolle
            Ditte de bouche femenine,
            Qui doit estre, selon l'escolle
            D'Amours, humble, doulce, et benigne   276
            Envers tout ce que masculine
            Bouche veult requerir en bien;
            Car dame ne doit par nul signe
            Martirer le serviteur sien.   280

XXXVI   Se amant n'avoit autre martire
            Que les maulx que lui fait Dangier,
            Au pourchas d'Envie qui tire
            A lui en Tristresse logier,   284
            Si est ce assés pour de legier
            Mourir, sans ce que sa maistresse,
            En elle servant, abregier
            Face sa vie par rudesse.   288

XXXIII	But he found exactly the opposite,
	this lover of whom I speak,
	because of her several carefully crafted ruses
	engendered of deception;
	for, no matter what appreciation
	he showed for this woman,
	he did not receive in consolation
	a single drop of compassion.

XXXIV	And so that he would be
	even more grieved, she said to him:
	"A malady such as you have
	cannot be considered fatal.
	Indeed, if it is so cruel
	that one must die of it,
	then it is better that one be ensnared
	with this rope than two."[11]

XXXV	What horrible words
	to come from a woman's mouth!
	They should be, according to the school of Love,
	humble, sweet, and benevolent
	toward anything that a masculine
	mouth wishes to request in recompense;
	for a lady should not, by any gesture,
	martyr her own servant.

XXXVI	Even if a lover had no other torment
	than the blows inflicted on him by Resistance,
	still, by the force of Envy, who is intent on
	making him live with Sadness,
	he would experience enough to make him
	die, without his mistress
	shortening his life even more by her severity,
	despite his service to her.

XXXVII	Quant ceste femme rigoureuse	[34r]
	Martiroit fort l'amant loyal	
	Et comme une fiere et crüeuse,	
	Vouloit que seul portast tout mal.	292
	Pas n'estoit fait de cuer loyal	
	Puis qu'Amours, par sa grant bonté,	
	Veult que deux cueurs soient esgal	
	En pensee et en voulenté.	296
XXXVIII	Pour ce l'amoureux, sans amer,	
	A toudis eu son cuer entier,	
	N'oncques ne se voult entamer	
	Pour aultre maistresse accointier.	300
	Et ceste femme en maint quartier	
	A son faulx acueil departy	
	Par Malice, qui acointer	
	Lui fist d'amer plus d'un party.	304
XXXIX	Et pour donner plus de mesaise	
	A l'amant qui la requeroit,	
	Elle lui dist que d'Amours aise,	
	Espoir, ne desir ne queroit,	308
	Et que ja d'elle il n'aquarroit	
	Tant que perdue eust sa franchise,	
	Pour ce qu'elle trop surqueroit	
	Vouloir maistrier a sa guise.	312
XL	Je dy que se Espoir et Desir	[34v]
	Doivent estre en dames logiez	
	Pour faire a son servant plaisir,	
	Mais Desdaing les a delogiez	316
	Hors de ceste dame et changiez	
	A Reffus, Despit, et Rigeur,	
	Par lesquelz l'amant fust plungiez	
	Ou puis de mortelle douleur.	320

XXXVII This harsh woman
grieviously tormented the loyal lover
and, just as one haughty and cruel,
she wished that he alone might feel all the pain.
This was not the deed of a loyal heart!
For Love, by his great bounty,
desires that two hearts be equal
in thought and desire.

XXXVIII For this reason the lover, without bitterness,
has always kept his heart true;
never did he wish to place himself in jeopardy
by courting another mistress.
But this woman sent out her false welcome
to many different places
inspired by Malice, who had her seek out
lovers in more than one place.

XXXIX And in order to give greater discomfort
to the lover who was courting her,
she told him that from Love
neither comfort, hope, nor desire did she seek,
and that never from her would he aquire
anything that would have her lose her liberty:
she was too firm on this point,
in her desire to remain mistress in her own way.[12]

XL I say that Hope and Desire
must be lodged in ladies' hearts
in order to please their servants,
but Disdain has chased them
out of this lady and transformed them
into Refusal, Scorn, and Severity,
who have plunged the lover
into the well of suffering.

XLI
    Quant au point qu'elle dist que ja
    Son cuer ne seroit asservis,
    L'amoureux riens n'y chalenga,
    Si non de grace estre assouvis,   324
    Pour ce qu'il avoit bien l'advis
    Qu'elle a d'amours la seigneurie
    D'estre maistresse a son devis
    Et qu'en franchise l'a nourrie.   328

XLII
    Mais la merveilleuse nature
    De ceste femme fut conduite
    Au rebours de la nourriture
    D'Amours, par qui doit estre duite,   332
    Car incessamment s'est deduite
    De faire decepvans attraiz,
    Par lesquelz Plaisance s'est duite
    Et de l'amant et a mort traiz.   336

XLIII
    Car contre l'amant maintenoit   [35r]
    Que, pour plaisans bourdes confire,
    En belles parolles tenoit
    L'escolle pour la deconfire.   340
    A elle povoit bien souffire
    Pour lui faire ou feu de desir
    Son loyal cuer ardoir et frire,
    Sans lui dire tel desplaisir,   344

XLIV
    Attendu qu'i ne dist parolles
    Qui ne fussent confitez en honneur.
    Et quant par lettres ou par rolles
    Il monstroit sa tresgrant douleur,   348
    Car au loing sans estre flateur,
    Veritablement escripvoit,
    Pour quoy oncques ne fut bourdeur
    Vers celle, qui si bien servoit.   352

XLI   As to the point she made that never
would her heart be enslaved,
the lover did not challenge a word,
except to ask for consolation by her grace;
for he was of the belief
that Love had given her the power
to be mistress, in whatever way she liked,
and had nurtured her in liberty.

XLII   But the astounding nature
of this woman led her
to act contrary to Love's education,
by which she should be guided:
for she was continually amusing herself,
by showing off her deceptive charms,
charms with which Pleasure disguised herself
and attracted the lover, as well as his death.

XLIII   For to contradict the lover, she maintained
that by couching his words in decorous language,
he was just adhering to the teachings of the school of flattery
in order to to win her over.[13]
As if it were not enough for her to
have him burn up his loyal heart
in the fire of desire,
without telling him such mean things,

XLIV   given the fact that he spoke no word
that was not adorned with honor!
And when he showed her his great suffering
with his letters, whether folded or rolled up in a scroll,[14]
they were the furthest thing from flattery,
for he was writing truthfully,
which proves that he was never a lying flatterer
to her, whom he served so well.

XLV   Mais ouvriere estoit de bailler
           Plaisans bourdes en paiement
           A l'amant, qu'elle fist baillier
           Aprés sa mercy durement.   356
           Car Regart son consentement
           Mist que d'elle il auroit confort,
           Puis s'en repentit faulsement
           Pour le tenir en desconfort.   360

XLVI   Et pour plusieurs aultres meschiefz   [35v]
           Qu'elle lui fist en son service,
           Comme de lui dire 'entechiez
           Sont plusieurs cuers en vilains vices,   364
           Qui sont mal duisans et propices
           Avec une courtoise bouche,
           Mais Faintise, par son malice,
           Les assortist ensamble et couche.'   368

XLVII   Ces durs motz sont bien a reprandre
           Par devant vous, Amours, qui feistez
           Le vray cuer de l'amant emprandre
           D'elle amer, auquel proumistez   372
           Moult de biens et en lui mistez
           Loyaulté sans crainte et honneur;
           Et pour lui garder commistez
           Espoir, vostre bon procureur.   376

XLVIII   Et son cuer, de noblesse plain,
           Qui loyaulment vous a servi,
           A ellë est nommé vilain,
           Faintif, a malice asservi,   380
           Qui grace avoit bien desservi
           Pour pleurs et plains et longue attente,
           Tant avoit son cuer assouvi
           De loyaulté et bonne entente.   384

XLV

But she endeavored to give
sweet lies as recompense
to the lover, whom she made yearn for her
and her grace most desperately.
For Regard had consented
that he would receive comfort from her,
but then she treacherously took it back
to keep him in a state of suffering.

XLVI

I also accuse her of other injuries
that she inflicted on him while he was courting her,
such as when she said to him, 'Sullied
are many hearts with base vices
that are neither fitting nor becoming
to a courtly tongue,
but Dissimulation, by her perfidious nature,
associates and unites them.'[15]

XLVII

These harsh words should be condemned
before you, Love, you who have made
the most sincere heart of the lover undertake
to adore her; to him you promised
great and wonderful benefits, in him you placed
honor and loyalty without fear,
for him you commanded the protection
of Hope, your benevolent prosecutor.

XLVIII

And his noble heart
which has always loyally served you,
she called vile,
double-dealing, and malicious,
this same heart that deserved to receive her grace
in return for his tears, pleas, and patient waiting,
since his heart overflowed with
loyalty and good intentions.

XLIX   Mais elle mesme fut vilaine,   [36r]
        Et vint d'ung mauvaiz estomac
        Quant de sa bouche d'orgueil plaine
        Fist yssir de reffus tel dac;   388
        Qu'abatu se trouva au lac
        De la mort ly amans preudens.
        Et on dit qu'i ne peut du sac
        Yssir que ce qui est dedens.   392

L   Et son sac estoit toudis plains
        De rudes parlers rigoureux
        Pour escondire les griefz plains
        De son vray servant douloureux,   396
        Disant que melencolïeux
        Estoit par la puissance fole
        De son legier cuer amoureux,
        Duquel mal nul cueur ne s'affole.   400

LI   L'amant n'avoit pas cuer legier
        Ne garny de fole puissance,
        Qu'en son vivant voult changier
        Ceste dame ou fust sa fïance,   404
        Qui, par sa grande decevance,
        Lui monstra semblant d'amour lye,
        Puis lui fist avoir acointance
        A mortelle melencolie.   408

LII   Et pour lui doulanment desplaire   [36v]
        Disoit qu'a tous, si non a lui,
        Vouloit joieusement complaire,
        Affin de l'eschever d'anuy,   412
        Pour ce d'Amours est au jour d'uy
        Petit saige et croit de legier,
        Et qu'i prent bien souvent d'autruy
        Chose dont pou se peut aider.   416

XLIX   Instead, it was she herself who was vile,
                born of repulsive bile,
                for out of her arrogant mouth
                shot a refusal that cut like a dagger;
                beaten, the discreet lover
                found himself in the lake of the dead.
                As they say, "nothing can come out of a sack
                except what is already within."[16]

L   And her sack has always been full
                of harsh and severe words
                in order to rebuff the grieveous pleas
                of her true and suffering servant,
                saying that he was melancholy
                due to the foolish influence
                of his fanciful heart in love,
                a condition from which no heart perishes.[17]

LI   But the lover did not have a fanciful heart
                fed by foolish influence,
                for never in his life did he wish to be fickle
                toward this lady, to whom he had pledged his faith;
                but she, by great deception,
                showed him signs of joyful love,
                yet then introduced him to
                mortal melancholy.

LII   And to afflict him even more cruelly,
                she told him that toward everyone else, but not to him,
                she wished to be pleasant,
                so as to spare him pain,
                because, she said, Love these days
                is facile and credulous,
                and often takes something from one
                that benefits another not in the least.[18]

LIII   Avoir ne povoit deshonneur
            De faire a l'amant bonne chiere
            Comme aux aultres, puis qu'en honneur
            L'aymoit; mais la faulce sorciere,   420
            De charité estoit trop chiere
            Contre l'amant qui, pour tel pris
            Qu'aultrë en avoit, sans ranchiere,
            Devoit elle avoir grace et pris.   424

LIV   Car Amours, que pou sage appelle,
            Veult que les bons aient de ses biens,
            Et jamés il ne les rappelle,
            Tant est large; et contre les siens   428
            Vraiz serviteurs cotidïens
            Ne veult croire nul faulx rapport;
            Et aussi ne prent d'aultrui riens,
            Car tous biens on trouve a son port.   432

LV   Dont ceste femme ou ciel maint   [37r]
            Doit on par droit fole nommer,
            Qui maintenant qu'en Amours remaint
            Pou de sens, qui tant renommer   436
            On dit pour ce qu'i fait amer;
            Et qui bien Amours congnoistroit,
            Jamés ne l'oseroit blasmer,
            Mais ne cuide pas qu'Amours soit.   440

LVI   Car losengier crüel et fort,
            Doulx a mentir et aspre en euvre,
            L'appelle, et se venge a effort
            De tous ceulx qui cuident qu'il euvre   444
            Pour eulx ses secretz et desqueuvre.
            Et ces motz tesmoingnent assez
            Que son cuer trop plus dur que coeuvre
            Est en son cuider entachez.[19]   448

LIII   She could not have been dishonored
            by gladly greeting the lover
            as she did others, for he loved her with honor;
            but the deceitful witch
            put too high a charge on her compassion
            for this lover, who, for the same price
            as any other and with no additional cost,
            should have received grace and esteem from her.

LIV   For Love, whom she called foolish,
            wants good men to get what they deserve,
            and he never takes back his benefits from them,
            such is his generosity; and against his
            true and faithful servants
            he will believe no false witness.
            Moreover, he takes nothing from others,
            because everything good comes from him.

LV   This woman brought up into the sky
            should therefore rightly be called a fool,
            for she maintained that in Love was little sense–
            even though he is highly famed because
            he is the impetus to love;
            if she knew Love at all,
            she would never dare to blame him,
            but then, she does not even believe that Love exists.

LVI   For a cruel flatterer,
            sweet in lies and bitter in deeds,
            she called Love, and claimed that he avenges himself
            on all those who believe that he acts
            in their favor by the revelation of his secrets.
            These words alone are proof enough
            that her heart, harder than copper,
            is tarnished by her delusion.

LVII   Amours est en lui tout parfait,
        Atrempé, doulx et voir disant,
        Car par parolle ne par fait
        N'est aux vraiz amoureux nuisant;   452
        Mais de ce qu'il est desduisant,
        A son servant il en depart
        De franche voulenté plaisant
        Et se tient tousdiz de sa part.   456

LVIII   Et se celle eust Amours congneu,   [37v]
        Quant l'amant faisoit sa priere,
        Et le grant bien de lui sceü,
        Monstree ne se fust si fiere;   460
        Mais comme la lune lumiere
        Ne peut que du soleil avoir,
        Femme n'est de grace aumosniere
        Se d'Amours ne congnoist le voir.   464

LIX   Et pour tant ceste femme cy
        Ne doit estre dame nommee,
        Car n'a pas son cuer enrichi
        D'umble Doulceur, la renommee;   468
        De quoy du tout est surnommee
        Quant 'dame' on l'appelle 'en amours'
        Mais doit estre 'femme' appellee
        'Crüelle et plaine de faulx tours.'   472

LX   Encores ceste fiere femme,
        Plaine de malice et rudesse,
        Et qui doit estre ditte infame,
        A l'amant ou estoit largesse   476
        Disoit que c'estoit grant saigesse
        De soy traire de bien amer,
        Affin qu'on passast sa jennesse
        Et qu'on ne s'amuse en amer.   480

LVII   But Love is perfect unto himself:
moderate, sweet, and honest,
and neither by word nor deed
does he harm true lovers;
On the contrary, because he is so good-natured,
with his servant he shares everything
with open heart and goodwill,
and for his part he is always loyal.

LVIII   If she had known Love
during the time the lover was courting her,
and had known of his excellence, too,
she would not have shown herself so proud.
But, like the light of the moon,
which can come only from the sun,
so a woman can only grant grace
if she knows the truth of Love.

LIX   And for all of these reasons, this woman here before us
should not be entitled 'lady,'
for she does not have a heart enriched
by the presence of humble Sweetness, the famed one.
Consequently, she is given too much honor
when called a lady in love
and instead should be called 'woman,'
cruel and practiced at deceit.

LX   Moreover, this haughty woman,
filled with malice and hardness of heart,
and who should be hailed as disgraceful,
said to that lover in whom was such generosity,
that it was wise
to keep oneself from loving,
so that one might live one's youth
and not find amusement in bitterness.[20]

LXI   La muse dont n'entendoit notte   [38r]
      Le fist jusques a la fin muser:
      Et plus musoit, tant plus asote
      Pensee estoit pour soy user;   484
      Car lui, qui ne sçavoit ruser,
      Ne visoit qu'a loyalle emprise,
      Et ceste femme a l'abuser
      Avoit sa voulenté comprise.   488

LXII   Car Faulx Semblant, le cabuzeur,
      Fist la muse desordonnee,
      Et par Bel Acueil, l'abuzeur,
      Fust au vray amoureux donnee,   492
      Et tellement fut ordonnee
      Que tant plus y musoit et moins
      Estoit Mercy habandonné
      A le recevoir en ses mains.   496

LXIII   Et en oultre a l'amant comptoit,
      Pour plus mouteplïer ses dueilz,
      Que long descomfort tourmentoit
      Son cuer, qui apart soy pour deux   500
      Se troubloit; et que l'amoureux
      Le jeu d'atente perdre doit
      Et ne se monstre scïenteux
      De son double point faire adroit.   504

LXIV   Jaméz n'eust fait adroit son point   [38v]
      L'amant; car ceste femme aprés
      Le faisoit jouer mal appoint,
      Pour ce qu'elle changoit les dez.   508
      Aussi, Amours, vous commandez
      Qu'en vous servant deux cuers se tiennent
      Tout ung, car point vous n'entendez
      Qu'en double vouloir se maintiennent.   512

LXI	This Muse, from whom he expected nothing,
	kept him musing on her behalf to the end.
	The more he mused, the deeper into foolish
	thinking he fell, which wore him down.
	For he, not knowing how to beguile,
	sought only to act out of loyalty.
	But this woman had construed her will
	to deceive him.

LXII	For False Seeming, that charlatan,
	rendered his musing obsessive;
	and by Fair Welcoming, the deceptive one,
	this Muse was offered to the true lover.
	It was all arranged so
	that the more he mused and wasted his time with her,
	the less likely it was that Mercy
	might receive him into his arms.

LXIII	Moreover, this lady told the lover,
	in order to multiply his pains,
	that a lifetime of discomfort was tormenting
	his heart, which all alone
	was suffering for two;
	and that he would lose the waiting game
	if he did not show himself clever enough
	to roll his point number twice in his turn.[21]

LXIV	Never, however, would the lover have succeeded
	in rolling his point number, for this lady then
	made him play at a disadvantage:
	she was loading the dice.
	Furthermore, Love, you command
	that in serving you, two hearts must become
	one, for you do not mean
	to join them together with two separate desires.

LXV   Et elle faisoit a tous tours
             Son point double, c'estoit par l'art
             De ses malicïeux atours,
             Soy gardant de getter hazard.   516
             Et l'amant, qu'elle fist musart,
             Loyaument de bons dez jouoit,
             Sans les changier tempre ne tart,
             Et son point en riens ne venoit.   520

LXVI   Et puis dist que tous amoureux
             Sont goulïars ou temps qui court
             Et que le plus secret d'iceulx
             Veult bien que l'on die en la court?   524
             Que aucune dame a tenue court;
             Dont, pour riens qu'il dist a dame,
             A verité dire de court
             Et n'en doit plus estre creu d'ame.   528

LXVII   Dieu a fait avecques Nature   [39r]
             L'omme tant discret et saige,
             Que sus toute aultre crëature
             C'est le plus parfait, ce bien sçay je,   532
             Du quel le femenin ymage
             C'est yssue par sa noblesse,
             Par quoy femme lui doit hommage
             Et garder que s'onneur ne blesse.   536

LXVIII   Quant ceste femme tresdespite
             Le voult du tout degouverner;
             C'est raison qu'on ne la respite
             A pugnir, pour mieulx honnourer   540
             Nom d'omme, que vituperer
             Le veult publiquement juger
             De tout son vivant demourer
             Ung goulïart et mensonger.   544

LXV   At every turn she was throwing
       her number twice in a row,[22]
       thanks to the artifice of her cheating tools,
       thus keeping herself from throwing hazard and losing.
       But the lover, whom she made look like a fool,
       played faithfully with true dice,
       never switching them out early or even late in the game,
       and his number never came up.

LXVI   And then she said that all lovers
       these days are scoundrels,
       and that even the most discreet one among them
       wishes that it be said about him at court
       that he is the lover of some lady;
       For this reason, no matter what he says to a lady,
       he comes up short on truth,
       and should not be believed by a single living soul.[23]

LXVII   God, with Nature, created
       man to be so discreet and wise
       that above all other creatures
       he is the most perfect, of this I am certain.
       The image of woman
       came forth out of his nobility,
       which is why a woman must pay him tribute
       and keep from wounding his honor.

LXVIII   But since this disdainful woman
       wished to completely undermine the lover,
       it is reasonable that we not hesitate
       to punish her, in order to better honor
       the name of this man, whom she
       wanted to insult and publicly condemn,
       so that all his life he would be reputed
       a scoundrel and liar.

LXIX   Et aussy qu'Amours vous renomme
Crüel losengier et menteur,
Et que le franc amoureux homme
Qui estoit son vray serviteur   548
A part son regart barateur,
Fait decevablement murdrir,
Lequel ne peut ou decepteur
Pour d'elle le nom amendrir.   552

LXX   Pour quoy, Amours, conclure veul   [39v]
Avec Espoir, vo procureur,
Que ceste femme soit en dueil
Enclose, et par paine et douleur   556
Gardee et en dure langueur,
Et avec ce, soit desgradee
De nom de dame, qui d'onneur
Doit este nourrie et paree.[24]   560

LXXI   Car si bel non ne luy affiert,[25]   [144r Pe]
Veues les causes que j'ay dictes,
Et que de sa langue a tort fiert
D'Amours les vertus et merites.   564
Et se faire veult contredictes
Sur ce, nous le voulons prouver
A suffisance, sans redictes,
Pour d'Amours la droit esprouver."   568

LXXII   Lors Franc Vouloir, le president,
Dit a la femme: "ouÿ avez
Tout ce que Desir le prudent
A dit contre vous. Pour ce vees   572
Que voz salvacions trouvez:
Le cas requiert pugnition,
Et, s'excuser ne vous savez,
Jugier fault la correction."   576

LXIX

and also because she dared impute Love
as a cruel flatterer and liar,
and the honest and loving man,
who was her true servant
she treacherously murdered
with her deceptive glance—
killed he who was incapable of deceit—
for fear of tarnishing her reputation.

LXX

These are the reasons for which, Love,
I wish to conclude, in accordance with Hope,
your prosecutor, that this woman be locked up in suffering
and by pain and torment
kept in overwhelming languor;
and above all, that she be stripped
of the name of lady, for a true lady
should be governed and adorned by honor.

LXXI

And such a beautiful name does not suit her,
given the evidence I have just introduced,
in addition to the fact that her tongue wrongly attacked
the virtues and merits of Love.
If, however, she wishes to object,
we reserve the right to prove our case
beyond a shadow of a doubt and above reproach,
in order to find in favor of Love."

LXXII

Then Free Will, the presiding judge,
said to the woman: "You have heard
everything that Desire, the prudent,
has said against you. See that
your defense is in order:
the case requires retribution,
and if you cannot successfully defend yourself,
the sentence will be carried out."

LXXIII   Et celle conseil demanda,
       Pour respondre ad ce qu'on disoit.
       Adonc Franc Vouloir commanda
       Qu'elle eust conseil, maiz nul n'osoit   580
       Estre pour elle; et s'excusoit
       Ung chacun pour ce que d'Amours   [144v *Pe*]
       Et de l'amant trop mesdisoit,
       Dont Espoir faisoit ses clamours.   584

LXXIV   Quant la dame vist l'apparence
       Que conseil n'auroit, clerc ne lay,
       Estat demanda, par absence
       De conseil, pour avoir delay.   588
       On luy octroya. Lors m'allay
       Esveiller, et puis a parfaire
       La balade me travaillay
       Pour mon devoirs vers Amours faire.   592

LXXV   Et quant faicte fut la balade,
       Mon chemin prist a aller veoir
       Sur toutes aultres la plus sade
       En beaulté, honneur, et savoir;   596
       Et luy supplïay moult qu'avoir
       Voulsist ma ballade en sa grace,
       Moy pardonnant se bien devoir
       Ne faysoie a louer sa face.   600

LXXVI   Aprés je luy feiz vray recort
       Du songe qu'avoye songé,
       Requerant que son cueur d'accort
       Ne fust que j'eusse tel congié,   604
       Ne mon soulas en dueil changé,
       Comme eut l'amant qui droit mena
       Son cueur, qui de mort fut chargé
       Par celle ou point de mercy n'a.   608

Explicit

LXXIII

Then she requested counsel
in order to prepare her defense.
Free Will ordered
that she have counsel, but no one dared
to take her case; they all recused themselves
because she had spoken too harshly
against Love and the lover,
the same reason for which Hope had brought the case forth.

LXXIV

When the lady saw that
no lawyer, neither cleric nor layman, would defend her,
she requested a delay,
and it was granted her. Then I woke up
and set my mind to work
on finishing the ballad in order to fulfill
my duty to Love.

LXXV

And when the ballad was written,
I set out on the path to go see
her who over all others is the most appreciable
in beauty, honor, and wisdom;
and I begged that she receive
my ballad with grace,
pardoning me if I failed in my effort
to praise her countenance and appearance.

LXXVI

Afterward, I gave a complete account
of the dream that I had dreamed,
and begged that her heart never consent
to receive me in the same way,
nor that my delight be changed to suffering
as it happened to that lover who kept his heart
faithful but who was stricken to death
by her in whom there was no mercy.

The End[26,27]

Notes

1. Line 1: the French court until the middle of the sixteenth century dated the New Year from Easter, between the end of March to late April, thus giving a New Year's Day that corresponded with the renewal of springtime.

2. Baudet Herenc has been identified as the author of a treatise on poetry, *Doctrine de Seconde Rhetorique*, in which are given instructions on the rules of poetry writing. Baudet seems to find himself in the position of knowing the rules of the art, but not its practice.

3. The variant "de Paris et de Helainne" has been adopted because it justifies the plural verb "servirent." The editor has two choices: one is to alter the verb to the singular in order to keep the original reading, which only mentions the Châtelaine de Vergy—a reading that makes good sense and reveals that the narrator is looking at a tapestry, but which would give a hypometric line; the second is to change the reading to that of the majority of manuscripts and keep the plural verb and a correct syllabic count.

4. Line 68: Paris and Helen were the lovers who caused the Trojan War. Line 69: The Châtelaine de Vergy was heroine of a thirteenth-century tale. She died of heartache when her lover revealed their affair. A copy appears in Valenciennes, Bib. Mun. 417, with the *Belle dame sans mercy* and the *Hospital of Love*. A prose account of the story was written in the fifteenth century, usually called *La Châtelaine du Verger*.

5. Hoffman suggests that Desire is the attorney for the dead lover's estate. See *Alain Chartier* p. 71.

6. Line 140: Desire is preparing his case based on the words of the lady recorded in Chartier's *Belle dame sans mercy*, words that he will claim prove that the lady is responsible for her lover's death.

7. Lines 164–68: an adaptation of the first words of the lady in Chartier's *Belle dame*, vv. 221–24.

8. Line 195: *Belle dame*, v. 224.

9. Lines 210–16: *Belle dame*, vv. 233–40.

10. Lines 237–40: *Belle dame*, vv. 253–55.

11. Lines 266–72: *Belle dame*, vv. 265–66 and 271–72. Desire alters the citation to integrate a hunting metaphor not present in the original.

12. Line 307–12: see *Belle dame*, vv. 281–88.

13. Lines 338–40: *Belle dame*, vv. 299–301.

14. At this point in the fifteenth century, both paper and parchment were in use. These supports were sometimes folded, as in manuscripts, or sometimes rolled, especially if the text was not very long.

15. Lines 363–68: citation adapted from *Belle dame*, vv. 361–64.

16. Lines 391–92: proverb that means "nothing can come out of her mouth that was not in her heart," a confirmation of this lady's essentially evil nature.

17. Lines 397–400: *Belle dame*, vv. 377–80.

18. Lines 410–16: *Belle dame,* vv. 393–400.

19. Lines 441–45: *Belle dame,* vv. 313–20. The complicated syntax confuses the subject of "se venge"—is it the lady or Love who is seeking vengeance? The translation presented assumes that the subject is the lady, who is claiming that Love seeks vengeance.

20. Lines 477–80: *Belle dame,* vv. 479–80.

21. Lines 499–504: *Belle dame,* vv. 493–96.

22. It is not clear whether she is throwing her number twice and thus winning at this game of hazard (a more complex version of today's craps) or if she is throwing a two, today's "craps," and deliberately losing the game (of love).

23. Lines 521–28: *Belle dame,* vv. 715–20.

24. "Explicit le traittie du jugement de la belle dame sans mercy en la cour du dieu d'amours" The poem ends at this point midpage in Pf and Pj, perhaps because the scribe tires of copying the poem, or more likely the scribe is copying an earlier version that does not yet include the device to invite continuation of the trial, the Belle dame's request for representation in court, and deferral of the trial. The belle dame here is considered judged and sentenced by the final words of Desire, a conclusion supported by its attributed title in these manuscripts.

25. The poem is continued according to Pe, a manuscript that is dated to the mid-fifteenth century (like Pf and Pj) and which also only contains the first continuation.

26. *Accusations,* rejected readings: 18. ale Pf; 23. entreprendre (+1) Pe; 44. la pourpasse PcPePn; 49. m'aprouche PcPn; 51. darbres et de c. Pf; 59. chardonneres (-1) PcPe; 63. Qui Pn; 68. Faite de palaiz et de laigne PbPbPe; 85. missing line supplied by PbPc; 86. fait son s. (-1) PbPc; 103. se mirent Pc; 133. fait deux ensemble rime PbPe; 134. En seul a. (-1) PbPcPe; 145. d. le trespuissant d. (+1) Pc; 159. par dur a. (-1) PbPc; 167. missing line PbPcPe; 221. d'amer (-1) Pf; 229. en leur douleur (+1) PbPc; 237. cuider PbPc; 240. Et sen v. (-1) Pb; 251. Qui en c. (-1) PbPc; 254. Ne p. (-1) Pc; 265. plus g. (-1) Pb; 287. Et illec le servant herbergier PbPc; 288. sa voye PbPc; 295. deux soient (-1) Pb; 313. Et dit PbPcPe; 330. est conjointe Pc; 346. cousttez or conftez scribe misread original PbPc; 352. huiet PbPc; 355. probably baer/ baier, a mistake in all the MSS; 360. la Pf; 388. dart Pc; 417. peut Pb; 425. pour Pb; 432. ont PbPc; 435. maintenant counts 2 syllables; 440bis. PjPf add a line: si maugracieux lozengier; 447. cueur plus fort qui ne treuve Pb; 449. lui p. (-1) PcPd; 463. que de (+1) PbPc; 481.Et de muse ou estoit note Pb; 485. lui ne (-1) Pb; 488. emprise Pb; 500. S. c. a. s. (-1) Pf; 518. de bons (-1) PbPc; 519. jetter PbPcPn; 536. son honneur (+1) Pc; 539. qu'on l'en respite PbPc; 541. Non dist que v. PbPc; 542. p. et j. (+1) Pf; 543. et d. (+1) PbPc; 550. decevamment (-1) PbPc; 565–66 copied twice.

27. *Accusations,* variant readings: Pn: Traittie fait par Baudart hereng corespondant a la belle dame sans mercy; 19. la ballade PcPePn; 26. compter Pn; 27. El ne pourroit Pe; 29. aprester PcPePn; 32. le f. Pn; 36. mon c. PbPePn; 47. luysans pierres de toppasse PcPe; 49. m'approchay Pc; 54. faicte d. Pc; 57. Pave PcPn; 63. jardin Pc; 66. Je y vys PbPc; 67. Ou de maintes f. PbPcPe; 68. comme d. P. Pn; 70. Qui furent amours jadiz Pe; stanza X omitted in Pc; 74. flouries genettes PbPcPe; 76. geroflees et MSS;

78. Et de lavende losengiés MSS; 79. r. et alloettes MSS; 82. Au dessoubz d'une liaison Pb, De soussies en ung gason PcPePn; 89. deux p. PbQh; 92. Que PbPe; 98. Amans et amantes Pb, Ames et amees Pc, Amis et amies s. Pn; 102. peussent a. Pn; 105. D. Penser Pc; 111. Pe adds la ballade; 119. En plourant lermes plus de vingt PbPcPePn; 125. Comment par graces allosees Pn; 126. Amer fait ung cuer son c. Pn; 129. p. mobille Pn; 130. D. penser Pc; 138. fut Pe; 139. Eut Pe; 142. Par l. PbPe; 146. Il vous pleust PbPe; 148. sentremettre Pe; 150. [fame Pc] que vous vees Pe; 151. vous feïstes PcPe; 157. le PbPc, Maiz elle du tout au contraire Pe; 167. Et pour ce fut ellë acquise Pf; 168. Fust paix pour tieulx maulx eschiver PbPcPe; 176. grace PbPcPe; XXIII not in Pc; 182. toutes nuys en PbPcPePn; 186. D. amoureuse et a. Pn; 196. l'amant venoit requerir PbPcPePn; 197. concquerir Pn; XXVI not in Pc; 199. acquerir Pn; 208. Si quau cuer est p. Pe; 219. mais PbPc, f. semblans Pb; 221. amer Pf; 223. Et ilz PePn; 224. leur d. Pb, i. adonnent Pc; 227. Et Pc; 245. ennuirer Pb; 248. porteroit PbQa; 254. ne [ny Pe] peust avoir d. PcPe, avoir difference Pb; 258. l'amant Pb; 261. admonicion Pb; 268. pourriez vous trouver PbPn; 270. quamans PbPePnQa; 272. l'un lié PbPcPePn; 277. tout sexe m. Pn; XXXVII is omitted in Pc; XXXIX-XLIV are omitted in *Le jardin de* plaisance; 281. D'amours n. Pn; 285. Sest assez mal p. Pb; 287. En elle servant, abregier PbPc; 288. vie PbPc; 290. feal Pb; 293. feal Pn; 299. le v. PbPc; 303. convoitier PbPc; 304. la fist Pf; 326. d'aucuns Pn; 330. c'est c. PbPe; 335. seduite PbPc; 336. Fut Pb; 346. conficte PbPc, toutes Pf; 345. nest dist Pe; 348. A elle moustroit PbPcPe; 349. Loyaulte, par sa grant doulceur PbPcPe; XLV missing in Pc; 371. a prendre Pe; XLIX displaced in Pe; 390. pendens Pf; 395. contredire PbPc; 396. languoureux PbPcPn; 398. sa pensee Pb, la plaisance Pc; 402. plaisance PbPcPe; 403. voulsist Pf; 407. Pour l. Pe; 421. De crainte se tenoit trop chiere Pb, Honte, sy la tenoit trop fiere Pn; 428. sage PbPcPn; 433. fierté PbPcPe; LV stanza order restored in Pe; 437. On doit Pf; 448. en fol cuider entassez Pb; 450. Atempre Pn; 457. l'amant c. Pn; 469. Quant dame on l'appelle en amours Pc; 470. M. digne de non estre amee Pn; 471. sonnee PbPc; 479. en passant s. PbPc; 478. soy retraire Pb, soy remettre Pe; 480. On ne muse a vivre en amer PbPc; 485. sauroit Pe; 499. conmetoit Pc; 505. ades PbPePn; 510. s'ajoingnent Pc; 512. voulenté [se joignent Pc] se tiegnent Pe; 513. a tous jours PbPcPn; 518. de vos d. Pe, deboutz Pf; 520. muoit PbPc; 525. a. [foys Pc] il en tienne c. PePn; 527. forcourt PbPcPn; 530. discret et noble et sage PbPcPn; 531. qui Pf; 538. deshonnourer PbPcPn; 545. qua. fol r. Pe; 546. flateur Pc; 549. En la seruant tout par honneur Pc; 551. Lequel onques ne fu vanteur Pe; 556. et cremeur Pn; 560. et gardee PbPe; 567. sur les parolles avant dictes Pb; 568. damours le droit PbQa, le fait approuver Pn; 585. ouÿ Pc; 591. m transportay Pc; 599. bon d. Pb.

The Lady Loyal in Love

Anonymous

S'ensuit la dame lëalle en amours

I   Se tristre penser me fust joye,   [89r]
                Et plains et plours me fussent ris,
                Et mercy pour refus avoye,
                Ne vouldroie aultre paradis.   4
                Mais il m'est bien aultrement pris,
                Quant de ma tresdoulce maistresse
                Ne puis avoir n'estre servis
                Fors de Reffus qui fort me blesse.   8

II   Et puis que je ne puis trouver
                Envers elle aucune allegance,
                Je sçay qu'i me fault retourner
                A celui le quel a puissance   12
                De ses servans mettre en plaisance,
                C'est le treshaultain Dieu d'Amours,
                Afin que par sa bien veullance
                J'aye confort de mes dollours.   16

III   Sy me submetz en sa mercy
                Pour acquerir joye prochaine;
                De ses biens doy estre enrichy,
                Puis que fail a remede humaine.   20
                Il puet bien allegier ma paine,
                Comme droiturier enseigneur,
                Et de toute joye mondaine
                Treshaultain et puissant seigneur.   24

IV   Ce fut par ung mois de septembre   [89v]
                Que tresdollant me complaindoye;
                Incontinent je m'en remembre,
                A pou soustenir me povoye,   28
                Car en ce point esté avoye
                Trois jours sans boire et sans mengier,
                Que nulle chose ne faisoye
                Fors le Dieu d'Amours invoquier.   32

Here Follows the Lady Loyal in Love

I

If doleful thoughts brought me joy,
and wails and weeping made me laugh,
and mercy I received rather than rejection,
I could wish for no other paradise.
But for me this is not so,
since from my sweet mistress
I am dealt only refusal,
which wounds me deeply.

II

And since I can find
from her no solace,
I know that I must return
to him who has the power
to put his servants at ease,
the great and mighty God of Love,
for by his benevolence
I might be relieved of my suffering.

III

I throw myself on his mercy
in order to find his joy soon;
from his bounty I require fortification,
for human remedy has failed me.
He can relieve my pain,
as he is the just teacher
and noble and powerful lord
of all worldly joys.

IV

It was in the month of September
that I was complaining in this way:
my memory of it is still quite vivid.
I was barely able to stand up,
for at that point I had gone
three days without drinking or eating.
I could do nothing at all
except pray to the God of Love for help.

V   Moy estant en ce dur martire,
Ung jour bien matin m'esveillay,
Desirant appaisier mon yre,
Ma dolleur, et mon grant esmay.   36
Pour ce prestement m'en allay
Aux champs atout ung esprevier,
Et deux espaignos y menay,
Comme il appartient en gibier.   40

VI   Ainsy trachant les champs alloye
Alöes de gibier querant,
Sy en trouvay une en ma voye
Que mon oysel fu convoitant.   44
Trop estoit forte, a mon samblant,
Et se volloit de sy rade elle
Que par son bien voller fist tant
Que mon oisel failly a elle.   48

VII   Quant mon esprevier ot failly,
L'esoir commença a surprendre,
La challeur et le vent cueilly
Sy hault que ne le peult comprendre,   52
Et sembloit qu'il voulloit contendre
A moy eslongier durement.
Sy commencha sa voye prendre
En sus de moy trop mallement.   56

VIII   Plus de deulx lieues le sievy   [90r]
Courant a tire de cheval,
Mais oncques ne la consievy.
Lors me trouvay en ung grant val   60
Qui trop bien sembloit lieu ou mal
Deuist souvent estre excercéz:
Couvert y ot de noir cendal
Maintz sarcus de corps trespasséz.   64

V   Suffering in this way like a martyr,
one day I awoke very early in the morning,
anxious to find ease for my affliction,
suffering, and dismay.
To do this I parted without delay
for the fields with a sparrow- hawk
and took two spaniels with me,
as is customary for hunting.

VI   I was tracking through the fields like this,
looking for young larks as prey.
I found one on my path,
and my bird took chase.
The lark was exceptionally strong, it seemed to me,
and it flew away swiftly,
with such speed
that my bird lost its trail.

VII   After this failure
my sparrow hawk soared above,
whirling around in the wind and heat,
so high above that it
appeared to be making every effort
to be as far from me as possible.
And it began to follow a course high above me
so it was difficult to track.

VIII   For more than two leagues I pursued,
riding at top speed,
but I was never able to catch it.
Then suddenly I found myself in a large valley,
which had the air of a place where evil
was often practiced.
There, wrapped in black silk cloth
was a multitude of coffins filled with dead bodies.

IX   Ceste vallee me dura
        Plus d'une demie lieue grant.
        Assés de paine y endura
        Mon cheval; pour ce fuz en grant   68
        D'estre oultre ce lieu desplaisant
        Ou aucune verdeur n'avoit.
        Ains sambloit lieu obeïssant
        A dueil, qui bien le regardoit.   72

X   Tant plus tenoye ce chemin,
        Tant plus me sembloit ennuyeuse
        La voye, et quant vins vers la fin,
        Je oÿ une voix trespiteuse,   76
        Par semblant tristre et dolloureuse,
        Comme se fust corps rendant ame;
        Mais ne fu pas trop oultrageuse
        Car bien ressambloit voix de dame   80

XI   Ce non obstant, je chevauchoye,
        Tousjours au Dieu mon souvenir
        Qui les cuers amoureux maistroye.
        Sy perceuz devant moy venir,   84
        Tout pas pour pas, a beau loisir,
        Une dame plainne de plours:
        Trop sambloit estre en desplaisir,
        Qui bien regardoit ses atours.   88

XII   Tantost que la viz, j'arestay,   [90v]
        Pour vëoir la maniere d'elle.
        Ung petit mon cheval tiray,
        Et en ce faisant, oÿ qu'elle   92
        Nommoit Malle Bouche rebelle,
        Et se plaingnoit moult durement
        D'aulcune oultraigeuse querelle
        Dont on l'accusoit faulsement.   96

IX   This valley spread at least
a half league across
and crossing it was difficult indeed
for my horse. For this reason, I was anxious
to be out of this awful place
where nothing green could grow.
It appeared to be a place under the rule of
Sorrow, who watched over it carefully.

X   The longer I stayed on this path
the more difficult became
my progress, just as I reached the other side,
I thought I heard a pitiful voice
which seemed sorrowful and in great pain,
as if a body were giving up its soul;
but it was not too horrible to hear,
for it sounded like the voice of a lady.

XI   In spite of this, I kept riding along,
keeping my mind focused on the god
who governs all hearts that love.
But then I saw before me,
walking slowly and deliberately,
a lady lost in tears,
who seemed in great despair,
to judge by her demeanor.

XII   As soon as I saw her, I stopped
to get a closer look
and reined my horse off the path.
As I was doing this I heard her
call Foul Mouth a renegade
and complain loudly about
some outrageous scandal
of which she was falsely accused.

XIII   Tellement venoit gemissant
        Et plourant pour son dur affaire,
        Qu'oncques ne me fut regardant
        Si fuz par devant son vÿaire,   100
        Prestement se cuida retraire.
        Sy me hastay de salüer
        Et elle, comme debonnaire,
        M'en sceut bien autant presenter,   104

XIV   Dont trop grant pitié me rendy
        De ce que tant fut esplouree.
        Pour ce du cheval descendy,
        Et le laissay resne avallee   108
        Sy lui requis d'umble pensee
        Que tant contraindist son voulloir,
        Qu'elle me deïst la riens nee
        Qui plus faisoit son cuer doulloir.   112

XV   "Lasse!" dit elle, "mon doulx sire,
        Ce vous puet moult peu proufiter.
        Vous ne m'en poëz estre mire,
        Ne vous chaille d'en enquester,   116
        Car de sa dolleur reciter
        Empir on assez, ce me samble.
        Joye et dolleur au vray compter
        Ne poevent remanoir enssemble.   120

XVI   Car se ma doullour ramentoy   [91r]
        Tant plus me croistra ma tristresse,
        Combien que je n'ay que bien poy
        De joye. Mais trop plus se blesse   124
        Cil qui deulx fois chëoir se lesse
        Que cil qui chiet tant seullement
        Une fois; dont est ce simplesse
        De chëoir tout a euscïent."   128

XIII   She was shuddering and weeping so violently
        about this grievous affair
        that she never even saw me
        until suddenly we were face-to-face.
        She acted as though she would turn away
        so I hastened to greet her,
        and she, well raised as a lady,
        knew how to respond in kind.

XIV   A great feeling of pity overwhelmed me
        for the tears that she had shed,
        and so I dismounted from my horse
        and let the bridle fall to the ground,
        asking her with humblest consideration
        to pull herself together
        so that she might tell me
        what was causing her heart such grief.

XV   "Alas!" she cried, "my dear lord,
        that could profit you little.
        You cannot be my physician,
        so why bother to question me?
        Telling of one's pain
        only makes it worse, or so it seems,
        for joy and suffering
        can never rest together in company.

XVI   For if I call to mind my distress
        my sadness will grow all the more—
        although there is precious little
        joy left in me now. But he is wounded all the more
        who lets himself fall twice
        rather than just once,
        for it is pure stupidity
        to fall again when you know already of the trap."

XVII   "Madame, il est bien verité:
                Ce que vous dictes vous congnois,
                Mais on prend bien joyeuseté
                Par bon conseil aucunesfois.   132
                On ne doit pas en tous endroiz
                Croire le veul de son courage,
                Et aussy nous remonstre drois
                Que folleur n'est pas vasselage."   136

XVIII   Lors dit elle: "Bien vous veul dire
                Partie de ma desplaisance,
                Quombien qu'en France et en l'Empire
                On a bien de moy congnoissance: 140
                On m'a mis sus par ignorance
                Ung criesme, dont j'ay sy grant dueil
                Que je ne puis prendre plaisance
                Ains suis de morir en l'escueil."   144

XIX   Ainssy que la dame parloit,
                Moy cuydant dire sa pensee,
                Une clarté aönda droit
                Sur nous, qui tant fut esmeree   148
                Et d'estranges rayz dÿapree
                Qu'elle sambloit, tant estoit nette,
                De fine flambe figuree,
                Plus clere qu'eselistre ou comette,   152

XX   Dont nous eusmes sy grant frëur   [91v]
                Que pasméz cheïsmes a terre,
                Car la clarté, par sa vigueur,
                Nous sceut en pou d'eure concquerre.   156
                Riens n'eust vallu effort de guerre:
                Sans deffence nous couvint rendre
                Et le vray Dieu d'Amours requerre
                Pour sa doulce mercy attendre.   160

XVII   "Madam, it is true.
You know of what you speak,
but one can take comfort
sometimes in the advice of others.
One mustn't always
follow the will of one's heart,
for as the law proves,
acting compulsively is not worthy or wise."

XVIII   Then she replied, "I wish to tell you
a bit about my distress:
in France and all over the empire
I am known.
Out of ignorance has been attributed to me
a crime, which causes me such grief
that I can find no pleasure in life,
and so I am on my way to die."

XIX   As the lady was speaking,
eager to share with me her thoughts,
a flash of light suddenly enveloped us
Which was so pure and refined
and diapered with rays so strange
that it seemed by its intensity
to be created of sheer fire,
brighter than a star or comet.

XX   We were so struck with fear
that we fell to the earth in a faint.
The light's brilliance, by its vigor,
struck us down in a flash.
Calling for help would have been futile;
we had to surrender without a fight
and then pray to the God of Love,
while waiting upon his mercy.

XXI   Si comme estiesmes en tel trance,
Une tresdoulce voix oÿs
Qui nous dit: "N'ayés pas doubtance,
Car nous sommes a vous transmis   164
Du tresamoureux paradis,
Comme messagiers invisibles,
Affin que soyez advertis
Des doulleurs qui vous sont nuysibles."   168

XXII   Et puis fut a la dame dit:
"Le Dieu d'Amours noble et haultain,
Dont nul lëal cuer ne mesdit,
Veult estre adverty et certain   172
De ton fait. Car nul cas villain
Ne veult impugny demourer,
Ains sommierement et de plain
Veult droit pour chacun ordonner.   176

XXIII   Pour ce, veult devant sa personne
Ta cause estre determinee,
Pour vëoir s'elle est faulse ou bonne."
Puis me dist: "La chose ordonnee   180
Est par Amour et disposee
Que tu compaignes ceste dame;
Son veul et plaisir s'y agree,
Afin que de ce fait soit fame."   184

XXIV   Aprés ces motz fusmes ravis   [92r]
Et en hault en l'air eslevés,
Et nos corps materïelx vifs
Angeliquement ordonnés,   188
Et puis impalpables müés,
Et plus, car par especïal,
Nos membres sembloient fourmés
De matiere de fin cristal.   192

XXI

As we were in this trance
I heard a sweet, soft voice
say to us: "Have no fear!
We have been sent to you
from the Paradise of Love
as invisible messengers
so that you might be advised
on the sufferings that torment you now."

XXII

And then was directed at the lady:
"The glorious God of Love,
whom no true heart despises,
desires to recognize and ascertain
the circumstances of your plight, for no case of villainy
should remain unpunished;
rather, summarily and without delay
he wishes to grant justice for all.

XXIII

For this reason, he requires that before him
your case be presented
to see if it is flawed or justified."
Then he turned to me: "It has been decreed
by Love and ordained
that you accompany this lady.
This is his wish and desire
so that the case might be publicized."

XXIV

After these words, we were suddenly swept away
high up into the heavens,
and our bodies of mortal material
were transformed into one intangible,
and became like that of the angels
or, to be more exact,
our bodies seemed to be made
of a pure, fine crystal.

XXV   En ce point fusmes, se me samble,
               Portéz devers soleil levant,
               Moy et elle tousjours enssemble.
               Lors entrasmes incontinent   196
               En ung ciel a merveilles grant
               De parfaicte rouge couleur,
               Que je percheus, a mon semblant,
               Hommes et femmes a dolleur.   200

XXVI   Lors me dist mon intelligence:
               En ce point sont les orguilleux,
               Qui n'ont point eu en reverence
               Les treshaultains faiz amoureux,   204
               Et qui ont esté curïeux
               D'amer presumptüeseté,
               Dont par leur semblant desdaigneux
               Ont lëaulx amans despité.   208

XXVII   De cestuy en ung aultre vinsmes,
               Qui de fin vert fu coullouré,
               Ou pluiseurs personnes veïsmes,
               Chacun d'estrange vert paré   212
               Et tres souvent renouvellé.
               Bien sambloient gens miserables
               Et c'estoient ly condempné
               Qui furent en amours müables.   216

XXVIII   Oultre ce ciel, ung en trouvasmes   [92v]
               De bleu et de blanc imparty;
               Tout au travers le trespassames.
               De cestuy envis me party,   220
               Car mainte amie et maint amy
               Y recepvoient tant de joye;
               De ce suy je bien adverty,
               Que recorder ne le sauroie.   224

XXV It was at this point, as I recall,
that we soared off into the rising sun.
She and I were still clinging tightly together
when suddenly we entered into
a sky of great marvel;
it was a vibrant red color,
and there I saw, I believe,
men and ladies in great pain.

XXVI And then I realized that this
was the place where the arrogant were lodged—
those who had held no reverence
for the holy acts of love,
who had been intent on
loving presumptuously,
and by this disdainfulness
had humiliated true and loyal lovers.

XXVII From this band we passed into another
that was colored vibrant green,
and within I saw many people
clothed in strange green garments
which changed shades of color rapidly.
They appeared to be miserable people,
indeed, they were those who had been condemned
for their fickleness in love.

XXVIII Beyond this sky we came upon another of
half blue, half white,
and all around it we circled.
I did not wish to leave this place
for many ladies and lovers
received great joy here.
Of this fact I was so well aware
that I could not make myself depart.

XXIX   Et me dist cil qui me portoit:
              "Ce sont les amoureux loyaulx
              En qui Humilité manoit
              Et non mie les desloyaulx.   228
              Gardez vous d'estre en amours faulx,
              Se bon conseil croyrre voullez,
              Et ne plaindez pas les travaulx
              Dont tel joye acquerre povez."   232

XXX   Dessus cestui ciel ert fondé
              Ung ciel comprenant grant espere,
              Car tout avoit avironné
              Les aultres. Et fut de matiere   236
              La plus resplendissant et clere
              Que je viz oncques en ma vie.
              Nulle aultre a lui ne se compere,
              Tant fut ceste clarté pollie.   240

XXXI   La avoit ung trosne comprins
              De tres exellente haulteur
              Sur lequel Amour fut assis
              Comme souverain empereur;   244
              Mais tant fut de clere coulleur
              Avironné et d'ardans rais,
              Qu'il n'est sy vif ymagineur
              Qui de sa fourme eust veu les trais. 248

XXXII   Dessoubz avoit a tous costés   [93r]
              Judicïaires sieges grans,
              De fines pierres äournés,
              Entretailliés de dÿamans   252
              Et d'escharboucques tant luysans
              Qu'a poy regarder les povoye,
              Sur lesquels estoient seans
              Pluseurs gens que je congnoissoye: 256

XXIX

And the one who had brought me here said:
"These are the loyal lovers
in whom Humility reigned
and who were never disloyal.
Take care never to be false in love,
if you wish to accept my good advice,
and never complain of the necessary travail
by which you, too, might attain such glory."

XXX

Above this heaven there was
another that was a great sphere.
It was surrounded by all of the others,
and was made of a matter
more resplendent and bright
than any I have ever seen in my life.
No other could compare to it,
so perfect was its light.

XXXI

And there was a throne
that rose to a most excellent height,
upon which Love was seated
as the sovereign emperor.
He was surrounded by color so bright
and such brilliant rays of light
that not even the best portraitist
could capture the features of his face.

XXXII

Below on all sides there were
large judicial seats elevated:
adorned with precious stones,
and incrusted with diamonds
and red carbuncles shining
so that I could scarce look at them.
Upon these were seated
many personages whom I knew well.

XXXIII   Premier y viz Honneur sëoir,
       Lëaulté, Verité, Celer,
       Souvenir, Doulx Regard, Espoir,
       Pitié, Mercy et Doulx Penser,   260
       Bel Acueil, Gracïeux Parler
       Franc Vouloir, Desir et Largesse,
       Qui ne fait pas a oublïer,
       Car c'est de donner la maistresse.   264

XXXIV   Et ou millieu d'un ciel plus grant,
       Plus que mille riens par dessus,
       Y avoit une estoille errant,
       Laquelle on appeloit Venus,   268
       Qui ses rais avoit estendus
       Par dessus tous ceulx de la court
       Tant doulcement qu'a dire plus
       On pourroit bien faillir tant court.   272

XXXV   La fut la dame jus posee
       Et moy; puis ouÿs prestement
       Que sillence fut imposee.
       Et lors amesureëment   276
       Amours parla moult doulcement,
       Disant: "C'est nostre voullenté
       De faire lëal jugement
       En nostre rëal magesté,   280

XXXVI   Pour une cause encommencee   [93v]
       Entre Espoir, nostre procureur,
       Qui fut par Desir prononcee,
       En cas de criesme ou deshonneur   284
       De ceste dame, pour l'erreur
       Oster, que nostre court n'empire.
       Espoir et Desir, sans faveur,
       Dictes ce que vous voullez dire."   288

XXXIII	First I saw Honor sitting there,
	and Loyalty, Truth, Concealment,
	Memory, Sweet Look, Hope,
	Pity, Mercy, and Sweet Thought,
	Fair Welcome, Gracious Talk,
	Free Will, Desire, and Generosity,
	who must not be forgotten,
	for she is the mistress of giving.
XXXIV	And in the middle of the heaven, greater
	and higher than any other by far,
	there was a roving star,
	the one they call Venus,
	whose rays extended
	over all those of the court
	so sweetly and softly that to try to say more,
	quite frankly, would be impossible.
XXXV	It was here that the lady was placed on the ground
	and me as well. Then suddenly I heard,
	that silence had been ordered.
	At that moment, slowly and deliberately,
	Love spoke sweetly,
	saying, "It is our will
	to grant a true and binding judgment,
	in accordance with our royal majesty,
XXXVI	for this case brought forth
	by Hope, our prosecutor,
	and which was introduced by Desire,
	alleging the crime or dishonorable conduct
	of this lady, or to exonerate her from erroneous allegations
	which might tarnish the reputation of our court.
	Hope and Desire, speak impartially,
	and say what you wish."

XXXVII   Lors est Desir avant passéz
Et dist: "Amoureux Dieu haultain,
La Court est advertie assez
Pour quoy d'elle je me complain;   292
Je diz que par son cuer villain,
Et par son regart plain de vice,
Elle a ung amoureux certain
Murdry, estant en son service.   296

XXXVIII   Comme aultrefois ay proposé,
Je tens qu'elle soit condempnee,
Pour avoir vostre edit faulsé,
D'estre entierement desgradee   300
De non de dame estre appellee,
Et getee en chartre de dueil,
Et par plains et plours gouvernee;
A ce contens comme je sueil."   304

XXXIX   Tantost Amours arraisonna
Ceste dame et lui dist sans yre:
"Sachiés quel lieu sa raison a:
Il vous couvient response eslire;   308
Fort content a vostre martire.
S'excuser ne vous en savés,
Vous pourriés bien avoir du pire
S'aucune coulpe en cë avés."   312

XL   Adonc la dame simplement,   [94r]
A deulx genoulx, toute esplourée,
Dist: "Amours, vous savés comment
Je suy cy venue esseullee,   316
De conseil nue et esgaree;
Plaise vous a moy ordonner
Aucun conseil, s'il vous agree,
Pour ma bonne cause garder."   320

XXXVII   Then Desire passed to the front
              and said: "Exalted God of Love,
              the court is well informed
              of the reasons why I accuse this woman.
              I contend that by her base heart
              and by her glance, full of deceit,
              she has murdered a certain lover
              who was then in her service.

XXXVIII   As I have already stated,
              I believe that she should be found guilty
              of breaking your law
              be disrobed entirely
              of the name of lady
              and thrown in the prison of suffering,
              and thus governed by wails and weeping.
              This I contend and require, as I should."

XXXIX   Love then addressed
              the lady and said to her without anger:
              "Know well that his speech has merit;
              it would do well for you to respond,
              for he is intent upon your conviction.
              If you do not succeed in exonerating yourself,
              you risk an even graver sentence
              if you are found to have any guilt in this affair."

XL   Then the lady, very humbly,
              sank down on her knees, weeping,
              and said: "Love, you know how
              I came here before all alone
              with no counsel, and completely lost.
              If it please you, order someone
              to be my lawyer, according to your will,
              in order to conduct my defense."[1]

XLI
"Quel conseil voullez vous avoir?"
Elle dist: "Je vueil Verité
Et Lëaulté, qui scet de voir
Mon courage et ma voullenté."   324
Lors dist Amours a Lëaulté
Et a Verité: "Levez sus
Par vostre debonnaireté,
Puis que ne veult fors vous sans plus."   328

XLII
Verité descendy adoncques,
Et Lëaulté, la demoiselle;
Deux meilleurs ne crea Dieu oncques.
Puis vindrent parler a la belle,   332
Et celle, qui de paour chancelle,
Les a d'une part appellés,
Ou elle leur dist sa querelle;
Puis sont arriere retournés.   336

XLIII
Verité premiere parla
Et dist: "Treshault et Puissant Sire,
Ceste dame requise m'a,
Ce que ne lui vueil escondire,   340
Puis qu'elle m'a volu eslire;
Sy requiers que, se sus personne
De la court me couvient rien dire
Pour sa cause, on le me pardonne.   344

XLIV
Il est vray, ad ce que j'entengs,   [94v]
Que Desir met sus ceste dame,
Et Espoir, qui cy est presens,
Injure, villennie, et blasme,   348
Pour lui oster sa bonne fame
Par leurs propos cy recitéz,
Qu'elle soit reputee infame
Par fais que je tieng repetéz.   352

XLI	"Which lawyer do you wish to defend you?" She said: "I want Truth and Loyalty, who in truth know my heart and my wishes." Then Love said to Loyalty and to Truth: "Get up, then, by your grace, for she will have no one but you."
XLII	Truth climbed down from her seat, as well as Loyalty, the damselle: two better creatures God has never made. They came to talk to the beautiful lady and she, quivering with fear pulled them to one side, where she told them her controversial story; and then they returned.
XLIII	Truth spoke first and said: "Your highness and most powerful lord, this lady has requested of me something that I do not wish to refuse, for she has chosen me specifically. So if it happens that I must say anything about anyone in this court in trying this case for her, I beg their pardon.
XLIV	It is true, from what I understand, that Desire accuses this lady, as well as Hope who is here present, of assault, vile deeds, and blasphemy, with the aim of stripping her of her good reputation in accordance with their indictment, repeated here, so that she be reputed in disgrace by facts that I hold to be hearsay.

XLV   Or, ne voullons nous mie prendre
               Contre la court conclusions
               Declinatores pour pretendre,
               Par aucunes exepcions,   356
               De plaidier par dillacions,
               Car nous n'y querons accessoires,
               Mais voullons par vives raisons
               Proposer nos fais peremptoires.   360

XLVI   Et disons en nostre mageur
               Que, selon droit, povons trouver:
               Tantost que dame a mis son cuer
               A vous servir et honnourer,   364
               Vous lui avez vollu donner
               Franchise, tout a son voulloir,
               Pour a son plaisir en user
               Qui que s'en puist plaindre ou dolloir.   368

XLVII   Et que se pluiseurs amoureux
               La requierent aucunement,
               Elle puet choisir l'un d'iceulx
               Qui sera mieulx a son tallent,   372
               Selon vostre loy proprement,
               Car pour la liberté qu'elle a,
               Puet retenir tout franchement
               Serviteur, tel qu'il lui plaira.   376

XLVIII   Mais il y a une aultre loy   [95r]
               Faitte en faveur de Lëaulté:
               Car puis q'une dame a pour soy
               Choisy servant a voullenté   380
               Et de lui prins la fëaulté,
               Et depuis aultres la requierent,
               Elle, sans varïableté,
               Doit refuser tout ce qu'ilz quierent.   384

XLV   We do not wish to call for
       a motion of dismissal before the court
       in order to present
       our several points of defense,
       nor to employ dilatory tactics to postpone the trial;
       we have no need to introduce additional witnesses,
       but rather will convince the Court
       by the exhibiting of indisputable facts.

XLVI   And we put forth as principal argument
       a point that can be proven according to the law.
       By the time a lady has set her heart
       to serve and honor you,
       you will have already given her
       Free Will, according to her wishes,
       to use at her pleasure, and without regard
       to the complaints or sufferings of others.

XLVII   And so if several lovers
       ask for her grace in some manner or another,
       she can choose among them
       the one who will be most to her taste,
       acting in accordance with your law;
       for within the liberty she has been granted,
       she can keep in good conscious
       the servant who pleases her.

XLVIII   But there is another law
       written in favor of Loyalty:
       once a lady has willingly chosen
       for herself a servant,
       and she pledges him her fidelity;
       if later others ask for her grace,
       she, without wavering,
       must refuse everything they ask for.

XLIX   Oultre, par le dessus dit droit,
        Quant aucune dame regarde,
        Et aucun ce regard rechoit
        Aultrement qu'elle n'y prent garde,   388
        Et par sa pensee musarde
        Son cuer juge trop de legier,
        Du vray jugement se retarde
        Par la coulpe du fol cuidier.   392

L   Or savez vous, Trespuissant Dieu,
        Que ceste dame de long temps
        A son cuer assiz en ung lieu,
        En acomplissant vos commans,   396
        Envers ung qui est ses servans,
        Qu'elle a tousjours lëal trouvé,
        Auquel mercy fut ottroyans,
        Comme il avoit bien concquesté.   400

LI   Sur quoy ma bouche vous dira
        Tout le fait au plus prez du droit:
        Nagueres elle se trouva
        En ung lieu ou on s'esbatoit,   404
        Et a son povair se penoit
        Illecq de dansser et chanter,
        Ainssy que faire le devoit,
        Sans nulle maulvaistié penser.   408

LII   Et fut la feste resjoÿe   [95v]
        De tout ce que dire on savoit,
        Et tant joyeusement servie,
        Que nul amender n'y povoit.   412
        Mais Fortune, qui pas ne doit
        Arrester ne dormir ung some,
        Y amena par son exploit
        Ce jour, pour y muser un homme.[3]   416

XLIX   Moreover, according to the aforementioned law,
                              when this lady casts a glance,
                              and someone else receives it
                              in a way other than she intended,
                              and by this foolish notion
                              his heart makes an impulsive decision,
                              he is only postponing acceptance of the true meaning
                              by fault of his ignorant presumption.

L   Now, you know, all-powerful God,
                              that for a long time this lady
                              had committed her heart in a certain place,
                              observing your commandments
                              with respect to one who is your servant
                              and who she has always found to be loyal.
                              She granted him her mercy,
                              for he had earned it.[2]

LI   Now I will tell you with my own lips
                              all the facts of the case.
                              Not long ago, this lady found herself
                              in a place where everyone was enjoying himself
                              and she made every effort
                              to dance and sing,
                              as well she should,
                              without the least malicious thought.[4]

LII   The party was enlivened
                              with every amusement one can imagine,
                              and the dinner was served with joy
                              in such a way that nothing could have been better.
                              But Fortune, who must not
                              stop or sleep even a short while,
                              in his urgency brought there
                              that day, to hide out, a man.[5]

LIII   Tout prestement que l'ot choisy,
           Assez perchut sa contenance,
           Car tousjours avoit enfouÿ
           Son visaige dedens sa mance,   420
           Et soubx umbre de decepvance,
           S'esbatoit de simple maniere,
           Faignant estre plain d'ignorance,
           Mais sous groz becq langue legiere.   424

LIV   A la foiz alloit et venoit,
           Parmy les gens en traversant.
           Et de pluseurs il s'acointoit,
           Ore assis et puis en estant,   428
           Son regart en travers portant,
           Affublé de decepcion,
           Et sur aucuns entregettant,
           Maniere d'abusion.   432

LV   Il avoit bel son voulloir faire,
           Nulz de son fait ne se gardoit.
           Bien savoit parler et bien taire,
           Les oreilles doubles avoit.   436
           Son samblant bien appoint menoit,
           Cy sa parolle, ailleur s'entente,
           Et celle que pou y penssoit
           Ne se gardoit pas de s'atente.   440

LVI   Sy advint que par aventure   [96r]
           Desir, par ung ardant voulloir,
           Avoit mis s'entente et sa cure,
           Comme il en a bien le povoir,   444
           A ung gentil homme esmouvoir
           De sa desordonnee flame,
           Et tant fist, moyennant Espoir,
           Que celle fist choisir pour dame.   448

LIII	As soon as the lady noticed him
	she realized his state of mind,[6]
	for he kept his face hidden
	in his sleeve,
	and, in the shadow of deception,
	he acted as if he were enjoying himself,
	feigning to know nothing,
	but as they say, a big beak hides a lying tongue.[7]

LIV	He went back and forth repeatedly,
	passing through the crowd.
	He met many people.
	Sometimes he would sit, sometimes stand.
	His gaze roved all around,
	cloaked in deceit,
	and cast on certain ones there
	his deceptive intention.

LV	He had no trouble acting out his intention,
	for no one was watching out for his trick.
	He knew how to speak and how to keep quiet.
	His ears, too, were very keen.
	He carried himself well,
	speaking of one thing but thinking of another;
	and she, who was not paying much attention,
	did not protect herself from his snare.

LVI	Then it happened by chance
	that Desire, motivated by ardent determination,
	set his mind and purpose
	to enflame a certain gentleman,
	as he has the power to do
	with his frenzied flame,
	and did it so well, with the help of Hope,
	that he made him choose this lady as his love.[8]

LVII
Combien qu'elle n'y ot pensee
Ne de lui riens ne lui challoit,
En ung seul lieu estoit fermee
Ou son cuer ostaige tenoit;   452
Et ainsy faire le devoit,
Par droit, a mon entendement,
Puis que de Lëaulté voulloit
User, sans double sentement.   456

LVIII
Par ainsy avoit sans partie
Cil de la dame enamouré;
Car vous l'aviez desja partie
Et son fait ailleurs ordonné,   460
De deux pars promis et juré.
Sy n'estoit pas chose legiere
De sy tost avoir discordé
Lëalle amour, ferme et entiere.   464

LIX
Nëantmoins, il ne laissoit mie
Vers elle sa requeste a faire,
Pensif, plain de merancolie,
Moult contendant a lui complaire,   468
Car tousjours prenoit son repaire
En tous les lieux ou elle estoit,
Et sy ne se voulloit retraire
De ce que plus fort lui nuysoit.   472

LX
Tousjours lui comptoit sa raison,   [96v]
Dont elle estoit moult annuyable,
Car celle estoit hors de saison,
Sans quelque tiltre raisonnable.   476
Pas ne lui sembloit recepvable,
Consideré ce que j'ay dit,
Et pour ce, sans parler müable,
Il n'ot d'elle fors l'escondit.   480

LVII However, the thought had not even crossed her mind,
  and she did not care a whit for him,
  for, locked in one spot,
  her heart had chosen its abode.
  And thus she acted as she should have,
  and legitimately, it seems to me,
  for she wished to carry out
  the practice of Loyalty and avoid any duplicity.

LVIII And so this is how he found himself in love
  without being loved in return,
  for you had already engaged her heart
  and determined her fate with another,
  on both sides promised and sworn.
  This was not something to be taken lightly,
  disturbing so soon
  a loyal love, thus far secure and true.

LIX Nevertheless, he would not stop
  pressing her with his request,
  pensive, full of melancholy,
  arguing against her resistance, and trying to please her.
  He kept returning
  to all the places where she was,
  and did not even try to avoid that
  which was doing him the most harm.

LX Instead he continued to argue with her,
  which she found quite exasperating,
  for his quarrel was out of place,
  without reason or justification.
  He never seemed acceptable to her,
  considering what I have told you,
  and for this reason, without the slightest equivocation,
  the only thing he received from her was refusal.

LXI

Car point n'estoit neccessité
Qu'el lui demandast a entendre
Qu'a aultruy eust habandonné
Mercy, a quoy vouloit pretendre.   484
Elle monstroit que condescendre
Ne voulloit pas a sa prïere,
Pour soy eschiver et deffendre
De faulseté et sa maniere.   488

LXII

Aussi Lëaulté ne veult mie
Que dame ait mercy de chacun:
Mercy ne seroit que follie
Qui la mettroit tout en commun.   492
Mercy puet tresbien avoir ung
Et non plus, selon Lëaulté,
Combien qu'il en soit bien aucun
Qui ne sont pas de ce costé.   496

LXIII

Ainsy celui recommenchoit
Par plus d'une fois sa requeste,
Et envers elle prononchoit
Pluseurs fois pour fournir sa queste.   500
Mais petite fut sa concqueste,
Riens a concquester n'y avoit.
Pour ce, se party de la feste,
Quant il perceut qu'il s'abusoit.   504

LXIV

En ce point tant poursuant fu   [97r]
Qu'il ne savoit tenir maniere,
Dont son fait fut apperceü,
Car ung estoit muchié derriere   508
Une haye de verde osiere,
Dont je vous ay parlé devant,
Qui oÿ refus et prïere
Dont il ne se tint pas atant,   512

LXI	For it was not at all necessary
	that she ask him to understand
	that she had pledged to another
	her grace, which was what he wanted.
	She showed plainly that she did not wish
	to yield to his request,
	in order to stay away from him
	and keep herself from any manner of infidelity.
LXII	Loyalty does not wish in any respect
	for a lady to accord her grace to just anyone.
	This gift would become only folly
	if it were appreciated by all.
	She can show pity to only one
	and no more, according to Loyalty
	(even though there are many
	who do not take this side).[9]
LXIII	And so this lover repeated
	his request more than once
	and declared his intent before her
	numerous times in order to carry out his quest.
	But his victory was small,
	for there was nothing to be won.
	And for that reason, he left the party
	as soon as he realized that he was deceiving himself.
LXIV	At this point he was so carried away
	that he could not control himself,
	and this state was perceived
	by one who was hidden behind
	a hedge of green willow branches,
	whom I have spoken of above;
	he heard the prayers and refusal of the lover,
	which he did not leave there,

LXV   Car tout alla en escript mettre
           Ce que ot veü et escouté,
           Et tant par bouche que par lectre
           Publiquement l'a raconté.   ·   516
           Et oultre, de sa voullenté,
           Pour ce qu'elle l'autre escondy,
           Il l'a par son escript nommé
           'La belle dame sans mercy.'   520

LXVI   Puis que dame a mercy donné
           Une fois, il puet bien souffire,
           Qui n'a cuer trop habondonné
           Et de par tous aultres le pire.   524
           Depuis ne chiet que l'escondire,
           Car mieulx vault Lëaulté amer
           Qu'estre condempné ou martire
           Du vert ciel qui tant est amer.   528

LXVII   Mais il ressemble, bien le sçay,
           Ceulx qui contrefont l'amoureux,
           Qui livrent a chacun assay
           Par Faulx Semblant, doulx et piteux.   532
           Qui octroye mercy a ceulx
           Qui scevent jouer de ce tour,
           Avoir convient plain deux orceulx
           De mercy pour sy folle amour.   536

LXVIII   Ce n'est pas amour, mais haÿne;   [97v]
           Ce sont, ensuyant la Guynarde,
           Rosiers poignans plus fort qu'espine,
           Toutes y doivent prendre garde.   540
           C'est dueil et pitié qu'on ne larde
           Ceux qui ainsy veullent avoir
           Mercy a toutes. Quoy qu'il tarde,
           Bien leur en pourra meschëoir.   544

LXV   for he went and put down in writing
what he had seen and heard,
and as much by word of mouth as by letter of the text,
he told the story publicly.
Moreover, by his will and deliberately,
because she had turned away this lover,
he named her in his poem
'the Belle dame sans mercy.'

LXVI   Once a lady has granted her mercy
the first time, it is enough—that is,
for anyone who has not too loose a hold on his heart
(which would make him of all others the very worst).
After this point refusal is the only becoming response,
for it is better to embrace Loyalty
than to be condemned to the suffering
of the green sky, which is so bitter.[10]

LXVII   But he resembles, I know well,
those who pretend to be in love,
who make a pass at all the ladies
in the guise of False Seeming.
She who grants her grace to those
who play this game
deserves two heaping measures
of pity for being deceived by such foolish love.

LXVIII   This is not love, but hate.
These are like the words of La Guignarde,[11]
lovely rosebushes with the very sharpest of thorns,
and all ladies should be on their guard against them.
What a shame! what a pity! that
those people are not burned alive
who would take the grace of all ladies.
Sooner or later, they will surely get their due.

LXIX   Du temps qu'il estoit amoureux,
        Que tant regrette sa maistresse,
        Estoit Mercy si trespiteux?
        Faisoit il lors tant de largesse?   548
        Mieulx vault que l'en tiegne a rudesse,
        Si se sache dame escondire,
        Que par trop user de simplesse
        On se puisse gengler ne rire.   552

LXX   Fault il, se dame est amoureuse
        D'ung qu'elle aura lëal trouvé,
        Qu'elle ait voullenté tant crüeuse
        Que de laisser sa lëaulté   556
        Pour ung de nouvel amusé?
        On la deveroit bien nommer folle
        Se sy tost avoit transmüé
        Son cuer, pour ung pou de parolle.   560

LXXI   Si me samble qu'on a grant tort
        De lë avoir ainsy nommee;
        Il vauldroit autant que la mort
        Fust a toutes habandonnee   564
        Que ce que telle renommee
        On leur portast communement.
        Au fort, mieulx vault tel, que trouvee
        Y fust mercy trop follement.   568

LXXII   Se de ceste dame a mesdit   [98r]
        Sy a il fait de vous, Amours,
        Assés et non mie petit,
        Qui sont tresfaulx et maulvais tours.   572
        Il a nonchié es haultes cours
        Qu'en toutes places mesdisans
        Ont voz povairs et voz honnours
        Tous apatis depuis dix ans.   576

LXIX

During the time when he was so in love
and languishing after his mistress,
did Mercy show pity?
And did he himself show much generosity?
It is better to be considered rude
and know how to say no
than, out of naiveté,
to be mocked and laughed at.

LXX

Is it necessary, if a lady is in love
with a man that she has found to be loyal,
that she submit to a cruel impulse
to abandon her faithfulness
for the newest tease to come along?
This lady should rightly be called crazy
if she so quickly altered
her heart, all for a few pretty words.

LXXI

In this light, it seems they were very wrong
to have named her as they have.
It would be better that death
be decreed to all women
rather than such a reputation
be attributed to them collectively.
Indeed, even this would be better than
to grant one's grace too liberally.

LXXII

And if this man spoke ill of the lady,
so much more did he of you, Love,
often and not lightly,
striking malicious and perfidious strokes.
He proclaimed in the highest courts
that everywhere slanderers
in the past ten years have
diminished your power and honor.[12]

LXXIII   Etes vous donc si pou cremu
             Qu'on se loge sus vostre garde?
             C'est de vous poy de bien tenu,
             Mais je ne prens mie a ce garde.   580
             Quant Bien Celer son avangarde
             Vouldra bien conduire et mener,
             Il fauldra forte arriere garde
             Aux mesdisans pour rencontrer.   584

LXXIV   Ce me samble grant niceté
             De telz parolles mettre avant;
             Ont gengleurs tant de poësté
             Ne tant de force maintenant?   588
             Que sont devenus ly vaillant,
             Qui tant ont honnouré des dames?
             Ou sont ceulx qui ont concquis tant
             Par lëaulté d'amours et d'armes?   592

LXXV   Qu'est devenu Pallamedés
             Lancellot, Tristran et Gauwain?
             Qu'est devenu Dÿomedés?
             Que ne tiennent ilz cy la main?   596
             Fault il pour ung parler villain
             Aux dames perdre renommee,
             Que les bons ont, et soir et main,
             En maint lieu sy tresbien gardee?   600

LXXVI   Il se veult a vous excuser   [98v]
             Que ce n'est fors que l'escripvain,
             Disant qu'on ne le doit blasmer
             S'il est d'aucun fait recitain;   604
             Mais saulf sa grace, il est certain
             Que de son voulloir la nomma
             'Sans mercy' ou coupplet derrain,
             Dont par cë acteur se fourma.   608

LXXIII
Are you so little feared
that one such as this dares lodge under your protection?
He is surely holding you in low esteem,
but this is not my main point.
When Well Concealed decides
to command his front guard to action,
he will need a strong rear guard
to hold off the calumniators.

LXXIV
It seems to me pure folly
to publicize such words.
Do the scandal mongers have such power
and influence in our time?
What has happened to the valiant ones
who so honored the ladies?[13]
Where are they who conquered so much
through loyalty in love and skill at arms?

LXXV
What has happened to Palamidés,
Lancelot, Tristan, and Gauvain?
What has happened to Diomedes?[14]
Why do they not offer us a hand?
Need it be that because of such base talk
we lose before women the fame
earned by the noble ones, fame that night and day
is carefully guarded in so many places?

LXXVI
He gives to you as his excuse
that he is only the copyist,
saying that he cannot be blamed
if he is only repeating what another told.[15]
But with all due respect, it is certain
that he named her quite deliberately
'without pity' in the final couplet,
and by this act proves himself the author of his words.

LXXVII	Ce point est contre lui tout cler:	
	Il ne puet dire le contraire.	
	Par son escript l'offre a prouver,	
	Qui en vouldra le procés faire.	612
	Mais du sourplus me vouldray taire	
	Et retourner a la querelle,	
	Pour entendre par quel affaire	
	Desir de criesme nous appelle,	616
LXXVIII	Disant que ceste dame cy,	
	Faulsement et deslëaulment,	
	A cest vray amoureux murtry	
	Par le regart d'abusement,	620
	Et refusé tant durement	
	Que la mort s'en est ensievye,	
	Comment que ne sçavons nëant	
	S'il est trespassé ou en vie.	624
LXXIX	A ce respons que ce regard	
	Lui sambla jugant son voulloir.	
	La dame dist que de sa part,	
	Ses yeulx ne fist oncques mouvoir	628
	Par quoy il peüst percevoir	
	Que le coeur d'elle fust content	
	Pour lui ne mal ne bien voulloir,	
	Et de ce fait a moy s'atent.	632
LXXX	Quant Nature premiers crea	[99r]
	Les yeulx ou sexe feminin,	
	Amoureux Regart leur donna	
	Humble, trescourtois, et begnin;	636
	Se par nature ilz sont enclin	
	A regarder d'amoureux trais,	
	Y fault il supposer venin,	
	Disant qu'ilz sont faulx contrefais?	640

LXXVII
On this point he is clearly guilty;
he cannot claim the contrary.
He offers the proof in his verses
for anyone who wishes to investigate the case against him.[16]
But I will refrain from saying anything further
and return to the debate at hand,
in order to hear for what reasons
Desire accuses us of a crime,

LXXVIII
saying that the lady before us,
wrongly and against loyalty,
murdered this 'true' lover
with a deceptive glance
and that she rebuffed him so severely
that death quickly ensued—
even though we know nothing really about his fate,
whether he be dead or still alive.

LXXIX
To this accusation, I respond that her glance
was interpreted according to his fancy.
The lady states that, for her part,
her eyes were never roaming in a way
by which he might perceive
that her heart was open to him.
She wished him neither harm nor goodwill,
and I will prove this fact on her behalf.[17]

LXXX
When Nature first created
eyes for the feminine sex,
she gave them Amorous Look,
who is humble, courteous, and benevolent;
if by nature eyes are inclined
to look about with an amorous expression,
must it be assumed that they be poisoned,
and then said that they are deceptive and counterfeit?

LXXXI	S'aucuns par ses yeulx abuséz,	
	Juge ce que son cuer desire,	
	Et dame n'aura de son léz	
	Pensee nulle qui y tire,	644
	Ce fait Desir, qui lui fait d'ire	
	Et nommer Doulx Regart murtrier;	
	Et sy ne fait en ce, chier sire,	
	Sy non son naturel mestier.	648
LXXXII	Et pour soy excuser disoit	
	Que franche voulloit demourer,	
	Mais cil croire ne l'en voulloit,	
	Ains se penoit de la remuer.	652
	S'elle lui eust fait esperer	
	Que mercy deust trouver en elle,	
	Faulse se fust faicte nommer	
	Et a cause tresbonne et belle.	656
LXXXIII	Aprés ce, Desir lui met sus	
	Que bien se congnoist en faulx déz	
	Et changier ceulx du mains ou plus.	
	Ne sçay de qui est advouéz,	660
	Mais s'il se fust bien informéz	
	Des responces par elle dictes,	
	Nulz faulx tours il n'y eust trouvéz,	
	Sy non prïeres escondictes.	664
LXXXIV	Encores Desir a proposé	[99v]
	Parolle et oultraigeuse et trop fiere,	
	Disant que tenu et amé	
	A plus d'un party, sans renchiere.	668
	Par ma foy, c'est laide maniere	
	De proposer contre une dame	
	Chose qui la sienne honneur fiere	
	De deshonneur et villain blasme!	672

LXXXI	If someone deceived by his own eyes
	interprets according to his heart's desire,
	and the lady, for her part,
	does not intuit the same response,
	it must be Desire who makes him, out of anger,
	name Sweet Look a murderer,
	even though he was only following, Your Honor,
	his natural instinct.
LXXXII	And in order to excuse herself, she said
	that she preferred to remain free,
	but he did not wish to believe her
	and so went to great pains to change her mind.
	But if she had given him hope
	that he might receive her grace,
	then she might have been called false,
	and with good reason.
LXXXIII	After this, Desire put forth the accusation
	that she knew all too well how to cheat at dice
	and to change them from lower to higher by loading them.[18]
	Well, I don't know whose lawyer he is,
	but if he had better informed himself
	of the responses she pronounced,
	he would have found no ruse in them,
	but only refused pleas.
LXXXIV	Furthermore, Desire made
	an outrageous and arrogant allegation,
	saying that she had taken and loved
	more than one suitor, and with no difficulty whatsoever.[19]
	Upon my soul, it's foul manners
	to accuse a lady of a
	thing that indicts her high honor
	with dishonorable and base claims!

LXXXV   Elle est de ce pure ignocente,
               Amours, sy vous en requiert droit,
               Tesmoing Lëaulté sy presente,
               Qui d'enfance bien la congnoit.   676
               On diroit bien moins qui vouldroit,
               Et on voit advenir souvent
               Que force de cuidier dechoit:
               Et petit pluye abat grant vent.   680

LXXXVI   On ne peut son honneur acroistre
               De dire d'aultruy villonie,
               Mais soy amendrir et descroistre.
               Car c'est une espesse d'envie,   684
               En cuer de fel gengleur nourrie,
               Qui ja nul bien ne pensera
               Combien qu'il ne s'en tenroit mie.
               Envis moeurt qui apris ne l'a.   688

LXXXVII   Desir dist qu'il ne puet yssir
               Du sac que ce qui est dedans;
               Pluiseurs ont de ce beau taisir.
               Mais nulz mesdisans n'est contens,   692
               Ains cuident acroystre leur sens
               Et leur los par losengerie,
               Disans mesparlers ou contens
               Des dames et de leur partie.   696

LXXXVIII   Que lui a Bel Acueil meffait   [100r]
               Qui ainsy l'appelle abuseur?
               On poeut bien vëoir que ce fait
               Luy procede d'aucune erreur.   700
               Bel Acueil est le conducteur
               De toute honneste conpaignie;
               Et puis qu'en lui a tant valleur
               Raison n'est pas qu'on en mesdie.   704

LXXXV
She is totally innocent of this charge,
Love; therefore, she begs your justice
according to the witness of Loyalty, here present,
who has known her well since infancy.
One could say even less favorable things about her;
it can oft be observed
that the force of imagination can deceive,
and as we know, a little rain can overcome a big wind.[20]

LXXXVI
One cannot increase his own honor
by speaking ill of another,
but in fact only belittles and depreciates his own worth.
For this is just another form of envy,
nourished in the heart of a foolish scandalmonger
who will never have a benevolent thought
and yet does not know how to shut his mouth.
He will die of his envy who does not learn this lesson!

LXXXVII
Desire himself says that nothing can come out
of a bag except that which is already within.[21]
And so many have good reason to keep quiet.
But slanderers are never satisfied:
instead they believe to enhance their conduct
and fame by flattery,
speaking lies and quarreling
about the ladies or their advocates.

LXXXVIII
What did Fair Welcoming do to him
to merit being called a dissembler?[22]
One can easily see that this claim
is based on some error.
Fair Welcoming is the guide
of all honorable company,
and because in him is such great merit,
it would not be right to speak ill of him.

LXXXIX   Quant ad ce qu'il a proposé
Qu'elle a dit que pas n'estes saige,
Mais de losengiers composé,
Et que mentir est vostre usaige: 708
Cuident ilz avoir avantaige
A telz malvais parlers retraire
Pour porter a dame dommaige
Dont l'entendement est contraire?   712

XC   On prende bien garde a le clause
Qui de tout ce fait mencion:
Et on poura veoir qu'ils n'ont cause
De mettre varïacion,   716
Car ce n'est son intencion
Que de l'amour de ceulx parler
Qui tantost, sans quelque raison,
Voeullent estre améz sans amer.   720

XCI   Ils ont dit que tous amoureux
Elle a appellés goullÿars,
Et que le plus secret d'iceulx,
Quel que part qu'ilz soient espars,   724
Veullent bien que de toutes pars
Les gens dïent qu'ilz sont améz,
Et que nul, soit large ou escars,
Ne sera ja de moy faméz.   728

XCII   Quant a ce point, c'est mal reprins   [100v]
De lui imposer sus telz maulx,
Car elle n'y a nulx comprins
En ceste clause que les faulx,   732
Qui sont malvais et desloyaulx,
Dont on ne puet trop de mal dire,
Mais des humbles et des lëaulx
Ne vouldroit elle pas mesdire.   736

LXXXIX	As for his claim
	that she said you, Love, are not wise,
	that your words are just flattery,
	and that your habit is to lie—[23]
	do they believe it to be beneficial to themselves
	to come back with such perfidious lies
	in order to inflict injury upon a lady
	whose intention is in fact quite the contrary?
XC	Careful attention should be paid to the clause
	where this point is made;
	then one will be able to see that they have no justification
	for the slightest difference of interpretation on this point,
	for it was never her intention
	to speak of love with those
	who, on the spot and without reason,
	wish to be loved without loving in return.
XCI	They declared she said that
	all lovers are rakes
	and that even the most discreet among them,
	wherever they might find themselves,
	wish that in every corner
	people talk about them and say that they have a lover.[24]
	And (she added) no one, be he generous or stingy,
	will ever gloat like that at my expense
XCII	On this point, it is wrong
	to impute to her such injurious words,
	for she meant only to include
	the false lovers in her accusation,
	those who are degenerate and faithless and
	about whom one cannot speak critically enough.
	But the humble and the loyal lovers
	she had no wish to blame.

XCIII   Aussy ce qu'elle respondoit
A cest amoureux mal content
A nulle aultre fin ne tendoit
Sy non appaisier son tourment,   740
Par quoy il sceust vrayement
Qu'il perdoit a elle sa paine
Et qu'il peüst plus plainnement
Percevoir sa requeste vaine   744

XCIV   Et pour la matiere conclurre,
Et nostre fait mettre en briefté
Et esclarchir la cause obscure,
Disons aussy que Lëaulté   748
Avoit receu la fëaulté
Et le serment de ceste dame,
Laquelle a bonne voullenté
De la servir tant qu'elle ait ame.   752

XCV   Par quoy elle ne devoit mie
Estre en plus d'un lieu amoureuse,
N'a plus d'un seul amant amie
Pour prïere, tant fust piteuse;   756
Ainchois devoit estre gracieuse
De bien sa promesse garder
Et d'escondire curïeuse
Pour son bon renom amender.   760

XCVI   Et par ainsy n'est point coulpable   [101r]
Se pour ce l'amoureux est mort.
Desir en seroit plus cappable,
Car desirer le fist a tort   764
Et le meist en mer loing de port
Par desirer sans congnoissance;
Car trop desirer sans confort
Fait chëoir en desesperance.   768

XCIII	In addition, what she said
	to this unhappy lover
	had no other aim
	than to allay his torment,
	so that he would know truly
	that he was wasting his time on her,
	and so that he would be able to perceive
	plainly the futility of his pleas.

XCIV	To conclude this matter,
	I will sum up our argument briefly
	and enlighten the unknown point of our case.
	We adjoin that Loyalty
	did receive the faithfulness
	and promise of this lady,
	whose firm intention
	it was to serve her as long as she lived.

XCV	This is the reason she should not have
	placed her heart in more than one place,
	nor had more than one single lover,
	no matter how piteous the prayers.
	However, she should certainly have been careful
	to keep her promise
	and to ward off any curious eyes
	in order to maintain her good reputation.

XCVI	Therefore, she is not guilty
	even if the lover died because of her action.
	Rather, Desire would be the more likely suspect,
	for in error did he inspire the desire for her
	and put the lover out to sea, far from any port,
	when he made him desire without any understanding.
	For too much desire with too little consolation
	makes a man fall into despair.

XCVII   Le tresardant voulloir Desir
            Contendoit sa voullenté faire
            Et ne pensoit qu'a son plaisir
            Et a son desirier complaire;   772
            Ce povoit plus l'amant deffaire
            Que la dame, a ce que je sens,
            Car il ne se povoit retraire,
            Tant lui fist Desir de tourmens.   776

XCVIII   Et ainsy Desir l'aveugla,
            Par quoy tantost Espoir perdy,
            Car sa raison trop mal rigla,
            Tant qu'en desespoir descendy.   780
            Puis qu'Espoir s'en estoit fuÿ,
            La Mort y voult callengier droit,
            Et cil pas ne se deffendy
            Car Desir son scens empeschoit.   784

XCIX   Et pour ce, puissant Dieu Haultain,
            Qui de tout ce le vray savez
            Et que vous en estes certain,
            Je dy aussy que vous devez   788
            Ces faiz savoir tous aprouvéz
            Pour de ce la sentence rendre
            'Et jugïer, se c'est voz grés,
            Car prestz sommes de droit attendre   792

C   En concluant que ceste dame   [101v]
            Soit de son honneur reparee
            Et remise en sa bonne fame
            Et Lëalle Dame appellee,   796
            En revocant la renommee
            Qu'on lui a porté jusques cy,
            Car trop a esté surnommee
            D'appeller 'Dame Sans Mercy.'"   800

XCVII   The ardent determination of Desire
         was intended to accomplish his will,
         and he considered only his own pleasure
         and the enjoyment of this desire.
         This could have been the lover's undoing,
         even more so than the lady's action, I believe,
         for he was unable to disengage himself
         as long as Desire continued to torment him.

XCVIII   And thus Desire blinded him,
         causing him to lose all Hope on the spot
         since he could not control his thoughts,
         and so he descended into despair.
         Since Hope had left him,
         Death came and called forth his due,
         and the lover knew not how to defend himself,
         for Desire had shackled his reason.

XCIX   And so, most powerful God on high,
         you who know the truth of everything
         with the greatest certitude,
         I say to you that you must now
         recognize these facts as proven beyond doubt
         and therefore render your opinion accordingly
         and make your judgment, if it be your will,
         for we are ready to hear your justice be served

C   by your concluding that this lady
         be restored her honor
         as well as her good reputation
         and that she be called 'loyal lady'—
         revoking thus the bad name
         that she had been carrying up to this point,
         for she was named too cruelly
         when called the 'lady with no mercy.'"[25]

CI
Lors reprist Desir la parolle
Aveuc Espoir le procureur,
Tout plainement, sans parabolle,
En disant: "Trespuissant Seigneur,   804
Vous savez que comme accuseur,
Nous avons proposés noz fais,
Qui se proeuvent sans nulle erreur
Par les livres qui en sont fais.   808

CII
Et quant est aux fais de deffences
Qu'elle a fait contre proposer,
Aussy de toutes les offences
Dont oÿ l'avés accuser,   812
Sans aultres tesmoings deposer,
En vous nous nous en rapportons.
A ce nulz ne puet opposer:
Vous savez qui est faulx ou bons."   816

CIII
Tantost le Dieu d'Amours parla,
Et dist: "Nous savons tout de voir
Que ceste dame qui est la
A de pieça fait son devoir   820
De noz haultains biens recevoir
Soubx le penon de Lëaulté,
Pour quoy lui feïsmes avoir
Ung servant a sa voullenté.   824

CIV
Or avons nous bien entendu   [102r]
Toutes ses excusacions,
Et comment Desir contendu
Avoit par ses conclusions;   828
Et pour ce, jugier en voullons
Par entre vous tous, noz subgétz
Cy presens, afin que soyons
Tousjours droicturier reputés."   832

CI	Then Desire took the floor,
	with Hope, the prosecutor,
	and plainly, without embellishment,
	he said, "Almighty Lord,
	you know that, as prosecutors,
	we have presented our case
	and proven the facts beyond a reasonable doubt
	with the words from the books that have been written.

CII	As to the defensive argument
	that she has proposed
	as well as all the accusations
	you have heard her cast,
	without even deposing any additional witnesses,
	well, we leave the case in your hands,
	for this no one can deny:
	you know who is false or true."

CIII	Without hesitation, the God of Love spoke,
	and said, "We know to be true
	that this lady before us
	has done what is required of her, and for some time now,
	having received our holy goods
	in the name of and under the flag of Loyalty:
	for this reason, we gave her
	a servant according to her desire.

CIV	Indeed, we have heard
	all of her justifications
	and how Desire has contested her defense
	in his rebuttal.
	And so we wish to conduct our deliberations
	in consultation with you all, our subjects
	here present, so that we shall
	always maintain our reputation for fairness and justice."

CV   Adonc se mirent tous enssemble,
            En conseil et longtemps parlerent
            A Amours, si comme il me semble,
            Et pluseurs livres retournerent.   836
            Puis incontinent appellerent
            Les parties pour oÿr droit,
            Et presentement ilz ordonnerent
            Que la sentence renderoit.   840

CVI   Je croy que Gracïeux Parler
            Fu ordonné d'icelle rendre;
            y commença a recorder
            Toutes les fins, pour mieulx entendre   844
            A quoy chacun voulloit pretendre.
            Puis pronuncha moult doulcement,
            En languaige doulx a comprendre,
            Ce que vous orrés prestement: 848

CVII   "La court vous dit, par jugement
            Et par arrest, que ceste dame
            Va delivre tout plainnement
            Des conclusions et du blasme   852
            Contre elle prises comme infame,
            Et veult qu'elle ait non a tousjours,
            Sans ce que nuls plus la diffame,
            'La Dame Lëalle en Amours.'   856

CVIII   Et oultre, pour pluseurs meffais,   [102v]
            Dont la court vouldra poursivir
            Desir et Espoir, qui ont fais
            Aux serviteurs d'Amours sentir,   860
            Et la mort de mains consentir,
            On les adjourne sans delay
            Par devant Amours pour servir
            Au premier jour du mois de may."   864

CV	Then they all gathered together
	behind closed doors and spoke at great length
	with Love, according to what I gathered.
	They requested many different books
	and then without delay called
	the parties together to hear the opinion;
	then they quickly ordered
	that the judgment be rendered.

CV

Then they all gathered together
behind closed doors and spoke at great length
with Love, according to what I gathered.
They requested many different books
and then without delay called
the parties together to hear the opinion;
then they quickly ordered
that the judgment be rendered.

CVI

It was Gracious Speech, I believe,
who was ordered to declare the verdict.
He began by recalling
all the terms of the case, to ensure a clearer understanding
of the claims that each side wished to make.
Then he spoke quite courteously,
in a language sweet to hear,
saying what you will hear now:

CVII

"The court declares its judgment
and verdict: that this lady
will be acquitted fully
of the accusations and charges
made against her as if she were dishonorable,
and orders that she be named from this time forward
the loyal lady in love,
and commands that no longer may she be dishonored or shamed.

CVIII

Moreover, in view of several crimes
that the court will wish to pursue,
Desire and Hope, who made
the servants of Love feel too strongly,
and consented to the death of many such lovers,
are hereby required to appear without delay
before Love in order to surrender to his service
on the first day of the month of May."

CIX   Tantost que Parler Gracïeux
             Ot ainsy sa raison finee,
             Prestement je me trouvay seulx,
             Lez mon cheval en la vallee   868
             Ou la dame avoie trouvee,
             Cuidant comme tous esperdus
             Que ce fust songe ou destinee
             Des parlers que avoie entendus.   872

CX   Mais nëantmoins, consideray
             Que ce fut quelque advision
             Pour oster mon cuer hors d'esmay
             Et de grief lamentacion,   876
             Tant que bonne informacion
             Eusse fait pour appercevoir
             De ma dame l'intencion,
             Et moy garder de decepvoir.   880

CXI   Sy supplie a tous ceulx qui veullent
             Ou service amoureux entrer,
             Que d'ardant desir ne s'aveuglent,
             Car moult est dur a encontrer,   884
             Si comme Verité monstrer
             Le voult adonc pour ceste dame:
             Le service fait bon doubter
             Que ung franc cuer mort et entame.   888

Explicit

CIX	As soon as Gracious Speech
	had finished his declaration,
	I suddenly found myself alone,
	beside my horse, in the valley
	where I had found the lady,
	believing that I had lost my senses
	or that it was a dream or even some premonition of the future
	in those voices that I had heard.

CX	Finally I decided
	that it must have been a vision
	that came to me in order to lift my spirit from despair
	and lamentation
	until that time when I discovered
	some reliable information
	of my lady's intentions,
	so that I might guard myself from deception.

CXI	And so I plead with those who wish
	to enter into the service of Love,
	not to let themselves be blinded by ardent Desire,
	for he is very difficult to resist,
	as Truth wished to show
	in the case of this lady.
	It is well to beware this service of Love,
	which wounds and kills a free heart.

The End[26,27]

Notes

1. Line 320: the Belle dame has been granted a continuance at the end of the *Accusation* (line 589) because no lawyer was willing to take her defense.

2. Line 397: there has never been mention of this secret lover until this point.

3. Line 416: *muser* or *nuiser* (to do harm). Interference from the descending stroke of the letter *x*, above, makes it difficult to determine the reading; both make sense and both appear in other manuscripts.

4. Lines 403–10: *naguere*—the reader's attention is immediately pointed to recall the first word of Chartier's *Belle dame* just as the author will begin to reference this work in the construction of the lady's defense. The party referred to is the one at the beginning of the *Belle dame*, vv. 64 and following, where the narrator first spies the lover and lady.

5. Line 416: this man is Alain Chartier, the narrator of the *Belle dame.*

6. Line 417: there is nothing in the *Belle dame* or the *Accusations* that indicates that the lady ever noticed Chartier at the party.

7. The meaning of this proverb is unclear. *Bec* may be taken to mean "mouth," "nose," "face," or "words"; *legiere* can be understood as "thoughtless," "light," "frivolous," or even "perfidious." Alain Chartier was reputed to be quite ugly, and the expression is directed at him.

8. Lines 441–48: the "gentil homme" is the lover of Chartier's *Belle dame*, of course. Truth goes on to cast the blame for the lover's passion on Desire and Hope, a standard defensive tactic of transferring guilt onto another party.

9. A reference to the *Cent ballades*, a poetic debate written at the end of the fourteenth century in which the old knight Hutin supports the side of Loyalty in love, and a young lady called La Guignarde maintains the opposing side. See Note 11.

10. Line 528: this bitter green sky, reserved for unfaithful lovers, is described earlier in verses 209–16.

11. Line 538: another reference to the *Cent ballades*. Near the end of the series of ballads, the young lover meets La Guignarde, "the Flirt," who proposes that undying love is folly, especially when unrequited, and that it is not disrespectful of Loyalty nor is it false to believe it better to discreetly place one's love in several places.

12. Lines 573–76: reference to the *Belle dame*, vv. 785–92.

13. Line 590–600: the poet is using the ancient elegiac and philosophical motif called *ubi sunt*. This motif, made famous by Villon ("Where are the snows of yesteryear?"), was quite popular in the fifteenth century as a means of showing the fragility of human effort in the passing glory of noble men, ancient civilizations, etc. See Gilson, pp. 31–38.

14. Lines 593–95: well-known lovers from the prose literature. Palamidés is a Saracen knight who falls in love with and kidnaps Isolde the Blond in the *Tristan en prose*; Lancelot is the famous knight who loves Guinevere, King Arthur's queen; Tristan is Isolde the Blond's lover; Gauvain or Gawain is the courteous knight and nephew of King Arthur who is known for his gallantry toward all women. All of these are char-

acters in the Vulgate Cycle. Diomede is the bold Greek warrior in the Troilus legend who wins Cressida's (or Briseida's) love and causes her betrayal to Troilus in the *Roman de Troie*. It is quite curious that the narrator cites as examples of good and loyal love these lovers whose affairs were so destructive.

15. Line 604: a reference to the *Excuse of Master Alain*, verse 216.

16. Line 612: in the prose letters to Alain, a lawsuit is threatened against the author by the ladies and courtiers and a date set for a hearing, the first of April. Alain himself mentions the threat in his *Excuse.*

17. Line 632: the Belle dame's response is recorded in vv. 233–40 of Chartier's poem.

18. Line 659: accusation made by Desire in *Accusations* v. 508 that the Belle dame was loading the dice.

19. Lines 667–68: *Accusations* vv. 301–4. In fact, Desire declared that the Belle dame had used her deceptive "fair welcoming" to attract more than one lover.

20. Line 680: "petite pluie abat grant vent"—proverbial expression that means "the smallest thing can change the course of fortune."

21. Lines 689–90: citation from the *Accusations,* vv. 391–2.

22. Line 698: *Accusations* v. 491.

23. Lines 706–8: reference first to the *Belle dame*, vv. 313–14, 397, but also to the *Accusations*, vv. 413–16, 425, 441–42.

24. Lines 722–26: *Accusations*, vv. 521–25.

25. Line 800: note that it is at line 800 that Alain Chartier, too, names his character "la belle dame sans mercy."

26. *Rejected Readings, Lady Loyal in Love,* : 20. fait Pc; 27. I. m. (-1) Pd; 34. Ung bien (-1) Pb; 37. Pour p. -1 PbPk; 38. Au c. 52. que ne pos c. (-1) Pb; 110. Que c. (-1) Pb; 114. mon p. Pb; 137. Lors me dist celle je vous vueil bien dire (+2) PbPc; 152. eselistre counts two syllables; 202. point les -1 PbPc; 212. de vert -2 PbPc; 274. y ot p. PbPc; 284. et de d. +1 PbPc; 312 ce cas Pc; 314. esplouré PbPc; 382. le PbPc (picardism); 424. son PbPc; 455. lui v. +1 Pc; 477. missing line Pc; 481. point nec-cessite (-1) PbPc; 482. elle; 499. procuroit PbPc; 510. Dont il vous eut p. PbPc; 518. ce l'autri (-1) PbPc; 521. mercy de homme PbPc; 535. Avoir convient deux orceulx Pq; 538. Aussy n'est pain blanc mais guignarde Pc; 550. Se toutes dames l'escon-dire Pc; 558. deveroit counts two syllables; 568. follemement; 569. Le de Pb; 577. cremir PbPc; 579. tenir PbPc; 596. il PbPc; 599. ont soir (-1) Pc; 606. le PbPc; 615. attaindre PbPc; 653. Delle l. e. f. espererer PbPc; 654. Mercy devoit Pb; 559. ou du plus (+1) PbPc; 665. Encores count 1 syllable; 673. pure et i. (+1) Pc; 676. le; 706. plus n. PbPc; 748. Disans Pq; 750. E. s. (-1) Pc; 752. le PbPc; 853. elles PbPc; 878. pour percevoir Pc; 888. tre dur.

27. *Variant Readings, Lady Loyal in Love,* : 1. ne fust Pp; 2. ne f. Pp; 6. ma dame et ma m. Pg; 8. trop PbPc; 15. benivolence Pc; 18. haultaine Pd; 20. q. seul a mercy h. Pg; 22. et seigneur Pb; 27. Inconvenient m. Pc; 31. n. savoye Pq; 44. qui Pb, f. desirant Pd; 46. si v. PbPc; 47. b. volloir Pc; 50. pourprendre PbPc; 52. ne le sceus Pc; 55. v. a prendre Pb, apprendre Pc; 57. heures PbPq; 59. le PbPc; 61. ressembloit Pc; 65.

volee Pq; 70. nulle verdure PbPc; 83. c. a. avoie Pb; 105. m. tendy Pc; 100. mon PbPc; 110. Quel me declarrast s. Pd; 111. Et quelle estoit sa destinee Pd; 113. Hellas Pc; 125. Car Qa; 137. bagaige Pb; 144. A. tost mourir desire et vueil Pb; 147. c. arriva droit Pb; 152. P. reluisans quune planecte Qa; 157. effort ne g. Pb, effray de g. Pc, v. fait de guerre Pg; 160. P. la sienne mercy Pc; 170. D. Amoureux treshaultain PbPc; 189. Et pres Pb, p. que imparables innez Pd; 190. Et pur coral especial Pg; 201–2: L. m. d. en celle indigence/Sont les faulx amans o. Qa; 218. my parti PdPq; 224. Q. racompter [PdPgQa: recorder] n. le pourroye PbPdPgQa, partir je ne m'en povoye Pc; 251. couronnez Pb; 264. Car elle est d'onneur l. m. Pd; 277. p. courtoisement Pb; 307. que son lieu raison a Pb; 314. esgaree Pd; 320. c. moustrer Pc; 333. p. de cautelle Pb; 350. P. les proces Pb; 352. P. motz q. j. t. repetes Qa, reputez Pd, proposés Pc; 362. voulons trouver Pg, pouvons prouver Pc; 374. Car la liberte Pc; 375. t. plainement Pc; 393. treshaultain d. Pc; 396. v. sermans Pb; 397. u. de voz bons s. Pb; 410. saroit Pc; 412. pourroit Pc; 416. l. nuisir PbPq, luy m. PcPkQa; 432. d'informacion PbPc; 448. avoit choysy PbPc; 452. atachie t. Pb; 456. amer doublement PbPc; 457. amoit Pb, estoit Pc; 482. donnast PbPc; 487. P. ly e. et d. Pq; 508. Car cilz e. PbQa; 518. qu'elle l'autre PbPc; 523. desraisonné PbPc; 531. chacune Pc; 532. doublier piteux Pc, double et piteux Pq; 535. A. comme p. d. hostieulx Pq; 548. de noblesse Pd; 550. se face d. Pb; 551. tenir de PbPc; 552. On ne p. gaber Pd; 580. il ne prent pas a Pc; 581. vostre a. Pc; 584. l'encontrer PbPc, lencompter Pk; 590. gardoyent l'onneur Pc; 601. se fait Pq; 608. Dont le propre a. Pb; 613. de son fait PbPc; 638. damours les traiz Pb; 641. par faulx y. Pd; 645. fait frire PbPc; 647. Neantmains ne fait, bien l'ose dire PbPc; 651. chilz c. Pq; 651. ne la vouloit PbPc; 652. la rouver PbPqQa, le nommer Pd, la prïer Pc; 654. Que m. deust t. Pb; 677. b. pis Pc, b. mieulx quil v. Qa; 687. tairoit Pc; 695. D. mains p. au c. Pq, D. faulx parlers Pc; 705. qu'ilz ont PbPc; 711. a dame PbPc; 729. aprins Pd; 739. Qui a a. f. Pc; 741. il sceut vraiement Pb, percheust clerement Pc, il sensuit Pd; 742. perdroit PcPb; 757. soigneuse PbPc; 763. dampnable PbPc; 778. t. party Pc; 793. Si conclüons Pc; 809. infames Pc; 811. diffames Pc; 812. excuser Pc; 813. aucuns t. depposer Pb, disposer Pc; 822. l. pouair Pc; 824. Ung s. Pb; 835. Aux acteurs Pb; 839. Et prestement ilz o. Pb; 840. Lequel Pc; 843. regarder Pc, raconter Qa; 859. ilx ont Pc; 874. occasion Pc; 882. d'Amours PbPc; 888. Qui si tres dur m. PbPc, tres dure m. entame Pk.

The Cruel Woman in Love

Achilles Caulier

S'ensuit La cruelle femme en amours

I   Ne tout aidié, ne tout grevé,[1]   [103r]
                Moitié en vie et moitié mort,
                Ne tout cheü, ne tout levé,
                Entre leesce et desconfort,   4
                Plus triste que joyeux, au fort,
                Fus nagueres long temps pensis,
                Mon cuer ayant plain de discort
                D'avoir ou tout mieulx ou tout pis.   8

II   En cest estat maulvais et bon,
                Dont je ne me loe ne plains,
                Froit que glace et chault que charbon,
                De toutes müabletés plains,   12
                De Crainte et de Desir contrains,
                Chevauchoie apart moy seullet,
                Ainsy logié, ne plus ne mains,
                Comme homme qui ne scet qu'i fet.   16

III   Si vins, comme par aventure,
                Dedens la plus belle forest
                Qu'oncques, je croy, crea Nature.
                Mais je n'y fis pas long arrest,   20
                Car joye a triste cuer desplaist,[2]
                Ce me fu bien lors apparent;
                Car pour approuver qu'ainsy est,
                Pis me fu apréz que devant.   24

IV   Ce fut le premier jour de may,
                Avant le soleil descouchié,
                Que seul estoie en cest esmay,
                Matin levé et tart couchié,   28
                Quant me viz illecq adrechié
                En ce lieu joyeux et nouvel,
                En ung aultre me suy lancié,
                Umbreux et loingtain de revel;   32

Here follows The Cruel Woman in Love

I   Neither fully at ease nor utterly afflicted,
        half alive and half dead,
        neither fallen nor exalted,
        somewhere between joy and pain,
        though more sad than joyful, it is true,
        I was, not so long ago, forever pensive.
        My heart, full of discord,
        overflowed with good or bad, I could not tell which.

II   It was in this state, neither good nor bad,
        which I can neither praise nor blame,
        cold as ice and hot as burning coal,
        plagued with incessant alterations,
        constrained by both Fear and Desire,
        I went out for a ride all alone
        in this shaken state, no better and no worse,
        like a man who knows not what he is doing.

III   Thus I entered, by pure chance,
        into the most beautiful forest
        that ever Nature created, I believe.
        But I did not stay there for long,
        for joy weighs heavily on a sad heart,
        it was never more obvious to me than at that moment;
        and to prove the point,
        I was worse after I entered than before.

IV   It was the first day of May,
        just before sunrise,
        that I found myself so alone and full of dismay,
        having gotten up early and gone to bed late.
        As soon as I saw myself headed
        into this place so joyful and fresh,
        I abruptly veered away down another path
        that was full of shadows and far from all revelry,

V   Lequel estoit une vallee   [103v]
        Ou ne luisoit soleil ne lune,
        Empréz ung flun d'eauwe salee
        Gectant une fumee brune.   36
        Ne sçay par ou m'y mist Fortune,
        Car tant est ce lieu sollitaire
        Qu'oncques n'y vey voye commune:
        Bien moustre qu'ame n'y repaire.   40

VI   En ceste vallee diverse
        N'avoit herbe, fleur, ne verdure;
        Nulle plaisance n'y converse.
        En ce lieu tousjours yver dure: 44
        Püanteur, horreur, et froidure
        Y sont en may comme en janvier,
        Et n'est saison doulce ne sure
        Qui y puist valloir n'empirier.   48

VII   En ce lieu furny de tristresse
        Me commença a souvenir
        De ma gracïeuse maistresse.
        Ne sceuz adonc que devenir,   52
        Bien voulsisse vëoir venir
        La Mort a moy, ou poing la darde,
        Pour faire ma vie fenir,
        Dont le demourant trop me tarde.   56

VIII   Quant pensoye a mes biens passés
        Et a mes presentes dolleurs,
        De vivre tant estoye lasséz
        Que de morir n'avoie peurs.   60
        En grant habondance de pleurs
        M'eust on trouvé, baignant en larmes.
        "Helas!" et müables coulleurs
        Estoient mon cry et mes armes.   64

V	into a valley
	where neither sun nor moon shone,
	next to a pool of salt water
	from which spewed a tawny smoke.
	I know not how Fortune put me there,
	for this place was so isolated
	that I saw no open path,
	a sign that clearly showed that not a soul lived there.

VI	In this dismal valley
	there was no grass, flower, or greenery;
	nothing cheerful was living there,
	for it was always winter.
	Stench, horror, and cold
	remain in May just as in January,
	and no season, mild nor bitter,
	could do anything to make it better or worse.

VII	In this place filled with sadness,
	I started to remember
	my gracious lady.
	I did not know what would happen there,
	but well I wished to see
	Death come to me, his dagger in hand,
	to end my life, because my remaining days
	were passing too slowly to bear.

VIII	When I thought of my past pleasures
	and then of my current suffering,
	I became so tired of living
	that to die no longer scared me.
	Racked by great sobs,
	I could always be found, bathing in tears.
	"Alas!" and constantly changing composure
	became my battle cry and my arms.[3]

IX   En ce doulloureux pensement,   [104r]
      Puis plaisant et puis anoyeux,
      Fus en ce lieu sy longuement
      Que ne fus tristre ne joyeux.   68
      Ung oubly tel dedens moy eulx
      Que je ne scay que je faisoye,
      Et fus grant temps que je ne sceuz
      Se je parloye ou me taisoye.   72

X   En ce fantasïeux estat
      Ou m'avoit ma tristresse mis,
      Fuz grant temps oublïeux et mat,
      Sans memoire, sens, ou advis.   76
      En cest estat, ou riens ne vis,
      Me vint ymaginacion,
      De la quelle fuz sy ravis
      Que j'en entray en vision,   80

XI   En laquelle me fu semblant
      Qu'en ung grant pallais me trouvay,
      Sy diversement en emblant
      Que je ne sçay par ou j'entray.   84
      Sa fourmë en escript mettray
      Au plus prez de ma retenance,
      Et les choses que j'encontray,
      Qui sont de diverse ordonnance.   88

XII   En ce lieu avoit grandes arches
      Fondees sus pilliers divers;
      La pierre n'est point de ces marches.
      Les murs estoient tous couvers   92
      D'ystoires, de diz et de vers,
      En grans ymages eslevéz;
      De merveilles fus tous ouvers
      Comment ilz furent achevéz.   96

IX   Locked in this heartrending reverie,
now pleasing, now distressing,
I stayed in that place so long that
finally I felt neither sadness nor joy.
Such an apathy overcame me
that I was no longer conscious of myself,
and for a long while I did not know
if I was speaking or silent.

X   In this bizarre state of mind
that my sadness had provoked,
long was I dazed and demoralized,
without memory, mind, or reason;
and then, though I could see nothing,
Imagination came to me
and swept me away
so that I entered into a dream,

XI   in which it seemed
that I found myself in a great palace,
so strangely devised
that I had no idea how I had entered.
I will write down a description of it here
as closely as I can recall,
as well of all the things I encountered there,
though it all seemed so bizarre.

XII   In this place were huge arches
set upon extraordinary pillars.
The stone did not come from this area.
The walls were covered
with stories, writings, and poetry,
painted on large mounted canvases.
I was overwhelmed by these marvels
and how they had been made.

XIII   Toutes les choses advenues   [104v]
            Presentes, celles advenir,
            Qui puent estre soubx les nues,
            Au moins dont il puet souvenir,   100
            Et maintes qui ja advenir
            Ne pourroient et n'ont peü,
            Pourroit on bien illecques vëir,
            Qui d'avis seroit pourveü.   104

XIV   Ce lieu n'estoit rond ne quarré,
            Trïangule, ne de mesure.
            D'ymaiges estoit tout paré,
            Les parois et le couverture,   108
            Et de matiere clere et dure
            Et plus pollie que cristal
            Estoit pavéz dessoubz l'allure,
            Pour quoy g'y alloye moult mal.   112

XV   Par la volte des personnages[4]
            Qui estoient cler et polly,
            Choppoye par pluiseurs usages,
            Et mal gré moy souvent cheÿ   116
            Par ce qu'il fist si mal onny.
            N'y pos mon regard arrester
            Sur une chose. Et riens n'y vy
            Dont proprement seusse parler.   120

XVI   Ces histoires dont je vous dis
            Sont de sy subtille nature
            Qu'on les puet percevoir toudis,
            Et aussy bien par nuit obscure   124
            Comme aultrement, quant le jour dure,
            Et aux yeulx serréz comme ouvers;
            Voit on de chacun sa figure
            Transmüer en estas divers.   128

XIII   All the things that have happened,
those present, and those to come,
everything that could happen under the clouds,
(or at least what all can be remembered)
as well as many things that have never,
could never, or were never allowed to happen.
All of this could be seen there
by one who was in the proper state of mind.

XIV   This place was neither round nor square,
nor triangular, nor of any other form.
Everything was adorned with paintings,
the walls as well as the ceiling,
and the paths were paved
with a material clear and hard,
more polished than crystal,
which is why I had a difficult time walking there.

XV   Because of the tiles arranged on the floor,
which were clear and polished,
I stumbled several times,
and in spite of my efforts, I kept falling down
because of the uneven surface.
I could not fix my eye on a single thing,
and I saw nothing there
of which I might speak with clarity.

XVI   These stories of which I spoke
were painted with such subtle skill
that they could be seen at any moment,
by dark night
as well as by the brightness of day,
and with eyes closed as well as open,
and each figure metamorphosed
from one form to another and back again.

XVII   Ce lieu en pluseurs pars trachay   [105r]
       Ou ces choses sont amassees
       Tant qu'envers la fin adrechay
       Ou je viz lettres compassees   132
       De fin or en pierre encassees,
       Les quelles disoient ainsy:
       "Ce lieu de diverses pensees
       Firent Fantasie et Soussy."   136

XVIII Quant j'euchz ceste place veüe,
       Ne sçay combien, poy ou plenté,
       Je fuz ravis en une nue
       Et hault enmy l'air transporté   140
       Dedens la plus belle cité
       Qu'onques regardast creature,
       Ou furent tout li bien porté
       De quoy pourroit finer Nature.   144

XIX   Les murs estoient de cristal,
       Dont la cité fu close entour;
       Combles de precieux metal
       Y avoit sur chacune tour.   148
       Les rues cherchay plus d'un tour
       Pour mieulx voir les choses nouvelles
       Affin qu'en sceusse a mon retour
       Raporter aucunes nouvelles.   152

XX   Les rues estoient pavees
       De jaspre et de fin cassidonne,
       Sans estre enfraintes ne cavees.
       Plus cler y fait que cy a nonne;   156
       Riens qu'armonie n'y rezonne;
       La nuit n'y puet donner eclipse.
       Assez y a merveilleux tronne
       Pour en faire ung Apocalipse.   160

XVII   I went from corner to corner in the place
              where these things were gathered
              until finally at the back I stopped
              at a spot where I saw letters traced
              in pure gold and encased in stone,
              which said in these words:
              "This place of bizarre thoughts
              was made by Fantasy and Worry."

XVIII   After seeing this place—
              I don't know how long I spent there—
              I was ravished in a cloud
              and transported high up into the air,
              until I reached the most beautiful city
              that any living creature has ever seen,
              in which had been brought
              all of the most beautiful things that Nature had ever made.

XIX   The walls were made of crystal
              and enclosed the city;
              each tower was topped
              with precious metal.
              I explored each road more than once
              in order to better see the marvels therein,
              so that I would know upon my return
              how to tell about this amazing news.

XX   The roads were paved
              with stones of jasper and pure chalcedony[5]
              that had been neither broken nor cut.
              The light there is brighter than at noontime,
              and only the sweetest harmony rings out.
              Night has no power to eclipse any of this.
              There were enough marvelous thrones
              to represent the Apocalypse.[6]

XXI   Ou millieu de celle cité   [105v]
                   Avoit ung grant pallais assis,
                   Fondé par grant subtillité
                   Sur cent pillers groz et massis,   164
                   Fais a chincq costés ou a six,
                   Rassamblés par belles archieres;
                   Par dessus avoit maint cassis
                   Plains de pierres fines et chieres.   168

XXII   Empréz ce pallais avoit fait
                   Amours ordonner ung vergier,
                   De tout delice si parfait
                   Comme pour ung dieu herbegier.   172
                   Nuit et jour le gardoit Dangier.
                   La croit gencienne et li balsmes.
                   Sans mercy n'y puet nulz logier,
                   Car c'est le refuges des dames.   176

XXIII   C'estoit le Pallais de Justice
                   Ou se tenoit le parlement,
                   Parfait en ce qui est propice
                   Et pertinent en jugement.   180
                   Quant j'euz veu le commencement,
                   Je m'en allay de le vëoir
                   Ung aultre lieu fait proprement,
                   Qu'on nommoit le Pallais Espoir,   184

XXIV   Ou se logent les amoureux
                   Poursuivans l'amoureuse queste:
                   Qui y demeure, il est eureux.
                   Une aultre place a empréz ceste,   188
                   Que Beaulté fist a la requeste
                   D'Amours, ou demeure Desir,
                   Qui en ce lieu par trop s'arreste:
                   Il a de chauffer bon loisir.   192

XXI	In the middle of this city there was a great palace, founded with ingenious design on a hundred massive pillars, each having five or six sides, and they were all connected by beautiful arcades. Above, the frames of the arches were decorated with the most precious and expensive stones.
XXII	Beside this palace, Love had planted a garden filled with the most perfect delights, as if to host a god. Resistance kept watch over it night and day. Juniper and balsam trees grew there. Those without mercy cannot lodge there, for it is the refuge of ladies.
XXIII	This was the Palace of Justice, where the court held session to discuss anything pertaining to courtliness and justice. After I had seen this first place, I went to see another that also had been perfectly constructed and which was called the Palace of Hope.
XXIV	This was where lived the lovers who were seekers on the quest of love. He who lives here is quite content. There was another place next to this one that Beauty had made upon the request of Love. Here lives Desire, who stops by often, for he has plenty of time to heat up hearts!

XXV   Quant j'eux illecq prins mon exemple   [106r]
             Et que plus n'y voulz demourer,
             Je m'en allay envers le temple
             Venus, la deesse äourer.   196
             Ce jour lui seult on celebrer
             La plus haulte feste de l'an,
             Et n'y ose nulz labourer
             Sur encourre en criminel ban.   200

XXVI   Ce jour y avoit grant aport
             De pelerins et pelerines.
             Tous y arrivoient a port,
             Seigneurs, dames, varletz, meschines.   204
             Pour partir a ses medecines,
             Lui mis ung verd chappel ou col,
             Et se lui fiz en piteux signe
             Sacrefice d'un rossignol.   208

XXVII   Quant faitte euz ma priere entiere,
             Je suis hors du temple passéz,
             Et entré ens ou cymentiere
             Ou gisoient les trespassés;   212
             Par les tombes congneus assez
             De ceulx qui gisoient en terre,
             Qui oncques ne furent lasséz
             D'amer lëaulment sans meffaire.   216

XXVIII   G'y congneus Helaine et Paris,
             Dido, Piramus, et Thibee,
             Leander, Hero, qui peris
             Furent tous deux en mer sallee,   220
             Et Philis qui fut affinee
             Pour Demolphon, et Achillés,
             Peneloppe, la bien amee,
             Aveucq son ami Ulixés.   224

XXV   When I had seen what I wished to see
and no longer wanted to stay there,
I went directly to the temple
of Venus, to give homage to the goddess.
This was the day on which to celebrate
her greatest feast of the year,
and no one dares to work
on pain of punishment for breaking the law.

XXVI   That day there were great offerings
from the pilgrims, both men and women.
They all arrived there with favor,
lords, ladies, squires, and maidens.
In order to participate in the goddess's cures,
I put a green garland around her neck[7]
and, begging her mercy,
offered the sacrifice of a nightingale.

XXVII   When I had finished my prayer,
I went out of the temple
and entered a cemetery
where the dead had been laid to rest.
By the tombstones I recognized the names of many
who were buried there,
who never had tired
of loving loyally without fault.

XXVIII   I recognized Helen and Paris,
Dido, Pyramus and Thisbe,
Leander and Hero, who both perished
in the salty sea,
and Phyllis, who killed herself
for Demophon, and
Penelope, the well loved,
with her lover Ulysses.[8]

XXIX   Apréz ce, m'en vins au pallais   [106v]
           Pour oÿr les causes plaidier.
           Quant vins au lieu, qui n'est pas lais,
           Viz hors d'une salle wydier   228
           Ung gracïeux jenne escuier
           Vestu de noir et faisont dueil:
           De confort avoit bon mestier
           Car il plouroit de cuer et d'oeul.   232

XXX   Quant Amours et les presidens
           Se furent en leurs lieux assis,
           Ains qu'on appellast la dedens,
           Vis cest escuier tres pensis   236
           Mettre a genoulx et lui oÿs
           Devant Amours compter son cas,
           Dont pluiseurs furent esbahis,
           Car ce sambloit ung advocas.   240

XXXI   Quant il ot de bouche parlé
           Et remoustré l'occasion
           Pour quoy il estoit la allé,
           Il prist sa supplicacion,   244
           Ou estoit son intencion,
           Et la presenta au greffier,
           Qui en fist la relacion
           Et le lisy de cuer entiers.   248

XXXII   Ainsy commenchoit sa clamour:
           "A vostre Rëal Magesté,⁹
           Trespuissant Roy et Dieu d'Amour,
           Vray sousteneur de Lëaulté,   252
           Contre qui riens n'a poësté,
           Victorïeux sur les plus fors,
           Vray engendreur d'humilité,
           Et la sourse de mes confors,   256

XXIX
Afterward, I went back to the palace
to hear the court arguments.
When I got to the place, which is far from ugly,
I saw coming out of a room
a handsome young squire
dressed in black and lamenting;
he desperately needed consolation,
for tears were streaming from his heart as well as his eyes.

XXX
When Love and the judges
were seated in their places,
and just before we were called to enter,
I saw this squire, gravely pensive,
get on his knees, and before Love
I heard him outline his case clearly,
which astonished many there,
for he had the air of a lawyer.

XXXI
After he had finished speaking
and explaining the circumstances of the case
that had brought him here,
he took his formal complaint,
in which his grievances were outlined,
and filed it with the bailiff,
who then presented it to the court,
reading it aloud quite willingly.

XXXII
His claim began in this way:
"Before your Royal Majesty,
Almighty King and God of Love,
defender of Loyalty,
against whom nothing has power,
victorious over even the strongest,
font of all true humility
and source of all my consolation,

XXXIII	Supplie humblement le dollant,	[107r]
	Triste et desrobé de leesse,	
	Jadiz l'amy et bien veullant	
	Du povre amant plain de simplesse,	260
	Traittié a mort par la rudesse	
	De sa maistresse sans mercy,	
	Laquelle en deuil et en tristesse,	
	L'a par son dur regard occy;	264
XXXIV	Que, comme il eust esté espris	
	Par le premier esmouvement	
	Doulx Regart de soy rendre pris	
	A sa dame, et puis humblement	268
	L'euist requise que temprement	
	Luy pleust adoulcir sa dolleur,	
	Et le voulsist tant seullement	
	Retenir pour son serviteur,	272
XXXV	La quelle lui ait reffusé	
	Mercy, par son felon couraige,	
	Et par son regard abusé	
	Dont il soit mort, qui est dommaige,	276
	Et depuis soubx ung faint langaige,	
	Par ung avocat contrefait,	
	Ait esté ce crüel oultraige	
	Contourné et jugié bien fait,	280
XXXVI	Dont pour elle restitüer	
	Et remettre en sa bonne fame	
	L'ayés voullu faire nommer	
	'En Amours la Lëalle Dame,'	284
	Pour quoy est demouré ce blasme	
	Sur le deffunct, que Dieu pardoinst,	
	Pour, aprés le corps, pugnir l'ame,	
	A qui la desserte n'est point.	288

XXXIII   humbly begs your grieving servant,
sad and stripped of all happiness,
who was the friend and well-wisher
of the poor sincere lover
who was rewarded with death by the severity
of his mistress who had no pity,
she who killed him by her cutting glance
in grief and sadness,

XXXIV   that, as he had been captured
by the first movement
of Sweet Look and surrendered himself as prisoner[10]
to his lady, and then humbly
requested that without hesitation,
if it pleased her, to soothe his suffering
and to be willing, at least,
to accept him as her servant,

XXXV   she who refused to grant him
her grace, so perfidious in her heart,
and who, by her deceptive glance,
killed him, though it be a shame;
and since then, in a misleading speech,
with the help of a counterfeit lawyer,
twisted and misinterpreted this cruel affront
and judged it a good deed,

XXXVI   for which in order to restore
and reestablish her good reputation,
you wished to call her
'the Loyal Lady in love,'[11]
which is why all the blame
has been lain upon the deceased, God rest his soul,
so that, after the body, his soul might also be punished,
even though he does not deserve it.

XXXVII   Il vous plaise que le procéz,   [107v]
           Prouvé par cavillacion,
           Qui est jugé pour aucuns faiz
           Sceüs par informacion,   292
           Soit remis en son action,
           Pour oÿr nos fais peremptores
           Et la vraye accusacion
           Des meffais, qui sont tous notoires,   296

XXXVIII   Et que lui, Desir, et Espoir
           Ayent a conseil Verité
           Et Lëaulté, qui main et soir
           Tint compaignie au trespassé,   300
           Pour apparoir la faulseté
           Qui fut contre Espoir et Desir.
           Et il vous en saura bon gré,
           Car vous lui ferez grant plaisir."   304

XXXIX   La supplicacion oÿe,
           A dit Amours au supplïant
           Que Verité se fist partie
           Et Lëaulté contre l'amant,   308
           Et que pour riens qui soit vivant
           Ne seroit a nul jour deffait
           Ne rappellé et fait nëant,
           Ce que Verité auroit fait.   312

XL   Celui respond que Verité
           Ne soustint oncqz la querelle
           De celle ou n'a que crüaulté,
           Et s'en rapporte bien a elle,   316
           Car elle savoit la cautelle
           Et la crüaulté que on fist faire,
           De quoy Leaulté ne s'en mesle
           Car Faulseté est sa contraire.   320

XXXVII	May it please you that the trial, argued through trickery and judged according to facts introduced through hearsay, be overturned and retried, so that our indisputable facts might be presented before the court and the real indictment of the offenses made, which are all well known;
XXXVIII	and that this squire, with Desire and Hope, engage as counsel Truth and Loyalty, who morning and evening keep company with the deceased, in order to expose the fraud that was committed against Hope and Desire. This squire will be grateful to you for so doing, and you will make him very happy."
XXXIX	After having heard the request, Love said to the plaintiff that Truth and Loyalty had testified against the lover, and that for no reason on earth might be rescinded nor overturned nor annulled the testimony that Truth had given.
XL	The plaintiff responded that Truth had never supported the case of her in whom there is only cruelty, and he refers back to Truth, who knew of the trickery and the cruelty that was done. Loyalty certainly does not engage in such foolery, for Falsity is her contrary.

XLI   Quant Amours entendy cela   [108r]
              Tantost appella Verité,
              Qui tout lui dit, rien ne cela,
              Comment trestout avoit esté: 324
              "Moy, dist elle, ne Lëaulté
              Ne savons riens de tout cecy,
              Se ce n'est ce qu'en a compté
              Cest escuier qui est icy.   328

XLII   Celle qui se mist en mon nom
              Pour ceste cause soustenir
              Ne fut aultre que Fiction.
              Poëterie lui fist venir   332
              Et ma semblable devenir;
              Et se transmüa Faulseté
              Pour la traÿson parfurnir
              En la samblance Leaulté.   336

XLIII   Non obstant que, qui veult voir dire,
              Nulz ne vous pourroit abuser,
              G'y vouldroie bien contredire,
              Mais on puet bien, par cabuser,   340
              Vostre conseil faire muser
              En tel cas, et le faire abus;
              Et quant par lui voullés user
              Vous n'y prendés garde au sourplus."   344

XLIV   Amours lui dist, "Monstrés moy dont,
              Vous que je tieng pour Verité,
              Que ce fut Fiction adont
              Qui commist ceste faulceté."   348
              "Vous savés, mon tres redoubté,
              Comme, selon l'acteur premier,
              La dame horrible sans pité
              Se monstra plaine de dangier,   352

XLI	When Love heard this, he immediately called forth Truth, who told him, concealing nothing, how everything had happened. "Neither I," she said, "nor Loyalty knows anything about all of this except what has been told by this squire before us.
XLII	The one who presented herself in my name in order to defend the lady's case was none other than Fiction, conjured up by Poetry to appear in my image; she then transfigured Falsity to resemble Loyalty in order to complete the deception.
XLIII	Notwithstanding, if truth be told, no one could deceive you, Love, and I would not wish to assert the contrary. Nevertheless, one can, by trickery, play your council of judges for fools in such a case, and thereby mislead them into making an error. And thus, when you consult their opinion, you do not know to be on your gaurd."
XLIV	Love replied to him: "Show me, then, you whom I hold to be Truth, that it was indeed Fiction who committed this fraud." "You know, my respected lord, how, according to the first author,[12] this lady, horrible and without pity, demonstrated only refusal,

XLV   Non pas tant seullement au mort,   [108v]
           Mais a tous, quant elle disoit:
           'Choisisse qui vouldra.' Au fort,
           Franche vers tous estre voulloit,   356
           Et dist que telle demourroit
           Sans soy dessaisir de son cuer,
           Car ja ne s'en dessaisiroit
           Pour en faire ung aultre seigneur.   360

XLVI   Et vous savez par le tiers livre
           Comment en l'ombre de nous deux
           Fiction dist tout au delivre
           Qu'elle avoit ung aultre amoureux,   364
           Et elle, atout son cuer crüeux,
           A dit de sa bouche que non,
           Dont ment Fiction, c'est ly neux
           Par le quel j'aprreuve son nom.   368

XLVII   Encores y a mainte clause
           Pour mon nom contre elle aprouver."
           "Il souffist, quant a ceste cause,"
           Ce dist Amours, qui fist lever   372
           Son noble conseil pour trouver
           Se le jugement tient effect.
           "Ce n'est pas ore a esprouver,
           Se dist Advis, il soit deffait!"   376

XLVIII   Adonc fist Amours appeller
           La Belle Dame Sans Mercy
           Et la sentence rappeller.
           A peu qu'elle adonc ne s'ochy   380
           Et si fist appeller aussy
           Espoir et Desir sans sejour
           Car s'ilz ont droit, sy convient y,
           Qu'ilz viengnent servir a leur jour."   384

XLV	not only toward the deceased but to everyone, when she said: 'I will choose whom I wish.' Indeed, she wished to remain free from everyone, and she added that she would remain free and not let another take over her heart, for never would she let go of it in order that another might become her master.[13]
XLVI	And you know by the third book[14] how in the appearance of the two of us, Fiction told before the court that she had another lover;[15] and yet she, with her cruel heart, has said with her own lips that this is not so.[16] It is therefore, that Fiction is lying about it; this is the crux of the matter, whereby I prove his identity.
XLVII	And there are many other reasons for which to accuse her on account of my name." "This is sufficient for the case," said Love, who then assembled his noble council in order to determine whether to uphold the previous verdict. "This judgment is no longer valid," said Opinion, "and should be overturned!"
XLVIII	Then Love summoned the beautiful lady with no mercy in order to rescind the verdict. She was on the verge of killing herself, and so Love also called forward Hope and Desire, without delay, for if they are in the right, as it seems to be in this case, they must be present on the appointed day.

XLIX   Espoir et Desir sont venu   [109r]
              Eulx deulx au greffier presenter,
              Et puis fu contre eulx maintenu
              Ce cy par Gracïeux Parler: 388
              "Il est vray que par desirer
              Et esperer trop follement
              Avés vos deux fait definer
              Ung amant doulloureusement.   392

L   Par Desir prinst il voullenté
              D'estre amoureux, loing de confort,
              Et par Fol Espoir enchanté,
              En qui il se fïa trop fort,   396
              Lui vint le mortel desconfort;
              Car lors qu'il failly a s'emprinse,
              Perdy espoir, dont il fut mort;
              S'en soit l'amende a vous deux prinse.   400

LI   Pour ce, contre vos deux conclus
              Que vous soyez mis prisonnier
              Dedens la prison de Reffus.
              Que dirés vous? Il est mestier   404
              Que vous vous sachiés deschargier."
              "Nous respondons a l'abregié
              Qu'on ne nous puet riens callengier
              Car nous n'avons point delinquié."   408

LII   Verité respond pour eulx deux,
              Et dist qu'ilz n'ont riens meffait.
              Müer ne puet le povair d'eulx,
              Le Dieu d'Amours les a parfait.   412
              Se mal y avoit en leur fait,
              La cause en seroit sur Amours,
              Car telz qu'ilz sont, il les a fait,
              Et sy l'ont bien servy tousjours.   416

XLIX	Hope and Desire then arrived
	and presented themselves before the bailiff,
	and Eloquence maintained
	the following against them:
	"It is true that by desiring
	and hoping too excessively
	you both have brought about the death
	most grievously of this lover.[17]
L	At Desire's instigation, he was inclined
	to fall in love, leaving behind comfort.
	And then, bewitched by foolish Hope,
	in whom he had too much faith,
	mortal discomfort overtook him,
	for when he failed at his enterprise
	he lost Hope, and from this loss he died.
	Thus penalty should be imposed on the two of you.
LI	Which is why against you two I conclude
	and hereby order that you be taken prisoner
	and held in the prison of Refusal.
	What say you? For you are obliged
	to respond to the charges."
	"We respond in brief
	that we cannot be charged with any offense,
	for we have not committed any crime."
LII	Truth then spoke for them both,
	saying that they had not done anything wrong;
	their power cannot be altered,
	for the God of Love made them.
	If there is harm in their actions,
	then the cause must be attributed to Love,
	for he has made them as they are,
	and they have always served him well.

LIII   Amours, qui savoit de laval   [109v]
            Quel meffait y povoit avoir,
            Leur dist, "Puis qu'il n'y a nul mal,
            Je vous remetz en vo povoir.   420
            Faictes tousjours vostre debvoir
            Sans estre aux amans estrangiers,
            Et maintenant, de bon voulloir,
            Je vous mes hors de tous dangiers."   424

LIV   Lors Verité et Lëaulté
            Aveuc le dollant escuier
            Sont mis enssemble d'un costé
            Pour la matiere commenchier.   428
            Verité dist tout au premier:
            "Amours, pieca avez sceü
            Que chacun cuer jeune et entier
            Vous doit une fois son treü.   432

LV   Je le dy pour ung vray amant,
            Qui pour sa jennesse acquitter,
            Voult humblement, par cy devant,
            A vous son deü presenter,   436
            Et son cuer hostaige livrer
            Soubx le seël de Leaulté,
            Et a une dame donner,
            Cruelle en l'ombre de beaulte.   440

LVI   L'amant que Mort ainsy prins a,
            Par vostre gré, se rendy prins
            A celle qui peu le prisa,
            Qui des crüelles a le pris;   444
            Car, sans vers elle avoir mespris,
            Le reffusa en desprisant.
            Mais il lui rendy meilleur pris
            Car il mourut en la prisant.   448

LIII	Love, who knew ultimately
	what misdeed might have been committed,
	said to them: "Since there has been no harm done,
	I reestablish you in your rightful position.
	Continue to do your duty
	without ever being far from lovers.
	And now, with goodwill,
	I release you from all confinement."

LIV	Then Truth and Loyalty
	with the grieving squire
	together went off to one side
	in order to begin the trial proceedings.
	Truth spoke first, saying:
	"Love, forever you have known
	that every young and pure heart
	owes you tribute one time.

LV	I say this for a true lover
	who, in order to leave his youth behind,
	wished humbly once upon a time
	to pay you his due
	and render his heart hostage to you
	under the seal of Loyalty
	by offering to give it to a lady
	whose cruelty was masked by her beauty.

LVI	This lover, whom Death has taken away
	with your accord, gave himself as prisoner
	to her who had little appreciation for him.
	She wins the prize for most cruel,
	for even though he had done her no wrong,
	she refused him disdainfully.
	But this only makes him more worthy,
	for he died while still holding her in highest esteem.

LVII
    La crüaulté dont elle usa   [110r]
    Estoit dessoubx acueil enclose
    Par quoy l'amoureux abusa,
    Et Desir bien maintenir l'ose.   452
    Car s'il eüst sceü la chose,
    Comme il apporta de ma bouche,
    Encor vesquist, com je suppose,
    L'amant que Mort en terre couche;   456

LVIII
    Le quel congnoissoit bien l'acueil
    Que celle tousjours lui faisoit
    Acointance de bouche et de oeil,
    Mais Faulx Samblant en congnoissoit.   460
    Faulx Acqueil l'appelle de droit;
    C'estoit le las pour l'amant prendre,
    Que nulle chose ne voulloit
    Que sa doulce mercy attendre.   464

LIX
    Je suis bien de tout informé
    Par ung tres noblë escripvain,
    Bien congneü en renommé,
    Qui vit et oÿ tout aplain   468
    Comment l'amant, de doullour plain,
    Prioit et estoit reffusé,
    Dont on lui donne nom villain
    Pour ce que tout a accusé.   472

LX
    Fiction, dedens son procés,
    Dist que c'estoit ung decepveur
    Faisant de ses yeulx entregetz,
    Et l'appelle faulx informeur.   476
    C'est trop parlé en la faveur
    De celle ou n'a que crüaulté,
    Car l'escripvain y fut meilleur
    Que ce qui n'y eust pas esté.   480

LVII   The cruelty that she employed
      was hidden behind a cordial reception,
      by which she fooled the lover:
      a fact that even Desire dares to confirm.
      For if he had known the truth
      as it just came out of my mouth,
      this lover would still be alive, I believe,
      the very same lover that Death has now lain in the earth.

LVIII   And he knew well the reception
      that she always reserved for him
      by her lips and eyes,
      but False Seeming knew of it, too.
      In fact, I call him rightly 'False Welcoming,'[18]
      and this was the trap laid to capture the lover,
      who wanted nothing at all
      except to aspire to her sweet grace.

LIX   I am very well informed on this affair
      by an excellent writer,[19]
      well known by reputation,
      who saw and heard plainly
      how the lover, full of pain,
      pleaded, yet was rebuffed,
      for which he has been given the name of villain,
      and receives the blame of it all.

LX   Fiction, in the previous trial,
      said that he was a dissembler,
      conjuring up tricks before his own eyes,[20]
      and she calls him a false witness.
      This is going too far in favor
      of her in whom there is only cruelty,
      for the writer is a better authority
      than anyone who was not there.

LXI	Et tant que le fait revela	[110v]
	Qui, se Dieu plaist, sera pugny,	
	Bien fist quant point ne le cela,	
	Car demouré fust impugny,	484
	Et au mains ceulx qui sont honny	
	De telz meschiefs y prendront garde,	
	Car ilz craindront d'estre banny	
	Des biens qui sont en vostre garde.	488

LXII	Mais encores, celui qui ce blasme	
	Lui mist sus, savoit de certain	
	Qu'il estoit mort, Dieux en ait l'ame,	
	Car son engin fu si haultain,	492
	Et son bon renom sy loingtain,	
	Que s'il estoit encore en vie,	
	Je ne viz huy couraige humain	
	Qui l'osast blamer quoy qu'on die.	496

LXIII	Tant le parfist Nature actif	
	En tout qu'on vault encore mieulx	
	De ce qu'il fu une fois vif.	
	Or est il de ce monde escheux,	500
	Mais, se Dieu plaist, il est es cieulx	
	Comme vray amoureux parfait.	
	Je m'en tais et retourne es lieux	
	Ou il est tesmoing de mon fait.	504

LXIV	Il met que celui qui mort gist	
	Tousjours se penoit de prier	
	Celle qui durement lui dist:	
	'Se perchevoir vous fait Cuidier	508
	Que peu de chose vaille chier,	
	Et qu'elle doye plaire aussy,	
	Et vous voullez meismes blechier,	
	Ce ne fay je pas, quant a my.'	512

LXI   Inasmuch as it was he who revealed the crime,
                 which, if God wills, will be punished,
                 he was right not to hide the affair,
                 for then it would have remained unpunished;
                 at least now those who are guilty
                 of such misdeeds will take heed,
                 for they will fear being banished
                 from ever receiving the treasure under your guard.

LXII   Moreover, he put the blame
                 on the writer, knowing full well
                 that he was dead, God rest his soul.
                 For his talent was so laudable
                 and his good reputation recognized so far and wide
                 that if he were still alive,[21]
                 no human heart today
                 would dare cast blame on him, no matter what is said.

LXIII   For active Nature created him to be
                 so perfect in all aspects that this world is better off
                 now simply because he was alive at one time.
                 However, now he is exiled from this world;
                 but, God willing, he is in heaven,
                 as a true and perfect lover.
                 I will be silent now on his account and return
                 to the place where his testimony is relevant to the case.

LXIV   It was maintained that the one who is now lying dead
                 continually pleaded with
                 this lady, who harshly said to him:
                 'If Presumption makes you believe
                 that a little thing has value
                 and that that thing must give pleasure as well,
                 and you wish to do yourself harm, fine;
                 but as for me, I do not wish to do the same.'[22]

LXV   Elle entendoit qu'on fait follie   [111r]
             Qui se met en vostre service.
             La se fourme vostre ennemie,
             Quant tant vo povoir apetice,   516
             Et sy fait de grant vertu vice
             Quant vous appelle Fol Cuidier:
             Ce mot est a son prejudice,
             Combien que nul l'en saiche aidier.   520

LXVI   Qui dist que Cuidier seullement
             L'ait ocy, il fait a blasmer;
             Car se vous n'estes en present,
             Fol Cuidier ne puet faire amer.   524
             Nul que vous ne puet entamer
             Les cuers des hommes et des femmes;
             Aux corps povez tous drois clamer
             Jusques au partement des ames.   528

LXVII   Faire amer est vostre povoir,
             Le Cuidier est faire cuidier,
             Esperer est le fait d'Espoir;
             Ainsy a chacun son mestier.   532
             Quant ainsy est, il est mestier
             Q'ung amant feru de vo darde
             Voist a sa dame publïer
             L'amour et le bien qui lui garde.   536

LXVIII   Pour ce cest amant s'acquitta,
             Qui vaincu estoit par prison,
             D'amer ce qui le despita,
             A tresgrant tort, car nous lison   540
             Qu'onques ne pensa traÿson,
             Mais l'amoit de bouche et de cueur.
             Sa mort fu approbacion
             Qu'il ne fut oncques delinqueur.   544

LXV   The lady meant that it is folly
       to devote oneself to your service,
       and there she declared herself your enemy
       by belittling your power in this way.
       She makes great virtue into a vice
       when she calls you Foolish Presumption.
       This word is so detrimental to her case
       that there can be no help for her.

LXVI   He who claims that Presumption alone
       killed the lover deserves to be blamed himself,
       for if you, Love, are not present,
       Foolish Presumption cannot make one fall in love.
       Only you can engage
       the hearts of men and women;
       over their bodies you can claim all rights
       until the day their souls depart.

LXVII Inspiring love is your power;
       that of Presumption is to make one presume,
       and hoping is the domain of Hope.
       In this manner, each one has his job,
       and thus it is necessary
       that a lover struck by your arrow
       go to his lady and make known
       his love and the esteem he holds for her.

LXVIII In this manner the lover fulfilled his obligation.
       He, vanquished and imprisoned,
       loved the one who held him in contempt,
       though she was wrong to feel this way, for we read
       that never a thought of treason crossed his mind;
       instead he loved her in word and deed.
       His death is the proof
       that he never failed in his duty.

LXIX   Non obstant, par merancolye   [111v]
           Lui dist, pour son orgueil sanchier,
           Que vous estes plaisant follie
           Que le mectiés vous ce dangier;   548
           Et ailleurs, pour vo nom changier
           Qui est tant plaisant a oÿr,
           Vous nomme 'cruel losengier,
           Aspre en fait et doulx en mentir.'   552

LXX   Celui qui l'en veult excuser
           Preuve vostre enemy fourmé,
           Combien que pour folz abuser
           Y a ung aultre scens tourné   556
           Soubx ung faint langaige äourné,
           Contourné soubx ung aultre sens;
           Nëant mains, vous bien informé,
           Vous y verrez ce que g'y scens.   560

LXXI   Quant l'amant treslëal adroit
           S'efforchoit de crïer mercy,
           Par grant desdaing lui respondoit
           Qu'on ne doit rien donner sans sy,   564
           Que honneur demeure; et quant ainsy
           Respondoit, ne pensoit nul bien,
           Et l'amant a riens n'entendy
           Qu'a son honneur sur toute rien.   568

LXXII   L'entendement d'elle estoit tel
           Que nul n'amoit sans deshonneur,
           Et banessoit de vostre hostel
           Vostre fëal amy Honneur,   572
           Qui est tresorier et donneur
           Des biens pour qui maint amant veille,
           Et qui est le vray semonneur,
           Qui vray Desir premier esveille.   576

LXIX   Nevertheless, out of annoyance,
she told him, in order to pacify his temerity,
that you, Love, are just a charming folly,
and that it is you who put him in this peril.
And elsewhere, so as to alter your name,
which is very pleasant to hear,
she names you 'cruel liar,'
bitter in deed and sweet in lies![23]

LXX   Anyone who would wish to excuse her
proves himself your sworn enemy.
Despite the fact that in order to deceive fools,
they find between the lines another sense,
hidden behind misleading and adorned words
that distort the primary meaning,
nevertheless, you who have been advised
will understand what I mean.

LXXI   When this loyal and upright lover
endeavored to beg for the lady's pity,
she responded with great disdain
that one should not give anything away,
so that honor be preserved; when she
responded thus, she showed him no benevolence,
and yet the lover meant only to protect
her honor above all things.

LXXII   But her understanding held
that no one could love without dishonor;
and she thereby banished from your abode
your faithful friend Honor,
who is the treasurer and grantor
of those good things for which many lovers keep vigil.
He is the real planter of seeds,
he who first awakens true Desire.

LXXIII	Fiction fainte et Faulseté	[112r]
	Disoient que ce qu'elle fist	
	Estoit pour garder lëaulté	
	Vers celuy qui son amy dist.	580
	Et oncqs ung mot hors ne mist	
	Que nul qui vive oÿst retraire,	
	Pour quoy ce propos averist,	
	Mais apreuve tout le contraire.	584
LXXIV	S'elle eust amé aultre que lui,	
	Sauf s'honneur, povoit tresbien dire	
	Bonnement: 'j'ay ailleurs choisy;	
	Retirez vostre cuer, beau sire,	588
	Avant que vostre mal empire.'	
	Mais nesnil, elle n'amoit pas;	
	Sa rigueur brassoit le martire,	
	Dont l'amant cheÿ en trespas.	592
LXXV	Encores pour mieulx aprouver	
	Qu'elle n'amoit aultre ne luy,	
	Pour le povre amant reprouver	
	Et monstrer qu'il avoit failly,	596
	Luy dist en faisant tout onny:	
	'Crïent, pleurent, rïent, ou chantent,	
	Car je pourverray, quant a my,	
	Que vous ou aultre ne s'en vantent.'	600
LXXVI	Ce n'estoit mie pour vanter	
	Qu'il s'estoit mis en celle queste,	
	Mais estoit pour soy creanter	
	D'estre leal puis sa concqueste.	604
	Pour neant donna mainte requeste	
	Que Leaulté lui escripsy;	
	Sy m'en raporte a toute enqueste	
	Qu'onques Pitié ne les lisy.	608

LXXIII	Fake Fiction and Falsity
	said that what she had done
	was done in order to remain loyal
	toward one she called her sweetheart.
	Yet she never spoke a word of this aloud
	so that anyone alive might have heard
	these words and verified them,
	but in fact she proves quite the contrary.

LXXIII

Fake Fiction and Falsity
said that what she had done
was done in order to remain loyal
toward one she called her sweetheart.
Yet she never spoke a word of this aloud
so that anyone alive might have heard
these words and verified them,
but in fact she proves quite the contrary.

LXXIV

For if she had truly loved another,
then, without losing honor, she could have very well said
in a friendly fashion: "I have chosen another;
take back your heart, dear sir,
before your heartache worsens."
But no, she had no other love.
Her harshness was the instigation of the torture
that brought about the death of the lover.

LXXV

Again, in order to affirm
that she loved no one at all, including him,
and in order to reproach the poor lover
and make him see that he had failed in his endeavor,
she told him, displaying complete indifference:
'Let them cry out, weep, laugh, or sing!
I will make sure, for my part,
that you nor anyone else can brag on my account.'[24]

LXXVI

But it was never in order to brag
that the lover set out on this quest,
but rather to prove himself truly
loyal, even after he had achieved his conquest.
For nothing he presented her with many requests
that Loyalty had written for him;
yet I confirm to anyone who might ask
that never did Pity read a single word.

LXXVII	Sa lëaulté lui vailly mains	[112v]
	Que s'il eust esté desleal,	
	Car, dez qu'il fut entre ses mains,	
	Tousjours lui offroit bien pour mal,	612
	Jassoit ce qu'on scet de laval	
	Que mieulx lui vault que chacun die	
	Qu'il soit mort renonmé leal	
	Que ce qu'il fust faulx et en vie.	616
LXXVIII	Mieulx vault morir en ung bon nom,	
	Tant que le monde puet durer,	
	Qu'estre vif en mauvais renom.	
	Pour ce Pacïence endurer	620
	Fist a l'amant sans murmurer	
	Le dur cop de la mort obscure,	
	Que celle lui voult procurer	
	Avant son temps, mal gré Nature.	624
LXXIX	Ou est Nature a ce cop cy	
	Qui ne vient son droit pourchassier	
	De celle qui lui a ocy	
	Celui qu'elle prisa sy chier?	628
	Que n'ayde elle a faire trachier	
	Les articles faulsement fais?	
	Bien doit venir celle, sachiez,	
	Afin qu'il soit adroit refais.	632
LXXX	Tant le prisa a sa naissance	
	Que tout bel le determina	
	Et puis parfait en sa croissance	
	Tant qu'en bonne fin l'afina.	636
	Chacun l'ama tant qu'il fina,	
	Fors une femme, ce fut ceste,	
	Qui sa mort lui predestina	
	Par son regard faulx et deteste.	640

LXXVII	His loyalty was worth less to him
	than if he had been disloyal.
	For, as soon as he was in her hands,
	she returned to him only bad for good.
	This affirms what we knew before:
	that it is better for him that they say
	he died with a reputation for loyalty
	than that he have been unfaithful, yet still alive.

LXXVIII	Better to die with a good name,
	as long as the world remains,
	than to live with a bad reputation.
	This is why Patience makes
	the lover endure, without complaint,
	the hard blow of dastardly death
	that the lady wanted to inflict upon him
	before his time, and against Nature.

LXXIX	Where, indeed, is Nature in all of this?
	Why does she not come to claim her rights
	from her who killed him,
	this man whom she prized so dearly?
	Why does she not help to track down
	these falsely asserted claims?
	She should come forth, to be sure,
	so that he might be restored to his right position.

LXXX	Nature so esteemed him at his birth
	that she made him quite beautiful
	and then perfected him as he grew,
	so that finally he was of exquisite proportions.
	Everyone loved him as long as he lived
	except one woman, this one before us,
	who ordained his death
	by means of her false and cursed glance.

LXXXI	Toute chose estoit son amie,	[113r]
	Tout l'amoit ce qui avoit sens,	
	Dont elle est a toute ennemie,	
	Nulle aultre chose je n'y sens.	644
	Or, soit dont, Amours, votre assens,	
	Que l'ennemie a toute chose	
	Soit pugnie et lui soit exemps	
	Bon Renom ou encor repose.	648
LXXXII	Puis que homme du monde n'amoit	
	Et heoit l'amy de chascun,	
	Par ces deux offences veult droit	
	Qu'elle soit haÿe en commun,	652
	N'ait ami ou monde nesun,	
	Mais soit de toute amour privee.	
	Dieu veult, soit aucune ou aucun,	
	Qui het trestout que tout le hee.	656
LXXXIII	Encores fist pis ceste femme,	
	Qui par espreuve congnoissoit	
	Qu'il estoit tristre jusqu'a l'ame,	
	Tant que prez se descongnoissoit:	660
	Quant party fut, peu y penssoit,	
	Car aux dansses revint virant;	
	Aprés meffait, s'esjoÿssoit,	
	Selon la guise de tirant.	664
LXXXIV	Et puis que le tirant ressamble	
	Bien la puis 'tirande' nommer,	
	Encor pis, pour ce qu'elle samble	
	Au vëoir doulce et sans amer,	668
	De mercy briefve a entamer,	
	Plaine de chiere ouverte et grande,	
	Pour quoy la puis, sans surnonmer,	
	Appeller la Faulse Tirande.	672

LXXXI	All creatures were his friend; every being with reason loved him. But she is the enemy of all of them; there is nothing further to say. Wherefore may we have your accord, Love, that this enemy of all be punished and banished from Good Reputation, whose company she still enjoys.
LXXXII	Since she loved no man on this earth and hated this friend of everyone, for these two offenses it is just that she be hated by all and that she have no friend in this world, but instead be deprived of all love. For God wills that, woman or man, if one hates everyone, then let everyone hate that one.
LXXXIII	Even worse was this woman, who knew by personal experience that he was sad to his very soul, such that he was almost unrecognizable. Yet as soon as he left, she scarcely thought of him, for she returned immediately to the dance. After scorning him, she was having fun, according to the way of a tyrant.
LXXXIV	And since she acts like a tyrant, I might rightly name her 'tyrant,' or even worse, because she appears to be sweet and without bitterness, ready to grant her grace, full of good cheer and encouragement; which is why I might, without exaggeration, call her a 'false tyrant.'

LXXXV   On ne puet d'elle assés mesdire   [113v]
Pour ce que seulle est sans mercy,
Car il n'est plus, qui voult voir dire,
De telz dames que ceste cy;   676
Des biens d'elles sont enrichy
Tous ceulx qui vivent soubx les cieulx,
Et cestë a celui ocy
Qui d'elle devoit valloir mieulx.   680

LXXXVI   Et samble que tel chose infame,
Selon ce que d'elle est escript,
Ne soit pas comme une aultre femme,
Mais soit quelque maulvais esperit   684
Qui ymage de femme prit
Pour mettre a mort vrais amoureux,
Dont cest amant en soit perit,
Qui tant fut bon et gracïeux.   688

LXXXVII   S'il n'est ainsy, sy couvient y
Qu'elle soit de malle heure nee,
Et que Sathan lui ait sorty
Quelque mauvaise destinee,   692
Car en mal est tant obstinee
Que bien ne puet dedens son corps;
Rigueur fut en elle assignee
Des qu'elle ot sens, bien m'en recors;   696

LXXXVIII   Non pas sens, maiz maulvais malice
Et art pour faire amans morir:
S'est bien raison qu'on abolice
Son faulx povair, qui fist perir   700
Le leal, sans le secourir,
Qui bien fut digne d'estre amé,
Se fait ne lui eust rencherir
Mercy, par faulte de pitié.   704

LXXXV   One cannot speak too ill of her
              because she is uniquely without mercy:
              for, truth be told, there are no more
              ladies like this one before us.
              All who live under heaven
              are enriched by the virtues of ladies,
              but this one has killed him who
              should have grown more worthy by her love.

LXXXVI   It seems that such a dishonorable creature,
              judging by what has been written about her,
              is not like other women
              but must be some sort of evil spirit
              who has taken the form of a woman
              in order to put true lovers to death,
              by which this lover perished,
              he who was so good and courteous.

LXXXVII   If this is not the case, then it must be
              that she was born at an inauspicious hour,
              and Satan reserved for her
              some wicked destiny,
              for she is so steeped in evil
              that good cannot enter her body.
              Hardness of heart was her lot in life,
              evident as soon as she could reason, I am sure.

LXXXVIII   No! Not reason, but wicked malice
              and ruses to bring on the death of lovers.
              It is right, then, to abolish
              her false power, which has killed
              the loyal one, to whom was offered no help
              even though he was worthy of being loved.
              If only she had not made her grace too costly,
              out of a lack of pity!

LXXXIX   Vray Dieu d'Amours, je te requier,   [114r]
            Oy tes subgés crïer justice!
            Ilz ne te cessent d'invocquier.
            Fay que de ta bouche juste ysse   708
            Raison, que ce meffait justice.
            Voy les leur bon frere plourer,
            Qui leur force moult rapetice,
            Car ce leur fait ung grant pillier.   712

XC   Tant ne me griefve pas sa mort,
            Puis qu'il estoit homme mortel,
            Qu'il me desplait quant me remort
            De ce que lui, qui n'est son tel,   716
            Ama femme qui n'estre el [ne soit el
            Que mal. Helas! Pour quoy loga
            Tant noble en sy rudë hostel
            Duquel la Mort le desloga?   720

XCI   Puis q'onques de Pitié n'usa
            Ou le dollant prinst allegance,
            Et que vray Desir abusa
            Et fist muer Doulce Esperance,   724
            Rigueur doit estre sa nuisance,
            Sans ce que Pitié la deffende:
            A tel desserte, tel vengance;
            Et a tel meffait, telle amende.   728

XCII   En oultre, je dy au sourplus
            Que celui qui la chose escript,
            Qui fut ou ciel, rapporta plus
            De pluseurs choses qu'il n'y vit.   732
            Il le convient, quant il a dit
            Que de vo bouche deposastes
            Qu'a celle ou n'a fors escondit
            Par avant aultre amy donnastes."   736

LXXXIX	True God of Love, I beg of you,
	hear your subjects crying out for justice!
	They call upon you without ceasing.
	Let come from your just lips
	your decision, which will punish this crime.
	See these who weep for their good brother!
	Their force restores him to you,
	for he is a great pillar among them.
XC	It is not that his death grieves me so much—
	after all, he was a mortal man—
	but it offends me when I remember
	that this man, who had no equal,
	loved a woman who was nothing
	but evil incarnate! Alas! Why
	did such a noble one lodge in so rude an abode,
	from which Death then dislodged him?
XCI	Because she never called on Pity,
	in whom the sufferer might have found relief,
	and she deceived true Desire
	and held back sweet Hope,
	Severity should dispense her castigation,
	with no intervention from Pity.
	For one gets what one deserves,
	and the punishment should suit the crime.
XCII	Moreover, I will add
	that he who put this earlier trial into writing,
	who was transported into the heavens, revealed more
	on several points than he actually saw.
	This is obvious, especially when he said
	that you yourself, by your very lips, declared
	that you had already given another lover
	to her in whom there is only refusal."[25]

XCIII   "Certes," dist Amours, "je tesmoingz
            Qu'onques de ma bouche n'issy,
            Et sy emprens par mes tesmoings
            Tous mes hommes qui sont icy.   740
            Celui qui le rapporte ainsy,
            Combien qu'il est saige et discret,
            En retint pou, ou trop oÿ,
            Car il ne dit pas verité.   744

XCIV   Sy l'aproche en deux faiz premis   [114v]
            De crisme tant manifesté.
            Premiers, je dy qu'elle a commis
            Crisme de leze magesté,   748
            Quant de sa bouchë areté
            Que pour pluseurs cas estes vice,
            Sy conclus que lui soit osté
            Son nom, que mal lui est propice.   752

XCV   Et soit deboutee a tousjours
            De vostre court et puis nommee
            'La Crüelle Femme en amours.'
            Et puis enjoinct a Renommee   756
            Que la voix soit par tout semee
            Qu'elle est crüelle et sans mercy,
            Quant de sa voix envenimee
            A des bons le meilleur ocy.   760

XCVI   Secondement, pour ceste mort
            Qui est criesme venu d'orgueil,
            Commie sans cause et a grant tort,
            Contens qu'en la chartre de dueil   764
            Soit plongié, contre son vueil,
            Et noyée ens ou puys de lermes,
            Afin que de son faulx acueil
            N'use jamais contre voz termes.   768

XCIII   "Of course," said Love, "I attest to the fact
that I never spoke these words,
and I take as my witnesses
all my men here present.
He who reported such a thing,
no matter how wise or discreet he might be,
remembered too little or imagined he heard too much,
for he is not telling the truth."

XCIV   "I accuse her, then, of these two acts I put forth before you,
which constitute manifest crimes.
First of all, I declare that she committed
the crime of lèse-majesté[26]
when from her own mouth she passed judgment and said
that in many cases you inspire vice;
and so I conclude that her good name
should be taken away from her, for it ill befits her.

XCV   And furthermore, that she be banned forever
from your court and renamed
'the Cruel Lady in love,'
and then let Reputation be enjoined
to spread the word far and wide
that she is cruel and without mercy,
for by her poisoned words
she killed the best of the best.

XCVI   Second, for this murder,
which is a crime issued of pride,
committed without cause and wrongly,
I contend that in the prison of torment
she be thrown, against her will,
and then drowned in the well of tears,
to the end that her false welcoming
never again be employed to thwart your intentions.

XCVII   Et soit l'amant, a tort finé,   [115r]
             Qui des bons portoit le penon,
             Glorifïé et ramené
             Ou paradis de bon renom   772
             Ou il vint en glore et en nom
             Aveuc les lëaulx trespassés,
             Et porte de lëal surnom
             Pour les biens dont il ot assés.   776

XCVIII   Et s'il est mestier d'aprouver
             Les fais de celle au cuer plain d'yre,
             Et aussy de tesmoings trouver
             Pour les biens de l'amoureux dire,   780
             J'ay preuves tant que pour souffire,
             Tant estrangiers comme privés,
             Tous prestz des faulx propos desdire
             Dont l'amant fut de vous privéz.   784

XCIX   La dame adoncques supplïa
             Qu'elle oÿst les tesmoingz nommer.
             Le Dieu d'Amours lui octrya;
             Verité les fist appeller.   788
             Quatre en y ot pour approuver
             La vie de l'amant finé,
             C'est a savoir: Honneur, Celer,
             Largesse aveuc Humilité,   792

C   Sans Verité et Lëaulté,
             Et l'escuier nommé dessus,
             Pour ce qu'ilz se furent fourmé
             Partie, n'en oÿ on nuls.   796
             Et s'en y ot quatre au sourplus,
             Certifïans l'enorme criesme:
             Bel Acueil, Dangier, et Refus,
             Et Souvenir, qui fut quatriesme.   800

XCVII	And may the lover, wrongly put to death,
	who carried the banner of good men,
	be glorified and returned
	to the paradise of Good Reputation
	that he may live in glory and honor
	with the loyal lovers who have died heretofore,
	and that he carry the name 'loyal'
	in recognition of his many good qualities.
XCVIII	And if it is necessary to prove
	the crimes of her whose heart is full of ire
	or to find witnesses
	to testify to the goodness of the lover,
	I have proof enough to suffice,
	which comes from strangers, as well as intimates,
	all of whom are ready to debunk the lies
	by which the lover was taken from you."
XCIX	At this point the lady made supplication
	to hear the names of these witnesses.
	The God of Love consented,
	and Truth had them summoned.
	Four of them appeared to testify
	to the life of the deceased lover,
	to wit: Honor, Concealment,
	Generosity, and Humility,
C	but not Truth or Loyalty
	nor the squire named above,
	because they were part of the plaintiff's case,
	and so nothing more was heard from them.
	And then there were four more
	who testified to the enormity of the crime:
	Fair Welcoming, Resistance, Refusal,
	and Remembrance, who was the fourth.

CI   Ung livre grant comme ung messel   [115v]
        Qui a deux chaines d'or tenoit,
        Fist on ouvrir, dedens le quel
        Le Dieu d'Amours pourtrais estoit;   804
        Verité en garde l'avoit.
        C'estoit le livre de la foy
        Sur le quel Amours sermentoit
        Les huit tesmoings par devant soy.   808

CII   Les quatre premiers deposerent
        Par leur serment pour ce juré
        Qu'onques l'amoureux ne trouverent
        Envers la dame parjuré,   812
        Et qu'ils avoient demouré
        Aveuc lui depuis son venir,
        Et l'avoit Honneur gouverné,
        Ce disoit il, jusqu'au morir.   816

CIII   Aprés fist on les quatre oÿr,
        Lesquelx ceste dame accusoient;
        Devant moy les vis maintenir
        Ce qui s'ensuit: premiers, disoient   820
        Dangier et Reffus qu'ilz n'avoient
        Oncques ceste dame laissie,
        Et en oultre plus, maintenoient
        Qu'en desdaing fut tousjours nourrie.   824

CIV   Puis Bel Acueil, l'umble et le doulx,
        Dist qu'oncq n'avoit a sa prïere
        Fait meilleur chiere a ung qu'a tous:
        C'est bien en prouvant qu'elle est fiere!   828
        Et puis dit Souvenir arriere,
        A qui bien de tout souvenoit,
        Qu'a tort avoit gecté en biere
        L'amant qui nul mal ne chassoit.   832

CI	A book as dense as a missal
	attached by two chains of gold
	was opened, in which could be found
	the portrait of the God of Love.
	Truth had the job of keeping this book, for
	it was the book of faith
	on which Love swore in
	the eight witnesses before him.

CII	The first four were deposed,
	and under oath for the jury of judges
	they swore that they had never found that the lover
	perjured himself to the lady,
	and furthermore, they swore that they had stayed
	with him since his arrival.
	Honor had governed him,
	he swore, until the lover's death.

CIII	Afterward were called the four
	who were testifying against the lady;
	before me, I saw them maintain
	the following: first, Resistance and Refusal said
	that they had never left this lady,
	and furthermore, they stated
	that she had forever been schooled in disdain.

CIV	Then Fair Welcoming, gentle and humble,
	said that despite her pleas,
	this lady had never shown a warmer welcome to one
	than to others, a fact that proves her haughtiness!
	Then Remembrance,
	who recalls everything so well, in turn
	said that the lady had unjustly thrown in the coffin
	her lover, who sought to do no harm.

CV   Quant le Dieu d'Amours et la court   [116r]
       Les orent oÿs, il me samble
       Qu'ilz se leverent sus tout court
       Et se retrayrent tous enssemble   836
       Au lieu ou le conseil s'assemble.
       Ne sçay qu'ilz dirent, trop fuz loing,
       Mais celle qui de dollour tramble
       Percheuz en crainte et en grant soing.   840

CVI   Quant ilz orent deliberé,
       En leurs lieux les vis revenir.
       Nulz n'y avoit riens differé.
       Lors par adveu dist Souvenir: 844
       "Dame, voullés vous bien tenir
       Tout ce que Verité depose?
       Il fault les jugemens finir
       Ou recevoir ce qu'il propose."   848

CVII   Lors viz ceste dame lever,
       Qui estoit plus morte que cendre;
       D'yre sembloit que deuist crever.
       Et ne vis de ses yeulx descendre   852
       Lermes: c'est bien pour condescendre
       Au tesmoing de sa crüaulté.
       Ne se sceut ou daigna deffendre
       Contre les propos Verité.   856

CVIII   Adoncques Gracïeux Parler,
       Par ung doulx langaige äourné,
       Lui dist: "N'est mestier de celer,
       Dame: congnoissiés verité,   860
       Et on aura de vous pité."
       Lors, par remors de conscïence,
       Confessa ceste crüaulté
       Comme Verité le recense.   864

CV   When the God of Love and his court
                              had heard the witnesses, it seemed to me
                              that they got up quickly
                              and retired together
                              to another room in which the council assembles.
                              I do not know what they said, for I was too far away,
                              but I watched her, who, suffering, trembled
                              in fear and with great worry.

CVI   After they had deliberated,
                              I saw them return to their places.
                              Not one of them had dissented in any regard.
                              Then Remembrance declared:
                              "Lady, do you wish to confess
                              all that Truth said in his deposition?
                              It is necessary to move forward in the trial
                              or else admit to what he claims."

CVII   Then I saw this lady rise;
                              she was as gray as death
                              and seemed as if she might die of anguish.
                              But I did not see fall from her eyes
                              any tears, and that supports
                              the testimony about her cruelty,[27]
                              for either she did not know how or she did not deign
                              to defend herself against Truth's indictment.

CVIII   Then Gracious Speech,
                              in a sweet voice and with well-chosen words,
                              said to her: "There is no need to dissimulate,
                              lady; admit to the truth
                              and the court will have pity on you."
                              At this point, full of remorse,
                              she confessed to her cruel act
                              exactly as Truth had exposed it.

CIX   Et croy que se n'eust esté Honte,   [116v]
Qui ung petit l'umilia,
De la court tenist pou de compte.
Mais Honte ung pou la maistrïa,   868
Car a moitié mercy crïa,
Disant: "Je me rapporte, au fort,
A ce que la court en fera.
Grace requiers, pour Dieu confort!"   872

CX   Aprés dist Amours au greffier
Que tous les procés allast querre,
Comme il fist, et les fist baillier
Au grant conseil pour a fin traire   876
La cause et le procés parfaire.
Ce furent Scens, Raison, Advis,
Memoire, et Crainte de Mal Faire,
Qui mal conseillaissent envis.   880

CXI   Les quatre sont docteurs es loix;
Memoire vault ung coustumier.
Sy estudïerent es drois,
Pour eulx meïsmes conseillier.   884
Quant fait eurent, au repairier,
Raison vint dire en jugement
Qu'Amour devoit tresbien jugier
La fin ou Verité content.   888

CXII   Quant Amours oÿ le rapport,
Jugier alla en tel maniere:
"Je voeul que l'amant qui est mort
Soit suscités en ma lumiere,   892
Et ait sa place et sa chayere
Ou paradis de Bon Renom,
Et comme ma chose plus chiere,
Y soit vif en gloire et en nom.   896

CIX   And I think that without the presence of Shame,
who humiliated her a bit,
she would have paid no mind to the court.
But Shame was able to control her somewhat,
because she half cried out for mercy,
saying: "I submit, then,
to the decision of the court
and beg your compassion, by God's grace."

CX   Next, Love told the bailiff
to go collect all the written documents,
which he did, and he then gave them
to the council so that they might bring an end
to the case and complete the proceedings.
The council was composed of Sense, Reason, Opinion,
Memory, and Fear of Wrongdoing,
who would never wish to render an unjust opinion.

CXI   Four of them were doctors in law;
Memory was trained in customary law.
They examined the laws with care
to better inform themselves.
When they had finished and returned,
Reason announced before the court
that Love was prepared to make a judgment
according to the recommendation of Truth.

CXII   When Love heard their report,
he rendered the following verdict:
"I order that the lover who is now dead
be resuscitated in my light
to take his place on a throne
in the paradise of Good Reputation
so that, as my cherished one,
he live in glory and fame.

CXIII	Et afin que chascun me criesme,	[117r]
	Contre toy, treshorrible femme,	
	Dist la court pour ton premier crisme,	
	Qu'on ne t'appelle jamais dame	900
	Et soyes repputee infame,	
	Et de nous bannie a tousjours,	
	Et enjoingz qu'on te nomme et clame	
	'La Crüelle Femme en Amours.'	904

CXIV	Et pour l'autre criesme ou gist mors,	
	Te condampne a estre enchartree	
	En chartre de dueil sans deport,	
	Et toy illecq ainsy gectee	908
	Soyes noyee et par oultree	
	Ou puys de lermes, je le vueil,	
	Le quel puys plain d'eauwe sallee	
	Est dedens la chartre de dueil."	912

CXV	Quant le jugement fu rendu,	
	Desespoir est sailly avant,	
	Qui maint meschant homme a pendu,	
	Et la print et maisne devant,	916
	Puis la boute en griefment lanchant	
	En la chartre ou n'a qu'amertume,	
	Et est la chartre en ung pendant	
	Du perilleux hostel Fortune.	920

CXVI	Doulx Penser, qui estoit huissier	
	Et publïeur, lieve sa mache	
	Et va de par Amour crïer	
	Que nul, jamais, en quelque place,	924
	Ne pense, die, tende, ou face,	
	Rien qui soit contre la sentence,	
	Sur paine de perdre sa grace	
	Et encourre sa malivollence.	928

CXIII And so that all might fear me,
       against you, most horrible woman,
       the court orders that for the first crime,
       you nevermore be called 'lady,'
       and that you be reputed infamous
       and banished forever from our company.
       Furthermore, I require that you be named and hailed as
       'the Cruel Woman in love.'

CXIV   And for the other crime by which the lover lies dead,
       I condemn you to be incarcerated
       without delay in the prison of pain,
       and, once you have been thrown there,
       that you be drowned in the very bottom
       of the well of tears, as I command,
       in the well full of salt water
       that is found in the prison of pain."

CXV   As soon as the verdict was rendered,
       Despair sallied forth,
       he who has hung many an unfortunate man,
       and grabbed hold of her and led her away,
       shoving and brutally throwing her forward
       into the prison, where there is naught but bitterness,
       for this prison lies on a slope
       on the grounds of the perilous abode of Fortune.

CXVI   Sweet Thought, who was the bailiff
       and public crier, lifted his club
       and went out to proclaim in Love's name
       that no one, ever, in any place
       should think, say, attempt, or do
       anything that would be contrary to this verdict,
       on pain of losing Love's grace
       and incurring his ill will.

CXVII   Ce finé, ne me donnay garde;   [117v]
            Seul me trouvay en la vallee.
            La teste sours par tout regarde;
            Je ne viz Amours n'assemblee,   932
            Tout ainsy q'une chose emblee.
            Ne sceuz que tout fu devenu,
            La veue avoye si troublee,
            Ne sceuz qu'i me fut advenu.   936

CXVIII   De la party, moy retourné;
            Saisy enque, plume, et pappier.
            A escripre fuy atourné
            Tout le fait, sans riens oublïer,   940
            Pour la merveille publïer
            A vous, mes dames redoubtees,
            A qui je vieng pour Dieu prïer
            Que telles ne soyés trouvees   944

CXIX   Comme celle crüelle femme,
            Qui par son criminel meffait
            Est par tout reputee infame.
            Aussy fist elle ung crüel fait   948
            Quant, de tous bons, le plus parfait
            En toute chose treseureuse,
            Qui nullement n'avoit fourfait,
            Fist morir de mort dolloureuse.   952

CXX   A joye et a Amours deffaire
            Ceste dame estoit tres eslite.
            Jhesucrist garde d'ainsy faire
            La belle en qui tous biens habite,   956
            En qui de mort je me respite
            Seullement quant je la regarde!
            Si lui pry qu'elle se delicte
            A m'esjouÿr, si n'aray garde.   960

Explicit.

CXVII Thus it all ended, and before I knew what to expect
I found myself alone in a valley.
My head felt stunned, and as I looked around
I saw neither Love nor his assembly,
as if they had surreptitiously disappeared.
I do not know what became of them;
my vision was disturbed,
and I did not understand what had just happened to me.

CXVIII I left that place and returned to my house,
where I quickly took up ink, pen, and paper
and returned to writing
down the entire affair, without omitting a thing,
so that I could relate this marvelous story
to you, most respected ladies,
before whom I come to pray, in God's name,
that you never be found to resemble

CXIX this cruel woman
who, by her criminal offense,
is everywhere considered dishonorable.
Furthermore, she did a cruel deed
when, of all good men, the most perfect one
and most fortunate in all things,
who did not fall short in any respect,
she made to die an agonizing death.

CXX Attacking joy and Love
Came easily to this lady.
Jesus Christ, keep from doing the same my beautiful
Lady, in whom all perfection is gathered and in whom
Escape I find from death
Simply by looking on her countenance,
and I pray that she may delight[28]
in bringing me pleasure; then I will no longer worry.

The End[29,30]

Notes

1. Line 1: echo of line 383 of the *Belle dame*: "Je ne vous aide ne ne greve."

2. Line 21: another echo of line 154 of the *Belle dame*: "joye triste cueur traveille."

3. Lines 63–64: these exterior signs of melancholy are compared to the attributes of a warrior knight. In the *Belle dame* love was compared to war in lines 184 and 226. The mania of slogans and coats of arms during this period is manifested on the fly-leaves of Pj by the arms and slogan of the commissioner Marie de Clèves, integrated into the decoration.

4. Line 103: Godefroy attests the form *personnage* of *parçon, parson, person* to mean "partage," "distribution," arrangement;" as well as a localized meaning at Liège of "travée, espace entre deux parties." I translated the passage with some liberty to refer to the arrangement of tiles on the floor, the spaces between which may be deep cracks or bumps; in any case, they give the narrator trouble walking. All of the manuscripts give the same reading.

5. Line 154: the doublet "jasper and chalcedony" refers to ornamental quartz rock (onyx, agate); jasper is usually a reddish brown variety.

6. Lines 154–68: Achilles Caulier evokes the description of heaven presented in Revelations chapter 4, even as he cites the Apocalypse.

7. Line 206: Piaget suggests that Achilles Caulier was a member of the association of the "Chapel Vert," whose members wore a green hat or collar during mass or at dinner (Piaget, *Romania* 31, 1902: 317).

8. Characters from classical mythology who represent examples of true and faithful love. Helen of Troy, the most beautiful woman in the world, elopes with Paris, bringing about the siege and destruction of Troy in Homer's *Iliad* and the first books of Virgil's *Aeneid*. Dido, the founder and queen of Carthage, falls in love with Aeneas and kills herself in grief when he leaves her. Pyramus and Thisbe, lovers forbidden by their parents to marry, die in their attempt to elope. Leander loves Hero and swims out to meet her each night, guided by a light, until one night the light is extinguished and Leander, without guidance, drowns in the sea. Demophon, son of Theseus, loves Phyllis, the Thracian princess; when he leaves her she hangs herself in despair and is changed into an almond tree. Achilles leaves the fighting of the Trojan War to go after his kidnapped love Briseis. Penelope, the wife of Odysseus, remains true to him for the twenty years of his wandering, despite the pressure of many suitors. These figures are also cited in Caulier's *Hospital of Love* lines 102–4 and 109–12.

9. Lines 250–304: the complicated syntax of this long sentence imitates courtroom language, as it incorporates all the constituent requirements of a case presentation in court.

10. Line 267: *Belle dame*, lines 225–32.

11. Line 284: conclusion of the *Lady Loyal in Love*, poem that precedes this one and to which this poem responds.

12. Line 350: reference, of course, to Alain Chartier.

13. Lines 355–60: this passage takes up again citations from the *Belle dame* lines 285–88, and the *Lady Loyal in Love* lines 649–50.

14. Line 361: Achilles Caulier designates the *Loyal Lady in Love* as the third book, recognizing the Quarrel cycle in which the poem of Chartier is the first book, the *Accusation* the second. It is worth pointing out, however, that as often as the manuscripts refer to the cycle as such, the books are not always numbered identically. According to Piaget, for example, the Diesback manuscript (Qj), now lost, on which he based his edition refers to the *Accusation* as the first book, the *Lady Loyal in Love* as the second, and the *Cruel Woman* as the third.

15. Line *364*: *Loyal* lines 393–400.

16. Lines 365–66: by declaring that she wishes to remain free from everyone (lines cited just above), the Belle dame denies any lover, even secret.

17. Lines 389–92: *Loyal* lines 763–84, in which the blame for the lover's death is cast on Hope and Desire.

18. Lines 457–61: the author is deliberately playing with the names of two personifications made famous in the *Romance of the Rose*, Faux Semblant (False Seeming) and Bel Acueil (Fair Welcoming).

19. Line 466: the writer is Alain Chartier, who transcribed the dialogue between the lover and the Belle dame.

20. Line 475: *Loyal* line 431.

21. Line 494: allusion to the death of Alain Chartier, by which Piaget will date the poem to after 1430.

22. Lines 508–12: an approximate citation of *Belle dame* lines 253–56.

23. Lines 551–52: exact citation of *Belle dame* lines 313–14; also quoted in the *Accusation* lines 449–50 and the *Loyal* lines 705–12.

24. Lines 598–600: *Belle dame* lines 702–4.

25. Lines 730–36: Achilles Caulier is referring to the author of the *Lady Loyal in Love,* whose narrator, after being transported in a cloud to the heavens, reveals the heretofore unknown existence of the Belle dame's secret lover.

26. Line 748: lèse-majesté, the highest crime of treason against one's sovereign, here the God of Love.

27. Lines 852–54: tears in the Middle Ages were often referred to as "water of the heart," and crying was a sign of real emotion and sincere contrition (Baumgartner 197). The Belle dame's lack of tears, therefore, is the proof that she does not truly repent of her behavior towards the lover.

28. Stanza CXX: the author's name is in acrostic, A-C-I-L-E-S. See also the opening stanzas of the *Hospital of Love.*

29. *The Cruel Woman in Love, Rejected Readings*: 22. fu missing PbPc; 66. Plus plaignant et plus e. *Pb*; 98. P. c. et a (+1) Pc; 100. p. me s. (+1) Pc; 108. scribe corrects les c; 221. affamee PbPc; 263. missing line Pb; 293. revenus e. (+1) PbPc; 356. par tout PbPc; 419. Lui Pc; 433. ung amant (-1) Pc; 448. le PbPc; 453. silz eussent s. Pn; 468.

Quil v. ; 472. Pour q que; 498. encore (-1) Pc; 566. a nul (+1) Pc; 619. en mais renom ; 631. s'elle la chier Pb; 684. m. esperit count 2 syllables; XCI is placed after XCIII in Pn, the order is reestablished according to the MSS; 722. Ou d. (-1) Pc; 781. Je PbPc; 836. s. treyrent (-1) *Pq*; 837. la ou (+1) PbPc; 917. Et le b. Pc; 948. ung grant meffait Pc; 958. le PbPc.

30. *The Cruel Woman in Love, Variant Readings*: 7. A tout mon cueur PbPc; 14. C. p. m. seulement Pq; 15. A. mené Pc; 16. s. qui sent PbPq; 19. creast Pc; 28. Main leve et fort courouchie Pc; 31. muschié PbPc; 32 Tenebreux l. Pk; 35. u. flos Pc; 45. Langueur Pb, horteur Pq; 59. T. estoye d'estre Pc, triste et l. Pb, destresse l. Pq; 63. Diverses et Pk; 68. fut Pk; 74. ma maistresse PbPq; 75. long temps PcPk; 84. ne sceu Pb; 85. vous m. PbPc; 86. remembrance PcQl; 95. suis PcPk, m. fu Pq; 101. james venir PcPk; 106. daultre m. PbPcPk; 110. et pollie comme c. Pc; 112. plus m. Pc; 113. les boches Pc, la volee d. Pd, les bouches PbPdPkPo; 115. Coppees p. Pq 117. fust Pc, fut Pk; 122. faicture Pc; 125. C. len fait q. Pq; 127. s. future Qj; 129. pas t. Pb; 131. madrecay Qj; 132. l. composees Pq; 133. entassees Pb; XVIII *missing* PbPo; 147. gracieux m. Pc; 152. plus vrayes PbPc; 155. ne casses Pb; 156. Cler y fait comme si fust nonne Pk; 157. R. quamours PoPq; 167. chassis PbPc; 168. p. bonnes Pc; 169. Dessoubz c. PbPc; Stanza XXII *missing* in Po; 174. c. li cyppres PbPc; 180. appartient Pc; 188. Maiz une place Po; 191. souvent s. PbPc; 200. qu'il n'encoure Po; 204. d. cleres et benignes PbPo, clers et beghines Pq; 205. P. pourveoir Pc; 206. Lung deulx le v. Pc, Ly ung u. Pq; 207. Lui fist en tresgracieux s. Pc; 209. pensee e. PbPc; 212. estoyent Pc; 242. bien m. Pc; 248. De tres bon cueur et v. PbPoPq, Et le lisy tres voulentiers Pc; 255. V. tresorier Pq; 258. esgaré Pc; 264. respons PbPc; 267. luy r. Pc, se r. Qj; 269. Pria et r. PbPo, Leust r. Qj; 270. peust Pq; 275. f. nommer PnQj; 277. Et puis par u. subtil l. Pb; 280. Controuve PbPq; 283. appeller PbPc; 291. a. ses Pq; 292. Amis s. Pq, sans i. Pc; 296. En quoy le d. Po; 306. dist Pc; 314. ne submist Ql; 327. conté PbPc; 332. la f. Qj; 333. m. semblance Pc, Et moy samblant PqPo; XLIII-XLV *missing* in PqPo; 368. se preuve PbPq; 370. l'amant PbPc; 374. vault e. PbPc; 375. a exprimer Pc, p. chose Pq; 376. Et d. amis Pq, Dist le conseil si s. Pd; In PcPkQl, XLVIII-LXXI *are misplaced after* CV; 383. d. et non ly Pq, com je os cy Pc; 384. l. tour Qj; 387. elle m. Pc; 395. incanse PbPcPo; 400. Si s'en est l'ame a Pc, sen yert Qj; 404. Quen dictez v. Pb, Advisés vous Pc, Quen direz v. Pq; 440. Crüelle umbre de verité Pc; 450. soubz bel acoeul e. PqPo; 453. e. sceue Qj; 454. elle apparust Pc, C. e. apparra Qj; 456. qui Pc; 457. c. bel acqueil Pc; 460. s. ne c. Pc, f. devant Qj; 462. lacz Pc; 464. seulle m. PcPo; 466. tresnotable Pc; 467. B le congnoys Po; 472. encuse Pc; 484. C. damours seroit i. PoPq; 493. si certain PbPc; 496. par envye PbPcPo; 498. quen vint Pq; 502. prisier PbPc; 513. e. quil f. Qj; 521. follement PbPc; 527. Ausquelx pouez Pq; 533. Aussy et quant i. Pc; 539. c. quele d. Qj, c. quil le d. Pq; 545. o. que m. Pq; 546. changier Pc; 549. le n. Pc; 556. trouve PbPc; 557. franc l. Pq; 558. Controuve PbPqQj; 574. maintenant v. Pq; 575. droit s. Pc; 581. hors n. m. PqQj; 582. Sauve Qj; 590. elle navoit p. PbPq; 606. rescripsi PdPq; 617. M. v. mort vivre en ung bon non Pc, M. v. mort v. e. b. renom Pd; 619. Que vif mourir en mal renon Pc, mains r. Pq, maix r. Qj; 626. Qu'el Pc; 629. Que d'elle faire tant t. Pc; 640. tout plain de feste Pc; 643. a tort e. Pq; 644. autre glose PqQj; 647. S. privee Pc; 648. o. tout heur Pc; 654. toute a. PbPcPdQj; 655. Droit v. PbPc; 656. Que on hee tout ce que tout hee Pc, Qui h. tout que tout la h. QjQlPq [le h.]); 662. r. riant Pb, r. errant Pc; 663. A. mal fait Pc; 666. t. appeller Pc; 669. merci. a e. Pk; 679. a

aultre c.Pc; 687. c. enfant Pc; 688. sage et Pc; 698. a. de f. PqQj; 699. quon n'obeïsse
Pc; 708. t. grant bonte y. Pc; 709. m. pugnisse Pc; 711. l. sorte PcQj; 712. fu Pc; 724.
mentir Pc; 734. v. bouches Pc; 742. discret Pc, est s. PqQj; 744. Ou il ne dit pas ce
quil scet Pb n. dist pas v. PqQj; 745. Elle est perverse a mon adviz Pc; 748. C. a vostre m. Pc; 750. Et p. p. este niche Pc; 765. logee Po; 776. ilz ont a. Po; 777. de prouver Pc; 781. qui doivent s. PbPo, qu'il peust s. Pc; 789. eust Pc; 796. nen y ot il plus
PbPcPo; 797. eust Pc; 828. bien apparant Pc; 816. dist Pc; 819. leur v. PbPo; 824. ny
c. Pb; 825. a sa c. Pb; 834. eurent Pc; 838. fu l. Pq; 839. päour Pc; 843. r. desire Pc;
845. bon t. Qj; 848. reprochier PbPc; 855. scait ou daigne Pc; 871. dira Pc; 874.
querir Pk; 893–948 *missing in* Pq *due to loss of a folio*; 896. Il s. PbPcPo; 917. b. si
rudement Pb, en languissant Pc; 925. d. tense PbPc; 937, 939: retournai/tournai Pc;
*Piaget suggets a play on words "a tourné/a Tournai" to indicate that the poem was
written in that town*; 948. ung piteux fait Pb; 950. toutes choses treseureux PbPc;
951. meffait Pc; 952. envieulx Pb, dolloureux PcPo.

The Errors of Judgment of the Belle dame sans mercy

Anonymous

Cy commencent les erreurs du jugement de la Belle dame sans mercy

I   Non pas pour la court corriger   [90r]
                 Qui ne sauroit jamais faillir,
                 Mais pour son jugement changer
                 Et certains erreurs abolir   4
                 Qu'on a tousjours volu tollir
                 Contre une dame jusques cy
                 Nommee, pour son bruit desmollir,
                 "La belle dame sans mercy,"   8

II   Ses heritiers si ont fait dire
                 Qu'elle fut moult notable femme,
                 Si belle qu'on pourroit eslire,
                 Passans toutes sans blasmer ame,   12
                 Jeune, gente, joyeuse dame,
                 Nourrie ou service d'Amours
                 Tant que savoit par cueur sa game
                 Avecques les faintes et tours.   16

III   Or fut vray que ung jeune galand
                 Tout fin, droit venant des escolles,
                 Qui estoit amoureulx vollant
                 Et ung bailleur de parabolles,   20
                 La voult amuser de parolles
                 En taschant a la decevoir.
                 En voyant ses approches folles,
                 Pour son honneur y voult pourvoir.   24

IV   Et advint que lui remonstra   [90v]
                 Qu'il n'avoit pas trouvé sa charge.
                 Mais aux fievres plus en entra,
                 Cuidant, par ung desir volaige,   28
                 La tourner a son avantaige,
                 Pour en jouïr legierement;
                 En quoy il se monstra peu saige
                 Et faillit y l'a lourdement.   32

Here begins The Errors of Judgment of the Belle dame sans mercy

I

Not to correct the court,
which could never be wrong,
but to alter its decision
and abolish certain errors
which we have always wanted to eradicate,
against a lady named until this time,
in order to sully her reputation,
"the Belle dame sans mercy."

II

Her descendants have made it known
that she was a very respected woman,
so beautiful that one could easily affirm
without slighting anyone that she surpassed all other women,
young, noble, a joyful lady,
brought up in the service of Love,
so that she knew by heart her game,
with all its pretense and cheating tricks.

III

Now, it was true that a young and refined gallant
coming straight out of school,
who was a fickle lover
and a smooth-talking liar,
wished to occupy her time with sweet words
in an attempt to deceive her.
But, seeing his foolish tactics,
she preferred to take care of her honor.

IV

And so it happened that she let him know
that he had not found consent in her,
but rather had entered into the fever of love,
believing only by his fickle desire
that he could turn her to his advantage
in order to take his pleasure from her easily.
But in this he proved himself unwise,
and he failed miserably in his endeavor.

V   Encores ne fut pas content,
         Ains, voyant qu'elle se enfuyoit,
         L'aloit de plus fort incitant,
         Et sa folie presumoit   36
         Que veritablement le amoit,
         Non obstant que l'eust reculé;
         Et ainsi le feu allumoit
         Dont il fut au derrenier brulé.   40

VI   Et pour ce qu'elle savoit bien
         La fin ou le gallant tendoit,
         Et que pour doulceur ne pour rien
         Il ne amolissoit ne amendoit,   44
         Ains soubz ung fol espoir cuidoit
         Avoir des biens de plus en plus,
         Lors luy dist que son temps perdoit
         Au derrenier, que n'en pouoit plus.   48

VII   Et combien que par ses langaiges   [91r]
         El n'eust l'amant vitupperé,
         Ne fait aucuns excés ne oultraiges
         Dont il fust gaires empiré,   52
         Nëantmoins l'en a conspiré
         La blasmer de ce cas icy
         Soubz ung proverbe coloré
         De belle dame sans mercy.   56

VIII   Or tout a prins en passïence
         Sans ce que lui en ait chalu
         Ne quë en ait requis vengence.
         Mais cela n'y a riens valu,   60
         Car, quant l'en lui a eu polu
         Son honneur sans cause et a tort,
         Je ne sçay quelz gens ont volu
         La chargier de crime de mort,   64

V   Yet he was not satisfied;
              rather, seeing that she was escaping him,
              he went to her even more forcefully;
              his folly assumed
              that she really loved him,
              despite the fact that she had refused him;
              and in this way she lit the fire
              by which he burned to death in the end.

VI   And since she knew well
              the end to which the gallant was striving,
              as well as the reality that he would never soften or amend his approach
              in return for her kindness or for anything else,
              but rather, under the influence of foolish hope, that he would believe
              to obtain more and more gifts,
              so she told him that he was wasting his time
              and then, by the end, she could take no more of him.

VII   And though by her words
              she would not have offended him,
              she made no excessive or outrageous remarks
              by which his condition might have been in the least bit worsened.
              Nevertheless, they have conspired
              to accuse her in this case now before us
              by means of a cautionary tale
              about "the Belle Dame sans mercy."

VIII   Now, she tolerated all of this patiently,
              without letting it bother her—
              not even asking retribution for it.
              But that did her no good,
              for even after they had sullied
              her honor without cause and wrongfully,
              there were those, I do not know whom, who wanted
              to charge her with murder,

IX   Disant qu'elle avoit amusé
        Cest amoureulx cy longuement,
        Et puis au derrenier reffusé
        Si tres malgracïeusement   68
        Que, du courroux et du tourment
        Qui l'en prinst, mort s'en est ensuye,
        Et par elle tant seullement,
        De quoy de puis l'en l'a poursuye.   72

X   Et fut vray que la povre femme,   [91v]
        Au jour que l'en la fist adjourner,
        Comparut pour tenir son terme
        Et ses deffences assigner.   76
        Mais chacun la vint blasonner
        Pour sa doleur tousjours acroistre:
        N'oncques de conseil peust finer
        Ne ame qui pour elle voult estre.   80

XI   Si eust la mains maulx a passer
        Et une passïon grevaine;
        Oultre, quant ne voult confesser
        Le cas dont se sentoit bien saine,   84
        L'en luy vint presenter la gehaine
        Dont elle se esmeut tellement
        Que de fraieur, doleur et paine
        Lors perdit son entendement.   88

XII   Et peut bien estre que a ceste heure
        Confessa tout ce qu'on vouloit
        Comme celle qui ja labeure
        A langueur qui la traveilloit,   92
        Car du monde ne luy challoit,
        Ains aymoit mieulx mourir que vivre
        Et contre elle mesmes parloit
        Pour estre de tous poins delivre.   96

IX   saying that she had retained
      this lover in question for a long time,
      and then in the end rebuffed him
      so maliciously
      that death ensued
      from the anguish and torment he experienced.
      They add that this torment came from her alone,
      which is the reason they prosecuted the case.

X   And it was true that the poor woman
      on the day that she was called before the court
      arrived at the appointed time
      to present her defense.
      But everyone came up to mock her,
      and, to add to her suffering,
      she was never able to procure counsel
      nor to find a single soul who wished to be on her side.

XI   She experienced in the courtroom many hardships to overcome,
      not to mention grievous suffering.
      Moreover, when she refused to confess
      to the crime of which she felt herself to be innocent,
      they threatened her with torture,
      which scared her so badly
      that from the fear, suffering, and pain
      she finally lost her senses.

XII   And it is possible that at that time
      she confessed to everything they wanted,
      like one who labors
      in the languor that makes her suffering.
      For she did not care about the world;
      she preferred to die rather than to live,
      so she spoke against herself
      in order to be left alone.

XIII	Et ja soit ce que de raison	[92r]
	La confessïon ainsi faicte	
	Par contrainte et hors de saison	
	Ne feust valable ne parfaicte,	100
	Toutesfois l'en en a extraicte	
	Une sentence si piteuse	
	Qu'il n'y a femme qui n'en caquecte	
	Et qui n'en soit trop doloreuse.	104

XIV	Par laquelle dure sentence	
	L'en a condempné ceste dame	
	A la nommer, par desplaisance,	
	En amour la Crüelle Femme;	108
	Puis, pour faire a la lignee blasme,	
	A souffir mort comme murtriere,	
	Ville, deshonneste, et infame,	
	Pour sa pugnicïon derreniere.	112

XV	Or, maintenoient ses heritiers	
	Qu'il y avoit eu jugement,	
	Par dix ou .xj. poins entiers,	
	Erreur ou erreurs clerement,	116
	En requerant consequemment	
	Qu'il fust de tous poins rescindé,	
	Au moins en tout avenement	
	Mis au nëant et amendé.	120

XVI	Le premier: car noblë estoit,	[92v]
	Et y a coustume notoire,	
	Gardee de tel temps qu'il n'estoit	
	Jamais memoire du contraire,	124
	Que en amours l'en ne peut forfaire	
	Le corps, posé qu'en mal s'aplicque,	
	Par quoy l'en ne la devoit faire	
	Mourir ainsi de mort publicque.	128

XIII   And now rightly it can be said
that the confession extracted in this manner,
by force and at an inopportune time,
was not valid or correct.
Yet they used it to extort
a sentence so pitiful
that there is not a woman alive who does not whisper
and grieve over it.

XIV   By this harsh sentence
they condemned the lady
to be named, because of their disapproval of her,
'the Cruel Woman in love';
then, to vilify her entire lineage,
she was made to suffer death as a murderer,
vile, dishonorable, and wicked,
as her final punishment.

XV   Now, her descendants maintain
that during the course of the trial
were introduced blatant errors
on at least ten or eleven points;
consequently they request
that the judgment be rescinded on all counts,
or at least in each circumstance
where facts were neglected or altered.

XVI   The first point: because she was nobility
and there is a customary law of note,
a custom upheld for so long a time that
no one remembers any different,
that out of respect one cannot vilify or harm
the body of a noble person, even given that harm was done;
by which we understand that one should not have made
her die thus a public and common death.

XVII
Secondement, y avoit erreur
Car envers l'amant s'aquicta
De le retraire par doulceur
De la folie ou se bouta;   132
Mais oncques ne s'en depporta,
Ains se y mist lors plus que jamais;
Ainsi, se mal en emporta,
Ceste dame n'en povoit mais.   136

XVIII
Tiercement: point ne le blessa,
Ne ne luy fist playe ou navreure,
Mais comme dit est, l'adressa
A son bien dont il n'avoit cure,   140
Ains vouloit mectre a l'aventure
L'onneur et vie d'elle en reprouche
Qui estoit prilleuse ouverture
Pour toutes a qui le cas touche.   144

XIX
Nulle n'est tenue ne asservie   [93r]
Des biens d'amours aucun saisir
Se de long temps ne l'a servie
Ou qu'en luy s'i preigne plaisir,   148
Car aux dames est de choisir
Ou le reffus ou le donner.
Donc fault prendre le desplaisir
Quant il vient, sans en mot sonner.   152

XX
Ainsi së avoit reffusé
Cest amant, comme l'en veult dire,
Elle auroit de son droit usé
Sans grever aucun ne luy nuyre,   156
Ne la cause de l'escondire
N'estoit pas assez souffisante
De luy brasser ung tel martire
Et si terrible mort dolente.   160

XVII
The second error was this:
she fulfilled her obligation to the lover
by asking him to withdraw out of kindness
from the pit in which he had thrown himself.
But he never did renounce it;
rather, he committed himself more than ever,
as if evil took over his mind.
This lady could have done nothing to prevent it.

XVIII
The third error is this: she never hurt him
nor inflicted any wound or any other injury.
Rather, as it is written, she spoke to his well-being,
about which he cared very little.
His lack of care for himself showed a wish to put in danger
of reproach her honor and life;
this was a risky proposition
for any lady who might be involved.

XIX
No lady is required nor subject
to grant just anyone the benefits of love
if he has not first served her in love for a long time
or if he does not please her.
For it is for ladies to choose
either to refuse or to bestow their grace.
And therefore, it is essential to accept displeasure
when it comes, without a word of complaint.

XX
In this vein, if she had rebuffed
this lover, as they like to say,
she would have only been exercising her right,
without vexing or harming anyone.
Nor was the cause of the refusal
sufficient
to instigate such torture
and painful, horrible death.

XXI   *Quarto*: la court aroit erré
                 Car touchant le cas principal
                 Elle adjoustoit foy au narré
                 D'un tel quel livre ferïal,   164
                 Fait par ung escripvain fiscal,
                 Qui y avoit du sien bouté,
                 Et d'elle dit cent fois de mal
                 Plus que jamais n'avoit esté.   168

XXII   *Quinto*: car par la Decretalle   [93v]
                 Des serviteurs aventureulx,
                 Et aussi par la Loy Finalle
                 Ou chapitre des douloureux,   172
                 Il est dit que nul amoureulx
                 D'une femme ne se doit plaindre
                 S'il n'a trois reffus rigoureulx
                 De distance d'un jour le moindre.   176

XXIII   Or, n'avoit cest amant parlé
                 Pas plus hault de deux fois a elle,
                 Ne esté que une fois recullé
                 Dont sourt toute ceste querelle;   180
                 Pour quoy a se plaindre d'icelle
                 Il ne faisoit a recevoir
                 Ne ne vault la sentence itelle,
                 Car il y a erreur pour voir.   184

XXIV   *Sexto*: ne fut jamais oÿe
                 Leans par conseil ne autrement,
                 Ains de tous advocats fouÿe
                 Par ce qu'ilz veoient clerement   188
                 Qu'on l'avoit en contempnement
                 Et qu'elle y eust perdue sa paine,
                 Qui estoit bien fait vengement
                 En icelle court souveraine.   192

XXI　　　　The fourth error is this: the court committed an error
with regard to the principal argument,
for it granted credence to the narrative
of a trivial book
written by a venal writer[1]
who inserted his own imaginings into the tale,
saying about her things one hundred times worse
than anything that had ever before been said.

XXII　　　　The fifth error, because by the *Decretal*[2]
of fortuitous lovers
and also by the book called the *Everlasting Law*
in the chapter for unfortunate lovers
it is stated that no lover
of a woman can complain
if he has not three times been firmly refused
in a space of at least one day.

XXIII　　　　But this lover had not spoken
any more than twice to her
and was only one time rebuffed,
from which stems this whole dispute.
This is why his complaint about her is in error:
he did nothing to receive
nor deserve such a judgment in his favor;
that it was a mistake is plain to see.

XXIV　　　　The sixth error: she was never heard
in court, neither by counsel nor otherwise;
instead all the lawyers abandoned her
because they saw clearly
that she was already considered guilty
and that she would have been just wasting her time,
which was a perfect revenge
in this sovereign court.

XXV	*Septimo*: la confessïon	[94r]
	Qu'elle fist estoit nulle et vaine	
	Car ce fut par impressïon	
	Et de paour d'estre mise en gehaine	196
	Dont n'eust sceu supporter la paine,	
	Car femme estoit delicative	
	Et de complectïon mondaine,	
	Non subgecte a doleur passive.	200
XXVI	Mais posé qu'elle eust revellé	
	Et congneu le cas dessusdit,	
	Veu qu'elle avoit le sens meslé	
	Et l'entendement interdit,	204
	Arrester l'en ne doit a son dit	
	N'a chose qui s'en est ensuÿe,	
	Car l'en ne scet lors que l'en dit	
	Quant la personne est esblouÿe.	208
XXVII	*Octavo*: quant l'en veult congnoistre	
	De mort et paine capitalle	
	Tous les seigneurs y doivent estre;	
	Mais plusieurs lors faisoient grant galle	212
	Et se pourmenoient en la salle	
	Quant le cas fut deliberé	
	Par quoy la sentence finalle	
	Si estoit nulle *ipso jure*.	216
XXVIII	*Nono*: cest amoureulx icy	[94]
	Ne prinst jamais la maladie	
	Du reffuz de grace et mercy	
	Fait de la dame, quoy qu'on dye,	220
	Mais d'une entreprinse hardie	
	Ou ne peult advenir jamais;	
	Et si a l'en la charge hourdie	
	Sur elle qui n'en povoit mais.	224

XXV

The seventh error: the confession
that she gave was null and void,
for it was obtained under pressure
and out of fear of receiving judicial torture,
of which she would not have known how to tolerate the pain,
for the woman was delicate
and of a temperament that prefers pleasure.

XXVI

Even assuming that she might have admitted to
and recognized the argument cited above,
given that her senses were muddled
and her understanding impaired,
one should not judge her by her word
nor by anything that follows from that,
for one does not know what one says
when one is so befuddled.

XXVII

Eight: when one wants to consider
death and capital punishment,
all of the lords must be there.
But several of them at that time were having a party
and were wandering about the room
as the case was being deliberated.
For this reason, the final sentence
is nullified, by the law itself.

XXVIII

Nine: this lover
was not made ill
by the refusal of grace and pity
from the lady, no matter what one says,
but from a difficult enterprise
that one can never achieve,
and so they placed too heavy a charge
on her, who could never tolerate it.

XXIX   Qu'i soit vray qu'i n'en mourut pas,
         Il sera clerement prouvé,
         Car de puis fist mains saulx et pas
         Sain, en bon point, et non grevé;   228
         Aussi estoit tousjours levé
         Et vescut bien ung moys aprés,
         En quoy le grief est approuvé
         De l'erreur sur ce point exprés.   232

XXX   *Decimto*: et le peremptoire,
         Cest amant par son testament
         Ne fist mencïon ne memoire
         De l'en chargier aucunement,   236
         Mais pardonna entierement
         A chacun, par quoy fut oultraige
         D'en nayer si villainement
         Ceste dame, dont est dommage.   240

XXXI   *Undecimo*: y eust erreur   [95r]
         En ce que la court ne advisa
         A la beaulté d'elle et doulceur,
         Et que Jeunesse ne excusa   244
         Et que Pitié si ne brisa
         La rigueur de Ferocité
         Dont la court aigrement usa
         Sans avoir l'oeil a equicté.   248

XXXII   L'erreur derrenier, pour abregier,
         Si fut car quant Misericorde
         Si volut venir au jugier
         Et y mener Paix et Concorde,   252
         L'en leur tira l'uys et la corde
         Pour ne point ouïr leurs requestes,
         Et si estoient, comme on recorde,
         Presidens d'Amours aux enquestes.   256

XXIX   That it is true he did not die of his illness
will be clearly proven,
for since that time he has taken many
healthy steps and leaps, at a good clip and without difficulty;
in addition, he was still on his feet
and lived a good month afterward,
by which the injustice of the error
on this point is undeniably certain.

XXX   The tenth error, and the irrefutable one,
is that the lover, in his last will and testament,
made no mention or record
to accuse her in this affair in any way whatsoever,
but pardoned in full everyone,
which is why it was an outrage
to drown so despicably
this lady, which is such a shame.

XXXI   The eleventh error: there was error
in that the court did not consider
the lady's beauty and sweetness,
nor did they excuse Youth; there was error
that Pity did not break down
the harshness of Ferocity,
which the court certainly made undue use of
without even an eye to fairness.

XXXII   The final error, to be brief,
was that when Compassion
wished to come to the trial
and bring with her Peace and Concord,
they employed every means to
prevent a hearing of their requests
and yet they were, as you recall,
presiding magistrates of Love's council.[3]

XXXIII   Ainsi la sentence crüeuse
Fut trop aigre de la moitié,
Car la dame estoit tant eureuse
Que tous si en avoient pitié   260
En desirant son amistié,
Et aussi quant l'en vit les termes
Du jugement qui fut gecté,
Chacun plouroit a grosses lermes.   264

XXXIV   Et en oultre, dit on plus fort   [95v]
Que quant ce vint a la noyer
Et que la faillut mectre a mort,
Le bourreau, qu'est de soy murtrier,   268
Si prinst si fort a lermoyer
Et a plourer soubz son chappeau,
Qu'on luy bailla pour se essuier,
Devant tout le monde, ung drappeau.   272

XXXV   Or peult estre que ne vouldroit
Pas estre de cest heure au monde,
Car elle a passé orendroit
Une grande doleur parfonde;   276
Mais pour ce cas icy, l'en fonded
Sur les hoirs d'elle aucun malice,
Qui est charge qui trop redonde
A leur grant fame et prejudice.   280

XXXVI   Non pas des hoirs tant seullement,
Mais de la lignee tant notable
Qui a vescu honnoreement
Sans faire cas vitupperable,   284
Dont le mal leur est plus grevable
Que qui leur vouldroit courre sus;
Pour le reprouche inreparable
Si concluoient comme dessus.   288

XXXIII   Thus the cruel sentence
was too severe by half,
for the lady was so blessed
that all had pity on her
and desired her friendship.
Furthermore, when they saw the terms
of the judgment that had been laid down,
every single one wept great tears.

XXXIV   Moreover, it was declared
that when it came to drowning her
and the fact that it was ordered that she be put to death,
the executioner, who is by definition a murderer,
started sobbing so hard
and crying under his hat
that they gave him a rag to wipe his eyes
in front of everyone.

XXXV   Now, it may be that she would not wish
to be of the world at this time,
for she has overcome recently
a profound and overwhelming grief.
But the question for the case at hand is that malice
is now being cast upon her descendants.
It is a charge that throws too much
extreme slander and damage on them.

XXXVI   And not only on her descendants
but on this entire notable lineage,
who have lived honorably
without ever doing anything despicable.
Thus the damage for the irreparable blame
concluded earlier
is more troubling for them
than him who wishes to attack them.

XXXVII   De la partie des ayans cause   [96r]
          Du feu amant, dont est memoire
          Tous deffendeurs en ceste cause,
          Si fut deffendu au contraire,   292
          Disans que chacun povoit croire
          Que le deffunct estoit renté
          D'un don de grace de douaire
          Dont nul n'est gaires herité.   296

XXXVIII   Il estoit tout premierement
          Tresbeau filz, courtois, amiable,[4]
          Soy vestant tousjours gentement,
          Saige, sachant, fort piteable,[5]   300
          Humble, graciëulx, serviable,
          De doulx parler et beau maintien,
          Portant couraige si notable
          Qu'il n'avoit en effect rien sien.   304

XXXIX   Il aymoit bien ce qu'il aymoit
          Sans ce qu'on l'en peut desmouvoir,
          Car par sa bonté presumoit
          Que chacun si devoit avoir   308
          Tel cueur que luy, a dire voir,
          Pour ayder et pour secourir;
          Dont cela le fist decevoir
          Et aprés, au derrenier, mourir.   312

XL   L'en ne savroit les biens penser   [96v]
          Que cest homme si soustenoit,
          Qu'il l'eust volu mesmes tencer
          De quelque argu, quant il venoit,   316
          En le voyant n'en souvenoit,
          Qui estoit a luy singulier don,
          Ne jamais debat ne prenoit.
          Dieu luy vueille faire pardon.   320

XXXVII   Then from the party presenting the case
             of the dead lover, or the memory thereof—
             all defendants, in this case—
             was presented a defense to contradict their argument,
             saying that everyone could certainly believe
             that the defunct had been endowed
             with a gift of grace
             that no one can now inherit.

XXXVIII   First of all, he was
             a beautiful son, courtly, friendly,
             always dressing himself as a gentleman,
             wise, knowing, and worthy of pity,
             humble, gracious, willing to serve,
             with a sweet manner of speaking and a pleasant demeanor
             that displayed a heart so generous
             that he considered nothing to be his own.

XXXIX   He loved well what he loved
             and no one could divert him from it,
             for his goodness presumed
             that everyone, truth be told,
             should have a heart like his,
             always willing to help and render succor;
             but this attribute allowed him to be deceived,
             and he died of it in the end.

XL   One could never comprehend the good
             that this man supported,
             which he would have wanted to present
             in persuasive argument himself. But when he arrived,
             seeing her, he forgot every detail
             of this gift that was singular to him,
             nor did he ever fight it,
             may God forgive him!

XLI   Or, estoit vray qu'il fut espris
                 De ceste dame en la malle heure,
                 Dont l'amour lui cousta bon pris
                 Et fut l'acointance bien dure,   324
                 Car il s'en ensuivit navreure,
                 De quoy l'amant est trespassé
                 Par le reffus contre Nature
                 Qu'elle luy avoit pourchassé.   328

XLII   Las! c'estoit mal consideré
                 L'ostel et lieu⁶ dont il estoit,
                 Et meschamment remuneré
                 Le service qu'il supportoit.   332
                 Bien pour mal si lui presentoit
                 Mais ne daignoit tourner les yeulx,
                 Et si tousjours sien se portoit
                 Ja soit ce qu'il eust trouvé mieulx.   336

XLIII   Elle estoit belle voirement   [97r]
                 Mais ceste beaulté naturelle
                 Si l'emploioit mauvaisement,
                 Car point në amendoit d'icelle,   340
                 Et si portoit doleur mortelle,
                 De toutes poisons assouvie.
                 Et qu'il soit vray, se ne fust elle,
                 Encores fust l'amant en vie.   344

XLIV   Pour cause de laquelle mort,
                 Elle, convenue en justice,
                 Si a, sans contraincte et effort,
                 Confessé tout du long le vice,   348
                 Et comment par mauvais malice
                 Elle avoit l'amant a mort mis
                 En requerant pardon propice⁷
                 Et que le cas lui fut remis.   352

XLI
Now, it was true that he was in love
with this lady, and at the wrong time.
Her love cost him a very high price,
and her acquaintance was harsh.
He received a deep wound
from the refusal that she gave him,
a refusal contrary to Nature.

XLII
Alas! It was not to be considered highly,
that dwelling and place where he found himself,
and his service there
was poorly paid.
He gave her good for bad,
but she did not deign to turn her eyes toward him;
yet he still considered himself hers
even though he might have found better.

XLIII
She was truly beautiful,
but she used this natural beauty
in a malicious way,
for he did not receive a bit of comfort from her
and so was laden with a mortal anguish
brought on by all sorts of poison.
And it is true that if it were not for her,
this lover would still be alive.

XLIV
This death is the reason
for which she, in a trial before the court,
confessed all of her sin,
without being constrained or forced to do so.
She revealed how out of malice
she had decided the lover's death,
and then she asked for forgiveness
and that the case might be remitted.

XLV   Or cela devoit bien souffire
             A la jugier et condempner,
             Mais affin qu'il n'y eust que redire,
             La court voult oultre ordonner   356
             Que l'en feroit examiner
             Tous les tesmoings devant sa bouche,
             Contre lesquelz ne voult donner
             Aucun contredit ne reprouche.   360

XLVI   C'estoient aussi tel gens notables,   [97v]
             De grant façon entre milliers,
             Tous preudommes et veritables,
             Rassis, fermes comme pilliers,   364
             Qui, devant tous les conseilliers,
             Disdrent la forme de l'excés,
             Mesmes ses servans familliers,
             Comme il appert par le procés.   368

XLVII   Et combien qu'elle, veu l'enorme
             Et horrible cas recité,
             Deust estre pendue en ung horme,
             Au mains son chief decappité   372
             Et le surplus du corps porté
             Au gibet, pour exemple prendre;
             Neantmoins, la court par pitié
             L'a volue de ce mal deffendre.   376

XLVIII   En quoy elle a les hoirs grevez
             Du trespassé, dont Dieu ait l'ame,
             Veuz les grans exés agrevés,
             Ensemble le cas tant infame.   380
             Et si les hoirs de ceste femme
             Ne s'en vuellent pas contenter,
             Ains pour faire plus grant wacarme
             Se viennent en erreur bouter.   384

XLV

That in and of itself should suffice
in order to judge and condemn her!
But so that there will never be reason
to recount the case again, the court wishes to order
that all the witnesses be examined
and the truth heard from their own mouths,
that their testimony
might not be contradicted or reproached by anyone.

XLVI

It was such notable people,
great even among many,
all prudent men and truthful,
upstanding, solid as pillars,
who before the judicial counselors
told of her outrageous acts and the form they took.
Even her close servants testified against her,
as was required by the law.

XLVII

Even though she, given the enormous
and horrible case repeated above,
should be hung on the boughs of an elm tree,
or at least have her head cut off
and the rest of her corpse carried out
and hung on the gallows to serve as example,
nevertheless the court, out of pity,
wished to keep her from this terrible fate.

XLVIII

And the court has hurt the heirs of the defunct lover
(by restraining their punishment), God rest his soul,
seeing that the outrageousness of her crime was compounded
when coupled with the infamous case itself.
And now the descendants of this woman
do not wish to be satisfied with the court's decision,
so they, in order to make a bigger fracas,
intrude on the scene to put forth their errors.

XLIX   Or disoient ilz que oncques procés   [98r]
            Ne fut si justement jugié,
            Ne qu'on a veu de telz excés
            Maindre prouffit estre adjugié,   388
            Et que au surplus avoient congié
            En ceste cause et les despens,
            Car la deffuncte avoit nagié
            Dessoubz l'eaue plus de cent arpens.   392

L   Ces deffendeurs disoient en oultre,
            Que ou congié ne pourroient avoir
            Et qu'il leur fauldroit passer oultre,
            Que ces demandeurs cy pour voir   396
            Ne faisoient a recevoir
            De erreur contre l'arrest poser,
            Car celle qui y deust pourveoir
            Si mourut sans le proposer.   400

LI   Mais encores au regard d'elle
            Jamais receue n'y eust esté,
            Car en matiere crimminelle,
            Quant le jugement est gecté,   404
            Il fault qu'il soit excecuté
            Tout a coup, sans dilacion,
            Autrement tout seroit gasté
            Qui n'en feroit pugnicion.   408

LII   Mal aux mauvais prouffiteroit   [98v]
            Et aroient retribucion
            Pour leurs vis qui en eslognneroit
            Contre des droiz l'entencion;   412
            Qui oultre disoient que l'action
            Ne transist point aux hoirs du corps
            Pour d'erreur faire mencion,
            Car seroit susciter les mors.   416

XLIX	However, the defendants said, never
	had a trial been more justly deliberated,
	nor had there ever been seen from such excessive crime
	so little profit in the sentence.
	Moreover, they said that they had carried
	even greater expense in this case,
	for the dead lover had swum
	under the water for more than one hundred measures.
L	In addition, the defendants said that
	they could not let this go
	and that they would need to proceed.
	They said that these plaintiffs here, in truth,
	were not here trying to propose a motion
	to show error against the judgment,
	for she who should make such a request of the court
	had already died without making any such complaint.
LI	But again, with regard to her,
	she never would have been granted such a request,
	for in a criminal matter
	when the judgment is rescinded
	it must be executed
	immediately, with no delay,
	otherwise all would be wasted
	and the guilty would not be punished.
LII	Evil would profit the bad people
	and they would have retribution
	for their lives, which would be prolonged,
	going against the intention of the law.
	Moreover, the punishment of the body does not translate to the heirs,
	as stated in the error regarding this point,
	for that would be reviving the sins of the dead.

LIII
Et pour respondre par articles
A telz quelz "erreurs" baptisez,
Dont ces acteurs font leurs boticles
Cy tenuz pour pressupposez,   420
Dient que en vain se y sont admusez,
Veu le procés et la sentence,
Et que sont tous faiz supposez
Ou il n'y a coleur n'apparance.[8]   424

LIV
Et au regard du premier point
Par lequel ilz ont volu dire
Que femme noble ne peut point
Mourir de publicque martire,   428
La raison ne se doit deduire
Au cas de ceste femme cy,
Car estoit faulse, plaine de yre,
Et si fut trouvee sans mercy.   432

LV
De avoir parlé de sa noblesse,   [99r]
Il n'estoit gaires grant besoing,
Car l'outraige de sa rudesse
Si fut du contraire tesmoing   436
Le pouvre homme prenoit grant soing
De la servir et honnourer,
Et si tousjours le gectoit loing
Pour enfin le deshonnorer.   440

LVI
Mais posé que noble eust esté,
Cela ne se entend ou applicque
En cas de leze magesté,
Comme elle commist tout publicque,   444
Car par sa langue baselicque[9]
Appella Amours "losengier"[10]
Et *sic*, par la tierce auctenticque[11]
L'en la devoit ainsi jugier.   448

LIII   And so to respond article by article
to what they have baptized as "errors,"
on which these plaintiffs base their claims,
presented as if they are indisputable,
the defendants say that in vain are they seeking their amusement,
given the trial and the judgment
and that all of their "facts" are assumed
and hold no water.

LIV   As to the first point,
by which they wish to say
that a noble woman should not ever
die a public death:
the rule does not apply
in the case of this woman,
for she was false, full of ire,
and was found to be without mercy.

LV   To have spoke of her nobility
was really unnecessary,
for the outrageousness of her hard heart
testifies to the contrary.
The poor lover took great trouble
to serve and honor her properly,
and yet she tossed him aside
in order to dishonor him.

LVI   Even assuming that she was noble,
the law would not apply
in a case of a crime of lèse-majesté,
which she committed quite publicly against Love,
for by her basilisk tongue
she called Love a lying slanderer,
and thereby, according to the third book,
she had to be sentenced in such a manner.

LVII   Au second point que s'aquicta
                D'oster le deffunct de folie,
                Ce fut elle qui le y bouta,
                Car il esperoit chiere lie;   452
                Comme beau temps aprés la pluye
                La suivoit et servoit tousjours
                Et y print la merencolie
                Dont il est mort avant ses jours.   456

LVIII   Au tiers erreur, ou veulent dire
                Qu'il n'y eut navreure ne bateure
                Du costé d'elle, ne martire,
                Fors que d'une response dure,   460
                Respondoient que ceste bleceure
                Vault pis que de cousteau fraper
                Car elle est de tele nature
                Que nul ne s'en peut eschapper.   464

LIX   Quant l'en frappe de glaive ung coup,   [99v]
                Posé qu'on ait doleur grevaine,
                Au moins l'en en meurt tout a coup
                Et ne languist on plus en paine.   468
                Mais il eust fievre traversaine
                Qui lui dura plus de trois moys,
                Sans qu'il trouvast viande saine
                Et devint aussi sec que boys.   472

LX   De son honneur contregarder
                Il n'en estoit que trop songneux,
                Car autant l'eust volu garder
                Que le sien, voire cent fois mieulx.   476
                Les lermes luy veoit aux yeulx
                Comme a ung cerf qui veult mourir,
                Mais son cueur fut tant furieulx
                Que ne le daigna secourir.   480

LVII

As to the second point raised,
that she tried to relieve the folly of the dead lover:
it was she who shoved him into madness!
For he was hoping for a joyful welcome,
like beautiful weather after the rain.
He followed her wishes and served her continually,
and thereby was afflicted with melancholy,
which killed him before his time.

LVIII

As to the third error, where they want to claim
that he received no wound or injury
from her, nor death,
but only a harsh response,
the defendants retort that this wound
was worse than that of a gouging knife,
for it was of such a nature
that no one could escape its pain.

LIX

When one is struck by a spear,
it is a given that grievous pain follows,
but at least one dies quickly
and does not languish long in one's pain.
But this lover had a spiking fever,
which he endured for over three months
without being to keep down any meat,
and so he became as dry as a stick of wood.

LX

To protect his honor,
he was only too careful,
though he wished to do the same
a hundred times more to guard hers.
Tears pooled in his eyes[12]
as in those of a deer that wishes to die,
but her heart was so enraged
that she did not deign to help him.

LXI   Quant est du reffuz ou choisir,
           Les dames n'y ont d'avantaige
           Si non de prendre leur plaisir,
           Et si se entend sans nul dommaige,   484
           Car de commectre excés ne oultraige
           Pour dire "il ne me plairoit point,"
           Amours, qui est tant noble et saige,
           Jamais ne consentit ce point.   488

LXII   Au quart erreur, touchant le livre   [100r]
           Qu'ilz disoient estre controuvé,
           Leur entendement estoit yvre
           Et avoient cela controuvé,   492
           Car il fut depuis approuvé
           Par tant de conseilliers notables,
           Voire quant ilz eurent trouvé
           Les faiz d'icelui veritables.   496

LXIII   L'escripvain si estoit entier,
           Si fut de ce livre facteur
           Le noble maistre Alain Chartier,[13]
           Jadis excellent orateur   500
           Et si parfait explanateur
           Des comedies et faiz d'amours
           Qu'il n'y a seigneur ne serviteur
           Qu'il ne prie pour lui a tousjours.   504

LXIV   Au vme, n'a decretalle[14]
           Qui peult ceste femme excuser,
           Tant fut trouvee rebelle et malle
           Et faicte pour gens abuser: 508
           Pas n'y eust ung seul reffuser
           Ains plus de dix, a tout voir dire,
           Ne ne le faisoit que amuser,
           Pour aprés s'en mocquer et rire.   512

LXI

As for refusing and the right to choose,
ladies have no more this right than anyone,
excepting that they choose according to their pleasure;
yet this is meant to be done without hurting another,
for to commit such an excessive or outrageous act
in order to say "he does not please me at all"—
well, Love, who is noble and wise,
never consented to that.

LXII

As for the fourth error, which refers to the book
that they claimed to have been fabricated,
their interpretation was inane
and they must have made it up,
for it was later proven, in truth,
by many notable counselors,
when they had recognized
the facts of this book to be true.

LXIII

The writer was of great integrity;
the author of this book,
the noble Master Alain Chartier,
was an excellent orator of old
and masterful exegete
of the dramas and deeds of love,
and there is neither lord nor servant
who does not constantly offer up prayers for his soul.

LXIV

As for the fifth error, there is no law
that could excuse this woman,
for she was much too rebellious and evil,
and crafted to deceive people.
Nor was there just one refusal,
but more than ten of them, truth be told,
and it was just an amusement for her
so that afterward she might mock and laugh.

LXV   Il faisoit bien a recevoir,   [100v]
                 Qui l'eust volu aymer et prendre,
                 Mais oncques n'en fist son devoir
                 Car mieulx aymoit sa grace extendre   516
                 Sur estrangiers et a pris vendre,
                 Que a cestui qui plus en offroit
                 Et a qui loyer devoit rendre
                 Du mal que pour elle souffroit.   520

LXVI   Pour le .vj.^me erreur et point,
                 En la court ont volu chargier
                 Par ce que on ne luy bailla point
                 De conseil pour la solagier,   524
                 Sur cela ne se fault targier,
                 Car en criminelle action
                 L'en ne doit point laisser forgier
                 Jamais la disposicion.   528

LXVII   Au viime, qu'elle confessa
                 Tout par contraincte et paour de gehaine,
                 Oncques nul si ne l'en pressa,
                 Ainsi elle, rassise et seine,   532
                 Et sans lui faire grief ne paine,
                 Depposa qu'elle fist mourir
                 L'amant, par angoisse inhumaine
                 Et par faulte de secourir.^15   536

LXVIII   Ainsi de proposer tel fait   [101r]
                 Et dire qu'elle estoit troublee,
                 C'estoit aux demandeurs mal fait,
                 Car la ne fut riens fait d'emblee   540
                 La court si estoit assemblee
                 Qui scet comment y doit pourvoir,
                 Et se on l'eust a gehaine acomblee,
                 L'en n'eust ja fait que son devoir.   544

LXV	He did everything he could to be received well,
	but she never did her duty;
	she should have tried to love him and accept him as her lover.
	But she preferred to extend her grace
	to strangers and sell it at a high price
	rather than give it to this lover, who offered her more.
	She should have rendered him his due
	for the pain he suffered for her.
LXVI	For the sixth error,
	they wished to rebuke the court
	for the fact that she was not given
	a lawyer to help her,
	but there is really no need to defend this action,
	for in the case of criminal activity
	one should never let the decision
	of the judges be manipulated.
LXVII	As to the seventh error, which concerns the confession
	extracted from her by force and for fear of prison,
	never did anyone press her to make her admission,
	but she, confident and in her right mind,
	and without the infliction of any grief or pain,
	testified that she caused the lover to die
	an inhumanly agonizing death
	by her refusal to help him.
LXVIII	So to make such an assertion
	and say that she was troubled by his death
	was insulting on the part of the plaintiffs,
	for there was nothing done in secret there.
	The court was assembled
	and it knows how it should be understood.
	Besides, even if they had threatened her with prison,
	they only would have been doing their duty.

LXIX	Il n'estoit ja besoing, au fort,	
	Veu qu'elle du commencement	
	Confessa le meurdre et la mort	
	Sur quoy se assist le jugement,	548
	Et combien que sans ce largement	
	Y avoit enqueste et tesmoings	
	Qui en depposoient tout clerement	
	Comme elle fist, ne plus ne moins.	552
LXX	A l'erreur de la nulité[16]	
	Des seigneurs qui n'y estoient pas,	
	Sauve leur grace, a la verité,	
	Tous y furent au derrenier pas	556
	En deliberant par compas,	
	Touchant ce procés ric a ric,	
	Et le jugement pas a pas	
	Par la voye du Saint Esperit.	560
LXXI	A l'erreur mesmes ou ilz dient	[101v]
	Que d'ailleurs l'amant fut malade,	
	Ceulx qui le soustiennent mesdient,	
	Car se ce n'eust esté la darde	564
	Du reffuz en arriere garde	
	De ceste dame sans mercy,	
	De mourir jamais n'avoit garde	
	Ne autre qu'elle ne l'a occy.	568
LXXII	Aussti n'y avoit apparance	
	De venir ce fait baptiser	
	Apres l'arrest et la sentence,	
	Et ung alibi proposer,	572
	Combien qu'il n'eust fait que amuser,	
	Car ou a depposicion	
	De faiz, l'en ne doit point user	
	Ne jugier par presumpcion.	576

LXIX	There was never a need to do such a thing, in truth,
	given that at the beginning
	she confessed to the murder and the death
	on which the judgment was based,
	and even though beyond that
	there were many questions and witnesses
	who testified clearly as to what
	she had done, adding no more or less.
LXX	As to the error claiming nullification due to
	the lords who were not there:
	by their grace, in truth,
	they were all there for the final stage,
	deliberating carefully,
	considering with great precision every detail
	presented in the trial, and deciding the decision
	with the help of the Holy Spirit.
LXXI	With regard to the error in which they claim
	that the lover had been ill beforehand:
	those who make such a statement misspeak,
	for the cause of his malady was only the arrow
	of the refusal that came from the rear guard
	of this lady with no pity.
	He never had cause to fear death
	nor anything else except that she might kill him.
LXXII	And there was no apparent reason
	to bring this fact to the court
	after the decision and sentencing,
	offering up an alibi,
	for that would only have confused the issue.
	In laying out the facts
	one should not waste time,
	nor make a judgment based on presumption.

LXXIII   Au dix.^me, ou il pardonna
            Le meffait par son testament,
            Respondoient qu'il n'avoit ne n'a
            Trop bien; peult estre voirement   580
            Qu'il, estant au derrain tourment,
            Dist adieu[17] en plourant adoncques,
            Mais qu'il parlast expressement
            De ce cas icy, non fist oncques.   584

LXXIV   Mais posé qu'il eust pardonné,   [102r]
            Cela feroit beaucop contre elle,
            En tant que lui aroit donné
            Grant loyer pour doleur mortelle,   588
            Et que d'autant que fust cruelle
            Plus piteux monstré se seroit
            Par sa grant bonté naturelle
            Qui en mourant si la prisoit.   592

LXXV   Luy pardonner le malefice
            Si ne la povoit exempter
            De l'interest de la justice
            Ne de pugnicion quicter,   596
            Ains la failloit excecuter
            Pour a tous vray exemplë estre:
            Qui fait mal, mal en doit porter;
            Barat deçoit toujours son maistre.   600

LXXVI   Au regard de la xj^e erreur,
            Disant que la court fut cruelle,
            Trop si ne usa que de doulceur
            Contre ceste femme rebelle   604
            Qui fut tant rude et criminelle,
            Qu'on n'y povoit mal coup ferir,
            Car selon raison naturelle,
            Elle devoit deux fois mourir.   608

LXXIII   As to the tenth error, which refers to the fact that the lover
pardoned the misdeed in his last will and testament,
they responded that he did not hold
anything against anyone; perhaps, verily,
being in the final throes of torment,
he did say adieu with tears of forgiveness in his eyes,
but that he was referring specifically
to this case—well, he never did such a thing.

LXXIV   But let us assume that he did pardon everyone;
that would be contrary to her benefit,
inasmuch as he would have given her
a great boon in exchange for mortal pain,
and for as much as she was cruel,
he would have showed himself as more worthy of pity
by the great goodness that came to him naturally,
for even in death, he cherished her dearly.

LXXV   His pardon of her maliciousness
does not exempt her from responsibility
in the interest of justice,
nor does it release her from punishment;
therefore it was necessary to execute her
that she might be a true example to others:
he who does evil will see evil come back to him,
and the trickster is always tricked.

LXXVI   As to the eleventh error, where it was said
that the court was too cruel,
in fact they were only too lenient
on this rebellious woman,
who was so coarse and wicked
that no blow could be harsh enough.
Common sense would dictate
that she should die two times for such crimes.

LXXVII   A l'erreur de Misericorde   [102v]
                  Que au procés point l'en ne appella
                  Pour y mener Paix et Concorde,
                  Illecques l'en ne les rappella,   612
                  Mais quant ilz virent ce cas la
                  Et la grant mauvaistié commise,
                  Chacun d'eulx tantost s'en alla,
                  Car ilz sont tous deux gens d'eglise.   616

LXXVIII   Encores plus, dame Pitié
                  Fut a la judicacion,
                  Mais quant ce vint a la moitié
                  Qu'on monstra la decepcion,   620
                  Elle prinst l'excusacion
                  Pour elle et pour sa seur Doulceur,
                  Disant que sa discencion
                  Se devoit faire par Rigueur.   624

LXXIX   Au fait du bourreau qui ploura
                  Quant il la voult mectre a mort,
                  Oncques lermes n'en souppira,
                  Non fist elle, qui plus est fort,   628
                  Car elle avoit cueur si tresfort
                  Endurcy de mauvais malice
                  Qu'il sembloit que l'en lui fist tort
                  De l'excecuter par justice.   632

LXXX   En cest estat son corps creva   [103r]
                  De grant raige, despit, et yre;
                  S'elle a bien fait elle le treuva:
                  L'ame va a joye ou martire.   636
                  Combien que Amours qui souspire
                  Les cueurs des bonnes gens tousjours,
                  L'en a deu rapporter et dire
                  Qu'elle estoit aux enfers d'Amours.   640

LXXVII   As to the error of Misericord,
who was not called to the trial
in order to bring along Peace and Concord:
these two were not called to the court,
for when they saw the case
and the great crime that had been committed,
each one of them fled the scene,
for both of them are men of the church.

LXXVIII   Moreover, Lady Pity
was at the adjudication,
but when they came to the part
where the deception was revealed,
she excused herself
and her sister Sweetness,
claiming that her dissention
should be presented by Severity.

LXXIX   As to the fact that the executioner cried
when he was putting the lady to death:
in fact, nary a tear fell from his eye,
nor from hers, which is even worse,
for she had a heart so hardened
by evil malice
that it seemed wrong even to execute her
in just punishment.

LXXX   In the state she was in, her body was crushed
by extreme rage, contempt, and ire;
if she had been a person who did good, she would have found good,
for the soul goes either to joy or to death.
Especially since Love always breathes life into
the hearts of good people,
they should have reported and let it be known
that she was in the hellfire of Love.

LXXXI	Or de cela ne leur challoit,
	Mais pour venir a leur matiere
	Erreurs proposer ne failloit
	Ne faire si grande baniere, 644
	Veu que la chose est toute clere
	Et en sont les parties polues.
	Si concluoient en la maniere
	Et aux fins que dessus esleues. 648
LXXXII	De la partie des gens d'Amours,
	Deffendeurs d'un autre cousté,
	Fut proposé que de leurs jours
	Crime de leze majesté 652
	Si grant commis n'avoit esté
	Ne jugement si tresbien fait,
	Requerans par leur recité
	Qu'il demourast en son effect. 656
LXXXIII	Ces demandeurs pour leur replicque [103v]
	Si parseveroient en leur fait,
	Disant qu'il y a erreur publicque
	Au jugement qui a esté fait: 660
	Erreur de droit, erreur de fait,
	Erreur en matiere et en forme;
	Par quoy devoit estre deffait
	Selon le jugement de tout homme. 664
LXXXIV	Premeierement, erreur publicque,
	Car ceste femme estoit clergesse
	Et ainsi, par la Pramaticque
	D'Amours, au tiltre de lïesse 668
	Et le chappitre de noblesse,
	Posé que de mort deust perir,
	L'en ne devoit, de loy expresse,
	La faire *publice* mourir. 672

LXXXI

But that did not bother them!
But to come to their subject,
it was not necessary to propose these errors
nor make such a grand stand,
given that the thing is quite clear
and the parties are set in their opinions.
Thus we conclude the matter
as outlined above.

LXXXII

From the party of Love's men,
defendants from another side,
was proposed that in their day,
the crime of *lèse-majesté*
was so great that
no sentence was too harsh to punish it,
and they requested in their speech
that the judgment remain unaltered.

LXXXIII

The response of the plaintiffs
continued to press their points,
saying that there was common error
in the judgment that had been made:
error of law, error of fact,
error of subject and of technicality,
by which the verdict should be rescinded
according to the good sense of any man.

LXXXIV

First of all, common error,
for this woman was a cultured woman
and thus, by the *Pragmatics of Love,*
under the title of happiness
in the chapter on nobility,
it is written that if one must die,
one should not, by law,
be made to die a public or common death.

LXXXV   Trop bien elle eust esté subgecte,
                 S'elle eust fait le murdre susdit,
                 D'estre misë en oubliecte
                 Certain temps qui eust esté dit,   676
                 Selon son meffait ou mesdit
                 Pour la pugnir secretement.
                 Et par ainsi, joinct cest edict,
                 Y eust erreur notoirement.   680

LXXXVI   Erreur de droit, car de raison   [104r]
                 Se aucun par Amours nommé,
                 Et qu'il n'ait en temps de saison
                 Fait le devoir accoustumé,   684
                 Il n'est pas disgne d'estre amé;
                 Ains le doit l'en envoier paistre,
                 Car ce seroit trop presumé
                 Que dame aymast sans recongnoistre.   688

LXXXVII   Et se de droit il est permis
                 Et qu'elle ait ainsi exploicté,
                 De son cousté n'avoit commis
                 Aucun crime de iniquité,   692
                 Car elle n'a que excecuté
                 Le droit et la loy ordonnee,
                 Et par ainsi, a la verité,
                 Injustement fut condempnee.   696

LXXXVIII   Erreur de fait, car le procés
                 Si fut jugié par ung faulx fait,
                 Coulouré de mort et excés
                 Que ceste dame n'avoit fait.   700
                 Aussi l'amant qui en fut deffait
                 N'en fist oncques nulle poursuite,
                 Mais, l'excusant dudit meffait,
                 Voult qu'ellë en demourast quicte.   704

LXXXV	She would have been subjected to far too much,
	even if she had committed the aforementioned murder,
	to have been put in an oubliette
	for the specified time
	in order to punish her secretly
	for her misdeed or misspoken words.
	By doing this, according to the edict attached here,
	there would be notable error in the sentence.

LXXXVI	There was error of law, for by reason,
	if one is called by Love
	and yet has not fulfilled the requirements
	by the appropriate time,
	then he is not worthy of being loved,
	and so he must be sent out to pasture.
	It would be much too presumptuous
	to expect a lady to love without recognition.

LXXXVII	And so by right it is permissible
	that she acted in this way,
	and for her part, she did not commit
	any sinful crime,
	for she did nothing except
	perform her right, by law ordained,
	and because of this, in truth,
	she was unjustly condemned.

LXXXVIII	There was error of fact, for the trial
	was judged based on a false fact,
	colored with death and outrageous action,
	something that this lady did not do.
	The lover who was destroyed by it
	never tried to bring her to court,
	but instead, excusing the aforementioned misdeed,
	wished that she be absolved of responsibility.

LXXXIX	Ainsi doncques, en cest endroit,	[104v]
	Les heritiers du trespassé,	
	Qui n'avoient adés plus grant droit	
	Que celui qui l'eust pourchassé,	708
	Avoient follement adressé	
	Leur conclusion et requeste,	
	Et fut ce fait yla mussé	
	Ou il n'y avoit os n'areste.	712

XC Erreur y eust en la matiere
Car, par le procés demené,
Qui tresbien si le considere,
N'y eust que ung seul reffus donné   716
Sans avoir de glaive assené,
Pour quoy la cause souffisante
N'estoit, tout bien examiné,
D'en ystre telle mort dolente.   720

XCI Et n'y faisoit riens au contraire
Que du reffus se ensuit mort,
Car elle n'eust peu pas retraire
Le trespassé de desconfort   724
Se de soy n'eust prins reconfort
Pour s'oster de merencolie,
Et s'il est courroucé en son tort
N'en devoit porter la follie.   728

XCII Dames si ne sont point marchandes,   [105r]
Ne tenues de amans garentir
Des maulx, travaulx, paines, amendes,
Que Amours souvent leur fait sentir;   732
Et si n'en est nul tant martir
Que les autres en tiennent compte,
Mais sont tous si duitz a mentir
Qu'il ne leur chault d'onneur ne honte.   736

LXXXIX
And so now in this place
the descendants of the defunct,
who had no greater right
than he who had pursued her amorously,
have foolishly directed
their request and opinion to the court;
the fact that the lover forgave the lady has been
buried away where there is neither ox bone nor fish bone.

XC
There was also error in the argument of the case,
for in the trial proceedings,
which are still well considered,
only a single refusal was given,
without even the strike of a sword,
which is why the cause
was not sufficient, if looked at closely,
for the outcome to have been such a grievous death.

XCI
And she did nothing, on the contrary,
by her refusal from which might follow death.
She could not have pulled back
the dead one from his discomfort.
If he could not take comfort from himself
to pull himself out of his melancholy,
and if he was upset by his own fault,
she should not carry the blame.

XCII
Ladies are not at all merchants,
nor are they required to preserve lovers
from the ills, labors, pains, and reparations
that Love often makes them bear.
And thus no one is the martyr
that the others hold him to be,
but they are all so trained to lie about it
that honor and shame mean nothing to them.

XCIII   Erreur y eust quant a la forme
           Du jugement et du condempner,
           Car quant elle eust tué ung homme,
           Murtry, pendu, et fait trayner,   740
           Ou autrement le villener,
           Si ne la povoit l'en pugnir,
           Ne plus aigrement terminer
           La mort dont l'en l'a fait finir.   744

XCIV   L'entree du procés fut terrible,
           La poursuite tres rigoreuse,
           La maniere du fait horrible,
           La sentence tres doloreuse,   748
           L'excecucion scandaleuse,
           La fin d'ellë orde et infame,
           La mort tres ignominieuse
           Dont il desplaist a toute dame.   752

XCV   Helas! L'en eust bien tost deffait   [105v]
           L'ouvraige que dame Nature
           Avoit en celle la parfait,
           Qui estoit belle oultre mesure.   756
           Tout pour une meschante ordure
           Qui ne valloit pas le parler,
           Dont par ce moien la blesseure
           Estoit plus dure pour avaller.   760

XCVI   Quant est de congié obtenir,
           Les hoirs d'elle sont partie
           Pour lesdiz erreurs soustenir,
           A qui le cas touche en partie   764
           Car, par la sentence impartie,
           Leur honneur fort grevé en est
           Et leur renommee amortie,
           En quoy ilz ont grant interest.   768

XCIII	There was error in the form of the judgment and the condemnation; for if she were to have killed a man, murdered, hung, or drawn and quartered him,[18] or vilified him in any other way, one could not have punished her more for it, nor more bitterly determined the death that they made her suffer.
XCIV	The beginning of the trial was terrible, the process too harsh, the presentation of facts horrible, the sentence too painful, the execution scandalous, her end heinous and disgraceful, her death ignominious: all of this is displeasing to ladies.
XCV	Alas! They quickly destroyed the work that Dame Nature had perfected within the lady, who was beautiful beyond measure. All for this malicious and unclean act that was not even worth speaking of, and for this reason the wound is too hard to swallow.
XCVI	As for trying to obtain permission to continue, the Belle dame's descendants, on one side, wished to sustain the aforementioned errors, for by a sustained verdict their honor is greatly harmed and their reputation destroyed, and so they have a great stake in it.

XCVII	A la fin de non recevoir	
	Bien recevables si estoient,	
	Comme vrais heritiers, pour voir,	
	De celle pour qui se mectoient	772
	Et laquelle representoient,	
	Affin de reparer l'outraige	
	Et le mal dont ilz se sentoient,	
	Et tous ceulx mesmes du lignage.	776
XCVIII	Et pour leur interest monstrer,	[106r]
	La deffuncte eust plusieurs parentes,	
	Dignes de grans biens rencontrer,	
	Tant estoient gracieuses et gentes,	780
	Doulces, belles, et plaisantes,	
	Dont plusieurs parlent en arriere,	
	Disant par parolles meschantes:	
	"Vé la les seurs de la murtriere!"	784
XCIX	Les autres dient: "Regardez cy	
	Les parens de la rude dame	
	Jadis appellee sans mercy	
	Et depuis la cruelle femme!"[19]	788
	Dont chacun d'eulx en est infame	
	Par le moien du jugement	
	Et qui leur portoit lourd diffame	
	Et prejudice grandement.	792
C	Les mors ne vouloient susciter	
	Ne ravoir la deffuncte morte,	
	Mais il leur souffisoit d'oster	
	Le faulx nom, le bruit, et la note,	796
	Tournant en malureuse sorte,	
	En requerant benignement	
	La court que les doleurs conforte,	
	De leur donner allegement.	800

XCVII	After such a long time of deprivation they were eager to receive; like real heirs, in truth, of her for whom they put themselves out and represented in this court, in the hope of repairing the outrageousness and the harm that they felt from from the judgement, they and all their family.
XCVIII	The defunct lover, too, had several relatives there to defend his interests, all of them deserving of great good for their graciousness and gentility; sweet, beautiful, and pleasant, among them several whispered behind their hand, speaking cruel words: "See there! There are the sisters of the murderess!"
XCIX	And others said: "Look there! the relatives of the rude lady they used to call 'without mercy' and now they call 'the cruel woman'!" That reputation stained every one of them because of the judgment that brought them such dishonor and damage.
C	They did not wish to have the two dead lovers resuscitated, nor have the dead woman die a new death, but it would have satisfied them to cast off the falsely attributed name, the scandal, and the gossip, which were causing their unhappy destiny; so they were requesting graciously that the court soothe their pains and lighten their burden.

CI	De parler de la trespassee	[106v]
	Et dire qu'elle feust cruelle,	
	Oncques femme mieulx entassee	
	Ne fut de amour naturelle	804
	Que estoit, car tous biens en elle	
	Habondoient pour estrë amee,	
	Aussi de sa vie et sequelle	
	En vouloient croire renommee.	808

CII   Obicer sa noblesse, en somme,
Le deffunct si ne povoit pas,
Car il se disoit gentilhomme,
Pour les faire noble repas,[20]   812
Ainsi fut abaissé d'un pas,
Qui n'est a croire ne songier;
Et qui se feust teu de ce pas
Il n'y eust eu guieres de dangier.   816

CIII   Oncques Amours ne reprouva
Ne ne nomma cruel losengier,
Mais aucun si le controuva
Pour le cuider a tort chargier;   820
Aussi tous biens pour habregier
Luy venoient de son service,
Ne n'eust sceu boire ne mengier
Qui ne lui eust fait sacrifice.   824

CIV   Au deffunct qui fut bien trios moys   [107r]
De desplaisir au lit malade,
Et qu'il devint sec comme boys,
S'il eust eu espoir, n'avoit garde,   828
Et si par secrecte ambaxade
Elle lui tremist, qui est grant chose,
Deux ou trois pommes de grenade
Et une fiolle de eaue rose.[21]   832

CI
To speak of the dead woman
and say that she was cruel—
well, never was there a woman better endowed
with natural love
than she was, for the perfections in her
to be loved abounded;
but about her life and what followed
they want to believe the worst of her.

CII
Objecting to her nobility, in sum,
the dead lover was unable to do,
for he called himself a gentleman;
nor could he make bait of a noble feast
and so was lowered a step,
which is not to believe or dream of;
he who might have been caught in this path
was never in any danger.

CIII
Never did she reprove
or call Love a deceitful slanderer,
but someone contrived it
so that he would believe he had been wrongfully charged.
To be brief, all goodness
came to him while he was in her service;
he did not know how to drink or eat,
but that did not make him a sacrifice to her.

CIV
As for the defunct who was for a good three months
sick in his bed from despair,
and the fact that he became dry as wood:
if he had had hope, he would have been unconcerned.
Yet by secret envoy
she sent to him,
two or three pomegranates
and a phial of rose water, which is a great thing.

CV   Ainsi doncques, ce n'estoit signe
              Que ne le voulcist secourir
              Quant lui envoya medicine
              Pour ayder plustost a guerir,   836
              Et se l'en pourroit recourir
              A lui pour parler de sa mort,
              Il disoit bien qu'on fist mourir
              La deffuncte pour lui a tort.   840

CVI   A ce qu'on dit qu'il trespassa
              Devant chacun piteusement
              Et que fierté ne la laissa
              Qui perturba son sentement,[22]   844
              C'estoit mal dit et meschamment,
              Car l'en ne vit a femme en ce
              Avoir si grant entendement
              Ne plus belle recoignoissance.   848

CVII   Les cordeliers qui l'ordonnerent   [107v]
              Ne virent oncques cueur si ferme,
              Car quant vint qu'ilz la confesserent,
              A l'ueil avoit tousjours la lerme,   852
              Parlant de Dieu et Nostre Dame
              En tous ses faiz et en ses ditz,
              Et brief certiffioient que l'ame
              Ala tout droit en paradis.   856

CVIII   Ainsi la revelacion
              De la deffuncte condempnee
              N'estoit que machinacion,
              D'une mençonge divinee;   860
              Car verité n'est certainee
              Qui ne la voit *ad occulum*,[23]
              Par quoy dire que fust dampnee
              C'est *ponere os in celum*.[24]   864

CV
And therefore this was not a sign
that she did not wish to succor him,
when she sent him medicine
to help him recover sooner!
If they would just go
to him to talk about his death,
he would tell that they put to death
the deceased lady wrongly, on his behalf!

CVI
As to what they said about him dying
in front of someone most piteously,
and (he said that) that haughtiness never left her
which had disturbed his mind so greatly:
it was ill spoken and malicious,
for one could not find a woman in whom
there was greater understanding
nor greater sensitivity.

CVII
The monks of Love's order who ordained her
never saw a heart so steadfast,
for when it came time for confession,
she always had a tear in her eye,
speaking of God and Our Lady
in all her words and actions;
in short, they confirmed that her soul
went straight to paradise.

CVIII
Thus the revelation about
the condemned defunct lady
was just a machination
based on a fabricated lie,
for truth is not ascertained
unless one sees with one's own eyes.
So to say that she was damnable
is just to turn one's face from the light of truth.

CIX   Et pour respondre aux gens d'Amours
      Du cas de leze majesté,
      En quoy perseveroient tousjours,
      Disoient que tel n'avoit esté,   868
      Car bien veu le fait recité,
      Il n'y avoit que delit commun,
      Dont n'estoit ja neccessité
      D'en mectre en procés ung chacun.   872

CX   Au residu des autres faiz   [108r]
      N'y convenoit solucion,
      Car trestous estoient satisfaiz
      Dessus en la narracion;   876
      Par quoy les acteurs mencion
      N'en faisoient arriere n'avant,
      Mais soustenoient leur action
      En concluant comme devant.   880

CXI   Ces deffendeurs, en dupplicquant,
      Disoient qu'il ne souffisoit pas
      Se le deffunct non delinquant
      Si eust de mort passé le pas.   884
      Mais pour plus agraver le cas,
      L'en lui donnoit chargë et blasme
      D'estre cause de son trespas
      Pour aprés le corps blasmer l'ame. 888

CXII   Qu'il se voult tuer n'est a croire,
      Car estoit bien moriginé
      De sens, engin, et de memoire,
      Autant que homme qui soit huy né; 892
      Et fut par contraincte mené
      A la mort de ça et de la
      Et estoit son jour assigné
      A mourir de cest heure la.   896

CIX
And to respond to Love's men
on the subject of the case of lèse-majesté,
a charge they were continuing to pursue,
they said that such an act never happened,
for, given the facts presented,
the case could only be considered a misdemeanor,
for which there was no need
to have a separate trial.

CX
As for the other facts, in sum,
there is no need for a rebuttal,
for everyone was satisfied
with the presentation outlined above,
which is why the parties made no mention
of them before or after,
but sustained their cause
by concluding as before.

CXI
These defendants, in their response,
said that it was not enough
that the nonculpable defunct lover
had already gone through the pain of death,
but now, to worsen further his situation,
they would put the blame on him
of causing his own death, so that after punishing
the body, they might also punish the soul!

CXII
It is not believable that he wished to kill himself,
for he was well endowed
with good sense, ingenuity, and a sound mind,
as steady as any man born today,
and he was brought against his will
to death, by this way and that,
and yet his day to die
was assigned for that very hour.

CXIII   Disoient, oultre, pour respondre   [108v]
            Aux erreurs de droit et de fait
            Et pour tous argumens confondre,
            Que ceste matiere en effect   900
            Si ne gisoit qu'en ung seul fait:
            C'est assavoir touchant la mort
            Et c'elle commist le meffait
            Car de la vint le droit ou tort.   904

CXIV   Or, tout ce cas l'en advera,
            Ainsi ne s'en puet excuser,
            Car recongneut et declaira
            Qu'elle avoit volu abuser   908
            L'amant, et que par reffuser
            Son temps s'en estoit abregié;
            Ainsi, a tout bien adviser,
            Le procés si fut bien jugié.   912

CXV   Se le jugement doncques est bon,
            Ergo, n'y peut avoir erreur,
            Et si n'y a ancre ne charbon
            Qui luy peult muer sa coleur,   916
            Mais s'il porte de soy doleur,
            C'est affin que nul ne mefface.
            Et n'y vault pitié ne doulceur:
            Il fault que justice se face.   920

CXVI   Mais ou l'en dira que l'en fist   [109r]
            Le cas ou que ne le fist point
            Si *primo* grandement mesprist
            Et s'il n'eust erreur en ce point;   924
            Si *secundo* n'estoit a point
            De le venir dire si tard,
            Car la court sur ce contrepoint
            N'y eust en jugeant son regard.   928

CXIII   Furthermore, they responded to the
errors of law and fact,
and to collapse the arguments,
they said that this case hinged
on one single fact:
that with regard to the death of the lover,
she committed the crime,
and from this fact was drawn right or wrong.

CXIV   So, since the whole case averred this,
she could not exculpate herself,
for she admitted and confessed
that she had tried to deceive
the lover, and that by refusing him
his time on earth was abridged.
Therefore, to all good advice,
the trial was well adjudicated.

CXV   If the judgment, therefore, is valid,
ergo, there cannot be error,
and thus no rhyme or reason
for altering its color.
And if the sentence brings dolorous consequences,
it is so that no one will commit this same crime.
Neither pity nor softness is called for:
justice must be done.

CXVI   But no matter whether they will say that
the case was retried or not,
first of all, it was greatly mistaken
to consider that there was error in the case;
and second, they had no business
bringing their request before the court at such a late date,
for the court on this counterpoint
would not be sympathetic in its opinion.

CXVII   Dire qu'elle en fut innocente
            Ou que²⁵ n'avoit riens offensé,
            La preuve estoit evidente
            Car elle l'avoit confessé!   932
            Si que bien poursuy, bien chassé,
            N'y avoit chose recevable
            Ne erreur qui ne fust renversé
            Par ce fait qui est veritable.   936

CXVIII   Et en tant que touche l'eaue rose
            Qu'elle envoya au trespassé,²⁶
            Ce n'estoit que eaue de buglose
            Destrempee en plantain cassé,   940
            Dont l'en se feust tresbien passé
            Veu que c'estoit mocquerie,
            Et qu'il estoit assez farsé
            Sans boire telle droguerie.   944

CXIX   Or prinst il tout en pacïence   [109v]
            Sans en faire semblant nesung,
            Ne requerir a Dieu vengence
            Contre elle ne contrë aucun.   948
            Si aimoit tant le bien commun
            Qu'i ne lui chaloit pas du sien
            Et estoit content que chacun
            Si eust des biens et qu'il n'eust rien.   952

CXX   Or, se Dieu plaist, le trouvera
            Es cieulx ou l'ame fut offerte,
            Car bien jamais ne se perdra:
            Chacun si avra sa desserte,   956
            Combien que c'est de lui grant perte
            Car a l'eure qu'il estoit fait
            Et qu'il veoit sa gloire ouverte,
            Ceste femme si l'a deffait.   960

CXVII
To say that she was innocent
or that she never committed any offense—
well, the proof is evident
because she confessed it!
So, despite their best efforts,
there was nothing to base their appeal on,
no presentation of error that was not reversed
by the facts, which are true.

CXVIII
And as to the rose water
that she sent to the dead man,
it was really only bugloss water[27]
steeped in crushed plantains,
which one would do well to avoid,
being that it was given in mockery,
and he had already been ridiculed enough
without drinking such a concoction.

CXIX
So the lover bore all of this patiently
without showing a sign of displeasure,
nor asking God for vengeance
against her or anyone else.
He loved the common good,
though it did not care for him,
and he was happy for someone else
to receive blessings, even though he was given nothing.

CXX
So, if it be God's will, he will be found
in the heavens, where his soul was offered up,
for his heart was never lost,
and each receives his just deserts;
even though for him it was a great loss,
for at the hour of his making,
and the moment he saw his glory blossom,
this woman destroyed him.

CXXI   Ces deffendeurs, au residu,
        Des choses qui ont esté dictes
        Ou n'aroient assez respondu,
        Combien que soient baves redictes,   964
        Emploient leurs raisons et replicques
        Sans le recité et souffist,
        Concluans a leurs fins susdictes
        Pour obtenir a leur prouffit.   968

CXXII   Si y ont les parties bien esté   [110r]
        Oÿes en ce qu'elles ont volu
        Tout a plain de chacun cousté
        Et tant argué et solu   972
        Qu'a la dicte court a falu
        Vacquer aux erreurs longuement,
        Affin de conseil resolu
        Iceulx jugier plus meurement.   976

CXXIII   Et finablement, jus et sus,
        Ouÿ le debat sus narré,
        La court, vestue comme dessus,
        Si a au loing consideré   980
        Le premier procés declairé
        Et a diverses assemblees
        Pour en estre deliberé
        Toutes les chambres assemblees.   984

CXXIV   Veu lequel procés dessusdit
        Et erreurs dont on l'a chargé,
        La court si vous declaire et dit,
        Par arrest et second jugié,   988
        Qu'en tout ce qu'il fut adjugié
        N'y eust erreur aucunement;
        Ains fut le procés bien jugié
        Et l'arrest donné justement.   992

CXXI   These defendants, in sum,
                  with regard to those things that were said
                  or have not been responded to,
                  no matter that they were repetitive babble,
                  employed to the best of their ability arguments
                  and counterarguments that need not be repeated,
                  and made conclusions that would best
                  profit their own ends.

CXXII   Now both sides have been
                  heard openly and from every angle,
                  concerning what they would request of the court,
                  and so argued and acquitted
                  that the court was occupied for a long time
                  by the consideration of these errors,
                  so that mature judgment might be made
                  by a fully informed council.

CXXIII   And finally, from every side
                  the court had heard the debate narrated
                  just as above,
                  and then considered at length
                  the explanation of the first trial
                  at several meetings
                  so they might be consider thoroughly
                  with all the chambers assembled.

CXXIV   Given the trial aforementioned
                  and the errors that were claimed,
                  the court hereby declares to you
                  its decision and second judgment:
                  that for every point of law under consideration
                  there was no error whatsoever.
                  The trial, therefore, has been deliberated judiciously
                  and the sentence justly assigned.

CXXV	Que le jugement ainsi fait	[110v]
	Ne se muera ne changera	
	Mais demourra en son effect,	
	Tant que le monde durera;	996
	Oultre plus, que l'en levera	
	le chapeau consigné de flours,	
	Et que le tout se applicquera	
	Au prouffit du tresor d'Amours.	1000

CXXVI	Mais la court, pour aucunes choses	
	Qu'i n'est besoing de publïer,	
	Et par vertu des lectres closes	
	Quë Amours leur envoya hier	1004
	Touchant celle qu'on fist nayer,	
	Donne congié aux heritiers	
	De amasser en l'eaue et fouillier	
	Ses os par morceaulx ou quartiers.	1008

CXXVII	Oultre, en faveur de ses amis	
	Et a leur requeste et prïere,	
	De grace si leur a premis	
	Qu'ilz puissent lesdiz os en biere	1012
	Enterrer dedans ung cymentiere	
	Pres d'une croix ou d'un posteau,	
	Mais toutesvois la court declaire	
	Qu'il n'y aura tumbe ne escripteau.	1016

CXXVIII	Après ces deux arrestz premiers,	[111r]
	Survindrent deux damoissellez,	
	Jeunes amans, beaulx escuiers,	
	Qui apportoient leurs tierceletz	1020
	Mais point n'avoient de gantelletz,	
	Par quoy les oyseaulx les picquerent	
	Sur les doiz qui estoient tendreletz,	
	Et firent tant qu'ilz eschapperent.	1024

CXXV
Therefore, the judgment thus declared
will never be altered or changed
but will remain in effect
as long as the world shall last.
Moreover, let the chaplet of flowers
be lifted high in honor
and the judgment be applied
for the glory of the treasure of Love.

CXXVI
But the court, for reasons
that are not necessary to make public,
and on the strength of the letters
that Love sent to them yesterday
about her whom they had drowned,
grants permission to the descendants
to look for and collect
her bones, whether scattered or in quarters.

CXXVII
Moreover, the court, in favor of her friends
and in response to their request and pleas,
has promised them, in grace,
that they may bury on a bier
the aforementioned bones in a cemetery,
close to a cross or a post;
however, the court declares
that there will be no tombstone or epitaph.

CXXVIII
After these first two decisions,
in came two lads:
young men, lovely squires,
who were carrying their falcons,
but they had no gloves,
which is why the falcons were able to prick
their tender fingers,
and so the birds succeeded in escaping.

CXXIX	Ainsi les eussiez veu voler	
	Et lors bruire comme raquectes,	
	Tant que on ne oyoit point parler	
	Le president pour leurs sonnectes;	1028
	Si furent diligences faictes,	
	Affin de tous coustez les prendres,	
	Mais la court en ces entremectes	
	Chouma bien une heure a actendre.	1032

CXXX	Le president lors se courrouça	
	Aigrement a tous les huissiers,	
	Et de prison les menace	
	Faire tenir trios moys entiers,	1036
	Deffendans que nulz espreviers	
	Ne entrassent plus au Parlement;	
	Aussi trestous les conseilliers	
	En murmuroient grandement.	1040

CXXXI	Et pour ce qu'il estoit si tard	[111v]
	Que unze venoient de sonner,	
	Le president, ayant regard	
	Qu'il n'eust peu aussi bien finer	1044
	Les arrestz qu'il avoit adonner,	
	Par ung expedïant querant,	
	En se levant fist assigner	
	Au premier jour le demourant.	1048

CXXXII	Si diz aparmoy que y seroye	
	Quoy que coustast le sejourner,	
	Car de tout mon cueur desiroye	
	Ouÿr lesdiz arrestz donner,	1052
	Affin que aprés, au retourner,	
	J'en peusse parler seurement.	
	Et a tant m'en allay disner,	
	Car l'en ferma le parlement.	1056

Cy finent les erreurs du jugement de la belle dame sans mercy

CXXIX   And you could see them flying about
                      and making as much noise as banging racquets,
                      so that no one could hear a word
                      spoken by the president, due to their din.
                      Measures were taken
                      so that the birds might be caught,
                      but the court during this intermission
                      was idle for a good hour while waiting.

CXXX   Then the president flew into a sharp rage
                      directed at all the bailiffs
                      and threatened to hold them in prison
                      for three entire months,
                      then he prohibited any bird
                      to enter into the courtroom,
                      and the other judges murmured
                      their consent.

CXXXI   And because the hour was late
                      and eleven o'clock had just rung,
                      the presiding judge, having taken into account
                      that he would not be able to finish
                      rendering the judgment,
                      found an expedient solution.
                      Getting up, he reassigned the rest of the sentencing
                      for first thing the next day.

CXXXII   And I said to myself that I would surely be there,
                      no matter what the trip cost,
                      since I desired with my whole heart
                      to hear those sentences delivered,
                      so that afterward, at my return,
                      I would be able to speak about them with authority.
                      Thereupon I went off to dinner,
                      for they were closing the courtroom.

Here ends The Errors of Judgment of the Belle dame sans mercy.[28,29]

Notes

1.   The reference may be to Achilles Caulier, author of the *Cruel Woman in Love*, but more likely is to Alain Chartier, on whom blame has earlier been cast.

2.   "la Decretalle." One must assume that the *Cour amoureuse* or other social organization composed a canon or book of laws by which lovers must abide, much like the decretals of real laws that were copied and bound into books. Charles d'Orleans, for example, had one in his library.

3.   These magistrates handled minor offenses and—of more relevance here—were also responsible for conducting the inquest in preliminary hearings.

4.   This verse in the manuscript was originally hypermetric: "Tresbeau filz courtois et amiable"; *et* has been canceled.

5.   Here *piteable* (usually written *pitoyable*) within the context must mean "worthy of receiving the lady's pity and thus her attentions" as well as "capable of feeling pity," a description that pointedly contrasts with that of the lady, according to her accusers.

6.   Correction of *dieu* to *lieu*.

7.   Correction of *par propice* to *pardon propice*.

8.   This line scans if *y* is exceptionally elided or if we assume that the scribe has inserted *y* in the older monosyllabic expression *n'a*.

9.   The term *baselicque* refers to the basilisk, a mythic reptile frequently used to refer to the Belle dame. It has fatal breath as well as a deadly glance.

10. *Belle dame* lines 313–14; *Cruel* lines 543–44.

11. The phrase "le tierce auctenticque" probably refers to the third book of the Belle dame, the *Cruel Woman*.

12. These tears are proof of his sincerity and should be contrasted with the lack of tears shed by the Belle dame.

13. Pb indicates "Me Alain Chartier" in the outer right margin.

14. The refutation here is that even given the Love decree (apparently written in one of the aforementioned books), which requires that a lover be rejected at least three times before complaining (see lines 169–84), this woman, if one is to believe what one hears, has refused him more than ten times, and she does it just for fun.

15. See the confession *Cruel woman,* lines 841–64. She never sheds a tear, which the narrator takes as proof positive of her cruelty.

16. The refutation of the eighth error. *Pb* and *Qh* say that all the lords must be present for deliberations; *Qt* says that all the goddesses must be present. The *presidens* would be lords in reality; the scribe who first copied *seigneurs* instead of *deesses* must have forgotten the allegorical fiction and been drawn in by the realism of the text, or, conversely, the one who wrote *deesses* was attempting to render the narrative more poetic.

17. Piaget's edition reads "a Dieu."

18. *Trainer*—a traitor's penalty, to be dragged behind a horse until dead.

19. Another reference to the *Cruel woman in love,* in which the Belle dame was renamed the Cruel woman.

20. "Pour les faire noble repas" probably means "to make bait out of a noble meal," understood as "to make trivial something grand."

21. There is no reference to these items in the previous poems—an indication of a poem in the cycle that has not survived, or of the product of a fertile imagination.

22. The reference to a witness at the deathbed of the lover is not mentioned in the earlier poems, though it could be understood as a vague reference to the man who reported the lover's death to the narrator of the *Belle dame* (lines 781–84).

23. The phrase *ad occulum* means "by sight."

24. The phrase *ponere os in celum* literally means "to turn one's face or mouth to the heavens," that is, to hide one's eyes from the light of truth.

25. The *s* of the corrector has been added after *que.* He may have read *onques* instead of *ou que.*

26. Reference to line 832.

27. The bugloss, a coarse hairy plant from the borage-worts family (God. 8:393b). Huguet indicates an etymological joke that uses this word to indicate the culinary dish *langue de boeuf* (2:24a). Water made from this plant (or even ox-tongue stew) would not have the same value for romantic cure as rose water.

28. *The Errors of Judgment of the Belle dame sans mercy,* rejected readings: title of Qt, Les erreurs de la belle dame sans mercy Pb; 4. certaines (+1) Qt; 19. ung a. (+1) Qt; 33. f. il p. (+1) QhQt; 36. Et de s. (+1) Qh; 40. derrenier counts two syllables; 50. Elle n. (+1) Qt; 62. a c. Qt; 69. Qui de c. et de t. Qt; 73. feust QhQt; 81. maint m. QhQt; 101. Toutesvoies (+1) Qh; 115. point e. QtQh; 122. Et quil y a (+1) Qt; 132. ou il se (+1) Qt; 142. +1 all mss.; 143. e. trop publique aventure (+1) Qt; 147. Si l. t. n. Qt; 159. atelle replaced by luy; 168. naroit QhQt; 172. missing line in PbQh; 175. nya t. (+1) Qt; 184. y a eu (+1) Qt; 191. vengement canceled and replaced by rudement; 205. Sarrester Qt, all mss hypermetric; 206. all mss hypermetric; 227. fist missing Qt; 230. vestu b. Qh; Qt: vesquit; 239. Denvayr QhQt; 244. Ou q. Qt; 253. luy t. QhQt; 256. requestes Qt; 257. crueuse canceled and replaced with rigoreuse; 268. qui canceled and replaced by qu'est; 278. verse altered to: Sur ses hoirs aucun malefice from QhQt; 279. trope; 283. honnorablement (+1 all mss), correction suggested by Piaget; 294. Que la deffuncte estoit renté Qt; 310. P. a. et s. (-1) Qt; 330. L'ostel et lieu dont elle estoit Qt; 342. Et de toutes poisons assouvie (+1) Qt; 343. Qu'il soit vray se ne fust elle (-1) Qt; 379. Veu les grans asses aggravez QhQt; 385. Or disoient il que oncques mais Qt; 457–65 missing QhQt; 521. Pour le vij^{me} erreur point (-1) Qt; 524. De conseil pour le solagier QhQt; 530. gehaine counts one syllable; 574. Car ou il y a depposicion (+2) Qt; 616. Car sont tous deux gens d'eglise (-1) Qh; 635. S'elle a bien elle trouva Qh; 652. Comme de leze majesé Qt; 674. S'elle eust fait le meurdre subtil Qt; 682. Se aucun par Amours nommé Qt; 712. Ou il n'y avoit oz n'azecte Qt; 715. Qui bien si le considere (-1) Qt; 726. Pour estre de merencolie Qt; 729. Dames ne sont point marchandes (-1) Qt; 753. Helas l'en eust tost deffait (-1) Qt; 775. Et le mal dont ilz sentoient (-1) Qt; 791. Qui leur portoit lors diffame (-1) Qt; 883. Se le deffunct no declinant Qt; 884. S'il esut de mort passé le pas Qt; 893.

Car fait par contraincte mené Qt; 901. Si ne gisoit qu'en ung fait Qt; 905. Or tout ce cas bien advira Qt; 925. Si oyez n'estoit a point Qt; 931. La premiere estoit evidente Qt; 973. Et que a la court a faillu Qt.

29. *The Errors of Judgment of the Belle dame sans mercy,* variant readings: 17. est v. Qt; 19. vaillant Qh; 20. beau b. Qt; 23. Dont v. Qt; 34. s. ensuyot Qh, enfumoit Qt; 59. Ne quelle e. Qt; 70. Quil print Qt; 75. Comparaut Qh; 88. Perdit tout s. Qt; 101. Toutesfois Qh; 104. tresdoloreuse Qt; 119. evenement QhQt; 121. n. elle e. Qt; 126. quel Qh; 151. Car Qh, Et Qt; 153. selle a. Qt; 154. Ce a. Qh, Tel a. Qt; 159. De aelle b. Qh, De acelle b. Qt; 168. navoit Qt; 191. vengeement Qh, e. f. estrangement Qt; 192. itelle c. Qt; 195. par oppression Qt; 211. Les deesses y Qt; 213. le pramenoient Qh; 220. par l. d. Qh; 239. D'ennoier Qt; 248. acquite Qh; 264. chaudes lermes Qt; 265. Et encores d. Qt; 268. qest Qt; 279. Cest une c. q. r. Qt; 282. noble Qh; 286. vendroit Qt; 292. deffendue *Qh*; 300. Saige savant *Qt*; 305. se qu'il Qh; 308. se Qh; 310. aider a secourir Qh; 315. Qu'il eust Qh, Qui l'eust Qt; 317. le feminine pronoun; 332. Bien pour mal si lui presentoit Qt; 333. En sa presence lamentoit Qt; 334–35 missing Qh; 340. Car ame n. Qt; 342 passions Qh; 346. elle est c. Qh; 348. ledit malefice Qt; 357–58 inverted Qh; 361. a. gens Qh; 368. Ce qu'il faloit joindre ou p. Qt; 383 vaucarme Qh; 394. Que c. Qt; 399. C. elle Qh; 411. Pour leur vie Qh; 424. Ou n'y a Qt; 427. doit point Qt; 430. ycy Qh; 432. f. nommee s. Qt; 445. bassillique Qh; 452. esperant Qt; 522. Ou la Qt; 527. l. songer Qh; 528. deposicion Qt; 529. que c. Qt; 530. p.d. ghaine Qt; 532. Aussi e. Qt; 543. en ghaine c. Qt; 554. Des dames Qt; 555. la verté Qt; 556. Elles furent au QhQt; 561. l'erreur ixe Qt; 564. C. ce ce n. Qh; 565. et a. g. Qt; 574. Car ou a d. Qt; 575. vous ne Qh; 576. jugier pas p. Qt; 580. qu'il luy Qt; 598. toutes v. Qt; 612. Onques on Qt; 617. Et encor plus Qt; 623. la discucion Qt; 635. fait le trouvera Qt; 644. N'en Qt; 675. D'estre boutee en Qt; 682. a. n'est par Qt; 683. ait Qh; 688. congnoistre Qt; 704. volut Qt; 712. otz Qh; 715. Qui bien se c. Qh; 723. pas peu r. Qh; 727. sil est courroucé eu son tort Qt; 738. Du jugier et Qt; 742. Ne le p. Qh; 753. tout d. Qh; 762. Les heritiers d'elle s.p. Qt; 770. Trop bien r. s. e. Qt; 771. veoir Qh; 784. Veez les seurs Qt; 794. avoir Qh; 797. Tournant a m. Qt; 799. les dolans c. Qt; 805. Que e. Qh; 812. lec faire Qt; 815. qui ce f. Qh; 816. Gueres n'y eust eu Qt; 818. Ne nomma Qt; 829. Si que par. Qt; 836. tantost Qt; 837. povoit Qt; 840. par l. Qh; 841. que trespassa Qt; 849. diroit Qt; 860. devinee Qt; 883. delinquant Qt; 886. L'en l. d. cy c. et b. Qt; 891. d'engin Qt; 903. s'elle QhQt; 921. qu'elle fist Qt; 923. mesfist Qt; 924. Et sic Qt; 926. a tard Qh; 928. eut en j. Qt; 929. que ne fut impossible Qh, en feust i. Qt; 947. N'en r. Qt; 948. Encontre elle ne autre aucun Qt; 953. soit offerte Qt; 962. deduittes QhQt; 965. raisons escriptes Qt; 966. reciter Qt; 978. sur n. Qh; 980. au long Qt; 990. eut Qt; 1011. promis Qh; 1042. Q. onze heures Qh.

The Hospital of Love

Achilles Caulier

S'ensuit L'ospital d'amours

I	Assez joyeulx, sans l'estre trop,	[184v]
	En la conduite de Desir,	
	Le jour de l'an, survins a cop	
	En assemblee de plaisir,	4
	Ou je viz a mon beau plaisir	
	Le tresor d'amours desploier,	
	Comme en ung passé desplaisir	
	En ung passetemps emploier.	8

II	Ce noble lieu estoit fourny	
	De tout, fors de mal et de deul.	
	L'assemblement estoit uny;	
	Chascun y sembloit a son veul.	12
	Je y fuz plus liéz que ne seul,	
	Car je veiz d'onneur la montjoye,	
	Qui est rabaz de tout orgueil	
	Et mon tout ce que j'ay de joye.	16

III	Illec estoit le droit tresor	[185r]
	De dames et de damoiselles.	
	Riens n'y failloit de bout encor:	
	Tout estoit plain d'ommes et d'elles.	20
	La vëoit on dances nouvelles,	
	Gracïeuses et sans vanter;	
	Si oyoit on, des dieu scet quelles,	
	La doulce noyse deschanter.	24

IV	La fus des dames bien veigné.	
	Et comme se je le valisse,	
	Me requerant par amitié	
	Q'une chançon dire voulsisse,	28
	De quoy voulentiers m'escondisse,	
	S'excusance y puet estre belle,	
	Mais il couvint que j'obeïsse,	
	Si en diz une telle quelle.	32

The Hospital of Love

I

Amply joyful, though not to excess,
and guided purely by Desire,
I happened quite unexpectedly, on New Year's Day,
upon the gathering of a pleasant party
where I saw unveiled, to my great pleasure,
the treasure of love.
And it was as if the worry of the past dissolved away,
in this place so agreeable to pass the time.

II

Complete with everything was this marvelous place,
everything, that is, except evil and grief.
The assembly was of one mind
since everyone was there of their own free will,
and I, too, was happier than normal,
for I saw there the crown of perfection:
the nemesis of all arrogance
and all that I could ever hope for.

III

In this place was a veritable treasure
of ladies and maidens,
and nothing at all was missing,
since a number of men and ladies were there.
One could watch the newest dances—
they were charming and courtly, without exaggeration—
and hear the melodious singing of the ladies,
though God only knows which ones!

IV

Ladies welcomed me warmly
and, as if I merited the honor,
they requested sweetly and out of friendship
that I sing a song,
an offer I would have preferred to refuse
had it been proper or seemly,
but I obliged as I ought
and sang a song for them at random.

V   Et quant j'euz chanté, tout failly,
          Et se tira chascun a part;
          Si me tiray vers celle a qui
          Entierement j'estoie sans part.   36
          Quant je fuz venu celle part,
          Je la salüay humblement,
          Et elle redist: "Dieu vous gart,"
          Bien tost, sans faire grant semblant.   40

VI   Seul appart m'asseiz emprés elle,[1]   [185v]
          Sans dire rien, car je craindy;
          Mais ma doulour aspre et crüelle,
          Aprés craindre, me fist hardy.   44
          Et lors en soudain m'enhardy
          Et lui deiz en quel point je fuz.
          Sur quoy elle me respondy
          En petiz de motz, grant reffuz.   48

VII   Finablement tant la requis
          Que de m'oÿr plus se lassa.
          Grant paine y euz et poy conquis,
          Car tousjours vers moy s'excusa.   52
          Et tant en fin me reffusa
          Que je n'y euz plus d'esperance.
          Ma parolle en vain se usa
          Et m'en partiz sans alïance.   56

VIII   Ainsy parti d'elle en pleurant,
          En grant deul qui me conduisoit,
          Quictant a Dieu le demourant
          De ma vie, qui m'ennuyoit.   60
          La Mort malgré moy me fuyoit
          Et me laissoit d'elle delivre;
          Et ma voulenté me suyvoit,
          Qui mieulx amoit mourir que vivre.[2]   64

V   Even as my song was finished
      and everyone left,
      I went off to find the one
      to whom I felt I belonged, heart and soul.
      As soon as I found her,
      I greeted her without delay,
      and she responded in kind: "God keep you,"
      but her expression did not alter.

VI   I lead her off to one side to sit with me
      without saying a word, for I was nervous.
      But my pain, bitter and cruel,
      soon after this moment of crisis, gave me courage.
      Then, feeling stronger,
      I revealed my state of mind,
      and she gave me her response:
      in a few short words, she rejected me soundly.

VII   By the end, I had pled with her for so long
      that she tired of listening to me.
      Even though I put forth great effort, I gained no ground
      for she made many excuses
      and finally refused all my prayers,
      so that all Hope has now left me.[3]
      My words were spoken in vain,
      and I left her there without any sort of accord.

VIII   I left her with tears on my face,
      now guided by profound grief,
      offering to God the remainder of my days,
      which overwhelmed me with too much pain.
      But despite my wish, Death fled from me
      and would but free me from his grip;
      so my will followed suit,
      even preferring death to life.

IX   En ce seul vouloir de mourir   [186r]
Passay je toute la nuyttie:
Rien ne me povoit secourir.
En pensant a ceste partie,   68
Entray en une fantasie
Et en ymaginacïon,
Ou j'oublïay melencolie
Et entray en avision.   72

X   Ceste fantasie nouvelle
Me faisoit songier en veillant,
Qui est chose desnaturelle.
Mais ce m'avint, ce non obstant,   76
Et me fut en ce point semblant
Qu'en ung grant chemin me trouvoye
Qui estoit le plus desplaisant
Que jamaiz homme vivant voye.   80

XI   Ce chemin estoit espineux
Et plain de croulieres sans fin.
Oncques si grant desplaisir n'eux,
Et enduray tant le hutain: 84
Yssir n'en poz tout le matin.
Jamais plus n'yray, je y renonce,
Car on appelle ce chemin
En françois "Trop Dure Responce."   88

XII   En ce chemin ung peu avant,   [186v]
En l'abisme d'une valee,
Trouvay ung desert long et grant,
Comme une place desolee.   92
La terre y estoit desmellee
Toute de lermes et de plours.
De tous maulz y avoit meslee,
C'estoit monjoye de doulours.   96

IX   In the grip of this desire to die
                I passed the entire night,
                believing nothing could help me.
                While meditating on such thoughts
                I drifted into a state of fantasy,
                a hallucination of sorts,
                in which I forgot my melancholy
                and entered into a vision.

X   This fantastic state of mind
                made me dream while awake—
                certainly an unnatural state!
                But it happened to me nevertheless,
                and so it seemed very real
                when I found myself in the middle of a broad path—
                the most disagreeable place
                that ever a man has seen.

XI   The route was overgrown with thorns,
                hiding quagmires all throughout.
                I have never been so uneasy,
                and the commotion I endured there
                prevented my escape from that place all the morning.
                I will never go there again, I swear,
                for this path is called
                in French: Too Harsh Reply.

XII   On the path, a bit farther along
                in the deepest part of a valley
                I came upon a wasteland, long and wide,
                and completely devoid of life.
                The earth was inundated
                with streams of tears and sobs.
                Everything bad was tangled together in this place:
                it was the culmination of all grief and pain.

XIII   En ce lieu desert n'avoit arbre
Qui de gens pendus ne fust plains:
Hommes et femmes froiz com marbre,
Qui se pendirent a leurs mains.   100
Une dame y veiz que moult plains:
Ce fu Philus, qui se pandy
Pour Demophon, qui valoit mains
De ce que sa foy lui menty.   104

XIV   Soubz ces arbres de desconfort
Avoit fleuves, puis, et fossés
Plains de gens noiéz jusqu'au bort.
Entre les aultres trespasséz   108
Y veiz, dont j'ay de deul assez,
Lëander et Hero, s'amie,
Qui oncques ne furent lasséz
D'estre léal jour de leur vie.   112

XV   La fontaine estoit la entour   [187r]
Ou Narcisus son umbre ama.
Amours s'en venga de beau tour,
Qui de tel rage l'enflamma: 116
Ce fut pour ce qu'il reffusa
Echo, qui mercy lui crioit.
Trop fist pour luy a ce cop la
Quant dame estoit, et si prioit.   120

XVI   D'aultre costé veiz les espees
Emmoillés de sang humain,
Dont les vies furent ostees
A ceulx qui de leur propre main   124
S'occirent; celle y veiz aplain
De quoy Piramus et Tybee
Moururent, de tristresse plain,
Par douloureuse destinee.   128

XIII	In this deserted spot there was not a single tree
	whose branches were not laden with hanging bodies.
	Men and women, cold as marble,
	had hung themselves by their own hand.
	I saw a lady I felt great pity for:
	it was Phyllis, who had hung herself
	for Demophon, though he was hardly worth it
	given his unfaithful lies to her.[3]

XIV   Under these trees of desperation
were rivers, wells, and trenches,[a]
filled to the brim with drowned bodies.
Among the other corpses
I saw—which really broke my heart—
were those of Leander and his love, Hero,
who never tired of loving loyally
for a single day of their lives.[4]

XV   The fountain was there, too,
where Narcissus fell in love with his reflection.
Love used a really clever ploy to avenge himself
when he inflamed Narcissus with such a rage!
For he had rejected Echo
whose cries had begged for his pity.
(Though she really did go too far,
being a woman, and yet begging him!)

XVI   I saw on the other side swords,
dripping with human blood,
which had been used to take the lives
of those who wanted to kill themselves
by their own hand; I saw the one
by which Pyramus and Thisbe[5]
died, filled with sadness:
victims of a dolorous destiny.

---

[a] *Motes* doesn't seem to be the correct word. I can't find any dictionary definition, even from a 1913 dictionary, that refers to a hole or trench of any sort.

XVII   D'aultre part avoit ung grant fu
              Fait de gens ars en lieu de busche.
              La cendre de Dido y fu,
              Et maint aultre y firent embusche.   132
              Qui se veult ardoir, la se musse:
              En ce desert n'a frain ne bride;
              Douleur y est qui les gens husche
              Pour d'eulx mesmes estre omicide.   136

XVIII   Ce desert est tant hors des termes   [187v]
              De droit et contraire a nature:
              La ne pleut que pluie de lermes,
              La ne peut vivre crëature.   140
              Vent de souppirs y queurt et dure:
              Zefirus en est forbanis.
              La tonne et espart sans mesure
              Hydeulx tonnoirres de haulx cris.   144

XIX   Quant j'euz tout veu a mon povoir,
              Lors me dist mon intelligence
              Que c'est ung lieu de desespoir
              Ou ne queurt rien que pestilence.   148
              La fine deul ou qu'il commence,
              Et prins voulenté d'y aler,
              Quant Esperance et Pacïence
              Se vindrent dedens moy bouter.   152

XX   Invisiblement comme espris,
              Ces deux se bouterent en my,
              Dont je fuz a cop si espris
              Que ce vil desert en haÿ.   156
              Tout aussy tost je fus ravy
              Et emporté plus que le cours,
              Jusques a ung saint lieu que j'oÿ
              Appeller l'Ospital d'Amours.   160

XVII   In another corner there was a powerful fire
         fueled by burning people instead of logs.
         The ashes of Dido were there,
         and many others were lurking around
         who wanted to be consumed in that fire.
         In this desert was neither brake nor bridle;
         instead Anguish is there inciting people
         to take their own lives.

XVIII   This desolate place was beyond the limits
         of the law and was ruled against nature.
         Tears fall down like rain
         in this land where no creature can survive.
         The wind of moans blows without ceasing and
         the gentle breeze, zephyr, is banished.
         The hideous thunder of screeching cries
         rumbles and flashes constantly.

XIX   After seeing all that I could stand,
         my spirit whispered to me
         that this was a place of hopelessness:
         the beginning and the end of grief,
         where nothing could be found but misery.
         I had a fervent desire to leave there,
         and then Hope and Patience
         rose within me.

XX   Invisible, like spirits,
         these two slipped into my being,
         and suddenly I was overwhelmed
         with abhorrence for this vile desert.
         Then, just as quickly, I was whisked away
         and transported in a flash
         to a holy place that I heard
         called the Hospital of Love.

XXI

Fondé estoit cest hospital   [188r]
Sur une roche de rubiz,
Clos par hault de murs de cristal
Et par embas de marbre bis.   164
Et en maniere de pallys
Y avoit une haye espesse,
En quoy je sçay bien que je vyz
De toutes fleurs l'oultrelargesse.   168

XXII

Quant je fuz mis devant la porte,
Tantost m'aparut Bel Acueil,
Qui les clefz de l'ospital porte,
Qui me fist gracïeux acueil;   172
Et, en grant pitié de mon deul,
M'amena jusqu'a l'enfermiere,
Courtoisie, qui d'un doulx veul
Me fist ce dont est coustumiere.   176

XXIII

Treize hospitalieres y a,
Dont prïeuse est Dame Pitié,
Et Loyaulté aprés lui va,
Puis Simplesce, et puis Verité,   180
Congnoissance et Humilité,
Largesse, Richessse, Maniere,
Jennesse, Liesse, Beaulté,
Et Courtoisie l'enfermiere.   184

XXIV

Les trois conseilliers sont Honneur,   [188v]
Entendement et Souvenir;
Doulx Parler est le procureur,
Pour leurs affaires soustenir.   188
Regart et Humble Maintenir
Servent Pitié matin et soir,
Et, pour les malades guerir,
Le droit medecin est Espoir.   192

XXI
The foundation of this hospital
was a rock of ruby,
surrounded by curious walls: the top half was of crystal
and the bottom half of gray and brown marble
to serve as palisade.
Then there was a thick hedge
in which I must have seen
every kind of flower in the world.

XXII
As I was let down at the door,
Fair Welcoming appeared before me:
he keeps the keys to the hospital.
He welcomed me graciously,
taking pity on me for my sorrow,
and so led me to the nurse
Courtesy, who in her goodwill
treated me as is her manner.

XXIII
There were thirteen sisters in the order
of which Lady Pity was the prioress;
Loyalty was next in the hierarchy,
followed by Sincerity, then Truth,
Knowledge, and Humility,
Generosity, Wealth, Manners,
Youth, Delight, Beauty,
and Courtesy, the nurse.

XXIV
The three counselors there are Honor,
Understanding, and Memory;
Sweet Talk is the lawyer
charged with the defense of their affairs.
Sweet Look and Humble Manner[6]
serve Pity day and night,
and, to heal the sick,
Hope is, with good reason, the doctor.

XXV	Le droit office Courtoisie	
	Est des malades recevoir:	
	Lors que ma maniere a choisie	
	Me dist, en moustrant bon vouloir,	196
	Que je luy feïsse savoir	
	Ma doulour—c'estoit sa demande—	
	Pour me faire tel lit avoir	
	Que ma maladie demande.	200

XXVI	Lors, tant malade que Dieu scet,	
	Lui deiz quel doulour je sentoye	
	Et comme des foiz plus de sept,	
	Puis que premier amant estoie,	204
	Mercy d'amours requis avoie	
	A celle qui sien me vëoit,	
	En qui trouver je ne povoie	
	Le remede qu'il y chëoit.	208

XXVII	Et lui deiz comment au derrain	[189r]
	Reffuz mon espoir aboli,	
	Et moustra cueur plus dur qu'arain	
	Quant ma douleur ne l'amoly.	212
	Mon cueur avoit sien et ou lui	
	Qui n'a mais espoir de nul bien:	
	Onques depuis ne lui toly,	
	Ne veul tollir, car il est sien.	216

XXVIII	Mon cueur est sien, elle le garde,	
	Mais quant j'ay bien pensé, au fort,	
	Elle en fait bien petite garde,	
	Car, sans lui faire aucun confort,	220
	L'a tout donné a desconfort	
	Abandonné a tel dangier	
	Qu'il ne desire que la mort	
	Pour sa maladie alegier.	224

XXV	The duty of Courtesy
	is to admit the sick.
	After observing my condition
	she said, following her charge,
	that I should describe for her
	my misery. This was her request,
	so that she might assign me to the bed
	best suited to my illness.

XXVI	So, sick as I was, God knows,
	I told her about the pain I was suffering,
	and how more than seven times
	since I had first fallen in love,
	I had asked for loving mercy
	from the one to whom I was devoted;
	but from her I could not obtain
	the necessary cure I sought.

XXVII	And I revealed how, quite recently,
	Refusal had destroyed my hope when
	the one I loved showed me a heart harder than brass,
	for she did nothing to ease my pain.
	She holds my heart within her breast,
	this heart that now no longer hopes for any relief,
	and since that time I have not withdrawn my heart from her,
	nor do I wish to, for it belongs to her.

XXVIII	My heart belongs to her, it is in her hands
	and yet, upon reflection, I realize that
	she has taken precious little care of it.
	For, by not offering any sort of comfort,
	she has given it over to despair and
	abandoned it to such hardship
	that it desires only death
	to relieve its malady.

XXIX	Quant Courtoisie a entendu	
	Le mal dont si fort me douloye,	
	Elle n'a gueres attendu	
	Que vers la sale me convoye,	228
	Par une gracïeuse voye	
	Ou a mainte flour precïeuse;	
	Si veiz ainsi qu'ilec passoye	
	L'ostel de Pitié la prïeuse.	232
XXX	Aprés venismes en la sale	[189v]
	Ou a des malades grant tas;	
	Plus belle n'a jusqu'en Thesale,[7]	
	Car elle est par tout, hault et bas,	236
	Tendue de tresriches draps,	
	Ouvrés d'amoureuses ystoires	
	Ou fait estoient par compas	
	Tous les amans dont on lit ores.	240
XXXI	Le pavement estoit semé	
	De toutes fleurs qu'on puet penser,	
	Et estoient encourtiné	
	Les litz de draps de Bien Celer:[8]	244
	Entendement les fist ouvrer,	
	Et sont faiz ces litz de repos	
	Et les linceulx de Doulx Penser	
	Qu'Amours fist faire a ce propos.	248
XXXII	Au bout de ceste sale estoit	
	La tresgracïeuse chappelle	
	En quoy le service on chantoit	
	Qui oultre beaulté estoit belle.	252
	Pour descripre la façon d'elle,	
	Me fauldroit ung long jour d'esté:	
	Elle est bien digne qu'on l'appelle	
	La plus belle qui ait esté.	256

XXIX	When Courtesy heard about the grief that so pained me, she did not hesitate a second to usher me to a room, first passing through an exquisite corridor where there were many rare and precious flowers. Down that corridor I saw, as we were walking by, the dwelling of Pity, the prioress.
XXX	Then we came to a room in which there were many sick people. No more beautiful room exists from here to Thessaly, as it is covered from top to bottom with resplendent tapestries on which stories of love are embroidered in exquisite detail of all the lovers about whom we still read.
XXXI	The ground was planted with every kind of flower imaginable. To adorn the beds had been hung drapes and coverings made by Well Concealed, for Understanding had conceived the beds to be places of rest; and there were also sheets of Sweet Thought, which Love had commanded be made for this purpose.
XXXII	At the other end of the room was a beautiful chapel in which the service was being sung, with a beauty beyond all beauty. To describe it accurately would take all of a long summer's day, but it was indeed worthy of being hailed the most beautiful to have ever been sung.

XXXIII   La dedens avoit ung autel   [190r]
           Äourné commë il falloit:
           Jamais homme ne verra tel.
           Deux ymages dessus avoit⁹   260
           L'un estoit Venus qui tenoit
           En sa main, dont j'ay bien memoire,
           Ung brandon de feu qui estoit
           Plus ardant que feu de tonnoire.   264

XXXIV   La dame avoit ung dÿadesme,
           D'une estoille portant son nom:
           De sa clarté n'a pas la desme
           Le soleil qui a grant renom,   268
           Car lëans n'a clarté si nom
           Celle qui s'espart de ses raiz;
           N'est oriflambe ne penon
           Qui tant soit cler a cent foiz pres.   272

XXXV   En son geron tenoit son filz,
           Qui se deduisoit d'une darde
           Dont les plus fors sont desconfis
           Et conquis sans y prendre garde.   276
           Nully en faveur ne regarde:
           Grans et petiz lui sont tout ung.
           Nul n'a contre lui sauvegarde:
           Son povoir est par tout commun.   280

XXXVI   De ceste chappelle auctentique   [190v]
           Estoit chantre Dame Leesse,
           Qui savoit tout l'art de musique:
           C'estoit de chanter la deesse.   284
           Conscïence estoit la prestresse
           Qui celebroit ceste journee
           L'office de la feste en la messe
           De Piramus et de Tybee.   288

XXXIII   Inside the chapel was an altar
decorated as was appropriate.
Never has man seen one comparable:
on the altar were two sculptures,
one of Venus, who held
in her hand, I remember this well,
a burning torch whose flame burned
brighter than lightning.[10]

XXXIV   The lady wore a crown
adorned with a star and bearing her name.
The sun in all its glory
has not a tenth of its intensity bright
for in this place there is no light
other than the one that beams from the star.
No banner or standard
has even one hundredth of its brilliance.

XXXV   In her lap she was holding her son,
who was playing distractedly with an arrow
that can bring down even the most powerful
before they have time to notice.
He grants special favor to no one;
great and small are all one.
No one is safe from him
for his power is all-encompassing.

XXXVI   In this chapel of great fame
Lady Delight was the cantor
who knew everything about art and music:
she is the goddess of song.
Conscience was the priestess,
who on that day was celebrating
the office of the feast in the mass
of Pyramus and Thisbe.

XXXVII   Quant je fuz droit devant ce temple,
                Ouquel Amours fait maint miracle,
                Je prins a Courtoisie exemple,
                Car en vëant la tabernacle   292
                M'eclinay tout bas vers l'oracle
                Et besay le planchier de plastre;
                Puis vins en ung aultre habitacle,
                Tout fondé sur pilliers d'albastre.   296

XXXVIII   Illec trouvay ung beau lit fait
                Ou Courtoisie me coucha,
                Et quant elle eut de moy parfait,
                Espoir le medecin hucha,   300
                Qui tantost vers moy s'adreça
                Et senty mon poux droicte voye;
                Et puis sans faillir me nonça
                Prestement quel douleur j'avoye: 304

XXXIX   "Ton cueur bruit trestout en chaleur,   [191r]
                Et es en fievre continue.
                Mais pour adoulcir ta douleur,
                Qui gueres ne se diminue,   308
                Te donrray a ma revenue
                Ung buvrage de tel racine
                Que se ta douleur ne s'en mue,
                Jamais ne croy en medecine."   312

XL   Lors se party et je remains.
                Quant il eut fait, il retourna.
                L'empoule tenoit en ses mains,
                En quoy buvrage si bon a.   316
                Gracë en ait! Il m'en donna
                Ung bon trait au pot sans verser,
                Et depuis il la me nomma
                Eaue de Gracïeux Penser.   320

XXXVII

When I arrived in front of this temple
where Love had performed so many miracles
I followed the example of Courtesy,
and, seeing the tabernacle,
I bowed low in the direction of the altar
and kissed the floor of plaster,
before passing into another dwelling that was
founded on pillars of alabaster.

XXXVIII

Here I found a beautiful bed already made,
and Courtesy tucked me in.
When she had done what was necessary,
she called in Hope, the doctor,
who immediately came to me
and felt my pulse.
Without delay, he told me
from which pain I was suffering.

XXXIX

"Your heart is beating excessively,
and you have a fever that will not break.
But to ease this pain
that will not diminish,
I will give you when I return
a drink composed of such herbs
that if your pain does not lessen
I will never again believe in medicine."

XL

Then he left and I remained.
When he had finished his task, he returned,
holding in his hands the phial
containing the proper potion.
God bless him! He gave me
a large swallow directly from the phial,
and then he told me its name:
Distilled Essence of Pleasant Thought.

XLI   J'en feuz ung poy mieulx disposé
             Quant j'euz beu l'eaue precïeuse,
             Si dormiz. Quant j'euz reposé,
             Vers moy vint Pitié la prïeuse,   324
             Comme de mon mal ennuyeuse,
             Et me conforta doulcement;
             Et, de sa voix delicïeuse,
             Se dist en mon commandement.   328

XLII   Quant j'oÿs son doulx abandon,   [191v]
             Qui ma douleur fist apaiser,
             Je m'enhardy, car ung grant don
             Lui requis pour mon cueur aiser.   332
             Ce ne fut pas flour de fraisier,
             Car de telz flours ne me chaloit:
             C'estoit sans plus ung franc baiser,
             Qui a ma fievre moult valoit.   336

XLIII   Quant Pitié demander m'oÿ
             S'un tout seul franc baiser aroye,
             Elle dist doulcement, "Oÿ,
             Voulentiers voir, se je povoye.   340
             Combien au fort, se je vouloye,
             Vous en ariez maulgré Dangier,
             Mais trop enviz lui mefferoye,
             Car Raison l'a fait jardinier.   344

XLIV   Il vous donrroit tout le seurplus
             Du jardin, rosiers et cyprés,
             Avant q'un franc baiser sans plus:
             Cest arbre qu'il garde plus pres.   348
             Nuyt et jour le garde de pres
             Car 'la soussye' est sa devise.
             Cela donne il par moz exprés
             A tous ceulx a qui se devise."   352

XLI	I began to feel a little better

XLI

I began to feel a little better
after having drunk this precious cocktail;
and so I slept. When I had rested,
Pity, the prioress, came to me,
still worrying over my illness,
to console me sweetly.
And in her luscious voice
she offered to help me in any way she could.

XLII

When I heard such a sweet and unrestricted offer,
it did much to soothe my pain,
and I braced myself to ask for a greater gift
in order to put my heart at ease.
Not for a strawberry flower did I ask,
for such flowers do not touch my fancy at all,
but instead for a simple kiss, nothing more,
which I was sure would relieve my fever.

XLIII

When Pity heard me ask
if I might have this one simple kiss,
she replied sweetly, "Yes,
I will grant it to you willingly if I can.
All in all, if it were up to me,
you would have it in spite of Resistance;
but I wouldn't wish to dishonor him in any way,
because Reason has made him the head gardener.

XLIV

He would give you anything
in the garden, including the roses and cypress trees,
before giving up even a single little kiss,
for this is the bush that he guards the most closely.
Night and day he keeps a close watch,
since "worry" is his slogan,
and he makes it known in no uncertain terms
to all those who are intent on entering."

XLV   "Helas!" diz je, "ma chiere dame,   [192r]
             Pour Dieu, que me faictez avoir
             Ung seul franc baiser, par mon ame!
             J'en donne trestout mon avoir.   356
             Faictez Dangier mon mal savoir.
             Dictez lui que je meurs aprés,
             Et, par ma foy, vous direz voir,
             Car desja suis mort a peu pres."   360

XLVI   Lors Pitié pleurant se party
             De la chambre en quoy je gisoye.
             Elle tenoit ja mon party,
             Pour ce que verité disoie.   364
             A Dangier ala droitte voye;
             Sa requeste ne fut pas vaine,
             Car elle eut ce que je vouloie,
             Maiz ce fut a Dieu scet quel paine.   368

XLVII   Encores, s'il le consenty,
             Ce fut par signe seullement,
             Car oncques mot ne respondy
             Ou il accordast franchement.   372
             Aler m'en couvint prestement,
             Tout si malade que j'estoie.
             Si mouruz pres soudainement
             Mais a Espoir me soustenoye.   376

XLVIII   Tant alasmes que nous venismes   [192v]
             Ou jardin ou Nature ouvra,
             Ou dames sans numbre veïsmes.
             Celle y trouve qui me navra,   380
             Qui par Pitié me recouvra,
             Car d'elle prins ung franc baisier
             Qui de tout mal me delivra
             Et me rendy sain et entier.   384

XLV

"Alas!" I responded, "my dear lady,
for God's sake, do make it possible that I have
this one simple kiss, upon my soul;
I will give all that I own to have it.
Just let Resistance know of my illness.
Tell him that I am dying,
and, I swear, you will be telling him the truth,
because I am already as good as dead."

XLVI

Then Pity, with tears in her eyes, left
the room where I was lying.
She had already taken my side in the matter,
because I told the truth.
She went straight to Resistance;
her request was not made in vain,
for she got what I wanted,
but heaven knows at what price.

XLVII

However, if Resistance consented,
it was only by signs,
for he said not a single word
to express his agreement explicitly.
I had to go that instant,
even as sick as I was,
for I might have died at any moment,
had Hope not sustained me.

XLVIII

We went along until we arrived
at the garden that Nature had created,
where we saw many ladies.
There I found the one who had wounded me
and who would revive me with Pity's intervention,
for I took from her a simple kiss
that delivered me from all my pain
and rendered me sound and content.

XLIX   Je l'en merciay doulcement,
      Et m'en partiz a son congié;
      Et, par le doulx atouchement
      Du franc baiser dont j'ay touchié,   388
      Je fuz tellement alegié
      Qu'a grant paine se je savoie
      Se j'avoie veu ou songé
      Ce qu'a mes yeulx veü avoye.   392

L   Quant ainssy me veiz en bon point,
      Je m'en alay par l'ospital
      Pour adviser de point en point
      Les beaultéz amont et aval;   396
      Si trouvay ung riche portal
      Tout massonné de pierre entiere,
      Qui est le chemin general
      Par ou on entre ou cimitiere.   400

LI   En ce cimitiere gisoient   [193r]
      Les vraiz et loyaulx amoureulx.
      Leurs epitaphes devisoient
      Leurs noms. Jë y congneuz entre eulx 404
      Tristain, le chevalier tres preux,
      Lequel mourut de desconfort,
      Lancelot du Lac, et tous ceulx
      Qui amerent jusqu'a la mort.   408

LII   Tant en y avoit que le compte
      Seroit trop long a assommer.
      Maint roy, maint duc, maint per, maint conte
      Y veiz que je ne sçay nommer,   412
      J'en veiz de par deça la mer
      Chevaliers, clers, et escuiers;
      Et s'i veiz, qu'on doit bien amer,
      Le Seneschal des Heinuyers,   416

XLIX   I thanked her very tenderly
and then bade her goodbye.
And thanks to this sweet interval,
and the simple kiss that I obtained,
I felt so comforted
that it was hard to know
whether I had really seen or just dreamed
what my eyes had witnessed there.

L   When I realized how much better I felt,
I wandered around the hospital
so that I might see from one end to the other
all of the beautiful things there, high and low;
I found a splendid doorway
built of unbroken stone:
the main gateway
by which one enters the cemetery.

LI   In this cemetery were buried
true and loyal lovers.
The epitaphs on the tombstones revealed
their names. I recognized among them
Tristan, that very courageous knight
who died of despair;
Lancelot of the Lake; and all those
who had loved even unto death.

LII   There were so many that an account of all of them
would take too long to tell.
So many kings, dukes, peers, and counts
were there that I would not be able to name them all.
I saw, too, those who came from this side of the sea,
knights, clerics, and squires;
and one in particular who merits admiration:
the seneschal of Hainuyers,

LIII   Nommé Jehan en son propre nom,
          Qui moult lëal fut en son temps.
          De vaillance eut moult hault renom;
          A trestout bien fut consentans.   420
          Son pareil ne fut puis cent ans.
          Honneur fut en lui anoblye,
          Et vally mieulx, en tout son temps
          Que renommee ne publye.   424

LIV   Assez pres, au bout du sentier,[11]   [193v]
          Gysoit le corps de tresparfait,
          Sage et lëal Alain Chartier,
          Qui en amours fist maint hault fait.   428
          Par qui fut sceü le meffait
          De celle qui l'amant occy,
          Qu'il appella, quant il eut fait,
          La Belle Dame sans Mercy.   432

LV   Entour sa tombe, en lettres d'or,
          Estoit tout l'art de Rethorique.
          Oultre lui, vers ung aultre cor
          Soubz une tumbe assez publique,   436
          Couchoit l'amant tresauctentique,
          Qui mourut sans le secours d'ame,
          Par le regart du baselique
          Contre raison appellee dame.[13]   440

LVI   Aprés passay une posterne,
          Ou je trouvay ung triste val.
          Je cuiday que ce fust inferne,
          Car c'est ung abisme de mal.   444
          Il n'est homme a pié n'a cheval
          Qui en yssist jour de sa vie.
          Illec rue l'en en general
          Tous ceulx qu'Amours excommenie.   448

LIII   called by his first name, John.
                He was the model of loyalty in his time,
                and was famed far and wide for his valor,
                always taking the side of right.
                His equal has not been seen in over a hundred years.
                In him honor was recognized as noble,
                and he was worth even more in his time
                than his reputation indicates.[12]

LIV   Not far from there, at the end of a path,
                reposed the corpse of the most perfect,
                wise, and loyal Alain Chartier,
                who authored many great works of love.
                He is the one who made known to all the crime
                of she who killed her lover,
                whom he called at the end
                the Belle dame sans mercy.

LV   Around his tomb, in letters of gold,
                was engraved the whole of the art of rhetoric.
                Next to him in another corner
                was buried, in a tomb visible to all,
                the illustrious and true lover
                who died, without the least gesture of help,
                by the fatal glance of that Basilisk
                who, against Reason, is called Lady.[14]

LVI   Next, passing through a rear gate,
                I came upon a miserable valley.
                I thought it must be Hell,
                for it was a real abyss of evil.
                No man, on foot or horseback,
                can ever escape from there alive,
                and there it is customary to beat to death
                those whom Love excommunicates.

LVII   C'est a maniere d'un faulx atre   [194r]
        Ou l'en gecte les corps mauldiz.
        Jë y en congneuz plus de quatre.
        La sont espars, noirs et pourriz,   452
        Sur terre sans estre enfouïz;
        Tous descouvers sont la gecté.
        A pluie et a vent sont submis
        Pour le peché de faulseté.   456

LVIII   La viz je le corps de Jason
        Pour ce qu'il fut faulx a Medee.
        Emprés lui gisoit Demophon,
        Et d'autre part ly faulx Enee   460
        Par qui Dido fut forsenee.
        Et le desdaigneux Narcisus,
        De qui Echo fut refusee,
        Gisoit a la pluie tout nuz.   464

LIX   Entre ces faulx amants couchoit
        La ditte dame que l'en dit
        "Sans mercy," laquelle y estoit
        Gettee comme par despit.   468
        Elle avoit esté sans respit
        Nouvellement noiee en plours,
        Et la nommoit l'en par escript
        La Cruelle Femme en Amours.   472

LX   Avec eulx Brisayda couchoit,   [194v]
        Qui foy menty a Troÿlus,
        Et tant, briefment, en avoit
        Qu'a grant paine en y avoit plus.   476
        Quant je les euz assés veüz,
        Tantost je me partiz de la;
        Et n'euz gueres esté en sus
        Que mon desir renouvella.   480

LVII

There was a sort of makeshift cemetery
in which were thrown the cursed corpses.
I recognized four or more of them.
They had been scattered, blackened and rotting,
all over the ground, without being buried, but
thrown out for all to see
exposed to the wind and the rain
as punishment for their sin of infidelity.

LVIII

I saw the body of Jason,
discarded there for his unfaithfulness to Medea.
Close to him Demophon was lying,
and in another corner the traitor Aeneas,
for whom Dido lost her mind.
And the proud Narcissus,
who rejected Echo,
lay there in the rain completely naked.

LIX

Among these unfaithful lovers was
the aforementioned lady
named "with no mercy"; she had been
tossed away as if in contempt.
Condemned without appeal
and recently drowned in tears,
she was renamed in writing
the "Cruel Woman in Love."[15]

LX

With them lay Breseida,
who broke her troth to Troilus;[16]
there were so many faithless lovers there
that there was scarcely room for more.
After having looked at them carefully,
I left that place,
and hardly was I out of sight
when my desire was renewed.

LXI   Desir, embrasé comme fu,
          Qui sa feste recommençoit,
          Me fist plus chault c'onques ne fu,
          Car en ardeur me conduisoit   484
          Et me commandoit et louoit
          Que je m'en ralasse au vergier
          Ou la belle se deduisoit,
          Qui me donna le franc baisier.   488

LXII   Tout aussi tost me transportay
          Qu'il ot dit, dont ne fuz pas sage;
          Dure nouvelle en rapportay,
          Car gaittes avoit au passage.   492
          Mais, non obstant ce y passay je,
          Me cuydant du tout resjouÿr;
          Mais Danger me fist dur message,
          Car oncques ne me voult ouÿr.   496

LXIII   Lors, comme au boys refuit le lievre,   [195r]
          A mon premier mal reffuÿ,
          Et rencheu en ma chaude fievre.
          Mon cueur en ardeur rebruÿ;   500
          Ardant desir me remuÿ
          Et je m'escrïay sur Pitié,
          Maiz ce rescry poy m'esjoÿ,
          Car je fus arriere alitié.   504

LXIV   Si m'en retournay tout honteux,
          Plus fort malade qu'oncques maiz.
          Desir mauldiz, par qui honte euz,
          Et fus en tel point que jamaiz   508
          Ne cuidoye mieulx avoir maiz.
          Espoir me veult dire que sy:
          "Croy moy, et en ma main te metz,
          Et je t'osteray de soussy."   512

LXI   Desire was reignited like a fire,
                   and again began to celebrate his office,
                   making me hotter than ever before,
                   for he was transporting me with ardor.
                   He commanded and impelled me
                   to return to the garden
                   where the beautiful lady was enjoying herself,
                   the one who had given me the simple kiss.

LXII   I set off on my way as soon as
                   Desire had spoken, which was not very wise, for
                   I ended up with a harsh response since
                   the passage was too well guarded.
                   Nevertheless, I kept to my path,
                   still believing I would find my joy.
                   But Resistance met me with a cruel message,
                   for he refused even to listen to me.

LXIII   Thus, just as the hare flees into the woods,
                   I fell into my former sickness of heart
                   and suffered again from a hot fever.
                   My heart began to beat furiously;
                   burning desire invaded me.
                   I cried out for Pity,
                   but this call brought me little relief,
                   and I ended up back in bed.

LXIV   Thus I returned, completely ashamed,
                   and sicker than ever before.
                   I cursed Desire, who had brought me this shame,
                   for I was so far gone that never,
                   I believed, would I be healed.
                   Hope came to contradict me:
                   "Believe me, and put yourself in my hands:
                   I will deliver you from your distress."

LXV   Si tost que je l'oÿ parler,
Je le regarday par despit,
Et durement l'en fis aler,
Disant: "Point ne vault ton respit.   516
Je suis mort, Desespoir l'a dit."
Lors fuz porté, ne sçay de qui,
A moitié mort, jusqu'a mon lit,
Ou grant temps maugré moy vesqui.   520

LXVI   Quant Courtoisie, l'enfermiere,   [195v]
Sceut que tant fort malade estoie,
Vers moy vint et fut la premiere;
S'amena Pitié en sa voye,   524
Et deux aultres dont plus m'envoye
Veu que l'un estoit Souvenir,
Mais de l'autre je ne savoye
Encore en son nom revenir.   528

LXVII   Maiz quant je reuz mon sentement,
Je le recongneuz au parler:
On le nommoit Entendement,
Et se savoit de tout mesler;   532
En phisique estoit bachelier.
Premier vint a moy Souvenir,
Qui de tout savoit aparler,
Si non de choses advenir.   536

LXVIII   Tout premier commença a dire:
"Beau sire, avez vous oublyé
Comment d'Espoir, vostre bon mire,
Fustez doulcement bien veigné,   540
Quant beustez, pour estre alegé,
L'Eaue de Gracïeux Panser?
Comment l'avez vous desdaigné?
Et si fist vostre mal cesser.   544

LXV
As soon as I heard her speak,
I turned to look at her with contempt,
and brushed her off rudely,
saying: "Your words are worth nothing:
I am already dead; Hopelessness has decreed it."
And then I was transported, by whom I know not,
half dead, all the way to my bed,
where I continued living, against my will.

LXVI
When Courtesy, the nurse,
learned that I was so seriously ill,
she came to me (she was the first)
and brought with her Pity
and two others whom I had not seen for a long time.
One was Memory;
as for the other,
I could not quite remember the name.

LXVII
But once I came back to my senses,
I recognized him by his words.
They called him Understanding,
and he knew something about everything,
for he had a degree in physics.
Memory approached me first;
he knew how to orate on any subject
except, of course, the future.

LXVIII
He began by saying:
"Dear sir, have you forgotten
how Hope, your most excellent physician,
welcomed you so warmly,
and how you drank for your improvement
the essence of Sweet Thought?
How can you hold him in disdain?
Indeed, he brought an end to your pain.

LXIX   Ce qu'il vous promist avery   [196r]
Quant vous eustez le franc baiser;
Si ne povez estre gary
S'il ne fait le mal appaiser.   548
Qui vous voit ainsy degrecer,
Il semble que tout soit perdu:
Ung homme fait peu apriser
Qui pour ung seul cop est rendu."   552

LXX   Quant il eut fait son preschement,
Qui gueres ne me conforta,
Devers moy vint Entendement,
Qui de croire Espoir m'ennorta,   556
Et dist: "Quant Dangier t'aporta
Son reffus, il fist sa coustume.
Il fait ainsy, maiz grant tort a
Qui pour cela, mal y presume.   560

LXXI   Tu doiz penser, se tu scez rien,
Que si ne fust empeschement
Tu fussez venu aussi bien
Comme tu feuz derrenierement.   564
Tu doiz croire certainement
Que Male Bouche et Jalousie
Se sont parceuz aucunement,
Dont la chose est si ralongie.   568

LXXII   Il est ainsy, j'en suis prophete.   [196v]
Il ne t'y fault point varïer,
Ains te fault faire une retraite
Se tu y veulz droit charïer.   572
Faiz tant que Pitié voit prïer
A Dangier que dormir se taise;
Bien lui saura faire ottroyer
Sa voulenté, maiz qu'i luy plaise."   576

LXIX	He kept his promise to you:
	you had your simple kiss.
	Now, you cannot be healed
	unless he himself treats your pain.
	Anyone who saw you pining away thus,
	would think that all was lost:
	a man is not worth his mettle
	if he is defeated on the first blow!"
LXX	When he had finished this sermon,
	which really did very little to ease me,
	Understanding came before me
	and exhorted me to believe in Hope,
	saying: "When Resistance confronted you
	with his refusal, he acted as is his wont.
	He was made to be that way; however, it would be wrong
	to presume that his action was malicious.
LXXI	You must realize, if you know anything at all,
	that if there were no obstacle
	to achieving your desire,
	you would the sooner have had it.
	But you must believe, without a doubt,
	that Foul Mouth and Jealousy
	introduce themselves at some point,
	so that the process might be prolonged.
LXXII	This is how it will be; I am a prophet on this subject.
	You must not waver on your course,
	however, you must be willing to retreat
	if you would act wisely.
	Do whatever it takes to get Pity to see
	Resistance and beg him to go to sleep and thus keep quiet.
	She knows well how to make him
	do her bidding, as long as it is in accordance with her will."

LXXIII   Quant ce conseil en moy sentiz,
                Quoy que guerir ne me povoye,
                Vint ce medecin tresgentilz,
                Espoir, que voulentier oyoye,   580
                Lequel me dist, se je vouoye
                Au Dieu d'Amours mon sacrefice,
                S'aprés ce fait ne m'en louoye,
                Il vouldroit perdre son office.   584

LXXIV   Adonc chascun se departy,
                Si non Espoir, qui demoura.
                Mon poux encores resenty,
                Et dist: "Ton cueur pas ne mourra,   588
                Tant que conseil croire vouldra
                Je te pense a donner tel chose
                Qui a ta douleur plus vauldra
                Que ta pensee ne suppose.   592

LXXV   Mais il te fault garder d'egrun,   [197r]
                Pou penser, querir compaignie
                En pluseurs lieux, non pas en ung,
                Tousjours mener joyeuse vie;   596
                Et se tu as melencolie,
                Lys quelque gracïeuse hystoire,
                Et avec, sur tout je te prie
                Que tousjours m'ayez en memoire.   600

LXXVI   Ceulx qui n'ont pas Entendement,
                Comme toy, bien leur doy souffire
                Quant je leur faiz alegement.
                Je suis prophete pour voir dire;   604
                Pour gairir douleur, je suis mire,
                Voire, s'elle n'est trop mortelle.
                Mais Amours, le souverain sire,
                Est cellui qui la guerist telle.   608

LXXIII	I realized the wisdom of this advice, even if it were not enough to cure me; and then Hope, the most gracious doctor, came to me, to whom I listened quite willingly as he suggested that I dedicate a sacrifice to the God of Love. He added that if afterward I did not receive praise for this deed, he would be willing abandon his office.
LXXIV	After these words, everyone left except Hope, who stayed with me. Again he took my pulse and said: "Your heart will continue to beat as long as you believe in this advice. I am considering giving you something that will treat your pain even more effectively than you might imagine possible.
LXXV	But you must be on guard against bitterness! Don't think too much; try to be social in many places, not just one. Be sure to enjoy yourself always, and if you find yourself melancholy, read a happy little story; and above all, I beg you, keep me always in your thoughts.
LXXVI	Those who have not Understanding, as do you, must be satisfied when I grant them a morsel of comfort. I am a prophet who tells the truth; when I heal pain, I act as a doctor, that is, if the illness is not fatal. But Love, the ruler of all, is the only one who can heal so serious a malady.

LXXVII   Se ton desir est tant ardant
                Que je ne te puisse guerir,
                Fuiz a Amours, prans le a garant,
                Et lui va mercy requerir: 612
                S'il luy plaist, tu ne peuz perir,
                Car tant fera vers ta maistresse
                Que ce qu'elle fait rencherir
                Fera venir a grant largesse."   616

LXXVIII   Atant se teut Espoir, mon maistre.   [197v]
                Et lors je regarday cellui
                Dont mon plaisir estoit a naistre:
                C'estoit Amours. Pensant a lui,   620
                Mes yeulx de lermes aveugly;
                J'estoie devot a oultrance,
                Tant que bouche et cueur me failly,
                Et fuz adont mort jusqu'au trance.   624

LXXIX   Quant je fuz a moy revenu,
                Les mains joingny vers la chappelle,
                Disant: "Ha! mon dieu tres cremu,
                Par qui je bruiz et estincelle,   628
                A mon plus grant besoing t'appelle,
                Et te prie qu'a ce cop cy
                Guerissez le mal que je celle,
                Pour m'en donner mort ou mercy!   632

LXXX   Si vraiement que je congnoy
                Ta loy et y croy fermement,
                Et si vraiement que je croy
                Que jadis ancïennement,   636
                Par miracle tresevidant,
                Et par ta force merveilleuse,
                Fina Ulixes franchement
                De Penoloppee l'orguilleuse;   640

LXXVII	If your desire is so ardent
	that it is impossible for me to heal you,
	flee to Love; submit yourself to his protection,
	and ask him to grant you his mercy.
	If it pleases him, you cannot perish,
	for he will attend to your mistress and make it
	so that what she prizes most,
	she will dispense with utmost generosity."

LXXVIII	After these words, Hope, my master, fell silent.
	And then I set my sights on him
	from whom my joy would be born:
	it was Love. Thinking of him,
	tears blinded my eyes.
	I was obsessively devoted
	to such a point that my heart and mouth failed me
	and I fell into a faint, as if dead.

LXXIX	When I regained consciousness,
	I stretched out my hands to the chapel
	saying, "Alas! Most fearsome god,
	by whom I burn and spark,
	I cry out to you in great need
	and pray that
	you heal me now of the sickness that I carry inside.
	Grant me either death or your mercy!

LXXX	Even as I acknowledge
	your law and believe in it firmly,
	so do I believe
	that in olden days,
	by undeniable miracles
	and your marvelous power,
	Ulysses ended his story in honor,
	despite Penelope the Proud;

LXXXI   Et comme tu vengas Equo   [198r]
               De Narcisus le renoyé,
               Qui tant ne sceust nayer ano
               Qu'a ton plaisir ne fust noyé,   644
               Son cueur estoit bien desnoyé
               Quant par son crüel pansement
               Avoit ton povoir guerroyé
               Et enfraint ton commandement;   648

LXXXII   Et comme ce fut verité
               Qu'a l'ymaige Pimalïon
               Donnas vie par ta pitié,
               Et comme en nostre regïon   652
               Feiz pour Guillaume champïon
               Contre le chastel Jalousie,
               Ou il eut la possessïon
               Du bouton et de la feullye;   656

LXXXIII   Et si vray que tu condempnas
               La Crüelle Femme a noyer
               Et que crüel nom lui donnas,
               Veullez moy briefment envoier   660
               Ce que tu scés qui m'est mestier:
               Donne aide a ce qui est tien;
               Ne me veullez pas renoyer,
               Regarde mon piteux maintien."   664

LXXXIV   En parfaisant mon oroison,   [198v]
               M'endormis tout soudainement.
               Lors m'avint en advisïon,
               Dont j'euz grant esmerveillement,   668
               Qu'Amours se leva prestement
               Et avec une aspre clarté
               S'apparut a moy proprement,
               Dont je feuz tout espoventé.   672

LXXXI
Likewise you avenged Echo
for the rebuff of Narcissus,
who did not know how to swim well enough,
and so drowned according to your pleasure.
His heart was too defiant,
when, by his pitiless preoccupation,
he declared war on your authority
and disobeyed your commandment.

LXXXII
Similarly, it is true
that to the statue of Pygmalion
you gave life by the power of your pity,
and, even in our region,
you were the champion of Guillaume
in the battle against the castle of Jealousy,
so that he took possession
of the rosebud and its foliage.[17]

LXXXIII
And it is also true that you condemned
the Cruel Woman to be drowned
and you assigned her this name, 'cruel.'[18]
I beg of you, in so many words, to send to me
what you know I need so desperately.
Help him who belongs to you!
Please do not send me away,
but look with compassion upon my pitiful condition."

LXXXIV
Having finished my prayer,
I fell fast asleep.
And then I saw in a vision,
a thing that amazed me greatly:
Love got up without delay
and in a flash of light
he appeared before me,
and I was sore afraid.

LXXXV	En venant, son filz m'appella	
	Et me dist: "Point ne t'esbahys."	
	Asseur fuz quant je veiz cela,	
	Et voulentiers parler l'oÿs.	676
	A le oÿr tant m'esjoÿs	
	Qu'onques puis ne feiz malle chiere.	
	Lors commança par grant advis	
	Sa raison en ceste maniere:	680
LXXXVI	"O nostre filz, qui ja souloyes,	
	En ton premier commencement,	
	Tandiz que nostre devenoies,	
	Occupper ton entendement	684
	A faire gracïeusement	
	Chançons, dictiéz, plaisans et doulx,	
	Et tousiours a l'exaucement	
	De nostre povoir et de nous,	688
LXXXVII	Qu'est devenu ce doulx usaige?	[199r]
	Comment t'en puez tu tant douloir?	
	Es tu en faulte de couraige?	
	As tu perdu ton bon vouloir?	692
	Ta joye est elle en nonchalloir?	
	As tu laissé honneur pour honte?	
	Ou est ton desir de valloir?	
	Comment nous en renderas tu compte?	696
LXXXVIII	Que pensez tu a devenir?	
	Helaz! Et qui te desconforte?	
	N'as tu point de moy souvenir?	
	Te semble ma puissance morte?	700
	Est ta cause de deul tant forte	
	Que riens ne te puet secourir?	
	Ne veulz tu que mieulx te conforte?	
	Finablement, veulz tu mourir?"	704

LXXXV	As he approached, he called me his son
	and then said: "Fear not!"
	I was reassured on hearing these words,
	and listened eagerly to hear him speak.
	It brought such joy to listen to him
	that never again will I be gloomy.
	Then he commenced his speech to me
	with great wisdom, and it followed in this manner:
LXXXVI	"Our own dear son, you had taken up the habit,
	since the very beginning
	when you became ours,
	of occupying your mind
	with the composing
	of songs and poems, as charming as they are melodic,
	in order to glorify
	us and our supremacy.
LXXXVII	What has happened to this lovely practice?
	How is that you grieve and pain yourself so?
	Have you no courage?
	Have you lost your willpower?
	Has your joy become indifference?
	Have you abandoned honor for shame?
	Where is your desire for valor?
	What do you have to say for yourself now?
LXXXVIII	What do you think you are doing?
	Alas! What has overcome you?
	Do you not remember who I am?
	Do you believe my power to be dead?
	Is the cause of your pain so great
	that nothing can help you?
	Do you not wish for greater relief?
	Finally, do you wish to die?"

LXXXIX   "Nennil, sire, s'il ne vous plest,
                Car, quel que dueil que je recorde,
                Vous savez bien comment il m'est:
                Plaisir ou deul, paix ou discorde,   708
                Tout tient a vo misericorde.
                Du lïen de mon desconfort
                Ne peut nul deslïer la corde,
                Si ce n'estes vous, ou la Mort."   712

XC   Lors dist Amours: "Tu te meffais   [199v]
                Encontre moy quant tu te plains,
                Veüz les biens que je t'ay faiz.
                Que n'y as tu prins exemple, ains   716
                Que tu publïasses tes plains?"
                "Sire," dis je, "pour Dieu mercy,
                Ce sont les deulz dont je suis plains
                Qui m'ont le cueur taint et noircy.   720

XCI   Me guerir et vous honnorer
                Est le desir de m'oroison.
                Mon cueur ne veult pas ignorer
                Vostre povoir, ne la foison   724
                Des plaisirs qu'a vostre achoison
                Pitié et Espoir m'ont donné:
                Espoir me donne le poison
                Dont mon plaisir fut saisonné,   728

XCII   Et Pitié pour moy procura
                Tant que j'en euz ung franc baisier,
                Qui pour lors tout mon mal cura.
                Mais je resuis au point premier,   732
                Car j'ay depuis trouvé Danger,
                Qui m'a, par responce crüelle,
                Plus rebouté q'un estranger,
                Dont j'ay douleur toute nouvelle.   736

LXXXIX

"Not at all, Master, unless it please you.
For, in spite of the pain of which I complain,
you know exactly what this is all about.
Pleasure or pain, peace or strife,
all depends on your grace and compassion.
The ties of my distress
can be loosed by no one,
unless it be you or Death."

XC

Then Love said: "You do wrong
against me when you complain this way,
especially given the favors I have accorded to you.
Why did you not consider these
before voicing your complaints?"
"Oh, Master, God have mercy!
I am so full of these miserable thoughts
that have blackened and tainted my heart.

XCI

My healing and your honor
are the reasons for my prayer.
My heart cannot be ignorant
of your power nor of the profusion
of pleasures that, at your instigation,
Pity and Hope have given me:
Hope has given me the poison
to season my pleasure,

XCII

and Pity took me in her care
so that I might receive a simple kiss,
which for now has cured my disease.
But now I am again at the point where I started,
for I have encountered Resistance,
who, by his pitiless response,
has shunned me as if I were a stranger
and thus renewed my pain.

XCIII   Je pensay, quant tel le trouvay,   [200r]
             Qu'il se penoit de moy bien faire;
             Et, par ce penser, approuvay
             Qu'il me vouloit du tout deffaire,   740
             Car bien m'estoit sans le forfaire.
             Si me poingnoit aprés ointure
             Et me punissoit sans meffaire,
             Qui est ouvre contre droicture.   744

XCIV   J'ay par ce deul blessé mon sens
             Et ay, par mon oultrecuidance,
             Blasmé Espoir, je m'en repens;
             Et en offre cueur et puissance   748
             A en faire la penitance.
             Maiz je vous prie doulcement
             Qu'aprés ma bonne repentance,
             Donnez mon cueur alegement.   752

XCV   Ostez moy la dure douleur
             Qui le corps me tue et martire
             Jusqu'a l'abisme de mon cueur!
             Et mandez a Dangier, chier sire,   756
             Qu'il m'en doint ce que je desire.
             Pitié en fera l'ambassade:
             Envoiez lui de chaulde tire
             Ains que je soie plus malade!"   760

XCVI   Amours dist lors: "Ains que plus dies,   [200v]
             Veul savoir se tu me saroies
             Raconter les griefz maladies,
             Les veilles, les perdues voyes,   764
             Que pieça dis que tu avoyes
             Ains que d'amours eussez le bout.
             Or ne me mens pas toutesvoyes:
             Diz moy s'il te souvient du tout."   768

XCIII   I thought, when he treated me in this manner,
that he had decided never to do me a good turn.
And by this understanding, I realized
that he was determined to undermine my plan.
For everything was fine, I had done no wrong,
and then (as they say) he injured me after applying the ointment.
He punished me for doing no wrong,
which certainly is an action unjust!

XCIV   This pain has impaired my good sense,
and then, in my idiocy,
I blamed Hope, of which I really repent,
and offer my heart and body
to pay penance for these sins.
But I pray you graciously
that after my sincere repentance,
you will give my heart comfort.

XCV   Free me from this severe pain,
which martyrs my body and chokes me
even unto the depths of my heart!
And order Resistance, dear Master,
to give me what I desire.
Pity will be the ambassador;
send him now, without delay,
before my sickness worsens!"

XCVI   Love responded thus: "Before you say more,
I want to know if you can
describe for me the severe pains you suffer:
the vigils and the wanderings
that I predicted earlier you would experience
before reaching the goal of your love.
Do not hide anything:
tell me if you remember it all."

XCVII   "Par ma foy, il me souvient bien
          Que me deistes aucun propos,
          Mais quel il fu, je n'en sçay rien,
          Car j'ay eu si peu de repos   772
          Qu'onques depuis penser n'y pos.
          Mais selon qu'il me puet valoir,
          Je vous supply que aucuns motz
          Vous en plaise a ramentevoir."   776

XCVIII   "Or sus! Pour ton bien je le veul.
          Il est vray qu'anciennement,
          Quand je t'euz conquis de ton veul,
          Je te prïay treshumblement   780
          Et commanday expressement
          Que loyal feusses et secré,
          Et parlasses honnestement
          De chascun selon son degré.   784

XCIX   Aprés commandemens pluseurs,   [201r]
          Te protestay mal et fortune,
          Pour quoy tu sceus biens et douleurs.
          Ce fiz je affin que la rancune   788
          De Dangier te feust plus commune
          Et te grevast moins aporter.
          Et je voy par ton infortune
          Que tu ne t'en scez conforter.   792

C   Ne te souvient il que je deiz
          Qu'au commencement tu orroyes
          Contre ung bien des maulx plus de dix?
          Ainsi ont tous dont tu devoyes   796
          Tenir les chemins et les voyes,
          Dont nul par fort courre n'eschappe.
          Aussi eschapper n'en pourroyes
          Puis que tu t'es mis sur ma trappe.   800

XCVII	"By faith! I remember well that you gave me a lecture, but what you said, I don't remember at all, for I had slept so little that I could not even think. But as long as it will be to my benefit, I beg you to repeat, if it pleases you, these words."
XCVIII	"Up then, pay attention! It is true that in the beginning, when I won you over (according to your wishes) I beseeched you, in all humbleness, and ordered explicitly that you be loyal and discreet, and that you speak with honesty and respect to everyone according to their rank.
XCIX	After giving you a list of commandments, I testified to you of the good and the bad by which you would have happiness and pain. I did this so that you would be expecting the wrath of Resistance, and it would thus not harm you as grievously. But I see by your distress that you know not how to find solace.
C	Do you remember how I told you that at first you would hear for every good thing, more than ten bad? This is how it happens for everyone, and you should hold firmly to the way and the path from which no one escapes no matter how quickly he runs. Nor would you be able to escape, now that you have entered into my trap.

CI   Ne scez tu pas bien par plusieurs
            Q'un seul bien que je sçay donner
            Reboute cent mile doulours?
            Qui veult dont justement compter,   804
            Nul ne puet trop chier acheter
            Mercy, qui est le plus grant bien:
            Tel est que, qui en puet finer,
            Il n'a jamais faulte de rien.   808

CII   Les loyaulx en ont la douleur,   [201v]
            Et les faulx en eschappent sain,
            Car ilz n'y mectent rien du leur.
            Mais les bons n'ont pas mal en vain,   812
            Car ilz en ont le bien haultain,
            Le quel bien aux faulx rien ne monte,
            Car quant ilz ont ce bien a main,
            Ilz ont ce dont ilz ne font compte.   816

CIII   Qui le veult paier a son droit,
            Il ne fault or n'argent tirer;
            Car qui pour argent le vouldroit,
            Je le feroye martirer.   820
            Il se paie de desirer,
            Et requerir par long espace,
            Et de craindre, et continüer
            En loyaulté qui oultre passe.   824

CIV   Le loyal qui grace dessert,
            En suivant ma loyalle queste,
            Je te diray de quoy il sert
            De penser et rompre sa teste,   828
            De faire en vain mainte requeste,
            De perdre mainte longue voye,
            Faire vigille avant la feste,
            A grant deul et a pou de joye.   832

CI	Have you not yet learned from others
	that a single good that I might grant
	erases a hundred thousand pains?
	He who wishes to keep an accurate account, then,
	must admit that no one can pay too high a price.
	Mercy, the highest good of all,
	is such that he who attains it
	will never lack for anything.

CI
Have you not yet learned from others
that a single good that I might grant
erases a hundred thousand pains?
He who wishes to keep an accurate account, then,
must admit that no one can pay too high a price.
Mercy, the highest good of all,
is such that he who attains it
will never lack for anything.

CII
The loyal ones feel great pain;
the unfaithful escape without a scratch,
for they risk nothing of themselves.
But the good do not suffer in vain;
they receive in exchange for their suffering the highest good.
The faithless, of course, do not know what they have missed,
for even when they have it in hand,
they do not realize its merit.

CIII
If one wanted to pay its true price,
(not in silver or gold,
for he who would sell it for money
I would kill on the spot)
it can only be paid with desire
and with beseeching for long periods of time,
and even with anxiety, but most of all
with constant loyalty.

CIV
The loyal man merits grace,
by following me in this loyal quest.
Let me tell you how the following actions serve him:
to contemplate, nay, to crack his head open,
to ask again and again, always in vain,
to wander around endlessly,
to fast and keep vigil before the feast,
in piercing pain and with little joy.

CV   Au chemin le fayz deviser,   [202r]
            Ou long derriere ou long devant,
            Et soy a celle deviser,
            Qui est a Bruges ou a Gant.   836
            La requiert il grace en pleurant,
            Et celle qui ailleurs s'esjoye
            Puis se repent en ottroiant,
            Et en pleurant se rit de joye.   840

CVI   Quant il a en ce point pensé
            Une heure ou deulx, lors lui souvient
            De quelque desplaisir passé,
            Ou d'aultre homme qui va et vient   844
            A l'ostel sa dame et couvient,
            Ce dist il, qu'il soit retenu:
            Car ce qu'il fait mieulx lui advient,
            S'en doit estre ly mieulx venu.   848

CVII   Quant il est ainsy enflamé,
            Adonc se commance a maudire,
            Et dit qu'onques ne fut amé.
            Lors l'ahert une rage d'ire,   852
            Et va commencer a mesdire
            De moy et de ce que je puis,
            Qui le fait amer, et va dire
            Qu'il n'eut bien ne joye oncques puis.   856

CVIII   Lors emprant d'aler en essil,   [202v]
            Et dit que plus ne l'aimera,
            Et si l'ayme; si promet il
            Que jamais veoir ne la vouldra.   860
            Il ment: car, des ce qu'il revendra,
            Se ung jour devoit querir l'adresse,
            Devant son hostel passera
            Et ne tendra veu ne promesse.   864

CV

Along the path, I make him cast his mind
back into the past as well as far into the future
and have him converse inside his head with her
who is in Bruges, or perhaps in Ghent.
There in his imagination, he begs tearfully for grace,
and she who is really somewhere else having fun
then repents by bestowing upon him her grace,
and he laughs with joy while still crying.

CVI

Reaching a point where he has been engrossed in thought
for an hour or two, he suddenly remembers
some past unpleasantness,
or some man who comes and goes
regularly to his lady's house,
but he believes that surely he will be the one chosen,
for what he does is more attractive to her,
thus he must necessarily be better received.

CVII

While he is incensed in this manner,
he begins to curse himself,
saying that he has never been loved in return.
Then an enraged anger takes hold of him,
and he will begin to speak ill
of me and of what I, who made him fall in love,
am capable of, and goes on to say
that he has known neither happiness nor joy since meeting me.

CVIII

Then he decides to go into exile
and declares that he will love her no more,
yet he still loves; furthermore, he promises
that he will never want to see her again.
But he lies, for soon after his return from exile
he will happen to ask one day for her address.
Then he will pass by her house
and thus will not keep his vow or promise.

CIX   Et s'il advient que a ce passer
           Elle n'est a huis n'a fenestre,
           Lors a plus supplus a penser
           Et tence a cil qui le fist naistre;   868
           Et dit qu'a lui n'a daigne estre,
           Pour ce qu'elle l'a veu de loing.
           Ainsi ce demaine ce maistre,
           Pour nulle chose et sans besoing.   872

CX   Tantost qu'il sera descendu,
           Sans dire ce qu'il a trouvé,
           Et sans ce qu'il ait attendu
           Qu'il soit vestu ne deshousé,   876
           Rira passer, trestout croté,
           Puet estre a l'estable verra
           La vielle tordant son fillé,
           Et sa dame veoir cuidera.   880

CXI   Ainsy sera trompé ce fol,   [203r]
           Qui cuidera veoir sa maistresse,
           Et il verra le maigre col
           De la vielle, ou n'a sain ne gresse.   884
           Pour nëant perdra sa tristesse,
           Et la vielle, quant le verra,
           Le regardera par finesse.
           Ainsy de rien s'esjouÿra.   888

CXII   En ce point passera le temps,
           Jusqu'a ce qu'on clourra les huis.
           Encores n'est il pas contens,
           Car il y revenra depuis;   892
           Et fera avecques ce duiz
           Que l'uis congnoistra au fermer,
           Si y vendra toutes les nuyz
           A ung certain trou escouter.   896

CIX   And if it happens, by chance, that as he passes by,
she is not at the door or the window,
he has even more to think about,
and will bicker with himself for even imagining these thoughts,
concluding that if she does not deign to show herself
it is because she saw him coming from afar.
This is the way in which the man will act
over nothing and needlessly.

CX   As soon as he has dismounted,
without speaking a word of what he has found out
and without waiting to have his cloak put on
or have his boots taken off,
he will remount and set off only to pass by again.
Perhaps then at the stables he will see
the old hag spinning thread,
and will believe he has seen his lady.

CXI   And so this idiot will fool himself
into believing he has seen his mistress,
but he really will see the skinny neck
of the old hag, whose skin hangs wrinkled on her bones.
For no reason, then, his sadness will disappear,
and the old hag, when she sees him,
will give him a coquettish look.
Then he will realize that he was overjoyed for nothing.

CXII   Time will pass by slowly,
until the moment when they close the doors of the house.
But he is still not happy,
and he will return again,
and so get very good at this,
able to recognize the door even when it is closed.
He will come back every night
to listen at a certain chink in the wall.[19]

CXIII   L'oreille y mectra justement,
      Pour escouter et riens oÿr;
      Et sa teste emplira de vent,
      Qui luy fera les dens fremir   900
      Et esmouvoir, si que dormir
      Ne pourra trois ne quatre nuiz.
      Si s'en yra tout seul gemir
      Et recorder tous ses ennuiz.   904

CXIV   Quant il sera tresbien couchié,   [203v]
      Et endormir ne se pourra,
      Tout malade et tout couroucié
      Se levera et vestira;   908
      Yra et puis retournera,
      Et fera le Prestre Martin:
      Il chantera et respondra,
      Et ainsy venra le matin.   912

CXV   Or est quite de descouchier,
      Car il est levé davantage,
      Et puis s'en va vers le moustier,
      Sans penser a Dieu n'a ymaige.   916
      Il scet l'eure que par usaige
      Sa dame doit venir a messe,
      Si l'atent de l'eul au passaige,
      Et puis s'en vient a grant leesse.   920

CXVI   Quant elle est en son siege assise,
      Lors gambie par devant celle.
      Aler veult de nouvelle guise,
      Tant que pour bien aler chancelle. 924
      La teste adonc luy estincelle,
      Et puis regarde sa maistresse.
      Ainsi va et vient en tour elle,
      Tant com veult commencer la messe. 928

CXIII	He will situate his ear judiciously in order to listen, yet will hear nothing. His head will be filled with nothing but the wind, which will make his teeth shiver and chatter so severely that sleep will evade him for three or four nights. He will leave there alone and trembling to write down all his woes.
CXIV	When he gets in the bed, he will find that he cannot sleep. Feeling completely ill and overly anxious, he gets back up and dresses, pacing to and fro, and then acts like Father Martin:[20] he chants and provides the response himself, until finally the morning dawns.
CXV	There is no need for him to get out of bed, for he is already up. Then he makes his way to the church, without the slightest thought of God or the saints. He knows the hour when usually his lady comes to mass. He spies her on the path and continues now with great happiness.
CXVI	When she has taken her seat, he struts in front of her. Wanting to pass by again, he whips around so fast that he loses his balance and sees stars spin in his eyes; then he gazes at his mistress. This is how he comes and goes around her until the mass begins.

CXVII   Et quant ce vient a l'introïte,   [204r]
       Emprés elle va querir place,
       Ou il s'encline a l'opposite,
       Tant qu'il la voit en my la face.   932
       Nul povre a lui ne se pourchasse,
       Qu'il ne s'en tourne main fournie;
       Mais certes, quel semblant qu'il face,
       C'est aumosne d'ypocrisie.   936

CXVIII   Puis vient l'offrande, et celle y va
       Baiser le doy; et puis veez cy
       Nostre maistre, qui grant peur a
       Qu'aultre ne la suive avant lui.   940
       Puis baise le doy ou joingny
       La bouche ou tant a de beaulté
       Que bien vouldroit baiser aussi,
       Et le prestre eust le doy couppé.   944

CXIX   Et quant ce vient a celebrer,
       Tousjours a l'eul sus sa deesse:
       De Dieu ne se puet remenbrer,
       Et s'en voit deux a une messe.   948
       Il pense a l'un, et l'autre laisse.
       Aprés fait tant qu'il a la paix,
       Si la fait baiser sa maistresse,
       Et, s'il ose, il la baise aprés.   952

CXX   En faisant ces choses lui semble   [204v]
       Que de celebrer a scïence,
       Et que si bien de chacun semble
       Que nul ne congnoist ce qu'il pensc. 956
       De tout scet fin des qu'il commence:
       C'est des secréz le plus habille,
       Comme il cuide, et l'experïence
       De quanqu'il fait court par la ville. 960

CXVII   When it is time for the *introit*,[21]
             he seeks a place very close
             so that he can kneel opposite her
             and see her face clearly.
             No beggar who comes to solicit from him
             leaves without his hands full.[22]
             But of course, despite this show,
             they are just the alms of hypocrisy.

CXVIII   Next comes the offering, and she goes up
             to kiss the finger of the priest;[23] now here comes
             our young master, who fears
             that someone might follow her and separate them.
             Then he, too, kisses the priest's finger and thereby touches
             those lips in which there is so much beauty,
             those lips that he wishes to kiss himself,
             and may the priest's finger be cut off!

CXIX   When the time comes to celebrate the Eucharist,
             his eyes are still fixed on his mistress.
             He has no thought of God,
             for he sees two gods at this mass;
             he thinks of one, and completely forgets the other.
             After the celebration he manages to get the peace,[24]
             and offers it to his mistress to kiss
             and if he dares, he kisses her afterward.[25]

CXX   In going through the motions, he believes
             himself to be an expert at pretending to participate in the mass,
             and that he is so good at it
             that no one realizes what he is really thinking.
             He knows how everything will happen before he begins;
             keeping secrets is his specialty,
             or at least he believes it is. Meanwhile the truth
             of what is really going on spreads all over town.

CXXI   Lors quant elle sera partie,
         De ses yeulx la convoÿra
         Jusqu'a ce qu'elle est eslongie,
         Et plus vëoir ne la pourra.   964
         Et puis encliner s'en venra
         Sur le lieu ou s'enclina celle,
         Car pour certain lui semblera
         Que le lieu vaille mieulx pour elle.   968

CXXII   S'elle a baisé pierre ou autel,
         Si fera il ains qu'il s'envoye.
         A tant s'en tourne vers l'ostel.
         Soit court, soit long, y prent sa voye   972
         Devant celle, affin que la voye
         En passant, son salut lui fait,
         Et ung doulx regard lui envoye.
         S'elle respont, il est reffait.   976

CXXIII   Disner s'en va, tout esjouÿ   [205r]
         De ce qu'il a ouÿe sa voix:
         Pieça de tel bien ne jouÿ.
         Par luy dist 'Joyeulx m'en vois.   980
         Rien qui me desplaise ne vois.'
         Et quant je le sçay en ce point,
         D'un peu d'espoir je le pourvoys;
         Et ainsi se remet apoint.   984

CXXIV   Par le plaisir de ce propos,
         Ne se puet tenir qu'il ne chante,
         En alant comme font ces folz.
         A chascun fait chiere plaisantc;   988
         D'estre loyal sa foy crëante,
         Et pour ce salut fait tel feste,
         Qu'il cuide estre amé et se vante.
         Car en ce propos peu s'arreste: 992

CXXI   As his lady is going out,
           he follows her with his eyes
           until she is far away
           and he can no longer see her.
           Then he goes to kneel
           on the very spot where she knelt,
           for he is certain that this place
           is now even more sacred because of her.

CXXII   If she kissed a stone or an altar
           he will do the same before he leaves.
           Then he heads back toward her house.
           Whether it be shorter or out of the way, he takes the same path she did,
           and manages to pass in front in order to see her.
           As he passes by, he waves a greeting
           and sends her a sweet look.
           If she responds, he takes heart.

CXXIII   He goes off to dinner in a happy daze
           for having heard her voice;
           he cannot remember when he has been so happy.
           He says to himself: 'Here I go in joy;
           I see nothing that can distress me.'
           And when I see him in this state,
           I allow him a bit of Hope
           and thereby he regains his strength.

CXXIV   Basking in the pleasure of her words,
           he cannot refrain from singing,
           acting like one of those fools you see.
           He smiles pleasantly at everyone,
           and swears he will always be faithful.
           He makes such a big deal out of her hello
           that he believes she loves him, and congratulates himself.
           But he will not be humming this tune for long.

CXXV   Car, en retournant, d'aventure
                Voit ung aultre, frisque et bruisant,
                Qui salüe la crëature,
                Qui tant est belle et si plaisant,   996
                Et elle luy, en soubzrïant,
                Pour quelque vielle affinité;
                Dont il en a deul et si grant
                Que cellui est en serveté.   1000

CXXVI   Lors se het et mauldit sa vie,   [205v]
                Et tance a Fortune et a moy,
                Et a honte de sa folye,
                Et me dist que je le decoy,   1004
                Quant je lui faiz porter sa foy
                A une qui aime chascun,
                Et qui rit a chacun qu'a soy,
                Et qui fait bel acueul commun.   1008

CXXVII   Ainsi s'en va vers le disner,
                De nouvel desplaisir tout plain,
                Et, pour contenance monstrer,
                S'assiet et va disner sans fain.   1012
                Quant il deust boire, il prent du pain,
                Et comme s'il n'eust point de bouche,
                Ses morceaulx detire a la main,
                Et puis sur son trenchoir les couche.   1016

CXXVIII   Et affin que son deul n'apere,
                Joue du coustel et du pié.
                Son trenchoir sa douleur compere,
                Car il est trestout detrenchié.   1020
                Et quant il est bien deshachié,
                Et ne scet plus parler ne taire,
                De gens se deppart sans congié
                Et s'en va en lieu solitaire.   1024

CXXV   For, upon his return, by chance
he sees another man, cheery and lively,
who greets this creature,
so beautiful and pleasing,
and she smiles back at him,
thereby displaying evidence of some earlier friendship;
and he is so miserable over it
that he feels completely enslaved.

CXXVI   Then he hates himself and curses his life,
blames Fortune and me as well,
and, ashamed of his folly,
he claims that I tricked him
when I had him commit his faith
to a woman who loves everyone; indeed,
she smiles at everyone except him,
and gives to everyone a warm and fair welcome.

CXXVII   Off he goes to dinner,
completely overcome by this new displeasure;
but to keep up appearances,
he sits down to eat, though without appetite.
When he should be drinking, he takes some bread;
and, as if he had no mouth,
his bites are torn with his hands
and then he leaves the morsels in his bread bowl.

CXXVIII   In order to cover up his wretchedness,
he plays with his knife or wiggles his foot.
But his bread bowl resembles him in his misery,
for it is completely torn to pieces.
Now that it is all shredded,
he can no longer speak or keep silent.
He abruptly leaves everyone without saying goodbye
and goes off to a place to be alone.

CXXIX   Quant il est tresbien esseullé,   [206r]
                 Et de chacun asséz loingtains,
                 Et est de lermes aveuglé,
                 Lors fait ses regréz et ses plains,   1028
                 S'escrye en hault, detort ses mains.
                 Mon nom renye, et puis invoque;
                 Puis crye mercy a haulx claims,
                 Et ce qu'il a mesdit revocque.   1032

CXXX   Et quant il s'est tant demené
                 Qu'il ne scet plus n'avant n'arriere,
                 Et qu'il a tant forment plouré
                 Qu'en feroit des lermes riviere,   1036
                 Lors reprant nouvelle maniere,
                 Et tout coy au panser s'arreste,
                 Sans soy mouvoir, ne qu'une pierre
                 Et sans memoire, comme beste.   1040

CXXXI   Lors ymagine fantasies,
                 Une heure ou deulx, sans soy mouvoir,
                 Puis sault hors de ces frenasies;
                 Et dit qu'il s'en veult aler veoir   1044
                 Sa dame, et lui faire savoir
                 Sa voulenté a ce cop cy,
                 Et en deust il mort recepvoir,
                 Si lui requerra il mercy.   1048

CXXXII   Lors pense comment il dira   [206v]
                 Quant venra jusqu'a l'aprouchier,
                 Et comment son propos sara
                 En ung bel langaige couchier.   1052
                 Le penser ne couste pas chier,
                 Mais la maistresse est en faisant:
                 Car lors qu'il devra commencer,
                 Ne saura quel bout va devant.   1056

CXXIX   When he is all alone and
far away from everyone else,
his eyes blinded by tears,
he exclaims his sorrows and moans his complaints.
He cries out loud and wrings his hands.
He denies my name and then invokes it,
calling out for mercy in lofty lamentations,
and then takes back all his calumnies.

CXXX   And when he has worked himself up to the point
that he can no longer tell up from down,
and he has sobbed so profoundly
that his tears could form a river,
suddenly he adopts a new posture:
falling silent, and lost in thought,
he doesn't move, but stays as still as stone.
Like a beast, he has lost all memory.

CXXXI   Fantasies invade his imagination,
and for an hour or two he is transfixed and doesn't move.
Then he jolts out of his delirium,
declaring that he wishes to go see
his lady to let her know
this time what he desires,
even if it kills him.
He intends to ask her for grace.

CXXXII   He reflects on how he will say it
when he finally is before her,
imagining how his speech
will be cloaked in eloquence.
But thinking is cheap,
and mastery comes from doing.
So as soon as it is time to speak,
he won't know where to start.

CXXXIII	Or lui semble qu'il est bien duiz,	
	Et s'en va recordant ses motz.	
	Ains qu'il s'apparçoive, est a l'uis.	
	Sa dame treuve, et aussi tos	1060
	Qu'il la voit, pert tout son propos.	
	Son cueur perd sens, son corps pert force.	
	Devant tressue, et tramble au dos,	
	Pour neant de parler s'esforce.	1064

CXXXIV	En ce point entre en la maison,	
	Sousprins de honte et de päour.	
	Son salut fait hors sa saison:	
	'Dieu doint bon vespre,' doint 'bon jour.'	1068
	Il est en joye et en doulour;	
	Il desire et est assouvi.	
	Il traveille en joyeulx sejour,	
	Et sans esloingner est ravi.	1072

CXXXV	En ce point s'assiet emprés elle,	[207r]
	Et n'y a qu'eulx deulx en la place.	
	Or deust reveller, et il celle.	
	Ilz sont seul a seul, face a face,	1076
	N'est nul qui destourbier leur face.	
	De pouvreté doit bien finer	
	Le pouvre, qui ne se pourchasse	
	Quant il voit cil qui puet donner.	1080

CXXXVI	Le pouvre triste, desireux	
	Voit la financhiere de joye,	
	Et le meschant est tant honteux	
	Qu'il meurt de deul en la montjoye	1084
	De tous les biens dont cuer s'esjoye.	
	Devant son mire veult mourir.	
	Et n'est pas bien digne qu'il joye	
	Quant n'est hardy de requerir.	1088

CXXXIII   But for now he thinks he's very clever
                   and heads out, reciting his speech.
                   Before he knows it, he is in front of the door.
                   He finds his lady in, and as soon as
                   he sees her, he loses his words.
                   His heart loses feeling, his body loses strength;
                   his face sweats and his back quivers.
                   In vain he tries to speak.

CXXXIV   He walks into her house
                   overcome by shame and fear.
                   His greeting is inappropriate:
                   instead of good evening, he says good day.
                   He is taken by joy and pain;
                   he desires and is overwhelmed.
                   He is working in joyful repose,
                   and, without moving an inch, is ravished away.

CXXXV   Now he sits next to her;
                   only the two of them are there.
                   It is time to reveal his feelings, and yet he hides them.
                   They are alone, face-to-face!
                   No one is around to disturb them.
                   But a poor man will only die
                   of his poverty if he does not chase after
                   the one who can give to him, when given the chance.

CXXXVI   This poor man, sad and desirous,
                   is looking at the treasurer of all joy,
                   but he, miserable, is so shy
                   that he is dying of grief
                   at the height of the heart's happiness.
                   In front of his doctor, he wishes only to die.
                   Yet he does not deserve to enjoy something
                   if he has not even the courage to ask!

CXXXVII   Ainsi se doulant se maintient
            Sans dire ung seul mot de son fait,
            Et puis je ne sçay qui survient
            De la maison, qui tout deffait.   1092
            Il a grant paine et riens n'a fait;
            Lors se repent qu'il n'a riens dit,
            Car partir le fault tout deffait,
            Dont il het son cueur et mauldit.   1096

CXXXVIII   Lors prent congié et se depart,   [207v]
            Plus triste que quant il y vint.
            Tant est doulant a son depart
            Qu'il mauldit des foiz plus de vint   1100
            La personne qui leur seurvint;
            Car, s'il ne feust, il eust tout dit
            Le mal qui oncques lui advint
            Depuis qu'a Amours se rendit.   1104

CXXXIX   Maintes foiz y va en ce point,
            Sans descouvrir ce qu'il endure:
            Une aultre foiz, s'il chiet a point,
            En sa pensee se murmure,   1108
            Et sa dame, par advanture,
            Qui n'a pas froit quant il a chault,
            Qui est pointe de tel pointure,
            Lui demande lors qu'il luy fault.   1112

CXL   Et lui dit en ceste maniere:
            'Vous me semblez tout desplaisant.
            Que ne faictes vous bonne chiere?
            Estes vous dont aussi doulant   1116
            Que vous en faictez le semblant?
            Pensez vous que voz desconfors
            Sont si grans qu'un vo bien veullant
            Ne vous en pourroit mettre hors?'   1120

CXXXVII

So this is the way the poor man behaves,
without whispering a single word of his pain.
And then someone, who knows who, comes in
from the house, and that ruins everything.
He has suffered much and accomplished nothing;
now he repents of having said nothing,
because he must leave now, wretched and undone.
For this he hates and curses his heart.

CXXXVIII

He says goodbye and leaves,
even sadder now than when he arrived.
He is so miserable at his departure
that he curses more than twenty times
the person who interrupted them,
for had that not happened, he would have told her
all about the suffering he has experienced
since he devoted himself to Love.

CXXXIX

Many times he returns to her house in this fashion,
without revealing what he is suffering.
And then once, it so happens that
he speaks his thoughts,
and his lady, by chance,
who is not insensitive to his feelings
since she has been pricked by the same sting,
asks him what is wrong.

CXL

She says to him in this manner:
'You seem to be very unhappy.
Why are you not in a good mood?
Are you indeed in as much pain
as you seem to be?
Do you think that your suffering
is so severe that someone who wishes you well
could not help you?'

CXLI	Aprés ce, gueres ne demeure	[208r]
	Qu'il ne die, puis hault puis bas,	
	'Entre deux vertes une meure.'	
	Comme il appartient en tel cas,	1124
	En matiere entre pas pour pas,	
	Et comme chascun le scet bien.	
	La maniere ne diray pas,	
	Car le dire ne sert de rien.	1128

CXLII	Mais posé qu'il die a son aise	
	Tout quant que dire lui vauldra	
	Et qu'aussi a sa dame plaise,	
	Pour ce conforté ne sera,	1132
	Car elle le reffusera:	
	Pour esprouver lui fait ce mal,	
	Car en la fin lui semblera	
	Que, s'il endure, il est loyal.	1136

CXLIII	Et cil qui prie doit savoir	
	Que tant plus est la chose chere,	
	Tant plus doit couster a l'avoir:	
	La value y met la renchere.	1140
	Et dame, qui est financiere	
	De tous les biens qui sont pourpris,	
	Ne vault elle qu'on la requiere	
	Et qu'on l'achate a plus hault pris?	1144

CXLIV	Tout est fait pour homme servir,[27]	[208v]
	Et homme est fait pour servir dame:	
	Il ne s'en puet desassouvir	
	Il est sien jusqu'au partir l'ame.	1148
	La dame est en la haulte game,	
	Car elle est maistresse du maistre:	
	Qui ne le croit doit estre infame,	
	Et ne doit plus en honneur estre.	1152

CXLI　　　　　At this, he no longer hesitates
　　　　　　　but says in a faltering voice:
　　　　　　　'Between the two green, there is one ripe.'[26]
　　　　　　　As is appropriate in such a situation,
　　　　　　　he broaches the subject one step at a time,
　　　　　　　and since everyone knows this story well,
　　　　　　　I won't talk about how it goes,
　　　　　　　for to tell it would be a waste of time.

CXLII　　　　　But let us assume that he tells her, at his leisure,
　　　　　　　everything that is worthy for him to say
　　　　　　　and that all of this pleases the lady.
　　　　　　　Nevertheless, he will not obtain comfort from her,
　　　　　　　for she will still resist him.
　　　　　　　She does this in order to test him,
　　　　　　　for it seems to her
　　　　　　　that if he shows endurance now, he will prove loyal.

CXLIII　　　　He who begs knows well
　　　　　　　that the more he pays for something,
　　　　　　　the more dear it is to him:
　　　　　　　its value becomes even greater.[28]
　　　　　　　And doesn't the lady, who is the treasurer and keeper of
　　　　　　　all the riches to be had,
　　　　　　　deserve to be sought after
　　　　　　　and purchased at the highest price?

CXLIV　　　　Everything on earth was made to serve man
　　　　　　　and man was made to serve woman.
　　　　　　　He cannot disengage himself from this service;
　　　　　　　he belongs to her until death.
　　　　　　　The lady is the highest authority,
　　　　　　　for she is mistress of the master.
　　　　　　　He who thinks otherwise should be disgraced
　　　　　　　and should no longer be called honorable.

CXLV   La dame est mieulx dame du tout
                Que l'omme qui en est seigneur:
                Combien que povoir d'omme est moult,
                Est povoir de dame grengneur,   1156
                Car l'omme laisse en sa faveur
                Tout ce qui lui est ordonné,
                Et donne tout povoir et cueur
                A dame de sa voulenté.   1160

CXLVI   Puisque si grant chose est de dame
                Que plus grant ne puet devenir,
                A paine sçay je, par mon ame,
                S'omme est digne d'y advenir.   1164
                S'il ne devoit ja advenir
                A plus grant chose qu'estre sien,
                Et deust il en ce point mourir,
                S'est il eureux sur toute rien.   1168

CXLVII   De grans seigneurs assez treuv on   [209r]
                De qui on vient bien a plaisance;
                Mais dames sont d'aultre façon,
                Car, avec toute leur puissance,   1172
                Vient d'elles la grant habondance
                De tous les biens dont on s'esjoye;
                Et n'est honneur, bien, n'acroissance
                Qui leur haulte bonté ne voye.   1176

CXLVIII   Les hommes sont faiz pour servir,
                Et elles, pour faire valloir.
                Et n'est nul qui peust desservir
                Leur mendre bien, a dire voir,   1180
                Et y meïst force et devoir
                Et deust il mourir en servant.
                Voulenté vault plus que povoir
                En leur grant grace desservant.   1184

CXLV   The lady is a better master over all things
than man, who is lord.
No matter how mighty is the power of man,
the power of woman is greater;
for man leaves in her control
everything that has been given to him,
and he gives willingly
to the lady all his power and all his heart.

CXLVI   Since being a lady is such a noble position
that no higher honor can be granted,
I wonder, upon my soul,
if man can even approach such a level.
But even if the best thing that can happen to him
is just to be in his lady's service
and he dies in this state,
he is still the happiest creature alive.

CXLVII   There are plenty of grand lords around
who can provide one with nice things,
but with ladies it is another story,
for they are all-powerful,
and from them comes in great abundance
every fine and delightful thing that one might enjoy.
There is no honor, good deed, or enrichment,
that their noble benevolence does not see.

CXLVIII   Men are made to serve ladies,
and ladies to make men worthy.
There is no man who could deserve
the least of their riches,
even if he put all of his strength and obligation to it,
and had to die from the effort of serving.
Desire is worth much more than force, indeed,
to deserve their noble grace.

CXLIX   Et puis que leurs biens sont si grans
               Qu'on n'en peut pas ung desservir,
               Des maintenant soiez souffrans
               Et sers tousjours sans desservir;   1188
               Le paiement vient en servir.
               J'ay pitié de ta povre chere;
               Pourtant, te veul desasservir,
               Et veul exaucer ta prïere.   1192

CL   Si te command que tu voyes   [209v]
               Incontinent vers le vergier,
               Et va si avant que tu voyez
               Celle dont vint le franc baisier.   1196
               Endormy trouveras Dangier."
               Tantost aprés ceste parolle,
               Ainsi com pour tout abregier,
               Amours se taist et puis s'en vole.   1200

CLI   Ainsi s'en va, et je m'esveille,
               Et me trouve sain et hetié:
               Riens ne senty que la merveille
               De ce qu'ainsi fuz alegié.   1204
               Je saulz sus et, a l'abregié,
               Vers le vergier prins mon chemin,
               Ou je trouvay Dangier couchié,
               Qui dormoit soubz un aubespin   1208

CLII   Ung pou avant trouvay la belle
               Qui me navra et puis gary.
               De mon estat bien deiz nouvelle,
               Comment Dangier m'en feist marry   1212
               Quant le franc baisier renchery
               Entierement lui deiz mon fait;
               D'Amours lui parlay et aussi
               Du miracle qu'il m'avoit fait;   1216

CXLIX   And because the riches of ladies are so great
               that no one can deserve a single one,
               from here on, be patient
               and serve continually without discrediting yourself.
               Recompense comes by doing service.
               I take pity on your poor flesh;
               therefore, I wish to release you from your servitude
               and honor your prayer.

CL   I command you to make your way
               to the garden without delay.
               Continue until you see
               her from whom you received the simple kiss.
               You will find Resistance asleep."
               Immediately after these words,
               as if to abridge the account,
               Love fell silent, and then flew away.

CLI   He went away, and I woke up,
               feeling happy and healthy.
               I knew nothing except the marvelous state
               of relief that I found myself in.
               I jumped out of bed and, to be brief,
               made my way to the garden,
               where I found Resistance asleep,
               lying under a hawthorn.

CLII   A little further ahead I found the Beautiful One
               who had wounded and then healed me.
               I told her all about my condition,
               and how Resistance had afflicted me
               when he made the price of the kiss impossibly high.
               I told her everything
               and spoke to her of Love and also
               of the miracle that he had granted me.

CLIII   Et comment il m'avoit promis   [210r]
            Alegence de ma douleur.
            Et a ce propos lui requis
            Que point ne le feïst menteur.   1220
            A donc müa elle coulleur,
            Et dist lors, pour me resjouÿr,
            Qu'au vouloir de si grant seigneur
            Ne vouloit pas desobeÿr.   1224

CLIV   "Mais je vous demande, dist elle,
            Quel est le don que vous voulez
            La chose pourra estre telle
            Qu'a vostre requeste l'aurez."   1228
            "Certes, diz je, vous le saurez.
            C'est seullement ung seul baisier
            Que vous mesmes me donnerez,
            Pour toute ma peine alegier."   1232

CLV   Ung poy pensa en soubz rïant;
            Et moy, qui estoit plain d'espoir,
            Lui pris ung baiser tout prïant,
            Moictié force, moictié vouloir[29]   1236
            Et puis pour me tout dedouloir.
            Es bras ouvers ung m'en donna,
            Doulx a sentir et a vëoir,
            Qui toute ma joye acheva.   1240

CLVI   Plus nous feusiesmes devisé,   [210v]
            S'omme ne feust la entour
            Male Bouche ce desguisé.
            Je prins congié jusqu'au retour,   1244
            Et puis alay faire mon tour
            Vers la chappelle gracieuse
            Ou je rendy grace a Amour
            De sa miracle merveilleuse.   1248

CLIII

I told her how he had promised me
relief for my suffering,
and with regard to these words, I requested
that she not make him into a liar.
Then she blushed
and said, in order to make me happy,
that the wishes of such a great lord
were not for her to disobey.

CLIV

"But I ask you," said she,
"what is the gift that you desire?
It may be that
you will have what you wish for."
"Certainly," I said to her, "I will tell you.
It is only a single kiss
that you give me yourself
in order to relieve my pain."

CLV

She thought for a moment, smiling,
and I, who was full of hope,
still pleading, took a kiss from her,
partly by force, partly by desire,
and then, in order to console me completely
with open arms she gave me another kiss,
sweet and lovely
which gave me complete joy.

CLVI

We would have talked for a long time
if someone had not been sneaking around.
It was deceitful Foul Mouth,
so I took my leave until we might meet again,
and made my way
to the gracious chapel,
where I gave thanks to Love
for his marvelous miracle.

CLVII   Et pour achever mon office,
             Et pour le mieulx regracïer,
             Lui feiz ung devost sacrefice
             D'une tyge en feu de lorier   1252
             Et puis m'en retournay arrier
             Vers les dames de l'ospital,
             Que toutes allay mercïer
             De l'alegence de mon mal.   1256

CLVIII   Mon medecin n'oublïay mie,
             Espoir, qui tant de moy soigna,
             Ne l'enfermeriere Courtoisie,
             Ne Souvenir, qui m'enseigna,   1260
             N'Entendement, qui m'alega.
             Puis tressailly soudainement;
             A cop bruit de gens m'esveilla,
             Et ne veiz que moy seullement.   1264

CLIX   Toutesfoiz fuz je conforté   [211r]
             Par l'advisïon dessus dicte,
             Si n'ay oncques puis arresté
             Tant que la merveille ay escripte   1268
             Selon ma scïence petite,
             Et mis en rime telle quelle,
             A fin que celle se delite,
             Qu'i n'a ou monde telle qu'elle.   1272

CLX   Si lui requier a jointes mains
             Que le songe veulle averir;
             Et je ne requier plus ne mains,
             Ne plus hault ne veul advenir.   1276
             Je n'ay ou monde aultre desir,
             C'est tout le plus hault de mon veul,
             C'est le plusgrant bien advenir,
             Et la fin de ce que je veul.   1280

Cy fine l'ospital d'amours

CLVII	To finish my adoration
	and to thank him all the more poignantly,
	I made a devoted sacrifice
	of a burning branch of laurel;
	then I retraced my steps
	and directed them toward the ladies at the hospital,
	all of whom I wished to thank
	for their treatment of my illness.
CLVIII	Of course, I did not forget my doctor,
	Hope, who took such good care of me,
	nor the nurse, Courtesy,
	nor Memory, who taught me well,
	nor Understanding, who made me feel better.
	But suddenly I started;
	the sound of people awakened me
	and I no longer saw anyone but myself.
CLIX	Nevertheless, I felt comforted
	by this dream I told above
	and I did not waste a moment until
	I had written down all of this miracle,
	as well as my wit might allow,
	and put it into rhyme,
	so that she might delight to read it—
	the lady who in this world has no equal.
CLX	I pray to her, then, with hands joined together,
	that she might make this dream come true.
	I ask neither more nor less than this,
	nor could I even wish to ask for anything more.
	I have no other desire in this world;
	this is my highest wish,
	the greatest good that I might attain,
	and the end of all my yearning.

Here ends the Hospital of Love [30,31]

Notes

1. Just as in the final stanza of the *Cruel Woman in Love*, our author Achilles Caulier begins each of the first six stanzas with the letters of his name to build an acrostic: A-C-I-L-E-S.

2. The narrator has put us here in the position of the lover at the end of the Belle dame, who has been refused by the lady and leaves her in search of death. In the next stanzas the author rewrites the narrative and corrects the outcome. All of the poems that imitate the *Belle dame sans mercy* rewrite in to some degree the plot of Chartier's poem and by this distinguish themselves from the Quarrel poems proper, for the characters of the original poem are not principal actors.

3. See also the *Cruel Woman in Love* line 222. These are the victims of unfaithful love. Phyllis, upon finding out that Demophon had betrayed her love, hanged herself in grief. This episode is reconted by Ovide in the *Heroides* book, and was frequently used to illustrate the consequences of faithlessness, most famously in the *Roman de la Rose* (trans Daulberg 228). Note especially this passage from the author of a poetry manual, *Règles de la Seconde Rhétorique* which explains the meanings attached to the names: "Demophons fu un prince qui moult ama Philis, et en la fin la delessa pour une autre; pour quoy Philis se pendi de duel que elle en ot quant elle le sot ... Par Demophon est entendu fainte amour, comme par Narcisus est entendu amour desdaigneuse. Par Philis est entendu amour desesperé[e], comme par Equo est entendu l'amour soudainement séparée." (Langlois, 66)

4. The story of Hero and Leander is also told in Ovid's *Heroides*, XVIII and XIX. The couple was often referred to in the Middle Ages to illustrate the power of love; see also the *Cruel Woman in Love* line 219.

5. Pyramus and Thisbe, lovers from Ovid's *Metamorphoses* book III were famed in the Middle Ages for their tragic love. A 12th century French lay (ed. Baumgartner) documents its transmission into the vernacular. Readers of English will certainly remember Shakespeare's faithful, if hilarious, retelling of the sad tale in *A Midsummer Night's Dream*.

6. 'Regart' has been translated Sweet Look (see line 975); this is the character the author would have named if he scansion of the line had allowed it. But mostly, rendering 'Regart' in English with Look or Glance does not convey the real service of this allegorical figure to help Pity.

7. Thessaly; Central Greece along the Aegean Sea.

8. The scribe of Pl makes a little joke at this point; 'Bien Celer' is so well concealed, living up to his name, that the reader cannot even see him (a blank space has been left). Construction and decoration of this manuscript support the theory that this omission was deliberate: the writing is carefully executed and the margins are crawling with exquisite and imaginative creatures.

9. "ymages": these might be paintings or statues; the French does not distinguish between the two.

10. This is the famous brand of Venus which lights the fire of love.

11. Stanza LIV: Pl offers a reading which praises the rhetoric of Jean de Meun instead of Alain Chartier:

Soubz le portal par dit commun
Gisoyt le corps du sage de mehun
Sur sa tombe escrit en lettre d'or
Estoit de rethorique le tresor
Qui en amours fist maint hault fait
Et par luy acheve et parfait
Fut de la Rose le Romans
Pour lire aux loyaulx amans

A la chappelle pres de l'autel
Amours fist faire ung chevalier tombel
De plus riche et fin cristal
Que n'est or ne autre metal
Pour celle qui renommee
De beaute porte par tout le monde
Encores vit et est nommee
Par Amours la plus du monde

Pres du bout et tout de nouvel
De velour noir couvert sans Fame
Mort vy le corps qui tant fut bel
De l'amant qui tant ayma sa dame
Que toutes ses voyes en elle fina
Par ung reffus dont l'a occy
Dieu luy pardoint qui la nomma
La belle dame sans mercy.

The scribe then returns to the lesson of the other manuscripts.

12. Jean de Werchin, Seneschal of Hainaut and lord of Cysoing at the end of the 14th century and the beginning of the 15th, was famed as an ideal knight-poet of outstanding prowess. Named as an example of valor in the *Livre des faits de Jacques de Lalaing*, Christine de Pizan, too, praised him in ballad 245 (ed. Roy) and listed him among true lovers in her *Débat des deux amants* as well as requesting his adjudication for the *Livre des trois jugements* and the *Dit de Poissy*. In 1404 he composed his *Songe de la Barge* in which he, betrayed by a disloyal lady, finds himself in the allegorical Joyous Land of the Amorous Forest where the God of Love was holding court. In another work he exchanged ballads with his squire, Gilbert de Lannoy, and advised his younger friend not to stay attached to a woman who proves too cruel. Jean de Werchin was a Counselor of the Cour Amoureuse of Charles VI before he was killed at the battle of Agincourt in 1415.

13. Stanza LV: Pp replaces stanza with these lines:

Empres ung epitaphe vy fait
Grave des yeulx enfle de larmes
Dessus ung coron d'or pourtrait

Du bon thomas veecy les armes
Sans croire sorceries ne charmes
Grace attende d'une haulte dame
Comme en amours vray homme d'armes
Et dit qu'elle est belle sans blasme.

14. The tomb of the dead lover of Chartier's *Belle dame*.

15. Achilles Caulier is referring to his *Cruel Woman in Love*. This passage, as well as
     the previous mention of the Belle dame and the headstone and praise of Chartier are
     clearly deliberate attempts to connect this poem with the Quarrel series.

16. Breseida or Creseida, a character whose perfidy in love is revealed when she aban-
     dons Troilus, who loves her hopelessly, for the Greek warrior Diomedes. This Hom-
     eric tale was made famous in the English tradition primarily by Chaucer's account,
     and then by Shakespeare's comedy. Curiously, Diomedes, her new lover, is men-
     tioned in the *Lady Loyal in Love* (verse 595) among the knights who are loyal in
     love.

17. A reference to the *Romance of the Rose* begun by Guillaume de Lorris in the 13th
     century and finished by Jean de Meung some 50 years later. The poem became the
     ultimate reference in the allegorization of love for writers until well into the seven-
     teenth century. The episode referred to here comes at the end of the poem of Guil-
     laume de Lorris: the narrator, in love with the rosebud imprisoned by Resistance in
     the castle of Jealousy, is waging war against the castle with the help of Venus. In the
     continuation of Jean de Meung, the lover finally reaches the rosebud and possesses
     her. The *Hospital* is replete with echoes of this predecessor.

18. Another reference to the sentence of the Belle dame handed down at the end of the
     Cruel Woman, lines 909-10.

19. This episode recalls the hole in the Pyramus and Thisbe story through which the lov-
     ers revealed their passion and set up their rendezvous, however, our young lover will
     only get an earful of cold air, a reminder that the narrator's story of the actions of the
     lover are based on imagination. See also the *Romance of the Rose*, trans. Dahlberg p.
     65-70.

20. Prestre Martin, see *Response of the Ladies*, note 10.

21. The *introit* is the opening act of worship in the mass, announced by a bell which
     calls worshipers to take their places for the service, just as the priest enters. As the
     people move about before the service begins, our lover is jockeying for a position
     close to his lady.

22. It is important for the lover to show his generosity, this being one of the command-
     ments of Love in order to become a deserving lover.

23. As the participants of the mass offered gifts to the priest, they kissed his hand (or
     finger, here) as a show of reverence to him and his overlord, Christ.

24. The kiss of peace is one of the elements of the celebration of the Eucharist, in prepa-
     ration for communion. However, around the 13th century the exchange of the kiss of
     peace among the congregation began to pose a problem in the service and so, start-
     ing probably in England around 1250, the presentation of an "instrument of peace"

was adopted. This object, often a crucifix, reliquary, or patent, and eventually a "plaque" with handle depicting some iconographic scene, was passed around from person to person to kiss. (Dict. Enc. 1135) The theme of the kiss of peace in literature emphasizes the erotic, and is a clear manifestation of the slippage between Godly love and corporal desire. Chartier, too, employs the motif in the *Debat des Deux Fortunés d' Amours*:

> Et au matin, a la messe sonner,
> L'Amant s'en va l'eglise environner
> Et l'eaue benoiste a sa dame donner,
> Et la paix prendre
> Tout volentiers pour lui porter et tendre,
> Car c'est le bien ou il veult lors entendre
> Qu'apres elle baisier sans plus attendre (ed. Laidlaw 402-408)

25. The referent of the direct object "la" is deliberately vague: is it "la paix" that he dares to kiss or "la maitresse"?

26. Proverbial expression meaning that there is a right time for everything.

27. Echo of longer passage in the *Accusations*, stanza 67.

28. The God of Love quotes himself from the *Romance of the Rose*; "No one has anything good unless he pays for it. Men love a possession when they have bought it at a higher price and the good things for which one has suffered are received with greater thanks, (trans. Dahlberg 67).

29. This line is also used in the *Belle dame* v. 62.

30. *Hospital of Love, Variants*: 1. et non pas trop Po; 5. loysir Pc; 6. d'onneur Pc; 7. en place de plaisir Po; 8. Et en lieu a PcPl, A lieu et a temps e. Po; 19-20. Il nest argent avoir ne or/Qui vaille la compaignie delles PdPo; 22. Gracieusetés PcPl; 24. La bouche noue de chantes Pp, de chanter Pc; 25. b. festie Pl; 26. vausisse Pc; 27. requirent Pc; 35. trays lors v. celluy PcPp; 36. A qui j'estoye tout PcPp; 37. getant sur elle mon regart Pp; 38. maintenant PcPlPp; 50. d. moy ung pou s. 1. PlPp, moy oyr s. 1. Pn, Que de mes plains elle s. 1. Po; 56. allegance PcPoPp; 63. la s. Pc; 69. u. frenaisie Po; 72. E. en e. en visïon PcPo; 76. M. il. PdQa; 78. me tenoye Po; 82. groiseliers Pp; 84. Et nenduray Pn; 93. L. place Pc; 116. Quant Pc; 122. Esroullees Pc; 127. de destresse p. Pn; 149. L. f. joye dueil y c. PdPo; 150. dy entrer Pn; 163. par hors de Po; 168. a grantlargesse Po; 172. recueul PcPlPo; 181. R. et L. M. Pl; 186-187. missing Pl; 188. maintentir Pc; 189. contenir Pc; 192. vray m. PnPo; 196. bon devoir PbPnPoPpQa, son devoir. Pc; 213. luy scored and replaced with huit Po; 220. reconfort Po; 222. et l'abandonne a Pc; 231. com je Pc; 238. Tout plain Pc; 240. d. lison Pc; 244. bien celer missing in Pl; 245. Gentement Pl; 253. P. deviser Pc; 258. c. i. le f. Pl; 270. espend Pb, espart Pc, sextend Pd, se part PpQa; 267. disme Pc; 280. a tous c. Po; 287. l'office la feste et la messe PcPo; 310. un g boire Pl; 311. Se nes guery [Pb: ne garis] a ma venue PdPb; 312. ma m. Pl; 319. Depuis oy quil le n. Pn; 344. C. amours Pn; 348. Cest larbre PcPl; 349. Il n'est de rien donner sy pres Pc; 372. il lacordast Pn; 373. promptement Pn; 375. y couru s. Pc; 378. que n. Pc; 380. trouvay PcPp; 381. secourra Pc; 382 de luy p. Pc, je luy p. PnPpQa 395. P. regarder Pn; 396. Les b. Pl; 404. recongnueuz Pc; 409. y vy Pl; 420. b. il fu contendans Pn; 423. m. de cinq cens t. Pp, cent tans Pc; 425-440. different stanza in Pl, see note; 429. P. luy Pc; 435.

Emprés 1. Pc; 437. Gesoit Pc; LVII missing in Pp; 465. pecheurs [c. Pl] gisoit Pc; 480. Quant e m. Pc; 481. feu Pc; 484. ardant Pc; 490. Dy aller je n. Pc; 493. s'y p. Pc; 493-96: Celluy qui gardoit tout lestage/La porte ne me volt ouvrir/Pour prieres ou beaul langage/Ne pour don n. m. v. o. Po; 495. passage Pl; 502. Et me retray Pc; 503. c. retrayt Pc; 505. Si en Pc; 510. vint Pc; 516. veul Pc; 520. long t. Pn; 525. que plus veüs n'avoye Pc; 526. L'un estoit nommé S. Pc, Avecques luy estoit s. Pl; 532-561 missing in Pl; 567. Ce sont ceulx veritablement Pp; 572. plus c. Pc; 574. D. q. desoremais s. t. PlPn, que dormant s. t. Pc; 580. v. veoye Pn; 589. vourra Pp; 601. m'ont par e. Pc; 607. mon s. s. PbPd; 621. amolly Pn; 623. cuer et corps m. PnPo; 627. En disant Amours t. c. Pc; 628. j. brulle Pd; 637. tres cuident Pp; 643. au no Pp; 645. Pour ce que trop fu desvoyé PcPp; 646. vengement Pc, sentement Pp; 675. j'ouys Pc; 678. mate c. Pd, moyse chiere Pl; 696. m'en Pc; 701. si f. Pc; 703. que ame Pc, Ne voy tu que riens t. c. Pp; 709. Gist en vostre m. Po; 718. Haa sire PcPp; 727. donna Pc; 728. f. foysonné Pc, frissonné Pp, est forcene PbPd; 738. se repentoit de bien Pc; 739. esprouvay PnPb; 741. m'ostoit Pc; 745. Maiz se ce PcPlPp; 746. ma mescongnoyssance PcPlPp; 754. me tire et rnartire Pl; 758. sera PnPb; 766. q. de moy Pn; 767. m. par quel que voyes Pc; 774. se l'ouyr me PcPl; 778. v. que au conmencement Pc; 779. de tel. v. Pl; 786. predestinay [ta f. PcPp] mal et f. Pl; 794. aroyes PcPp; 796. Ainsi ont eu trestous leurs joyes Pd, Ainsy ont tous euz leurs royes Pn, Aussy ont en toutes leurs Pc, o. trestous heurs leurs royes Pp; 797. Ceux que j'ay chaint de mes couroyes Pc, ceulx que j'ay fains de mes couroyes Pp; 798. D. mal p. Pn; CII follows CIII in PbPcPdPnPp; 809. v. acquerre Pn; 813. s. acquiert Pn; 819. vendroit PcPp; 823. en m. PnPdPb; 828. D. veillier Pn; 831. De faire veille a mainte f. Pc; 833. f. je penser Pc; CII missing in Pc; 860. lors qu'il r. Pc, j. nyra ne vendra Pn; 866. El ne soit PdPb; 867. p. a luy p. Pl, sur plus Pp; 869. Car il dist que a l'uys Pc; 872. n. cause Pn; 877. Sy rapasser Pc, Re yra passer Pp; 878. e. que a luys viendra Pd, e. a la traille PcPp; 888. r. ne se fiera Qa; 893. sera Pc; 903. t. s. gesir Pn; 904. recordera Pl; 906. e. se cuydera Pc; 910. sera PlPn; 930. E.il s'en va q. Pp; 931. i. se mect PdPo, i. sassiet Pn; 934. m. garnie Qa; 936. amoureuse h. [experience Pl] PcPp; 938. vecy PcPlPp; 940. n. le s. a . ly Pn; 943. Q. bien b. v. a. Pl; 948. en u. PbPnQa; 951. sil a fait b. Pl; 952. Et puys si l'abaise a. Pl; 954. Qu'il a de celler la s. PcPl, Que de bien celer. a s. Pp; 957. fait f. PdQa; Et t. est sceu Pl; 959. c. a l. Pp; 960. bruit Pb; 965. s. yra Pc; 970. sen voye Pn; 973. avant qu'il la v, qu'el le voye Pc; 982. j. lai fait Pb, j.le sens Pn; 1000. infinité PcPp, infinitivé Pl; 1007, fors q. PdPlPo; 1009. vers le dangier Pl; 1015. deschire Pc, derompt Pn; 1016. taillouer Pd; 1025. esloignié Pp; 1029. En requerant Dieu et ses sains Pp; 1030. le mocque PdPb; 1039. ne q. PbPdQa, nez q. Pn; 1051. fera Pl; 1054. la maistrise Pc; 1066. Surpris Pn; 1069. e. tristour Pn; 1075. r. a icelle PdPb; 1081. doloreux PdPb, diseteux PcPp; 1084. Qui voit de joye Pc, m. de fain Pn; 1086. vient m. Pn; 1101. la s. PcPl; 1117. en moustrés Pc; 1119. Soient PnPdQa; 1120. puist m. dehors Pc, peussent m. hors Pn; 1124-25. verses reversed Pc; 1127. matiere Pl; 1129. M. prenez PbPdPn-PoQa; 1140. d. qui n'est f. Pp; 1142. b. de mon p. PcPlPp; 1143. veult e. Pc; 1147. desasservir PcPlPp; 1164. de parvenir PcPlPp; 1167. finir Pp; 1170. ne p. PcPp; 1175. b. ne vaillance Pn; 1176. n'envoye PcPp; 1181. avoir Pc, savoir Pp; 1183. puet PlPp; 1208. soubz [les Pc] u. sappin PlPnPp; 1211. luy dis nouvelle PcPlPp; 1213. b. m'enchiery Pc, les francs baisiers r. Pp; 1230. franc b. PcPlPp; 1232. abregier QaPo; 1234. qui yere Pc; 1242. Somme Pf, Se ame Qa, Se nully Pd, Senvye PcPl; 1243. est si desguise PcPlPp; 1246. glorieuse, PcPlPp; 1248. m. gracieuse Pc; 1249-50. p. de son grant benefice/A mon pouoir r. Pn; 1252. [teurtre en f. d. 1.PcPp; un tresbel chappel de l'orier Pl, teurtre fust d. l. PnPd; 1260-61. Souvenir and Entendement are reversed Pn; 1269. savance p. Pn, memoire p. Pb, souvenance p. Qa; 1277. C. m. p. g. bien a venir Pc, C'est mon plus eureux advenir Pl, C'est mon plus eureulx souvenir Pp; 1278. C'est tout le plus hault d. Pp; 1279. Et mon plus eureux advenir Pn, mon sollas, mon souvenir Pc, C'est mon plus joyeux souvenir Pl

31. *Hospital of Love, Rejected Readings*: 22. Gracieuses -1 Pp; 50. Q. ung peu de moy s. Pb; 62. elles Pc; 110. etara s'amie Pc; 122. priamus; 142. zephions; 136. m. e e. (+1) 147. desplaisir (rhyme) Pc; 193. o. est c. Pc; 197. fisse -1 Pc; 204. avant missing minim Pc; 238. O. de tresamoureuses y. (+l) Pc; 333. ne f. ne f. Pc; 442. luserne PcPp ; 508. suis Pc; 521. Rubricator mistakenly paints P over a clearly visible q of the scribe, giving "Puant"; 417. 'Jehan' count 1 syllable; 614. devers (+1) PcPl; 678. mai se chere Pc; 689. visaige Pc; 695. En Pc; 697. advenir (-1) Pc; 806. que qui (+1) Pc; 861. 'des ce qu'il' count 2 syllables; 903. dormir PcPlPp; 911. respondera Pc; 938. veez cy, count two syllables; 970. sera PcPl; 1016. Et sur (-l) Pc; 1047. Et e. d. je m. r. Pn ; 1062. part PcPlPp; 1075. reveillier Pc; 1105. en p.(-l) Pc; 1116. E. bien (-l) Pc; 1236. missing line Pc

The Belle Dame Who Has Mercy

Attributed to

Oton de Grandson

L'amant parle   **[39v]**

I   Belle qui Bon Renom et Los
                     Sont saiges de tous appellés,
                     Vers vous viens pour dire abriefz moz
                     Ce que je ne puis plus celer.   4
                     Et se mon tresrude parler
                     N'est mie de doulz moz enté,
                     Prenez en gré, sans regarder
                     Fors qu'a la bonne voulenté.   8

II   Veullez moy ouÿr humblement,   [40r]
                     Et par vo courtoisie entendre;
                     Si m'alegerez grandement
                     Sans que vostre honneur en soit mender.   12
                     Car ainsi m'aist Dieu que mesprendre
                     Vers vous ne veul, ne ja n'aviengne
                     Que vers celle face a reprandre,
                     Dont il fault que tout bien me viengne.   16

III   Toutesfoiz, humblement vous prie,
                     Ains que saichiez comme il m'est prins
                     Quant ma requeste aurez oÿe;
                     Ne me tenez pour mal aprins   20
                     Se j'ay si hault fait entreprins.
                     Pardonnez moy, car par mon ame,
                     Ce fait Amours qui m'a esprins,
                     Dont vient de lui s'il y a blasme.   24

La dame

IV   Des grans loz que vous me donnez
                     Qui viennent de vostre bien,
                     Car largement me blasonnez,
                     Sans qu'il y ait que pou de bien.   28
                     Vous parlez doulcement et bien;
                     Mieulx que dire ne sçay ou puis,
                     Maiz telz motz n'affierent de rien
                     A si nyce comme je suis.   32

The Lover Speaks

I

Beauty, whose loveliness is wisely spoken of by all,
and especially by Good Reputation and Fame,
I come to you to speak some brief words
about feelings I can no longer hide.
And if my clumsy speech
is not cloaked with eloquent words,
still take them in faith, with no other consideration
than that of goodwill.

II

Please listen to me;
graciously and by your courtesy, hear me out.
Thus you will comfort me greatly,
without compromising your honor at all.
For, so help me God, doing any wrong
to you I do not wish, nor may
anything ever happen to reflect ill on the one
from whom all good must come to me.

III

And so I humbly beseech you:
listen and know what has happened to me,
and when you have heard my request,
do not take me to be poorly raised.
If I have set myself too high a goal,
forgive me, for by my soul,
it was Love who lit my fire,
so any blame should be placed on him.

The Lady

IV

The high praise that you give me
comes from your own worthiness,
since you sing my praises too highly,
though there is little good there to speak of.
You speak sweetly and well,
better than I could or would know how,
but such words mean nothing
to one as naive as I am.

V	Se vous m'avez a dire chose	[40v]
	Qui a bien et honneur me touche,	
	Comme aultrement je ne suppose,	
	Je l'orray de voulenté doulce,	36
	Car je vous tiens si sans reprouche	
	Et de si treshaulte noblesse	
	Que ja n'ytra de vostre bouche	
	Ung mot qui l'onneur d'aultrui blesse.	40

VI	Je ne congnoiz votre pensee	
	Ne vostre seullë enterprise.	
	Aussi suis je pou a pensee,	
	Sotte et d'entendre mal apprise.	44
	S'elle est en honneur bien comprise,	
	Elle n'est oultrageuze ne haulte,	
	Mais sans ce que je vous desprise,	
	Se poise moy s'il y a faulte.	48

L'amant

VII	De ce qu'i vous plaist m'escouter,	
	Vous mercy. Saichiez que mes jours	
	Veul user a vous redoubter,	
	Comme ma princesse en amours.	52
	Mais tous mes plaisirs seront cours	
	Se vostre beaulté qui contraint	
	Mon cuer a vous servir tous jours,	
	N'adoulcist mes maulx et reffraint.	56

VIII	Et sy vous playst moy retenir	[41r]
	Pour vostre humble et loyal servant,	
	Vers vous me verrez maintenir	
	En l'estat d'un loyal amant.	60
	Car en vostre honneur bien gardant,	
	Vivray joieulx, cointe, et secret;	
	Et de bien servir feray tant	
	Que vous n'y aurez nul regret.	64

V   If you have something to say
    that affects my virtue and honor,
    (and I can't imagine otherwise)
    I will hear you quite willingly.
    For I hold you above all reproach
    and of such high nobleness
    that never could there slip from your lips
    a single word that might hurt anyone's honor.

VI I do not know your thoughts
    nor what your enterprise is.
    But I am weak of mind,
    silly, and slow to understand.
    If your undertaking is honorable and well intended,
    neither reckless nor proud,
    and involves nothing for which I would think badly of you,
    well, it pains me that it be in vain.

The Lover

VII That it pleases you even to listen to me,
     I thank you, and know that all my days
     I wish to use to honor you
     as my princess in love.
     But all my pleasures will be short-lived
     if your beauty, which binds
     my heart to serve you forever,
     does not soothe and quell my suffering.

VIII And if it pleases you to retain me
      as your humble and loyal servant,
      you will see me keep myself
      in the state of a loyal lover,
      safeguarding your honor
      and living joyously, graciously, and discreetly.
      And to serve you well, I will make sure
      that you never have a single regret.

IX
    Helas, mon douloureux cuer sent
    Mieulx que la bouche ne scet dire,
    Des douleurs dont j'ay plus de cent,
    De quoy je ne congnoiz la pire;   68
    Si ne me vueilliez escondire.
    Que vostre honneur ne me pourvoie.
    Faitez moy ou pleurer ou rire,
    Je suis vostre quelque je soye.   72

La dame

X
    A moy requerir de ce point,
    Vous perdriez langaige et paine;
    Si ne vous en traveilliez point.
    Fol est qui pour si pou se peine!   76
    S'amours vous tient en son demaine,
    Oncques par moy ne vous advint
    C'est une plaisance mondaine
    Qui s'en ira dont elle vint.   80

XI
    Se vous avez d'amer desir   [41v]
    Pour vivre en joyeuse plaisance,
    Autre amye povez choisir
    Qui plus que moy vous en avance.   84
    Or, en ostez vostre fiance
    Et pensez d'ailleurs requerir,
    Car je vueil sans vostre acointance
    A par moy mon honneur chairir.[1]   88

XII
    Se vostre cuer a aporter
    Des maulz assez plus qu'onquesmez
    A vous est de le conforter
    Puis qu'autre que vous n'en peut més   92
    Si ne croy pas quant en vous traiz
    Tant de douleurs comme vous ditez
    Quoy que vous en plangniez jaméz
    Car je croy que bien sont petites   96

IX
Alas, my stricken heart feels
better than my mouth can voice
the pains, of which I have more than one hundred,
and of which I know not yet the worst;
so please do not rebuff me.
May your honor not fail me.
Make me cry or make me laugh,
I am yours, whatever else I may be.

The Lady

X
Continuing to plead with me on this subject
would be a waste of words and effort,
so please, belabor the point no longer.
Foolish is he who pains himself for so little!
Even if Love holds you in his domain,
never through me will you obtain what you seek:
it is a worldly pleasure
that will disappear as fast as it came.

XI
If you have the desire to love,
so to live in joyful pleasure,
surely you can find another lover
who is willing to grant you more than I.
Do release yourself of this pledge
and consider seeking love elsewhere,
for I prefer to eschew your friendship
and, instead of love, to cherish honor.

XII
If your heart has brought to you
more than your share of pain and suffering,
it is up to you to give it relief,
for no one can comfort you but you yourself.
I do not believe that you suffer from
as many pains as you claim;
even though you complain about it constantly,
I think your pains are really minor.

L'amant

XIII   Belle de beaulté bien eureuze
                 Des autres belles l'examplaire
                 Vostre simple chere joyeuse
                 A fait mon cuer a soy retraire   100
                 Quar je vous ayme sans retraire
                 Et l'ay celé par plusieurs moys
                 Se j'en meurs puis qu'il fault faire
                 Mourir me fault il une foiz.   104

XIV   Onques Amours si ne me prist   [42r]
                 Pour autre dame ou damoiselle
                 Mais a mon gré pas ne mesprist
                 Quant yla me fist choisir telle   108
                 Ne me parlez d'amour nouvelle
                 Il est de moy tout ordonné
                 Car a vous comme a la plus belle
                 Est mon cuer tout entier donné.   112

XV   Helaz dame ad ce que je voy,
                 Vous ne congnoissez qu'Amours monte.
                 Et Dieu scet se je l'apparçoy.
                 Maintesfoiz que je n'en tiens compte,   116
                 J'ay de souspirer si grant honte,
                 Quant je m'entroublie en mains lieux.
                 Qui m'est pis que je ne vous compte;
                 Mais quant vous plaira, j'aray mieux.   120

La dame

XVI   Se mon maintien avez veü
                 Que vous louez oultre mesure,
                 Et voz yeulz vous ont deceü
                 Par mal aviser ma figure,   124
                 Le mal que vostre cuer endure
                 Ne fait pas la vie abregier
                 Mais plus maladie vit et dure
                 On ne meurt pas si de legier.[2]   128

The Lover

XIII
    Beautiful One, blessed with such loveliness,
    of all others the supreme model,
    your joyful and innocent countenance
    has called my heart to you,
    for I love you without reserve
    and have hidden it for several months now.
    So if I die from this distress, well then,
    I must die sometime.

XIV
    Love did not capture me
    me thus for another lady or damsel,
    and to my mind made no mistake at all
    when he made me choose such a one as you.
    Do not speak of a new love:
    for me it is already decided,
    since to you, Most Beautiful One,
    my entire heart is given completely.

XV
    Alas! Lady, from what I can see
    you do not recognize that Love grows.
    God knows if I can even understand it.
    So many times that I cannot keep count,
    I have wept and felt enormous shame,
    losing control of myself in places public and private.
    And what is worse, I mean nothing to you.
    But when it pleases you, I will be healed.

The Lady

XVI
    If you have really gazed upon my countenance,
    which you praise beyond all measure,
    and your eyes have deceived you by
    gauging incorrectly my expression,
    well, the pain that your heart endures
    will not shorten your life one bit.
    Graver sickness is survived and endured
    than this; one does not die of such a trifle.

XVII	Vous direz ce qui vous plaira	[42v]
	Et voulentiers l'escouteray,	
	Mais ja nulz homs mon cuer n'ara	
	Ne par amours je n'ameray,	132
	Fors ung a qui je garderay	
	Ma foy comme espoux et amy.³	
	Ja se Dieu plaist vouloir n'avray	
	De departir mon cuer parmi.	136

XVIII	Mais je me donne grant merveille	
	Que je vous voy tant enquerir	
	Car une dame a vous pareille	
	En tous biens deussiez acquerir.	140
	Vous ne l'avez mie a querir,	
	Car chascun peut assez sçavoir	
	Que qui scet si biau requerir	
	N'est pas sans belle amie avoir.⁴	144

L'amant

XIX	Jenne, gente, source et riviere,⁵	
	D'Onneur et de Joyeuse Chiere,	
	Qui font en vous Beaulté fleurir;	
	Vous estez ma dame premiere	148
	Car m'amour avez toute entiere	
	En ce point veul vivre et mourir	
	Et se ne voulez secourir	
	Mon cuer dont je vous ay fait don	152
	Or en faitez a vostre bon	[43r]
	Car je suis vostre, franc et quicte.	
	J'exploiteray, vueilliez ou non,	
	Car vous n'avez pas le renom	156
	D'estre orgueilleuse ne despite	

XVII
You will say whatever makes you happy,
and I will listen to you willingly,
but never will any man have my heart;
never will I love anyone willingly
except him to whom I keep
my troth and faith as husband and lover.
With God as my witness, never will I have the desire
to divide my heart in two.

XVIII
Indeed, I am surprised and amazed
to see you inquiring and begging so,
for a woman deserving of your worth
in every way should have your attention.
You do not even need to entreat her,
for everyone can see clearly enough
that one who can woo so appealingly
does not go without a beautiful lover.

The Lover

XIX
Young and gracious, the very spring and river
of Honor strong and Joyful Countenance,
who make Beauty bloom and grow within you;
you are my lady love, first and foremost,
for you have all my affection and love.
In this state I wish to live and to die,
even if you do not wish to soothe the heart
I gave to you as a precious gift.
So do with my heart what you would desire,
for I am yours, freely and entirely.
Zealous will I be, whether you wish it
or not, for you do not have the reputation
of being proud or disdainful

XX	En Espoir, qui m'en soit de mieulx.	
	Vous serviray jeunë et vieulx	
	Et m'en tiens pour bien honnouré.	160
	Et se je vous suis ennuyeulx,	
	C'est signe de cuer pou joyeulx:	
	Triste, doulent, et exploié,	
	Et largement enamouré,	164
	Mais s'il est ainsi qui vous plaise	
	Moy commander que je me taise	
	De vous requerir reconfort.	
	A tout le moins ne vous desplaise	168
	Se j'aimë en souffrant mesaize.	
	En ce ne vous faiz je nul tort.	
XXI	Je congnoiz bien et voy a l'ueil	
	Que les maulz que d'amer requeil	172
	Sans mort n'auront point de duree	
	Neant moins j'aime vivre en dueil	
	Encore plus que je ne sueil	
	Qu'autre dame avoir procuré.	176
	Et eussiez vous ma mort juree.	
	Ce qui vous plaist m'est agreable	[43v]
	Et ne me verrez variable	
	Pour assault que douleur me livre.	180
	Se vous ne m'estez aimable,	
	Combien que mort m'est prouffitable,	
	Si veulx je en vostre mercy vivre	

XX　　　　　　toward Hope, which is all the better for me.
　　　　　　　　I will serve you forever, young and old,
　　　　　　　　and will consider myself well honored.
　　　　　　　　And if I am despondent before you,
　　　　　　　　that is the sign of a heart full of woe:
　　　　　　　　sad, grieving, anxious,
　　　　　　　　and swelling with love.
　　　　　　　　But if it pleases you more
　　　　　　　　to command me to be quiet
　　　　　　　　and to stop asking you for solace,
　　　　　　　　at least do not be displeased
　　　　　　　　that I love and suffer such discomfort.
　　　　　　　　In this, never will I do you any harm.

XXI　　　　　　I know well and can see for myself
　　　　　　　　that the heartaches that loving requires
　　　　　　　　will not continue beyond death.
　　　　　　　　Nevertheless, I prefer to live in grief
　　　　　　　　even longer than is my due
　　　　　　　　rather than take another lady.
　　　　　　　　And so you have sworn my death.
　　　　　　　　Whatever pleases you is agreeable to me,
　　　　　　　　and never will you see me change my mind
　　　　　　　　for any attack that grief might launch against me.
　　　　　　　　If you are not receptive to me,
　　　　　　　　no matter how much Death might benefit me,
　　　　　　　　still I wish to live in your mercy.

La dame

XXII	Quant dame en honneur se maintient	184
	Et respont ce qu'il appartient,	
	Et qui la requiert de folie,	
	Fol est qui despite la tient.	
	Pour tant se femme se contient,	188
	Sans que beau parler l'amolie,	
	Si n'ayez ja melencolie.	
	Se je suis trop rude ou sauvage,	
	Car asséz aprés de langaige,	192
	Je vous dy bien ung mot pour tous;	
	Quique m'en tiengne folë ou saige,	
	Que je n'avray ja le courage,[6]	
	De me faire blasmer pour vous.	196

XXIII	Se vous voulez vous m'aimerés,	
	Et se non vous le laisserez.	
	Je ne vous y puis pas contraindre.	
	Mais quant d'amer me parlerez,	200
	Ja par moy hay n'en serez.	
	Cela ne devez vous ja craindre.	[44r]
	Un amant peut prier et plaindre,	
	Et puis qui veult si s'i consente.	204
	Bien sçay que pas ne vous contente,	
	Et que le reffus si vous greve	
	Ce poise moy, j'en suis doulente	
	Maiz se j'eusse d'amer entente	208
	Je feisse responce plus breve.	

The Lady

XXII When a lady conducts herself honorably
and always responds in proper fashion,
then he who requests something foolish
is a fool himself if he gets angry at her.
For these reasons, a woman conducts herself
so that pretty words shall not stain her.
So do not be melancholy,
if I am too ignorant or coarse;
But after so much talking,
I will conclude in a final word:
no matter who thinks me crazy or wise,
I will never have the heart
to be reproached or criticized on account of you.

XXIII If you wish to, you will love me,
and if not, you will leave it be.
I cannot keep you from either.
And if you continue to speak to me of love,
you will never be hated by me for it.
This you never need fear.
A lover can cry and complain,
and whoever wishes can consent.
Well I know that my reply does not satisfy you
and that refusal hurts you.
This weighs heavily on me; I am sad about it,
but truly, if I were intent on loving,
I would give you an answer more brief.

XXIV	Vous n'avez garde que je face	
	Chose qui vostre mort pourchasse,	
	Ne par quoy vostre cuer se dueille,	212
	Car oncques nul jour, que je sache,	
	Ne me feistes en nulle place	
	Chose pourquoy de riens me dueille.	
	C'est raison que beau vous aqueulle;	216
	Car vous m'avez maint honneur faite.	
	Et se vous avez paine traite,	
	Amours qui scet bien qu'a ce fault	
	Vous doint dame en tous biens parfaite,	220
	Telle que je la vous souhaite	
	Et que vostre doulceur le vault.	

L'amant

XXV	Se ma requeste me cases,	
	Je tiens mes bons jours pour passéz;	224
	Car nul plaisir ne me demeure.	
	N'ay je pas eu des maulx asséz	
	Je suis amoitié trespasses!	[44v]
	Il est temps qu'Amours me sequeure.	228
	Je ne fus pas né de bonne heure	
	Se d'Amours n'ay aucun solaz	
	Car oncques ne me trouve laz	
	De vous amer en loyaulté,	232
	Puisqu'ainsi prins suis en voz las[7]	
	Se j'ay dit maintesfoiz, helaz!	
	Ce n'est pas trop pour tel biaulté.	

XXIV

You need not be worried that I would do
anything that would bring about your death,
or even anything that would give your heart grief,
for never on any day, to my knowledge,
have you ever, in any place, done
anything that would hurt me.
That is why I have received you so well;
you have done me much honor.
And if you have suffered pain for it,
Love, who knows well what is necessary,
will give you a lady who is perfect in every way,
all that I might wish for you,
and what your sweetness deserves.

The Lover

XXV

If you refuse my request,
I will consider all my good days past
for no pleasure would remain for me.
Have I not suffered enough pain?
I am half dead!
It is time that Love came to help me.
I was not born at an unlucky hour
if from Love I receive no help.
Never will I tire
of loving you loyally,
for I am captured in your snare,
as I have told you so many times, alas!
Even so, it is not too much for such beauty.

XXVI

Sy vous requier a jointes mains,   236
Belle et bonne, qu'a tout le moins
De tous poins ne me deboutiez,
Et se les maulx dont je me plains
Sont de vous assez petit plains,   240
Aumoins que vous les escoutiez.
Il peut que de moy vous doubtiez
Qui suis votre, comment qui soit.
Et qui suis cellui qui feroit   244
Tout ce que commanderiez.
Et se desplaisir vous venoit
Qui autant doulant en seroit,
Ou plus que vous ne seriez.   248

XXVII

S'ainsi estoit qu'il advenist
Que vostre cuer tant devenist
Amoureux, que le mien fust oncques,
Et que par force convenist   252
Que autant de doulour soustenist,   [45r]
Comme moy ou aultre quelconques,
Seriez vous bien contente doncques?
Que amant feïst de vous reffus,   256
Que'en feriez vous au seurplus?
Vous n'y sariez nul conseil.
Et pour ce vous dy et concluz,
Qu'en ce point ne me teniez plus,   260
Combien que ce n'est pas pareil.

XXVI
So I beg you with joined hands
O Beautiful and Good One, at least
do not spurn me categorically!
And if the pains I bemoan
are to you just silly little complaints,
at least listen to them for me:
it might be that you doubt me,
I who am yours no matter what!
And I am he who would do
everything that you command.
And if you were displeased by this,
I would be distressed as much
or more than you might ever be.

XXVII
If it ever were to happen
that your heart might become
as loving as mine has ever been,
and by force it became necessary
that your heart sustain as much pain
as I have or another in like way,
then would you be satisfied?
If a lover were to refuse you,
what more would you be able to do?
On this subject you would find no advice.
And so I conclude and beg you
that on this point, you hold me no longer,
inasmuch as the situations are not the same.

La dame

XXVIII   Se vraye estoit vostre complainte,
                  Enduré avez douleur mainte,
                  Car vostre cueur forment se deult.   264
                  Mais on n'aime point par contrainte,
                  Autrement l'amour seroit fainte,
                  Nul n'aime qui amer ne vault.
                  Laisse chascun ce qu'i ne peust.   268
                  Il me plaist, se le voulsissiez,
                  Que de ce plus ne parlissiez,
                  Et que la chose en ce point fine.
                  Lors aultre dame choisissiez,   272
                  Dont mieulx que de moy vaulsissiez,
                  Car d'amer ne suis je pas digne.

XXIX   Il me desplaist bien qu'il conviengne
                  Qu'en parler longuement vous tienne   276
                  Mais c'est par vous, vous le scavez,
                  Car oncquesmaiz qui me souviengne   [45v]
                  Non vy nul qui son propos tiengne
                  Ainsi comme tenu l'avez.   280
                  Je ne scay se vous recevez
                  Tant que vous ditez de griefz maulx
                  Plusieurs ont des pensers nouveaulx
                  De jour en jour dont y font mal   284
                  Maiz se vrais sont voz diz tresbiaux,
                  Vous estez decevant ou faulx
                  Ou tresparfaitement loyal

The Lady

XXVIII
        If your complaint is true,
        then you have endured many pains
        for your heart laments exceedingly.
        But one loves not by force.
        If it did, love would be just deception.
        No one loves who does not wish to love;
        let him try who thinks differently.
        I would prefer, if you do not mind,
        that you no longer speak of this
        and that the subject be put to rest.
        Now choose another lady
        who, more than I, will merit your affections;
        for I am not worthy of loving.

XXIX
        It greatly displeases me that it be necessary
        for you to speak at such great length.
        But it is your doing, and you know this well,
        for never until now, to my memory,
        have I ever seen anyone who can keep up
        this kind of talk as you have.
        I do not know if you really experience
        the kind of grievous pains of which you speak.
        So many are quick to have a change of heart
        from one day to the next, which brings only harm.
        Nay, if your sweet talk is true,
        you are either deceptive and deceitful
        or else quite perfectly loyal.

XXX

> Me voulez vous mettre en danger   288
> De ces faulz parlans lozengier
> Dont riens fors mal n'est retrait?
> Ilz parlent assez voulentiez,
> Et dient souvent plus du tiers   292
> Qu'onques ne fust pensé ne fait
> Si ne veul riens faire de fait
> Qui soit a mon honneur nuysant
> Il vous en seroit desplaisant,   296
> Se vous estez de mes amis.
> Gens sont sans cause medisans
> Et qui les feroit voir disans
> Lors encore seroit du pis.   300

L'amant

XXXI

> Se mon service en gré prenez,
> Pour serviteur me retenez,
> Par grace et par grant amitié.   [46r]
> Et s'autrement l'entreprenez,   304
> Vostre honneur sauf vous mesprenez,
> En tant qu'estez si sans pitié.
> Se je suis pour vous mal traittié
> Et Mercy ne me reconforte   308
> Je prendray drap de noire sorte
> En ce moys que joye habonde
> En signe que ma joye est morte,
> Et comme cellui qui se porte   312
> Pour le plus maleureux du monde.

XXX   Do you really want to put me in danger
of the gossip of those liars,
which brings about nothing but harm?
They speak all too willingly,
and tell more than three times
of all that was ever even thought, much less done.
So I don't want to do anything, in truth,
that might compromise my honor.
It might be displeasing to you,
even if you are one of my friends.
People tell lies for no reason at all
and he who would make them speak the truth
would only come off looking worse for it.

The Lover

XXXI   If you accept my service willingly,
then keep me as your servant,
out of grace and dear friendship.
But if you decide to do otherwise
your honor will surely be harmed
insofar as you are portrayed as without pity.
If I am mistreated by you
and mercy does not comfort me,
I will put on a sullied black cloak
to wear during this month when joy abounds
as a sign that my joy is dead,
and act like one who is taken for
the most unhappy man in the world.

XXXII   Et se estre puis de vous acointe[8]
             Sans ce qu'autre m'en desapointe,
             Je puis bien dire sans mentir,   316
             Que j'aime la tresbelle et cointe
             Et tant que la mort nous depointe
             Vous ne m'en verrez repentir
             Et pour ce vueilliez consentir   320
             Que noz deux cuers soient en ung
             Qui sera a nous deux commun
             Sans que jamaiz nul autre y parte
             L'ung aime l'autre et l'autre l'un   324
             Et face son devoir chascun
             Jusques ad ce que Mort nous departe.

XXXIII   Si vous suppli et de rechief,
             Ditez moy a ung seul mot brief
             De ce dont je vous ay requis.   328
             Croissés ma peine et mon meschief   [46v]
             Ou que je viengne tout a chief
             Des biens que j'ay vers vous tant quis.
             Oncques autre dame ne quis,   332
             Estre ne me peut reprouvé.
             Vous eussiez bien amy trouvé
             Trop plus gracieulx et plus bel,
             Mais quant vous m'aurez esprouvé   336
             Il sera bien par vous prouvé
             Qu'en loyaulté n'en est nul tel.

XXXII

But if I can know you better
without anyone dismissing me,
I can say without lying
that I love the most beautiful and comely lady,
and until death doth prick us out,
you will never see me repent of my love.
So for this, please consent to my plea,
that our two hearts might be one:
one heart for us both to share
which no one can ever part.
One loves the other and the other loves the one,
and each is true to his duty
until the day when Death do us part.

XXXIII

And so I beg you once more,
give me in a single brief word
a response to what I have requested.
Cancel my pain and my distress
so that I might achieve
in you the good I have sought after.
Never will I seek another lady
nor can I be reproached.
You might have found a lover
more gracious and more handsome
but when you have tested me
you will find
that in loyalty, there is no one equal to me.

La dame

XXXIV   Mon cueur tressault, tramble et tressue.
               Je suis pres que toute esperdue,   340
               Ne je ne voy nulle deffence
               Car je me sens d'Amours ferue.
               Vostre beau parler m'a vaincue,
               Qui plus me plaist quant plus y pense.   344
               Dieu doint que ce soit sans offence
               Et que la chose en bien se passé.
               Je suis de vous reffuser lasse;
               Mon cuer se rent et se rendra.   348
               Jamés a nul jour ne cuidasse
               Que pour rien par amours amasse.
               Je ne sçay comme y m'en prendra

XXXV   Si vous plaist amer par amours,   352
               Et que pour pire ne meillieur,
               Vous ne me veulliez ja changier,   [47r]
               Je laisseray toute rigour
               Et vous ottroieray m'amour,   356
               Sans jamais en faire dangier,
               Si ne vous veul pas estrangier.
               Et combien que j'aye estrivé,
               De grace ne serez privé,   360
               Doncques dame doit estre large.
               Mais soiez secret et privé,
               Si sera tout blasme eschevé.
               Se sont les poins dont je vous charge.   364

The Lady

XXXIV

My heart pitter-pats, pulsates, and pounds;
I am almost completely overwhelmed,
and I have no more defenses,
for I feel myself struck by Love.
Your sweet talking has won me over,
which pleases me more the more I think on it.
God grant that this be above reproach
and that everything will work out well.
I am too tired to refuse you any longer;
my heart is paying its dues and now surrenders to you.
Never in a million years would I have thought
that for any reason would I fall in love!
I know not how I was captured thus.

XXXV

And if it pleases you to be in love
and for better or for worse
you will never want to betray me,
I will leave aside all hardness of heart
and grant you my love
without ever putting up any resistance
since I do not wish for you to be away from me.
And although I have resisted up to now,
you will never be deprived of my grace
for ladies ever should be generous.
But be discreet and keep our secret
so that we might avoid any blame,
these are the points with which I charge you.

XXXVI   Puis que nous sommes aliez
                 Ainsi que m'en avez priez,
                 Si feray je vous de bon cuer
                 Qu'en ma loyaulté vous fiez;   368
                 Et que pour riens ne m'oubliez
                 Je ne vouldroie a nul feur!
                 Mais ainsi comme frere et seur
                 Tout ung mesmes vouloir ayons,   372
                 Ne ja pour riens que nous oyons,
                 La nostre amour ne se dessamble;
                 Mais souvent nous entrevoions
                 Affin que plus joyeux soions,   376
                 Ainsi aurons bon temps ensamble.

L'amant

XXXVII   Je vous mercye humblement
                 Comme tout plain de reconfort,   [47v]
                 Car j'estoie bien pres de mort,   380
                 Se je n'eusse eu alegement.
                 Nous vivrons tres joyeusement
                 Sans faire l'un a l'autre tort,
                 Et tant que j'avray sentement,   384
                 Ne veul ailleurs faire deport;
                 Vous estez ma vie et le port
                 Dont vient tout mon esbatement.

Explicit le livre de la belle dame a mercy[9,10]

XXXVI	Since we are now together
	just as you begged of me,
	I will ensure with all my heart
	that you can trust in my loyalty,
	and that nothing can make you forget me:
	that I would not want on any account!
	But just like brother and sister,
	we shall have one single will,
	and never, for anything that we might hear,
	should we separate one from the other;
	instead we should see each other often
	so that we might be joyful,
	and thus we will have a good time together.

The Lover

XXXVII	I thank you most humbly
	as one now filled with comfort,
	for I was very near to death,
	if I had not received succor.
	We will live in joy
	without doing wrong to each other,
	and as long as I have my wits,
	I will not want to seek the favor of any other.
	You are my life and the harbor
	where all my pleasures are secured.

The end of the book of the Belle dame sans mercy

Notes

1. These words are similar to those spoken by the Belle dame 489-92.

2. The lady refers to the sickness of love in a manner quite similar to the Belle dame, lines 265-68.

3. Is this spouse dead (making one think of Christine de Pizan and the widow's vow to remain true to her husband even in death) or is he still alive?

4. Po: "Et ho," leaving a blank half page, recommences on the verso of the folio. This break makes a clear demarcation between the eight-line stanzas and the following thirteen-line stanzas.

5. The stanza form and rhyme scheme change at this point from the eight-line octosyllabic stanza to a thirteen-line stanza with the rhyme scheme of *aabaabbccdccd*. The manuscripts handle this abrupt shift in form in various ways. The scribe of *PjPf*, our base manuscripts, does not immediately recognize the shift and thus copies first an eight-line stanza followed on the next folio by another eight-line stanza, then a nine-line stanza, then eight lines, verso side a six-line stanza, then finally gets the thirteen line stanza; his exemplar must have left no stanza separations, as does Pl, whose copy does not mark stanzas at all, even though in earlier items stanzas were marked with spaces. Po, on the other hand, clearly marks the shift with "Et Ho" and treats the decasyllabic stanzas as if they are a new poem.

6. Another line that is similar to words spoken by the Belle dame, lines 701-704, words used to convict her in the trial poems.

7. Caught in a woman's snare is not an uncommon image to evoke being in love; the Belle dame's lover uses the same metaphor in line 260.

8. There is a *double entendre* here with 'acointer' which incorporates a sexual reference.

9. *Rejected readings:*. Apprés s'enssuit la dame a mercy title given by Pd; 21. Se j'ay trop hault entreprins -1 Pe; 22, Pardonnez moy car mon ame -1 Pf; 24. si sil Pf; 32. A ainsi n. +1 PbPcPe; 52. ma maistresse PbPlPoQx; 62. Vivre PbPePo; 78. advient PbPcPf; 93. Que vous aiez si ne croy pas PbPcPePlPp; 96. Mais bien croy PbPcPd-PePlPoPp; 109. ne belle PbPcPePlPoPp; 115. s. j. le l'apparcoy Pf; 161. faiz tout le mieulx PbPo; 225. me demande PbPcPdPlPoPp; 322. line missing PcPe; 346. de reffuser (-1) PbPcPe;

10. Variant readings. 1. B. que b. PcPdPo; 2. Fait s. de vous a. Pb, Font s. de tous a. PcPePp, Fait s. de tous a. PdPlQxPo; 8. Si non ma b. v. Pb; Stanza II-III placed after IV Qx; 10. E. de v. grace mentendre Pd; 11. Et v. Pb, Vous m. PcPp; 16. mon b. Pp 17. T. chierement v. PbPdPo; comment mespris Pb; 19. m. complainte Pe, aves o, Po; 22. Vueillez PbPdPlPo, Mais me p. Pe; 23. dont suis e. Pb; 24. Tout v. PdPfPlPo; 25. Sire du 1. PcPp; 26. Sire v. PbPdPlPo, Vous mercy c'est d. PcPp, Que v. Pe; 28. du mien PbPcPe; 30. qu'entendre PbPcPePlPoPp; 31. ne servent Pp; 34. b. ou a h. t. Po ; 35. c. je le croy et s. Pp; 40. Chose q. Pb; 42. v. celee PbPcPoPp, v. sense e. Pf; 44. Docte et de tender a. Pb, Et de l'e. PcPp; 46. Qui, Pb, II Pc, Et PePo; 47. Sans qu'aucunement v. Po; 49. Puis quil vous p. moy e. PcPp; 50. Vostre m. Pb, Saches [que Pp] je veul user m. Pc, 51. A vous amer server doubter PcPp; 52. Combien que

j'aye des doullours PcPp; 53. Tant que PcPp, m. plains s. bien c. Pe; 54. En vo loyaulte Pb, Se v. [leaulte Pc] qui [me Pc] vous c. Pp, 55. v. amer t. PlPePoQx, A vous requerir par amours PcPp; 55. Ne les adoulcist e. PcPp; 58. et petit s. PbPcPePo; 59. A tousious vous voudray servir Pc; 60. Comme doibt faire ung vray amant PcPp; 62. V. preux PbPe, Seray j. PcPp, V. piteux Pl, V. en paix Po; 63. b. amer seray Pb; 66. peust d. Pc; 70. v. grace PbPcPePoPp, n'y p. PePl; 72. ou que PbPdPePo; in Qx Stanza X placed after VII; 72. P. et 1. et. p. PbPcPdPe; 78. p. soubdain PcPdPlPoPp. 80. sen va PbPl; 81. damours d. Pc; 83. p. querir PbPc, A. dame povez ailleurs c. Pp; 85. Ostes de moy v. Pc; 86. regarder PbPdPlPoPp, E. veuilles a. regarder Pc; 88. h. garder PbPcPdPePlPoPp; Stanza XII: Qx begins to rearrange stanzas to alternate speakers; 90. quil not o. Pc; 91. de len c. PbPe; 92. Quant a. PbPcPePlPoPp; 93. Je ne c. p. que v. ayes PdPo; 95. Or ne v. PbPcPe; 100. Fait a [vous Pc] m. c. si actraire PdPo; 101. Que PbPc, Car Pf; 102. p. foys Po; 103. p. a faire faire PbPcPo, sen faire PdPe; 105. O. maiz a. [ne mesprist Pc] PoPp, 106. P. d. ne pour demoiselle Pe; 110. tant o. Pf; 112. Ay m. PbPc; 113. H. belle PbPe, Certes belle PcPp, Ha madame Po; 117. Jay souvent de s. h. Pc; 118. je me tienne Pb; 119. Il PbPcPePlPoPp; 120. v. vouldrez Pd; 124. adviser PbPcPoPp; 125. Si naves vous pas telle ardure PcPp; 126. Que vous en perdes le mangier PcPp; 127. Ayant p. Pc, Maint Pp; 128. Que Pb; Stanza XVII and XVIII reversed PcPp; 131. M. croiez ja mon cueur navrez Pb, M. ja n. honts m. c. Pd, 135. p. je le trouveray PcPp; 136. Tel cornrne [au tel que Pc] si fera il my Pp; 138. Quant j. Pb; 139. C. mainte aultre vostre pareille PcPp; 140. Deussiez en beaulte requenr Pb, En beaulte poves acquerir Pc, Vous ne lavez mie aquerir Pl, En beaulte deussiez requerir PdPo, En beaulte deussies vous choisir Pe; 142. Car il est legier a savoir PcPp; 143. Que homs Pc; 144. b. dame PbPp; 145. Mer de doulchour source de r. PcPl, Ma doulceur s. Pp, G. demourant sur r. Po; 149. Qui m. PbPoPe, Vous etes m. Pc, missing line Pp; 151. las vous ne v. Po; 153. f. v. baudon Po; 154. Comme du v. Pc; Jay espoir v. Pb, Jespereray v. PcPdPlPoPp; 155. Quev. Pb; Stanza XX-XXI missing in Po; 158. Je v. Pb; 161. j. faiz trop lennuyeulx PcPp, lenvyeux Pl; 163. Qui de douleur est esplouré Pp; 167. Du mal qu me charge si fort Pb, v. demander Pc, sans v. r. c. PdPl; 170. De vous requerir reconfort Pb; 174. jay plus chier v. PbPl; 175. Trop plus dassez que je ne sueil PcPp, veuil Pl, missing Pb; 183. missing PbPc; 186. A qui PcPlPoPp; 187. qui en desdaigne Po; 188. se elle s. PbPcPdPoPp; 191. Que je soye dure ne s. Pb, Que je vous soye t. PcPp, s. du tout s. PlPo; 193. mort p. Pp; 197. vous a. PcPd; 202. le refusser PbPo, vostre doulleur PcPp, aggreve Pl; 208. se javoie Po; 209. f. parole Qx, Qx ends; Stanza XXIV-XXV reversed PdPoPl; 211. Nulle nen qui m. vous p. Pc; 215. C. p. je vous desveuflle Pb, Nulle chose que [bien Pc] je ne vueille Pp; 216. bien vous vueille PbPlPo; 217. Pour lonneur que vous mavez f. PcPp ; 220. d. en honneur Pb, d. en amours Pc, d. joye en tout bien Pd, d. joye en amour Pp; 221. Qui soit tout a vostre s. Pb, Ainsi comme Pc; 222. Et que vostre gent corps se vault Pp; 226-27. lines reversed Pc, jai endure Pd; 231. fus 1. PcPl, missing line Po; 232, Ne ne [baisay Pp] brisay ma 1. Pc, 234. Sen la fin men fault dire hellas PcPp; 235. Jen en blasme que vostre beaulte PcPp, bien pou p. Po; 241-2448 lines rearranged Pb; 245. missing Pc; 247. Mon cueur tresdoulent PcPp, tant courrouce e. s. Pb; 248. Autant comme v. s. PcPp; Belle comme vous seriez PdPl, Belle dame que Po; 254. Seray vous content adoncques Pb, Il vous desplairoit moult adonques PcPp, Stanza XXVIII lines rearranged Pd; 261. Mais me faittes en cas pareil PcPp; 262. Je voy

bien par v. Pp; 265. o. doit amer sans contrainte Pp; 272. Et quaultre dame advisis-
siez PbPl; 273. line missing PbPc, qui feist ce que demandissiez Pp; 276-278
missing Pl; 279. Ne vy nul qui si ferme t. PcPp; 280. Son propos c. PcPp; 281.
retenez Pl; 282. Pour moy ou pour autre voz maulx PcPp; 283. Et [se Pc] vous avez
desires n. Pp; 284. De jour en jour ce seroit mal PcPp, dont ilz ont m. Pl, d. il font m.
PbPo; 285. M. veu vos ditz plaisans et beaulx Pp; 286. Ou v. e. [joyeulx Pp] maulves
et faulx Pc; Stanza XXX missing Pp; 289. mensongers Po; 291. Il pleut a. Po; 296.
Vous en seriez PbPc; 299. vray d. Po; 302. Et vostre amy me r. Pc, Je vous pry que
me r. Pp; 303. Vous serez dame de pitie Pb, Vous me feres grant amitie Pc, vostre
serviteur par amitie Pp; 305. Je vous dy que v. m. PbPl, Il me semble que m. Pc, je
diray que v. m. Po, 306. Et [qu Pc]estres [Comme une Pp] dame sans pitie
PcPdPlPo; 310. mayPcPdPl, Et diray que de j. h. Po; 312. se deporte PoPl; 314. Et se
je devieng vostre a. PcPp; 315. Et vostre doulce amour s'appointe Pb; 319. departir
Pb; 325. missing PbPc; 328. Des biens que j. PdPlPo; 329. Vivray toujours en
meschief PcPp; 330. Et me banisses de rechief Po, Ou se je vendrayja a chief Pp;
331. De vostre amour que tant j'ay q. Po; 338. Quon n'en trouveroit nul au tel Pp;
346. se parface Pc; 348. c. plus ne se combatra Pc; 348-349 reversed Pb; 349. J. en
nul temps n. Po; 352. garder mon honneur PcPp; 354-5 reversed PlPo; 355. Je veul
oster Pc; 356. tout mon cueur Pb; 357. Sans en faire plus de d. PcPp; 360. Vous ne
vous verrez ja privé Pp; 361. Dont d. ne d.e. l. PbPc, Des biens dont chascun n'est
pas large Pp; 363. Et de blasme tout delivré Pp ; 367. Je vous [supply Pc] require Pp;
369. que jamaiz n. PbPcPoPp; 370. Car je vous ay donné mon cueur Po; 375.
entretenons Pl, missing line Po; 377. in margin: Et ho Po, manuscripts except PjPf
end at this line. Pl offers a different final stanza from line 373: Pl offers a different
final stanza from line 373: "Afin que plus joyeux soyon/Et souvent nous entretenon/
Ainsi amours bon temps ensemble/Puis que veoir ne vous puis belle/Par devers vous
mon cuer s'en va/Qui de par moy vous comptera/De mon estat pouvre nouvelle/Or
vueillez done ma demoiselle/Moy mander ce qu'il vous plaira/Car vous estes la
seule celle/Pourquoy mon cuer joyeux sera/Ne pour autre ne vous changera/En con-
fortant vostre querelle."

This poem, coming immediately after the Excusation, without only a tiny and very
faint marginal explicit (Cy fine l'excusation envers Amours par l'acteur), seems to
directly comment on the tranformation to be seen in both of Chartier's characters:
Chartier's lover's "pouvre estat" is refreshed, and the lady by her consent to love will
find comfort for "vostre querelle." This may be interpreted as closure to the "quarrel," and explain why none of the sequel poems are included in the manuscript,
although, like Pf, it contains the *Hospital of Love*.

Bibliography

I. Principal Editions of the *Belle dame sans mercy* (in Chronological Order)

Les fais maistre alain Chartier notaire et secretaire du Roy Charles VIe, Paris: Pierre Le Caron, 1489.

La belle dame sans mercy, [Lyon: Mathieu Huss, 1490].

Les oeuvres de Maistre Alain Chartier, clerc, notaire et secrétaire des Roys Charles VI & VII, ed. André Du Chesne, Paris: Samuel Thiboust, 1617.

Pagès, A., "La belle dame sans merci d'Alain Chartier: Texte français et traduction catalane," *Romania*, 62 (1936): 481–531.

Alain Chartier, *La belle dame sans mercy et les poésies lyriques*, ed. A. Piaget, Paris: Droz, 1945; Textes littéraires français, Lille: Girard, 1949.

"The Major Poems of Alain Chartier: A Critical Edition," ed. J. E. White, Jr., diss., University of North Carolina, 1962.

The Poetical Works of Alain Chartier, ed. J. C. Laidlaw, Cambridge: Cambridge University Press, 1974.

Alain Chartier, *Poèmes*, ed. J. Laidlaw, Bibliothèque médiévale, Paris: Union générale d'éditions, 1988.

Le cycle de la Belle dame sans mercy, ed. and trans. D. Hult and J. E. McRae, Paris: Champion, 2003: 116–67.

II. Editions of Other Works of Alain Chartier

Alain Chartier, *Le livre de l'espérance*, ed. François Rouy, Bibliothèque du XVe siècle, LI, Paris: Champion, 1989.

Alain Chartier, *Le quadrilogue invectif,* ed. E. Droz, 2nd ed., Les Classiques français du moyen
    age, 32, Paris: Champion, 1950 [1st ed., 1923].
Alain Chartier, *Le quadrilogue invectif,* trans. Florence Bouchet, Paris: Honoré Champion, 2002.
Bourgain-Hemeryck, P., ed., *Les oeuvres latines d'Alain Chartier,* Paris: Editions du CNRS, 1977.
Rice, W. H., "Deux poèmes sur la chevalerie: *Le bréviaire des nobles* d'Alain Chartier et *Le psau-
    tier des vilains* de Michaut Taillevent," *Romania,* 75 (1954): 54–97.

III. Editions of Poems in the *Belle dame sans mercy* Cycle

The Accusations Against the Belle dame sans mercy (The Parlement of Love)

Le jardin de plaisance et fleur de rhethoricque, Paris: Antoine Vérard, 1501: cxxxix r–cxlii v.
Les oeuvres de Maistre Alain Chartier, clerc, notaire et secrétaire des Roys Charles VI & VII, ed.
    André Du Chesne, Paris: Samuel Thiboust, 1617: 695–710.
McRae, J. E., ed., "The Trials of Alain Chartier's *Belle dame sans mercy:* The Poems in Cyclical
    and Manuscript Context," diss., University of Virginia, 1997: 102–52.
Hult, D., and J. E. McRae, ed. and trans., Le Cycle de la Belle dame sans mercy, Paris: Cham-
    pion, 2003: 116–67.

The Lady Loyal in Love

Piaget, A., "La Belle dame sans merci et ses imitations," *Romania,* 30 (1901): 323–51.
McRae, J. E., ed., "The Trials of Alain Chartier's Belle Dame Sans Mercy: The Poems in Cycli-
    cal and Manuscript Context," diss., University of Virginia, 1997: 153–221.
Hult, D., and J. E. McRae, ed. and trans., *Le cycle de la Belle dame sans mercy,* Paris: Champion,
    2003: 169–243.

The Cruel Woman in Love

Le Jardin de plaisance et fleur de rhethoricque, Paris: Antoine Vérard, 1501: cxlii v–cxlvii r
Piaget, A. "La Bellle dame sans merci et ses imitations," *Romania,* 31 (1902): 322–49.
McRae, J. E., ed., "The Trials of Alain Chartier's *Belle dame sans mercy:* The Poems in Cyclical
    and Manuscript Context," diss., University of Virginia, 1997: 222–95.
Hult, D., and J. E. McRae, ed. and trans., *Le cycle de la Belle dame sans mercy,* Paris: Champion,
    2003: 244–325.

The Errors of the Judgment of the Belle dame sans mercy

Piaget, A. "*La belle dame sans merci* et ses imitations," *Romania,* 33 (1904): 179–99.
McRae, J. E., ed., "The Trials of Alain Chartier's *Belle dame sans mercy:* The Poems in Cyclical
    and Manuscript Context," diss., University of Virginia, 1997: 326–73.
Hult, D., and J. E. McRae, ed., *Le cycle de la Belle dame sans mercy,* Paris: Champion, 2003:
    501–23 (abridged).

The Hospital of Love

L'ospital d'amours, [Lyon, Gaspard Othuin, 1485].
Les fais maistre alain Chartier notaire et secretaire du Roy Charles VIe, Paris: Pierre Le Caron, 1489,
    fol. G.i. v–H.ii. v.
Les oeuvres de Maistre Alain Chartier, clerc, notaire et secrétaire des Roys Charles VI & VII, ed.
    André Du Chesne, Paris: Samuel Thiboust, 1617: 722–54.

Hult, D., and J. E. McRae, ed. and trans., *Le cycle de la Belle dame sans mercy*, Paris: Champion, 2003: 327–437.

The Belle Dame Who Has Mercy

Les fais maistre alain Chartier notaire et secretaire du Roy Charles VIe, Paris: Pierre Le Caron, 1489: fol. C. iii [as well as subsequent early editions of Chartier's work].
Les oeuvres de Maistre Alain Chartier, clerc, notaire et secrétaire des Roys Charles VI & VII, ed. André Du Chesne, Paris: Samuel Thiboust, 1617: 684–94.

IV. Other Editions

L'amant rendu cordelier à l'observance d'amours, poème attribué à Martial d'Auvergne, ed. A. de Montaiglon, Société des anciens textes français, Paris: Firmin-Didot, 1881.
André le Chapelain, *Traité de l'amour courtois*, trans. C. Buridant, Bibliothèque française et romane, Paris: Klincksiek, 1974.
Christine de Pizan, *Oeuvres poètiques de Christine de Pisan*, ed. M. Roy, 3 vols., Société des anciens textes français, Paris: Firmin-Didot, 1886–96.
Christine de Pizan, *Le débat sur le Roman de la rose*, ed E. Hicks, Bibliothèque du XVe siècle, 43, Paris: H. Champion, 1977.
Christine de Pizan, *The Love Debate Poems of Christine de Pizan*, ed. B. K. Altmann, Gainesville: University Press of Florida, 1998.
François Villon, *Le testament Villon*, ed. J. Rychner and A. Henry, Textes littéraires français, Geneva: Droz, 1974.
Guillame de Lorris and Jean de Meun, *Le roman de la rose*, ed. F. Lecoy, 3 vols., Les Classiques français du moyen age, Paris: H. Champion, 1965–70.
Guillame de Lorris and Jean de Meun. *The Romance of the Rose*, trans. C. Dahlberg, Hanover: University Press of New England, reprint 2nd ed., 1986.
Guillame de Machaut, *Le livre de voir dit*, ed. and trans. Paul Imps, rev. Jacqueline Cerquinglini-Toulet, Lettres gothiques, Paris: Librairie générale française, 1999.
Jean de Garancières, "Jean de Garancières," ed. A. Piaget, *Romania*, 22 (1983): 422–81.
Jean Régnier, *Les fortunes et adversitez*, ed. E. Droz, Société des anciens textes français, Paris: Librairie Edouard Champion, 1923.
Jean le Seneschal (with the collaboration of Philippe d'Artois, Comte d'Eu, of Boucicuat le Jeune, and of Jean de Crésecque), *Les cent ballades: poème du XIVe siècle*, ed. Gaston Raynaud, Société des anciens textes français, Paris, Frimin-Didot, 1905.
Jean de Werchin, "Ballades de Guillebert de Lannoy et de Jean de Werchin," ed. Arthur Piaget, *Romania*, 39 (1910): 324–68.
Jean de Werchin, "*Le songe de la barge* de Jean de Werchin, Sénéchal de Hainaut," ed. A. Piaget, *Romania*, 38 (1909): 71–110.
Marot, Clément, *Oeuvres complètes de Marot: revues sur les meilleures éditions, avec une notice et un glossaire par B. Saint-Marc*, 4 vols., Paris: P. Jannet, 1873–76.
Martial d'Auvergne (attrib.), *L'amant rendu cordelier à l'observance d'amours*, ed. A. de Montaiglon, Société des anciens textes français, Paris: Firmin-Didot, 1881.
Martial d'Auvergne (attrib.), *Les arrêts d'amour*, ed. J. Rychner, Société des anciens textes français, Paris: Picard, 1951.
Martin le Franc, *Le champion des dames*, ed. R. Deschaux, 5 vols., Les Classiques français du moyen age, vols. 127–31, Paris: Champion, 1999.
Martin le Franc, "Un poème inédit de Martin le Franc," ed. G. Paris, *Romania*, 16 (1887): 383–473.
Le mesnagier de Paris, ed. G. E. Brereton and J. M. Ferrier, trans. K. Ueltschi, Lettres gothiques, Paris: Librairie générale française, 1994.

Michault Taillevent, *Un poète bourguignon du XVe siècle: Michault Taillevent (édition et étude)*, ed. R. Deschaux, Geneva: Droz, 1975.

Le miroir aux dames: Poème inédit du XVe siècle, ed. A. Piaget, Recueil de Travaux publiés par la Faculté des Letters de l'Académie de Neuchâtel, fasc. 2, Neuchâtel: Attinger Frères, 1908.

Oton de Grandson, "Oton de Granson et ses poèsies," ed. A. Piaget, *Romania*, 19 (1890): 237–59, 403–48.

Oton de Grandson, *Oton de Grandson: sa vie et ses poésies*, ed. A. Piaget, Mémoires et Documents publiés par la Société d'Histoire de la Suisse Romande, 3e série, vol. 1, Lausanne: Librairie Payot, 1941.

Pierre de Hauteville, *La complainte de l'amant trespassé de deuil. L'Inventaire des biens demourez dudecés de l'amant trespassé de deuil de Pierre de Hauteville*, ed. R. M. Bidler, Le Moyen français, 18, Montréal: CERES, 1986.

Pierre Michault, *Ouevres poètiques*, ed. B. Folkart, Bibliothèque médiévale, Paris: 10/18, 1980.

Pierre de Nesson, *Pierre de Nesson et ses oeuvres*, ed. A. Piaget and E. Droz, Documents artistiques du XVe siècle, 2, Paris: [impr. par G. Jeanbin], 1925.

Pyrame et Thisbé, Narcisse, Philomena, ed. E. Baumgartner, Paris: Gallimard, 2000.

Recueil d'arts de seconde rhétorique, ed. E. Langlois, Paris: Imprimerie Nationale, 1902.

René d'Anjou, *Le livre du cuer d'amours espris* [The Book of the Love-Smitten Heart], ed. and trans. S. V. Gibbs and K. Karczewska, New York: Routledge, 2001.

René d'Anjou, *Le livre du cuer d'amours espris*, ed. Susan Whaton, Bibliothèque médiévale, Paris: Union générale d'éditions, 1980.

Le roman de Troy, ed. G. Bianciotto, 2 vols., Rouen: Publications de l'Université de Rouen, 75, 1994.

V. Studies on Alain Chartier and *La belle dame sans mercy*

Angelo, Gretchen, "A Most Uncourtly Lady: The Testimony of the Belle dame sans mercy," *Exemplaria*, 15:1 (2003): 133–57.

Armstrong, Adrian, "'The Deferred Verdict: A Topos in Late-Medieval Poetic Debates," *French Studies Bulletin: A Quarterly Supplement*, 64 (1977): 12–14.

Badel, P.-Y., "'Les yeux sont faits pour regarder': sur la fortune d'un vers d'Alain Chartier," in *"Ce est li fruis selonc la letre": mélanges offerts à Charles Méla*, ed. O. Collet, Y. Foehr-Janssens, and S. Messerli, Paris: Champion, 2002: 99–109.

Badel, P.-Y., "Les suites de la *Belle dame sans merci*," in *La litterature française aux XIVe et XVe siècles*, dir. D. Poirion, ed. A. Biermann, D. Tillmann-Bartylla, Grundriss der romanischen Literaturen des Mittelalters, vol. 8/1, Heidelberg: Carl Winter, 1988: 157–58.

Brami, J., "Un lyrisme du veuvage: étude sur le je poètique dans *La belle dame sans mercy*," *Fifteenth Century Studies* 15 (1989): 53–66.

Cayley, E., "Collaborative Communities: The Manuscript Context of Alain Chartier's *Belle dame sans mercy*," *Medium Aevum*, 71:2 (2002): 226–40.

Champion, P., *Histoire poétique du quinzieme siecle*, 2 vols., Paris: Champion, 1923.

Giannasi, R., "Chartier's Deceptive Narrator: *La belle dame sans mercy* as Delusion," *Romania* 114 (1996): 362–84.

Hoffman, E. J., *Alain Chartier: His Work and Reputation*, New York: Wittes Press, 1942.

Hult, D. F., "The Allegoresis of Everyday Life," *Yale French Studies*, 95, "Reading Allegory: Essays in Memory of Daniel Poirion," ed. Sahar Amer and Noah D. Guynn (1999): 212–33.

Johnson, L. W., *Poets as Players: Theme and Variation in Late Medieval Poetry*, Stanford: Stanford University Press, 1990.

Kibler, W. W., "The Narrator as Key to Alain Chartier's *La belle dame sans mercy*," *The French Review*, 52:5 (1979): 714–23.

Laidlaw, J. C., "The Manuscripts of Alain Chartier," *Modern Language Review,* 61 (1966): 188–98.

Laidlaw, J. C, "André Du Chesne's Edition of Alain Chartier," *Modern Language Review,* 63 (1968): 569–74.

Lamarque, H., "Autour d'Anne de Graville: le débat de la 'Dame sans sy' et l'épitaphe de la poétesse," in *Mélanges sur la littérature de la Renaissance à la mémoire de V.-L. Sulnier,* Geneva: Droz, 1984: 603–11.

Kelly, Douglas, *Medieval Imagination,* Madison: University of Wisconsin Press, 1978.

McRae, J. E., "The Trials of Alain Chartier's *Belle dame sans mercy*: The Poems in Their Cyclical and Manuscript Context," diss., University of Virginia, 1997.

Piaget, A., "Notice sur le manuscrit 1727 du fonds français de la Bibliothèque nationale," *Romania,* 23 (1894): 192–208.

Poirion, D., "Lectures de la *Belle dame sans mercy*," in *Mélanges de langue et de littérature médiévales offerts à Pierre Le Gentil,* Paris: SEDES,1973: 691–705.

Sansone, G. E., "La belle dame sans merci et le langage courtois," *Le Moyen Français,* 39–41 (1997): 513–26.

Shapley, C. S., *Studies in French Poetry of the Fifteenth Century,* Le Haye: Nijhoff, 1970.

Solterer, H., *The Master and Minerva: Disputing Women in French Medieval Culture,* Berkeley: University of California Press, 1995.

Walravens, C. J. H., *Alain Chartier: études biographiques, suivies de pièces justificatives, d'une description des éditions et d'une édition des ouvrages inédits,* Amsterdam: Meulenhoff-Didier, 1971.

VI. Other Studies

Aubert, Félix, *Histoire du Parlement de Paris de l'origine à François 1er,* 2 vols., Geneva: Mérariotis Reprints, 1894.

Badel, P.-Y., *Le roman de la rose au XIVe siècle: étude de la réception de l'oeuvre,* Geneva: Droz, 1980.

Bennett, H. S., "The Author and His Public in the 14th and 15th Centuries," *Essays and Studies by Members of the English Association* 23 (1938): 7–24.

Bidler, R. M., "De Pierre de Hauteville à Villon," *Le Moyen Français,* 8–9 (1981): 26–36.

Bouchet, F., "Alain Chartier et les paradoxes de la Guerre: *Le quadrilogue invectif*," in *Images dela Guerre de Cent Ans,* ed. D. Couty, J. Maurice, and M. Guéret-Laferté, Paris: Presses universitaires de France, 2002.

Bouchet, Jehan, *Les annalles d'Acquitaine,* Paris: Jehan Mace, 1537.

Bozzolo, C., and H. Loyau, *La cour amoureuse dite de Charles VI,* vol. 1: *Étude et édition critique des sources manuscrites,* Paris: Le Léopard d'Or, 1982.

Cerquiglini-Toulet, J., *La couleur de la mélancolie: la fréquentation des livres au VIVe siècle (1300–1415),* Brèves littérature, 1152–1279, Paris: Hatier, 1993.

Champion, Pierre, *La librairie de Charles d'Orléans,* Bibliothèque du XVe siècle, 11, Paris: Champion, 1910.

Champion, Pierre, *Histoire poètique du quinzième siècle,* vol. 1, Éditions Honoré Champion, Paris: Champion, 1923.

Champion, Pierre, "Un *Liber amicorum* du XVe siècle," *Revue des bibliothèques,* 20 (1910): 320–36.

Chatelain, H., *Recherches sur les vers français au XVe siècle, rimes, mètres, strophes,* reprint, Geneva: Slatkine, 1974 [orig. 1907].

Comte de Marsy, *Pierre de Hauteville, dit le Mannier, seigneur d'Ars en Beauvais, surnommé le Prince d'Amours,* Beauvais: 1900.

Conseils pour l'édition des textes médiévaux, fasc. 1: *conseils généraux,* coord. Françoise Vieillard and Olivier Guyotjeannin, Paris: École Nationale des Chartes, 2001.

Cook, Elizabeth, ed., "La Belle dame sans merci," in *John Keats*, The Oxford Authors, New York: Oxford University Press, 1990: 273–74.

Dictionnaire encyclopédique du Moyen Age, dir. André Vauchez, Paris: Éditions du CERF, 1997.

Dictionnaire des lettres françaises: le Moyen Age, Paris: Fayard, 1992.

Foulet, L., *Petite syntaxe de l'ancien français*, Les Classiques français du moyen age, Paris: H. Champion, 1998.

Furgeot, Henri, *Actes du Parlement de Paris: deuxième série—de l'an 1328 à l'an 1350*, Archives National: Inventaires et Documents, Paris: Plon-Nourrit, 1920.

Gilson, E. "Tables pour l'histoire du thème littéraire," in *"Ubi sunt?": les idées et les lettres*, Paris: Vrin, 2nd ed., 1955: 31–38.

Gossen, Ch. Th., *Grammaire de l'ancien Picard*, Paris: Klincksieck, 1970.

Hassell, J. W. Jr., *Middle French Proverbs, Sentences, and Proverbial Phrases*, Subsidia Mediaevalia 12, Toronto: Pontifical Institute of Mediaeval Studies, 1982.

Jodogne, O., *"Povoir* ou *pouvoir?* Le cas phonétique de l'ancien verbe pouoir," *Travaux de linguistique et de littérature*, 4 (1966): 257–66.

Jeanroy, A., and E. Droz, *Deux manuscrits de François Villon*, Documents artistiques du XVe siècle, 6, Paris: E. Droz, 1932.

Knudson, Ch. A., "'Hasard' et les autres jeux de dés dans le Jeu de Saint Nicolas," *Romania*, 63 (1937): 248–53.

Laborde, Comte de, *Les ducs de Bourgogne: études sur les lettres, les arts, et l'industrie pendant le XVe siècle. Seconde partie: preuves, tome III*, Paris: Plon frères, 1852.

La Grange, A. de, *Pierre de Hauteville et ses testaments*, Anvers: 1891.

Laidlaw, J. C., "Christine de Pizan—An Author's Progress," *The Modern Language Review*, 78 (1987): 35–75.

Laidlaw, J. C., "Christine de Pizan—A Publisher's Progress," *The Modern Language Review*, 82 (1983): 532–50.

Laidlaw, J. C., "The Manuscripts of Alain Chartier," *The Modern Language Review*, 61 (1966): 188–98.

Marchello-Nizia, C., *La langue française aux XIVe et XVe siècles*, Paris: Nathan, 1997.

Martin, R., and M. Wilmet, *Manuel du français du moyen âge: 2. Syntaxe du moyen français*, Bordeaux: SOBODI, 1980.

Maugis, E., *Histoire du Parlement de Paris*, Geneva: Slatkine-Megariotis Reprints, 1977 [orig. 1913].

Meyenberg, R., *Alain Chartier prosateur et l'art de la parole au XVe siècle: études littéraires et rhétoriques*, Romancia Helvetica, 107, Berne: Francke, 1992.

Olivier-Martin, F., *Histoire du droit français*, Paris: Éditions du CNRS, 1984 [orig. 1948].

Oulmont, C., *Les débats du clerc et du chevalier dans la littérature poétique du Moyen-Age*, reprint, Geneva: Slatkine, 1974 [orig. 1911].

Paris, G., "La poètique de Baudet Herenc," *Romania*, 15 (1886): 135–36.

Pastoureau, M., *Figures et couleurs: études sur la symbolique et la sensibilité médiévales*, Paris: Le Léopard d'Or, 1986.

Piaget, A., "La cour amoureuse dite de Charles VI," *Romania*, 20 (1891): 417–54.

Piaget, A., "Pierre Michault et Michault Taillevent," *Romania*, 18 (1889): 439–52.

Piaget, A., " Un poème de Baudet Herenc," *Romania*, 23 (1894): 256–57.

Piaget, A., and E. Droz, "Recherches sur la tradition manuscrite de Villon: I. Le Manuscrit de Stockholm," *Romania*, 58 (1932): 238–54.

Poirion, D., *Le poète et le prince: l'évolution du lyrisme courtois de Guillame de Machaut à Charles d'Orléans*, Université de Grenoble Publications de la Faculté des Letters et Sciences Humaines, 35, Paris: Presses universitaires de France, 1965.

Poirion, D., ed., *Précis de littérature française du Moyen Age*, Paris: Presses universitaires de France, 1983.

Rouy, F., *L'ésthétique du traité moral d'après les oeuvres d'Alain Chartier,* Publications romanes et françaises, 152, Geneva: Droz, 1980.

Rubin, M., *Corpus Christi: The Eucharist in Late Medieval Culture,* Cambridge: Cambridge University Press, 1991.

Santoni, P., "Les oeuvres latines d'Alain Chartier," *Journal des Savants* (1980): 217–24.

Schulze-Busacker, Elizabeth, *Proverbes et expressions proverbiales dans la littérature narrative du Moyen Age française: recueil et analyse.* Paris: Editions Slatkine, 1985.

Shennen, J. H., *The Parlement of Paris.* Ithaca: Cornell University Press, 1968.

Seronde, J., "The Lover in Achille Caulier's *Hospital d'Amours,*" *The Romantic Review,* 5 (1914): 177–85.

Siciliano, I., *François Villon et les thèmes poétiques du Moyen Age,* Paris: Nizet, 1967 (reprint 1992).

Stefano, G., *Dictionnaire des locutions en moyen français,* Montréal: CERES, 1991.

Thomas, A., "Une oeuvre patriotique inconnue d'Alain Chartier," *Journal des Savants,* n.s., 12 (1914): 442–49.

Wack, Mary Frances, *Lovesickness in the Middle Ages: The Viaticum and Its Commentaries,* Philadelphia: University of Pennsylvania Press, 1990.

Index

A

B

K

L

2 0 JUN 2018